Dictators and Dictatorships

Dictators and Dictatorships
Understanding Authoritarian Regimes and Their Leaders

Natasha M. Ezrow
Erica Frantz

continuum

2011

The Continuum International Publishing Group
80 Maiden Lane, New York, NY 10038
The Tower Building, 11 York Road, London SE1 7NX

www.continuumbooks.com

Library of Congress Cataloging-in-Publication Data
Ezrow, Natasha M.
Dictators and dictatorships : understanding authoritarian regimes and
their leaders / Natasha M. Ezrow, Erica Frantz.
    p. cm.
 ISBN-13: 978-1-4411-1468-6 (hardcover : alk. paper)
 ISBN-10: 1-4411-1468-8 (hardcover : alk. paper)
 ISBN-13: 978-1-4411-7396-6 (pbk. : alk. paper)
 ISBN-10: 1-4411-7396-X (pbk. : alk. paper)
 1. Dictatorship. 2. Dictators. 3. Authoritarianism.
 I. Frantz, Erica. II. Title.

 JC495.E97 2011
 321.9–dc22

                                        2010025328

ISBN: HB: 978-1-4411-1468-6
       PB: 978-1-4411-7396-6

Typeset by Newgen Imaging Systems Pvt Ltd, Chennai, India
Printed and bound in the United States of America by Sheridan Books, Inc

Contents

viii Contents

List of Illustrations

Tables

Figures

Acknowledgements

From Erica Frantz

When my sister, Natasha, first approached me about this project, I thought she was crazy. Having just finished a book-length project on dictatorships, I figured we both desperately needed a break from them. Luckily for us, the world of dictatorships is a colorful one and it is nearly impossible to not find it fascinating and engaging. I am extremely appreciative of Natasha for agreeing to work with me again and for putting up with all of my stubbornness and rigidity. Without her perseverance and positivity, this project never could have happened. I am also appreciative of my dissertation advisory group—Barbara Geddes, James DeNardo, and George Tsebelis—who were each integral in my development as a scholar, as well as Lawrence Ezrow, who provided invaluable feedback and advice on the project.

I want to thank my wonderful community of family members—Yvette, Jeff, Pam, Jim, Kamie, Mark, and LJ—each of whom has provided me with unwavering love and support in all of my endeavors, along with plenty of good humor. I also want to thank my sounding board in life, my husband Cliff. His vitality and optimism are a force to be reckoned with. Without him, my sun does not shine.

Lastly, I am extremely grateful for the record snow the DC area got in the 2009–2010 winter. Being snowed in on multiple occasions provided me with precious writing time, along with ethereal and inspirational scenery.

From Natasha Ezrow

I would like to first thank our wonderful acquisitions editor, Marie Claire for approaching me to write a book on dictatorships and for providing helpful comments and support.

I would also like to thank my co-author and sister Erica. After Marie Claire approached me about the book, I quickly enlisted Erica to come on board, because she has studied dictatorships for many years. Erica is incredibly talented and hard working and this book would not have been possible without her. She was however, not particularly optimistic about the chances of us finishing this book before our deadline. Erica is seemingly unaware of how productive and efficient she is at juggling many things at the same time.

I am also grateful to my brother-in-law Cliff, my husband Lawrence and our parents Jeff and Yvette. Lawrence is very helpful in ways that most people aren't aware of, such as making me laugh on a daily basis. My parents were also extremely helpful, by providing childcare, support and by being unintentionally hilarious.

Lastly, I would like to thank my little daughter Annika. In addition to being adorable, she also delayed herself from being born until I had a rough draft finished.

Introduction

Politics under Dictatorship

Though, much of the world lives under dictatorship, misperceptions about dictatorships abound. Dictatorships are typically viewed as unpredictable, brutal regimes, ruled by a single, outrageous individual with absolute power. As is often the case with stereotypes, there are partial truths to this depiction.

Some dictatorships are unpredictable. For example, in November 2005, the leader of the Burmese dictatorship, Than Shwe, abruptly moved the entire capital from Rangoon to Pyinmana, a remote jungle 250 miles north. Government employees and military officials were given two days' notice and transported to the new capital in massive trucks laden with furniture.[1] In Uganda, as well, Idi Amin in 1972 issued a decree expelling nearly one hundred thousand Asians who were not Ugandan citizens, sending the country into economic chaos.

Some dictatorships are brutally repressive. During the military dictatorship of Uruguay, for example, at one point the country had the highest percentage of political prisoners in the world. This statistic, however, pales in comparison to the nearly one million Cambodians who died in Pol Pot's tenure. The irrational brutality of Saddam Hussein's dictatorship in Iraq is also well documented. The French magazine *Le Nouvel Observateur* published an article referring to Hussein as a "perfect idiot," "killer," and a "monster." Hussein sued the magazine for libel and lost.[2]

Some dictators are eccentric. Saparmurat Niyazov of Turkmenistan, for example, named the months and days of the week after himself and his family. Ballet was banned because he found it dull. A course in the Rukhnama, a book of spiritual musings penned by Niyazov, was required to receive a driver's license.[3] Similarly, Kim Jong-il, leader of the North Korean dictatorship, is said to wear shoes with heels and sport a bouffant hairstyle in order to appear taller. Kim reportedly travels in armored trains, due to a fear of flying, and has lobsters airlifted to him daily while he travels, which he eats with silver chopsticks, historically believed to detect poison.[4]

Stereotypes about dictatorships, such as these, do describe many regimes and their leaders, but they do not accurately depict all regimes. Though there are dictatorships like that of Amin's Uganda, there are also dictatorships like that of Singapore, which on most days seems like a modern democracy.[5]

Such misperceptions about dictatorships persist partly because dictatorships are less studied in political science than democracies. According to Stanley G. Payne, "The political literature on authoritarian regimes is more limited and weaker than that on democracies and nominal parliamentary systems."[6]

Part of the reason for this is because it is simply more challenging to gather information about dictatorial regimes. As Paul H. Lewis writes, "It is more difficult to study dictatorships than democracies because the internal politics of the former are deliberately hidden from the public view. There is no free press, no free public opinion, no open lobbying or party competition."[7] Due to the closed nature typical of dictatorships, political information tends to be more difficult to obtain and government sources less reliable. Media outlets are often censored, government propaganda is widespread, and details of government administration are concealed.

Authoritarian regimes present us with unique challenges because of the very fact that they are authoritarian. An extreme example of this is the case of Laos, a single-party dictatorship. For many years in Laos, even the identity of the party leaders was unknown. In some dictatorships, obtaining the most basic facts about the regime is impossible. Because of this, testing hypotheses regarding dictatorial political systems can be difficult.

This study seeks to dispel many of the myths that shroud dictatorships and help clarify how authoritarian politics works. In doing so, this study synthesizes and examines the growing literature on autocratic rule. We integrate traditional theories about authoritarianism with cutting-edge research on dictatorships. We also discuss the various typologies of dictatorship emphasized in the literature, their uses, and how they have evolved. To illustrate our arguments, we offer an ample selection of case studies from a variety of regions in the world. Through these real-world examples, this study helps to bring theory to reality.

We should note that in this study we use the terms, authoritarian regime, non-democracy, autocracy, and dictatorship interchangeably, unless indicated otherwise. In addition, we examine political processes under dictatorships in the 20th century and later.

Two central points are woven throughout. The first is that *dictatorships are not one and the same*. Dictatorships differ from one another in important ways. As we show in the chapters that follow, these differences have systematic effects on the types of policies that result.

The second point is that *dictators are distinct from dictatorships*. The overthrow of the dictator is not synonymous with the overthrow of the dictatorship. Authoritarian regimes, in fact, often last well beyond the fall of any particular ruler. Conflating dictators with dictatorships can lead to misunderstandings of not only leadership survival and regime survival, but also a variety of other political outcomes.

In this study, we examine key questions in the fields of comparative politics and international relations. Why are some types of dictatorships more likely to be long-lasting and others highly unstable? In a similar vein, why do leaders in some dictatorships seem to rule forever, while others are easily overthrown? Why do some dictatorships exhibit unpredictable behavior, while others appear prudent and cautious? On the economic front, why do some authoritarian regimes have impressive economic growth, while others have been plagued by stagnancy and corruption? Why are some dictatorships aggressive and war hungry, while others are more prone to peace?

Though some of these questions have clear answers, others are still very much the subject of debate. This study disentangles the various approaches put forth to answer these questions and, where relevant, provides discussion of their relative weaknesses and strengths.

Authoritarian politics remains one of the most understudied areas of political science.[8] This is true despite the fact that many of the world's people live under some form of authoritarian rule, and dictatorships are by no means a thing of the past.[9] By offering a thorough and comprehensive analysis of authoritarian politics, this study enhances our understanding of how dictatorships work. Given the persistence of authoritarianism as a form of government, this is an effort that is as important as ever.

Overview of the Book

Chapter 1: Authoritarian Politics: Typologies

This chapter provides a thorough overview of the different ways in which dictatorships are categorized, both in the early literature on authoritarianism and in contemporary research. It also presents the typology of authoritarian regimes used in subsequent chapters—that of Barbara Geddes.[10]

Geddes classifies dictatorships as *military*, *single-party*, *personalist*, or a *hybrid* of these three. We supplement Geddes' typology with the category of *monarchy* to give a fuller picture of contemporary post-World War II dictatorships.

Chapter 2: The Causes of Dictatorship

This chapter examines the causes of authoritarianism. It looks at the factors that drive the emergence of dictatorial—as opposed to democratic—forms of government. It then discusses why different types of dictatorships arise and where they are most likely to sprout, with emphasis on regional trends in their distribution.

Chapter 3: The Survival of Authoritarian Regimes: Strategies and Trends

This chapter gives an overview of the strategies for survival that dictatorships employ and how they differ across regime types to influence survival rates. It also examines the role that elections and political parties play in prolonging the longevity of regimes. Lastly, this chapter looks at how and why dictatorships collapse.

Chapter 4: The Survival of Authoritarian Leaders: Strategies and Trends

This chapter focuses on the factors that influence the survival of authoritarian leaders. It explores the strategies that dictators use to stay in power, showing how these strategies are limited, or influenced by the type of regime they rule. It then discusses trends in the survival rates of authoritarian leaders, before turning to an examination of how they fall from power.

Chapter 5: Coups

This chapter examines coups d'états. Coups are central to many aspects of authoritarian politics; they are often a catalyzing force behind the rise and fall of authoritarian regimes, as well as the rise and fall of authoritarian leaders. It discusses why coups occur, where they are most frequent, and the factors that precipitate them.

Chapter 6: Dictatorships and Political Gridlock

This chapter focuses on how the type of authoritarian regime affects political gridlock, or how easy or hard it is to change policy. When it is difficult for actors to agree to policy changes, policy outcomes will be stable from one year to the next; when it is easy for actors to agree to policy changes, policy outcomes will be volatile. This chapter discusses which actors are critical to the policy-making process in dictatorships, and shows how the breadth and diversity of their policy preferences are influenced by regime types.

Chapter 7: Dictatorships and the Economy

This chapter discusses the literature on democracy, dictatorship, and the economy, with an emphasis on how domestic political institutions affect economic growth and performance. It also looks at the effectiveness with which different types of dictatorships use foreign aid. Lastly, it explores the propensity of dictatorships to engage in corruption, examining in detail the phenomenon of predatory states.

Chapter 8: Dictatorships and International Conflict

This chapter focuses on how authoritarian regime type affects international conflict behavior. It also looks at how the quality of military intelligence that dictators receive from their advisers differs across regimes. It shows that poor quality intelligence is associated with foreign policy blunders.

Chapter 9: Military Dictatorships in Latin America and Beyond

This chapter provides an in-depth discussion of a specific type of dictatorship: military dictatorship. It defines what military dictatorships are, examines the factors that influence their durability, and presents key theoretical work devoted to them. Lastly, it offers case studies from Latin America, where military dictatorships have been most common, as well as, Turkey, Thailand, and Nigeria.

Chapter 10: Single-party Dictatorships in Eastern Europe, Asia, and Beyond

This chapter explores single-party dictatorships; along with a detailed analysis of single-party dictatorships, it presents case studies from Hungary, Czechoslovakia, East Germany, China, Malaysia, Taiwan, and Mexico.

Chapter 11: Personalist Dictatorships in Sub-Saharan Africa and Beyond

This chapter is devoted to personalist dictatorships. It discusses the key facets of personalist regimes, before turning to a selection of case studies from sub-Saharan Africa (where personalist dictatorships have been most prevalent). It also includes a case study from the Haitian personalist dictatorship.

Chapter 12: Monarchies in the Middle East and Beyond

This chapter provides an in-depth discussion of monarchic dictatorships. It uses case studies from the Middle East, a region prone to monarchic rule, as well as a case study from Swaziland.

Chapter 13: Hybrid Dictatorships

This chapter offers a selection of case studies of hybrid dictatorships to show how these regimes differ from their "pure" authoritarian counterparts. The case studies are drawn from Pakistan, Cuba, El Salvador, and Egypt.

Summary and Review Questions

- Why is it important to study dictatorships?
- Why is so little known about dictatorships?

Key Points

- Dictatorships are not one and the same.
- Dictators differ from dictatorships.

Notes

1. Kurlantzick, *Burma's Dear Leader*, (2006).
2. Lamont, *In the Filing Line*, (2002).
3. Bloomfield, *Anxiety in Europe*, (2006).
4. Source: *Profile: Kim Jong-il*, BBC News, January 16, 2009, http://news.bbc.co.uk/2/hi/asia-pacific/1907197.stm (accessed March 10, 2010).
5. Though the Singaporean government does engage in efforts to damage the opposition's prospects in elections, ordinary citizens are usually free to live as they please. Source: Freedom House, www.freedomhouse.org.
6. Payne, *Twentieth-Century Dictatorships*, (1996, p. 1187)
7. Lewis, *Salazar's Ministerial Elite*, (1978, p. 622).
8. As Adam Przeworski noted in 2003, "Dictatorships are by far the most understudied area in comparative politics. We need to start thinking about it." Source: *Adam Przeworski: Capitalism, Democracy, and Science,* Interview conducted by Gerardo L. Munck, 2003, http://www.nyu.edu/gsas/dept/politics/faculty/przeworski/przeworski_munck.pdf (accessed April 22, 2008).

9. As the Economist wrote in 2008, "Following a decades-long global trend in democratization, the spread of democracy has come to a halt." Source: *Democracy Index: Off the March*, The Economist, October 29, 2008, http://www.economist.com/markets/rankings/displayStory.cfm?source=hptextfeature&story_id=12499352 (accessed November 18, 2008).

10. Geddes, Paradigms and Sand Castles, (2003).

Authoritarian Politics: Typologies

1

Chapter Outline

Dictatorships often vary from one another as much as they do from democracies. There are dictatorships like Malaysia under the National Front, but there are also dictatorships like North Korea under Kim Jong-il. These regimes differ from each other on multiple levels, ranging from their de facto institutional structures, to their political openness, to their interconnectivity with the outside world.

In this chapter, we begin with a brief discussion of how dictatorships are defined. We then present some theoretical background on how dictatorships have been categorized. Lastly, we discuss in depth the contemporary typologies of dictatorship and the typology used in the rest of this study.

Defining Dictatorship

In order to understand how dictatorships function, it is first important to define what we mean when we refer to them. There are, of course, a variety of ways in which scholars have defined dictatorships. This section will briefly review them.

According to Juan Linz, "authoritarian regimes are political systems with limited, not responsible political pluralism, without intensive nor extensive political mobilization, and in which a leader or a small group exercises power within formally ill-defined limits but actually quite predictable ones."[1] This definition is roughly echoed by Samuel Huntington,[2] who writes that authoritarian regimes are characterized by a single leader or group of leaders with either no party or a weak party, little mass mobilization, and limited political pluralism. Daron Acemoglu and James Robinson, by contrast, emphasize representation. They argue that dictatorships are regimes in which the government represents solely "the preferences of a sub-group of the population"[3]. Non-democracies are "for the elite and the privileged;"[4] decisions are made either by a single individual, the elite, a junta, or an oligarchy. In a different vein, Paul Brooker's definition focuses on the electoral process, with dictatorship defined as the "theft of public office and powers."[5] For this study, we use Adam Przeworski et al.'s simple definition of democracy and dictatorship: democracies are regimes in which "those who govern are selected through contested elections;"[6] dictatorships are "not democracies."[7]

Theoretical Background

Though our knowledge of dictatorships is less advanced than our knowledge of democracies, the literature on modern dictatorial regimes is increasingly growing. As Brooker notes, "theorists and analysts of totalitarianism, authoritarianism, one-party states, military regimes and personal dictatorship have made a major contribution to the development of political science."[8] In the sections that follow, we detail foundational work on dictatorships and how our conceptions of dictatorships have evolved across time.

Totalitarianism

Early studies of dictatorship are largely descriptive in nature and predominately focus on the notion of totalitarianism. Huntington[9] defines totalitarian regimes as rule by a single party led by an individual with a powerful secret police and a highly developed ideology. In totalitarian regimes, the government has total control of mass communications and social and economic organizations. Such regimes aim to create an ideal society through the use of government propaganda.

Hannah Arendt

Following World War II, the concept of totalitarianism gained traction in political science, likely as a result of increased international exposure to the regimes of Germany under Adolf Hitler and the Soviet Union under Josef Stalin. Hannah Arendt's[10] work on the subject is foundational in the field. In *The Origins of Totalitarianism*, Arendt highlights the uniqueness of totalitarianism, calling it a new and extreme form of dictatorship comprised of "atomized, isolated individuals."[11] Relying heavily on the cases of Hitler and Stalin, Arendt argues that ideology plays a prominent role in totalitarian regimes. Though the type of ideology used varies, the common thread among all totalitarian regimes is that the leadership wants *to transform human nature*, by providing a complete road map for the organization of human life.[12] The leadership seeks to exert full control over society, subjecting citizens to omnipresent terror as a means of ensuring compliance. Critical actors in maintaining such a tight grip over society are the leader, the secret police, and the party.

Carl Friedrich and Zbigniew Brzezinski

In a similar vein, Carl Friedrich and Zbigniew Brzezinski[13] highlight six features of totalitarian dictatorships in *Totalitarian Dictatorship and Autocracy*. These features are: the implementation of an official ideology, a single political party, party control over mass communications, party control over the military, a central economy, and a secret police. In later work, Brzezinski[14] defines totalitarianism as a new form of government that seeks to bring about a social revolution, based on the ideological assumptions declared by the leadership. In totalitarian regimes, power is "wielded without restraint."[15] The main goal of the leadership is to achieve the total unity of society and politicization of the populace via political organizations. These means are achieved through propaganda and terror. The leader has greater power than the party or security apparatus and typically possesses religious or charismatic appeal. Examples cited include Nazi Germany, Communist Eastern Europe and the Soviet Union, Fascist Italy, and Communist China.

North Korea: A Modern Totalitarian Regime?

The dictatorship of North Korea (a personalist/single-party regime) shares many characteristics with totalitarian regimes. Ideology plays a strong role in the North Korean regime. The state's ideology, Juche, serves to atomize the public and subordinate the people under the will of the state (Oh and Hassig 2000). The regime's first leader, Kim Il-sung, was credited with creating Juche, decreeing that the only way to understand the ideology was "to follow the party and the leader" (Ibid., p. 22). Juche is essentially a "state of mind" that focuses on putting North Korea first (Scobell 2006, p. 30). The ideology provides guidelines for "all fields of human endeavor from poetry to potato farming" (Ibid., p. 13). Where ideology fails to engender mass support, social control is used (Oh and Hassig 2000). The state's control over North Korean society is extensive; no individuals are exempt from investigation or monitoring (Ibid.). The goal of these measures is to create a "climate of terror . . . instilled not just by the visible elements of the coercive apparatus . . . but also by a fear of being informed on by a colleague, friend or even a loved one" (Scobell 2006, p. 34). Large-scale efforts to mobilize the masses are also undertaken, facilitated by one of the "most oppressive personality cults in the world" (Ibid., p. 28).

Totalitarianism vs. Authoritarianism

In *Totalitarian and Authoritarian Regimes*, Linz[16] builds on this body of work and develops a typology of political systems, disaggregating regimes according to whether they are democratic, authoritarian, or totalitarian. The key factors that distinguish totalitarian and authoritarian regimes are the degree of social pluralism and levels of political mobilization. Linz argues that authoritarian regimes are characterized by a mentality, whereas totalitarian regimes are characterized by an ideological belief system. The main goals of authoritarian regimes are political demobilization and depoliticization. Authoritarian regimes do not seek to homogenize society and instead allow for some degree of pluralism. By contrast, totalitarian regimes place great emphasis on political mobilization and use ideology as a main source of their legitimacy.

Authoritarian vs. Totalitarian Regimes (Linz)

Authoritarian Regimes

- Role of ideology is weak
- Goal is to depoliticize and de-mobilize society
- Small degree of pluralism is allowed
- Political parties, if they exist, are devoid of ideology and may not play an important role in the regime
- Regime does not exercise total control over society; masses have some political power
- Terror and propaganda may be used, but not to the same extent as in totalitarian regimes

Totalitarian Regimes

- Goals of the regime are social revolution, aiming to transform human nature
- Ideology plays a strong role, provides legitimacy
- Strategy to achieve these goals is to subject society to terror
- Regime has a high level of organization and total control over society
- Key holders of power are the leader, secret police, and party
- Emphasis on mass mobilization
- Regime exercises total control over society

Beyond Totalitarianism

In response to the literature on totalitarianism, other scholars have moved away from an emphasis on ideology. Rather than being central to the typology, ideology is instead one of the many factors that distinguish dictatorships from one another. Institutions—and how entrenched they are in society—are also key.

One-Party Dictatorship

Scholarship on the role of the dominant parties in totalitarian regimes soon expanded to include their role in dictatorships more generally. Huntington and Clement Moore's *Authoritarian Politics in Modern Society: The Dynamics of Established One-Party Systems*, for example, focuses on one-party dictatorship, which they claim is an example of authoritarianism in its "principal modern form."[17] The authors differentiate between weak and strong one-party states, based on the party's concentration of power. In weak one-party states, at least one other actor eclipses the role of the party (like a single individual, the military, or the police); in strong one-party states, the party plays the dominant role. Huntington and Moore argue that the strength of a one-party system is based on the intensity and duration of the party's struggle to acquire power.

Huntington and Moore discuss in detail the different types of strong one-party states. They categorize strong one-party dictatorships based on their level of institutionalization and the strategies the party uses for staying in power. The revolutionary one-party system, for example, is characterized by "social dynamism, autocratic and charismatic leadership, disciplined party, highly developed ideology, stress on propaganda and mass mobilization, combined with coercion and terror."[18, 19] Established one-party systems, by contrast, have characteristics that are more administrative than revolutionary in nature. They have lower levels of political mobilization and more pragmatic goals. Political leadership is less "personalist, charismatic and autocratic," and more "oligarchical, bureaucratic and institutionalized."[20] In all of the strong one-party states that Huntington and Moore identify,

Types of One-Party Dictatorships (Huntington and Moore)

Revolutionary

- Level of charisma: high
- Social dynamism: high
- Level of party discipline: high
- Role of ideology: high
- Strategies for achieving goals: subordinate and annihilate social divisions
- Level of institutionalization: low

Established

- Level of charisma: moderate
- Social dynamism: unimportant
- Level of party discipline: moderate
- Role of ideology: more pragmatic
- Strategies for achieving goals: administrative means, mediating policy initiatives that originate from technocratic and managerial elites
- Level of institutionalization: high

there is neither turnover in power among political parties nor low levels of pluralism.

Military Rule

Whereas Huntington and Moore concentrate on one-party rule, Amos Perlmutter[21] looks primarily at military rule. Perlmutter highlights two types of military-based dictatorships: the arbitrator type and the ruler type.[22] The arbitrator type of military dictatorship is professionally oriented, without an independent political organization or ideology. The officers are "civilian oriented" and more acceptant of the "existing social order."[23] The military is disinterested in interjecting its own viewpoints in government policy and does not seek to rule for a long period of time.[24] Rather, it sees itself as a guardian of the constitution, and a means of bringing stability to the country and restoring order. It is more likely to "operate behind the scenes as a pressure group."[25] The ruler type of military dictatorship, by contrast, employs a "coherent and elaborate political ideology."[26] The military seeks to maximize its power and views civilian politicians as incompetent and dangerous to stability.

Types of Military Rule (Perlmutter)

Arbitrator

- Time limit for military rule: willing to return to the barracks after disputes are settled
- Goals of the military: to settle disputes
- View of professionalism: concerned with professional improvement
- Level of political organization: no independent political organization
- Confidence in existing social order and civilian rule: accepts the existing social order
- Relationship with civilians: civilian-oriented, fears civilian retribution

Ruler

- Time limit for military rule: no desire to return to the barracks
- Goals of the military: wants to maximize time in power, convinced that military rule is the only alternative to political disorder
- View of professionalism: politicizes professionalism
- Level of political organization: high, has a strong political organization
- Confidence in existing social order and civilian rule: no confidence in existing order, challenges civilian rule
- Relationships with civilians: not civilian oriented, little fear of civilian retribution

Contemporary Typologies of Dictatorships

Multiple research strains have spawned from the original typological work on dictatorships. These research strains can broadly be grouped into two categories: continuous and categorical. The continuous typologies of dictatorship disaggregate regimes based on how "authoritarian" they are, whereas the categorical typologies of dictatorship view all dictatorships as equally "authoritarian" and instead focus on how they differ from one another.

Continuous typologies of dictatorship emphasize the various gradients of dictatorship. They identify the extent to which regimes are democratic or authoritarian and place regimes along a democratic-autocratic scale. Many scholars claim that there is a grey zone that lies between democracy and dictatorship. Regimes that lie somewhere in the middle of this scale are essentially "pseudo-democracies."[27]

Categorical typologies of dictatorship, by contrast, ignore the "level" of authoritarianism and instead focus on the heterogeneity that exists within the universe of dictatorships. They disaggregate dictatorships based on the meaningful ways in which dictatorships vary from one another.

In the sections that follow, we provide a review of the contemporary typologies of dictatorship.

Continuous Typologies

Grey Zone Regimes

According to Larry Diamond,[28] many regimes fall in the grey zone between authoritarianism and democracy.[29] Grey zone regimes have formally democratic institutions, which help mask "the reality of authoritarian domination."[30] They typically lack the means for contesting power that enable turnover in government and are characterized by illegitimate elections with high levels of fraud. Opposition victories are not impossible; but they are highly unlikely and difficult to achieve, often requiring international observation and intervention. Diamond points to the examples of contemporary Russia, Nigeria, Indonesia, and Venezuela.

Grey zone regimes are differentiated based on the degree of their competitiveness. Diamond develops a six-fold typology that places regimes into the following six categories based on a democratic-authoritarian scale: liberal democracy, electoral democracy, ambiguous regimes, competitive authoritarian, hegemonic electoral authoritarian, and politically closed authoritarian. Regimes are considered democratic if they have free and fair elections for all key positions of power. Regimes that have no political competition or pluralism, by contrast, are politically closed. Such a typology is useful because it captures the variety of regimes that have adopted the "form" of electoral democracy, but do not live up to the standards expected of electoral democracy.[31]

Competitive Authoritarian Regimes

Other scholars also differentiate regimes according to the degree to which they are authoritarian. In particular, Steven Levitsky and Lucan Way[32] focus on "competitive authoritarian" regimes. In competitive authoritarian regimes, democratic institutions are used to exercise political authority, but incumbents violate the rules often enough that the "regime fails to meet conventional minimum standards for democracy."[33]

They highlight four key minimum criteria for democracy: 1) the executive and legislative branches must be chosen through elections that are open, free, and fair; 2) all adults must be able to vote; 3) political rights and civil liberties must be protected; and 4) elected officials must be given the right to govern, instead of the military or clerical leaders. When violations of these criteria are such that they impede democratic challenges to the incumbent, regimes are classified as competitive authoritarian.

Competitive authoritarian regimes are unique in that they are neither fully democratic nor fully authoritarian. Though competitive authoritarian regimes hold elections in which the opposition is able to meaningfully challenge incumbents, the electoral "playing field"[34] is not even as it is in democracies. Instead, incumbents have access to a variety of state resources that can help them steer the election's outcome in their favor. They can deny the opposition, adequate media coverage, harass and threaten opposition candidates and/or supporters, and manipulate the electoral rules and results in ways that disadvantage opposition candidates.

These regimes are not fully autocratic, however. Electoral institutions not only exist, but can lead to "meaningful contestation for power."[35] According to Levitsky and Way, in spite of the dominance of the ruling group or party, elections are not entirely predetermined in competitive authoritarian regimes, as they are in "pure" forms of dictatorship. Though there are multiple advantages given to incumbents, as discussed above, elections in competitive authoritarian regimes are generally free of massive fraud. In pure authoritarian regimes, by contrast, elections are either nonexistent or the outcome is already decided well before the date of the election.

Competitive authoritarian regimes differ from pure authoritarian regimes in other ways, as well. In pure dictatorships, legislatures either do not exist or are controlled by a single ruling party; the judiciary has little independence or political power apart from the ruling group or party, and most forms of media are state owned and closely censored. In comparison, in competitive authoritarian regimes, though legislatures are weak, "they occasionally become focal points of opposition activity;"[36] the judiciary, though subject to subtle methods of coercion like bribery and extortion, is not totally powerless; and the media are generally free to operate legally, though they are often restricted in the scope of their reporting.

Competitive Authoritarian Regimes

- Elections are held and outcomes are not predetermined, though incumbents have large advantages and manipulate the formal democratic rules.
- Legislatures and the judiciary exist, but both are very weak.
- Opposition political parties are legal and the media is free to operate, but both are heavily restricted in their freedoms.

Electoral Authoritarianism

Other scholars also see regime type as continuous. Like Levitsky and Way, Andreas Schedler[37] focuses on the role of elections. Schedler uses a four-fold typology to differentiate regimes, based primarily on how leaders gain access to power. He classifies regimes—on a scale of the most democratic to the least democratic—as liberal democracies, electoral democracies, electoral authoritarian regimes, or authoritarian regimes.

Liberal democracies are regimes that go beyond the minimum requirements for democracy. Electoral democracies, by contrast, have free and fair elections, but "fail to institutionalize other vital dimensions of democratic constitutionalism," such as the rule of law, government accountability, and civil liberties.[38] Electoral democracies differ from electoral authoritarian regimes in that elections in the former are held regularly and are largely free and fair.

In electoral authoritarian regimes, elections are manipulated in favor of the incumbent to such a degree, that they are not considered truly democratic. Nevertheless, elections are a means of contesting power in these regimes, as there is some "degree of uncertainty"[39] about the outcome. Though the opposition rarely wins a majority of seats, it is typically allowed to win some seats. In this way, electoral authoritarian regimes are very similar to competitive authoritarian regimes, as described by Levitsky and Way. Lastly, in regular authoritarian regimes, elections—if they are held— are largely predetermined;[40] it is known ahead of time that the incumbent will win, and typically by large margins.

Drawbacks of Continuous Typologies

The strength of continuous typologies is that they allow regimes to fall in the "in-between" category of neither totally democratic, nor totally autocratic. It is likely that these "in-between" regimes differ from their "truly" authoritarian counterparts in meaningful ways, particularly in terms of the civil and political liberties enjoyed by their citizens.

The weakness of continuous typologies is their implication that as regimes become less authoritarian, they become closer to being democracies. This may not be true, however. The likelihood of democratization may be independent of how "authoritarian" a regime is.

Continuous typologies are also, by definition, restricted to differentiating regimes along a single dimension, which is typically the level of competitiveness of the regime. Yet, as Axel Hadenius and Jan Teorell point out, "If the degree of competitiveness were the only dimension along which authoritarian regimes differed, we would need no regime typology. Instead, a continuous measure of competitiveness—serving as a rough proxy for the level of democracy—would be sufficient."[41]

Categorical typologies capture more of the complexities of dictatorships, by allowing multiple dimensions to factor into the classifications. They also make no assumptions about whether the path from dictatorship to democracy is linear in nature.

Categorical Typologies

The contemporary literature on categorical typologies of dictatorship is quite extensive. Within this research tradition, classifications of dictatorship either emphasize the strategy the dictator uses to stay in power, or the structure of the dictatorship.

Typologies Based on the Strategy of the Dictator

Loyalty vs. Repression

Some scholars emphasize how dictatorships differ based on the goals, insecurities, and strategies of the dictator. Ronald Wintrobe,[42] for example, categorizes dictatorships using two dimensions: how much loyalty citizens feel toward the dictator and how much repression the dictator uses to control the citizenry.

There are potentially negative consequences for dictators using repression as a survival tool. According to Wintrobe, repression can create excess fear among the citizenry, lessening the likelihood that the dictator's subjects will signal to the dictator if they are dissatisfied with his rule. Absent any knowledge of the citizenry's intentions, dictators have no way of gauging their popularity, causing them to constantly suspect that their subjects are scheming to overthrow them. Wintrobe terms this predicament the "dictator's dilemma."[43] The more dictators repress citizens to deter efforts to oust them, the less information dictators have about such efforts. In order to solve the dictator's dilemma, some dictators choose instead to implement policies aimed at generating support and loyalty from their subjects, such as the distribution of rents.

The extent to which dictators will emphasize loyalty or repression depends partly on the preferences of the dictator. In Wintrobe's formulation, leaders either: 1) seek to maximize control over the population, or 2) seek to maximize consumption (retaining no more power than required to remain in office).[44] Those leaders who seek power maximization will often have highly loyal supporters, as they pay them well to ensure their loyalty. Those leaders who seek consumption maximization will often have supporters who are less loyal, as they are not as well paid.

Thus, Wintrobe asks two questions: 1) How loyal are the citizens to the dictator? 2) Does the dictator want to maximize loyalty or consumption? Based on these questions, Wintrobe identifies four types of dictatorships:

- Tinpots (characterized by low levels of repression and loyalty)
- Tyrants (characterized by high repression and low loyalty)
- Totalitarians (characterized by high levels of repression and loyalty)
- Timocrats (characterized by low repression and high loyalty)

A tyrant, for example, will spend just enough resources on repression and loyalty in order to stay in power. Any excess resources, the tyrant will devote to personal consumption. Loans and foreign aid may induce tyrants to cooperate by giving tyrants economic incentives to do so. Wintrobe uses this typology to explain variations across dictatorships with respect to a variety of political outcomes, such as economic growth and stability.

Launching Organizations

Stephen Haber[45] develops a theoretical framework that emphasizes the relationship between dictators and the organizations that launch them into power. According to Haber, once in power, the dictator is often engaged in a power struggle with members of this launching organization. The strategies dictators use to ensure their survival in power lead to three different institutional arrangements in dictatorships:

- Dictators who terrorize the leadership of their launching organizations
- Dictators who co-opt the leadership of their launching organizations
- Dictators who create a set of rival or complementary organizations

Haber examines what these scenarios imply for political repression, property rights, economic growth, and democratic transitions.

Dictators use the strategy of terrorizing the leadership of their launching organizations when they fear that the organization can easily remove them from power. The idea is that if the organization was powerful enough to launch the dictator into power, it should also be powerful enough to remove the dictator from power. By fomenting terror within the launching organization, members will have incentives to denounce one another, making it more difficult for them to coordinate to take action against the dictator. The dictator typically carries out this terror by creating a secret police or other paramilitary organization. According to Haber, dictators rarely rely on the strategy of terrorizing the leadership of the launching organization, because it is dangerous. The secret police, for example, could turn on the dictator at any moment. This strategy also undermines the ability of the government to function, as government positions are populated by members of the launching organization.

The strategy of co-optation of the launching organization is used by dictators more frequently. With this strategy, dictators seek the loyalty of the members of the organization by making it in their interest to cooperate with the dictator, as opposed to overthrow the dictator. To do so, dictators can give members easy access to jobs, loans, tax breaks, and other rents. The downside of this strategy, however, is that the "source of rents and the government are one and the same."[46] Without continued access to rents, the dictator cannot maintain the use of this strategy.

The final strategy is, to raise the costs of collective action within the launching organization by creating a new parallel organization. Organizational proliferation forces the leadership of the launching organization to coordinate with the newly created organization, and/or "raises the cost of coordination within the launching organization by aligning the incentives of its membership with the leadership of another organization."[47] This strategy can be costly, however, as none of the members of these organizations work for free.

Haber shows how each of these strategies yields different property rights' systems, helping to explain the high degree of variance in economic performance across dictatorships.

Drawbacks of Strategy-based Typologies

Strategy-based typologies capture real differences in the factors that motivate and drive the behavior of dictators. They largely ignore, however, the different domestic environments that leaders inherit. Underlying such typologies is the assumption that dictators enter structure-free domestic environments upon taking power, and create from scratch, any institutional arrangements that emerge. The extent to which such an assumption will be true, though, will depend on how tightly organized the seizure group is that launched the dictator into power.

The more formally constituted the seizure group is, the more likely the regime that forms will share similar structural characteristics as those of the seizure group, and the more difficult it will be for the leader to mold the structure of the regime in ways that will prolong the leader's political survival.[48]

Typologies Based on the Structure of the Dictatorship

Military and Party Institutions

Barbara Geddes[49] looks at how dictatorships vary with respect to their institutional structures. She identifies which groups in dictatorships hold political power and control policy, examining post-World War II regimes lasting three years or longer.

Dictatorships are grouped according to whether they are personalist, single-party, military, or hybrids of these three.[50] These categorizations are based on whether access to political office and influence over policy are controlled by a single individual (as in personalist regimes), a hegemonic party (as in single-party regimes), or the military as an institution (as in military regimes).

Governance by a political party, professionalized, military, or neither structures elite politics, and leads to very different strategies for survival pursued by elite factions, according to Geddes. Because elites in different institutional contexts use markedly different strategies to stay in office, regime survival rates differ systematically across dictatorships. As Geddes shows, military dictatorships are the most short-lived, followed by single-party dictatorships, and lastly, personalist dictatorships.

One weakness of Geddes' typology, however, is that many dictatorships exhibit some level of personalism as Hadenius and Teorell[51] point out. Many single-party and military dictatorships, for example, experience periods during which the leader is extremely powerful vis-à-vis the party or military. Geddes' typology may not capture such changes in the power structure of a regime that occur across time. In addition, because regimes vary in their levels of personalism, many regimes end up classified as hybrids, regimes for which it is difficult to generate theoretical expectations. Lastly, Geddes' typology excludes monarchies, leaving out a handful of key dictatorships.

In response to this, Hadenius and Teorell[52] develop their own typology, which is essentially a more nuanced version of Geddes'. They categorize regimes as monarchic, no-party, military, one-party, or multi-party. With the exception of monarchies, Hadenius and Teorell's typology maps well onto Geddes' groupings of regimes as personalist, military, or single-party.

Selectorate and Winning Coalition

Bruce Bueno de Mesquita et al.[53] develop a theory that identifies two institutions of governance, the selectorate and the winning coalition, that expose generic differences between democracy, monarchy, military junta, and other forms of government. They claim that differences in the make-up of the winning coalition and the selectorate explain a variety of outcomes, such as economic performance, political survival, and conflict behavior.

The selectorate is a subset of the population that has a say in the selection of the leader. In a democracy, the selectorate consists of all enfranchised citizens. The winning coalition is a subset of the selectorate large enough to maintain a leader in power. Without the support of the winning coalition, the leader cannot stay in office. If members of the winning coalition defect and lend their support to a rival, the leader must quickly be able to replace them with other members of the selectorate or risk being deposed. In order to secure the support of the winning coalition, the leader must confer special privileges to its members. Leaders naturally have an incentive to keep the size of the winning coalition small so that they can provide more concentrated benefits to members and ensure their continued loyalty. In a democracy, the winning coalition is the set of voters whose support is necessary to select and keep the leader in office (i.e. a plurality of voters in a plurality voting system).

According to Bueno de Mesquita et al., the sizes of the selectorate and the winning coalition have implications for the leader's political survival. The leader's position is the most secure when the selectorate is large and the winning coalition is small. In such a scenario, the leader can easily find replacements for defectors of the winning coalition given the large size of the selectorate. The sizes of the two groups also influence public goods' provisions. When the size of the winning coalition is large, doling out private goods to coalition members becomes too expensive; leaders instead provide public goods as a means of rewarding their supporters, which in turn benefit all members of society (as in democracies). When the size of the winning coalition is small, however, leaders do not have the same incentives to invest in public goods.

A key insight of the theory is that not all citizens have influence over the leader. Leaders will primarily cater their policy choices to the subset of the citizenry whose support they require to stay in office.

Though the concepts underlying Bueno de Mesquita et al.'s theory are very useful, one weakness is that the argument is difficult to evaluate, given that in most dictatorships it is not clear who the selectorate is. Apart from members of the winning coalition, it is not obvious which individuals in authoritarian regimes have a say in the selection of the dictator. In military dictatorships, for example, elites and leaders typically rely on other members of the military for the *regime* to last. These low-level members of the military, however, rarely, if ever, have any say in the selection of *leaders*.[54]

Despotic and Infrastructural Power

Many scholars are interested in how authoritarian regime type influences a regime's propensity for conflict. Brian Lai and Dan Slater[55] create a typology of dictatorship to address this. The authors criticize those typologies that emphasize the personalization of dictatorships, as well as those that focus on their decision-making structures. Instead, Lai and Slater emphasize in their typology the institutions that regimes require to ensure social control and "political incumbency."[56]

According to Lai and Slater, military regimes are less effective than single-party regimes at creating these types of institutions, making them more likely to use military conflict as a means of thwarting potential challenges to their rule. What matters is not how dictatorships "make decisions (personalized vs. collective procedures), but how they enforce them (party vs. military institutions)."[57] Though their typology incorporates personalist tendencies, the authors argue that the characteristic that drives conflict initiation is the regime's ability to control society.

Authoritarian regimes are grouped according to their despotic and infrastructural powers. Despotic power refers to whether the decision-making is autocratic or oligarchic (i.e. individual or collective); infrastructural power refers to whether the regime uses the military or a political party to stay in power. Thus, there are two key questions: 1) How do dictatorships make decisions? 2) How are decisions enforced? From these questions, four types of dictatorships emerge:

- Machine (oligarchic, party dictatorships)
- Bossism (autocratic, party dictatorships)
- Junta (oligarchic, military dictatorships)
- Strongman (autocratic, military dictatorships)

According to Lai and Slater, parties are better tools for deterring elite defections and mobilizing the masses. Militaries, though capable of providing security, are less capable of organizing elites and finding effective means for distributing patronage. Militarized dictatorships are more likely to provoke other states because they are seen as less legitimate in the eyes of the citizenry. They are also more willing to engage in risk-taking behavior to secure their continued power, as they have few other tools at their disposal to do so. Lai and Slater find that only infrastructural power influences conflict initiation; despotic power has little effect. Levels of personalization have little impact on the likelihood that conflicts will be provoked.

The ability of institutions to curtail dissent and instill a sense of the regime's legitimacy has greater impact on authoritarian politics in Lai and Slater's view than does the way in which institutions constrain the behavior of the leaders. Though Lai and Slater's theoretical argument provides many insights about authoritarian politics, it is unclear whether their categorizations are solely measuring the ability of regimes to ensure social control and *not also* elite constraints on the leadership. Embedded within both party and military institutions are organizational structures that provide elites with the tools to collectively checks leaders' powers. These domestic constraints may in turn influence the leader's decision-making calculus when it comes to inter-state conflict. It is also unclear how military organizations lack the tools necessary to distribute patronage. Though the subset of citizens targeted may be different in military dictatorships than in party dictatorships, it seems logical that militaries would be fully capable of distributing perks to members of their organization (i.e. lower-level members of the military).

Type of Leadership

Autocratic regimes are distinguished based on the type of leader in power. Jennifer Gandhi and Przeworski[58] group regimes according to whether the dictator is a monarch, a member of the military, or a civilian. The unit of analysis is the leader of the regime. Monarchs rely on the royal family or the court to organize their rule, while military leaders rely on the armed forces. Civilian leaders of dictatorships, by contrast, "do not have preexisting organizations on which to rely. They must create their own organization."[59] Because of this, civilian leaders typically rely on a political party to assist them in governance.

Such differences in the nature of the leader have implications for the incentives that leaders face to create institutions and, in turn, for dictators' survival rates. The logic is that dictators need the cooperation of other actors to maintain their power. Such cooperation can be induced by "sharing spoils or by making policy compromises."[60] The greater the dictator's need for cooperation, the more the dictator must rely on such concessions. Though rents can be directly doled out by the dictator, legislatures provide a key means by which dictators can provide policy compromises. Gandhi and Przeworski argue that civilian dictators face a higher need for cooperation than monarchic or military leaders, and therefore nearly always incorporate legislatures and one or more political parties in the political system. These institutions, in turn, prolong the survival of the regime.

This typology provides key insights regarding how the nature of leaders' support groups influences the types of decisions that leaders will make. It also shows that political institutions are not created arbitrarily; they can be tools by which leaders entrench their hold on power. One weakness of this typology, however, is that it conflates leaders with regimes. As we emphasize in this study, authoritarian regimes often last well beyond the fall of any one leader. The processes of regime change and leadership change are in most cases distinct. Viewing the dictator as synonymous with the dictatorship will lead to misunderstandings of these distinct processes.

How Dictatorships are Classified in this Study?

Each of the categorizations of dictatorships discussed in this chapter has merits and drawbacks; the typology used should depend on the question the researcher seeks to answer. In this study, we are interested in how elite-leader and elite-mass relations influence authoritarian politics. Because of this, we use the Geddes typology,[61] which identifies the key institutions that structure elite politics in dictatorships (i.e. parties and militaries).

Though Geddes' typology has weaknesses (as discussed earlier), we view its weaknesses as minor given the size of its strengths, which include: the simplicity of the categorizations, cross-national applicability, the emphasis on elites and leaders, and the incorporation of institutions (parties and militaries) as central to shaping politics. We should note that while Geddes' typology underlies many of the arguments presented throughout this study, we discuss other ways of conceptualizing dictatorships where relevant.

In addition to the categories of dictatorship that Geddes outlines, we also discuss monarchic dictatorships in this study where possible. We do so because monarchies comprise a sizeable portion of extant authoritarian regimes.

In the section that follows, we briefly define military, single-party, personalist, and monarchic authoritarian rule. We also discuss regimes that share features of two or more of these categories, referred to as hybrid regimes.

Definitions of Regimes

Military Dictatorships

Military dictatorships are defined by Geddes[62] as regimes in which a group of officers holds power, determines who will lead the country, and exercises influence over policy. Though some scholars classify regimes as military dictatorships if the leader of the regime is a member of the military, for Geddes, this is but one component. In addition to the leader being a member of the military, in Geddes' classification other high-level elites must also be members of the military.

Military dictatorships are characterized by rule by a professionalized military as an institution. In military regimes, elites are referred to as junta members; they are typically senior officers (and often other high-level officers) in the military.

Examples:[63]

- Algeria: 1992–present
- Argentina: 1943–1946; 1955–1958; 1966–1973; 1976–1983
- Brazil: 1964–1985
- Guatemala: 1970–1985
- Honduras: 1972–1981
- Nigeria: 1966–1979, 1983–1993
- Peru: 1968–1980
- South Korea, 1961–1987
- Turkey: 1980–1983
- Uruguay: 1973–1984

Single-party Dictatorships

Geddes[64] defines single-party dictatorships as regimes in which one party dominates politics. In single-party dictatorships, a single party has access to political posts and control over policy. Other parties may legally exist, compete in elections, and even hold legislative seats, yet true political power lies with the dominant party.

In single-party dictatorships, party elites are typically members of the ruling body of the party, sometimes called the central committee, or politburo. This group of individuals controls the selection of party officials and "organizes the distribution of benefits to supporters and mobilizes citizens to vote and show support for party leaders."[65]

Examples:

- Bolivia: 1952–1964, Revolutionary Nationalist Movement (MNR)
- Botswana: 1966-present, Botswana Democratic Party (BDP)
- China: 1949–present, Chinese Communist Party (CCP)
- East Germany: 1945–1990, Socialist Unity Party of Germany(SUPG)
- Kenya: 1963–2002, Kenya African National Union (KANU)
- Laos: 1975–present, Laos People's Revolutionary Party(LPRP)
- Malaysia: 1957–present, Barisan Nasional (BN)
- Mexico: 1917–2000, Institutional Revolutionary Party (PRI)
- Singapore: 1965–present, People's Action Party (PAP)
- Soviet Union: 1917–1991, Communist Party(CP)

Personalist Dictatorships

Personalist dictatorships, as characterized by Geddes[66] are regimes in which all power lies in the hands of a single individual. Personalist dictatorships differ from other forms of dictatorships in their access to key political positions, other fruits of office, and depend much more on the discretion of the personalist dictator. Personalist dictators may be members of the military or leaders of a political party. Yet, neither the military nor the party exercises power independent from the dictator.

In personalist dictatorships, the elite corps is usually made up of close friends or family members of the dictator. These individuals are all typically handpicked to serve their posts by the dictator.

Examples:

- Central African Republic: 1966–1979, Jean-Bédel Bokassa
- Dominican Republic: 1930–1961, Rafael Trujillo
- Haiti, 1957–1986, François and Jean-Claude Duvalier
- Iraq: 1979–2003, Saddam Hussein
- Philippines: 1972–1986, Ferdinand Marcos

- Somalia: 1969–1990, Siad Barre
- Spain: 1939–1979, Francisco Franco
- Uganda: 1966–1971, Milton Obote; 1971–1979, Idi Amin
- Yemen: 1978–present, Ali Abdullah Salih
- Zaire: 1965–1997, Joseph Mobutu

Monarchies

We follow Hadenius and Teorell and define monarchic dictatorships as regimes in which "a person of royal descent has inherited the position of head of state in accordance with accepted practice or constitution."[67] Regimes are not considered monarchies if the monarch's role is largely ceremonial (as in the United Kingdom). Real political power must be exercised by the monarch for regimes to be classified as such. Elites in monarchies are typically members of the royal family.

Examples:

- Afghanistan: 1929–1973
- Cambodia: 1953–1970
- Ethiopia: 1850s–1974
- Iran: 1925–1979
- Iraq: 1932–1958
- Jordan: 1946–present
- Libya: 1951–1969
- Oman: 1740s–present
- Saudi Arabia: 1927–present
- Swaziland: 1968–present
- United Arab Emirates: 1971–present

Hybrid Dictatorships

Hybrid dictatorships are regimes that blend qualities of personalist, single-party, and military dictatorships.[68] When regimes share characteristics of all three forms of dictatorships, they are referred to as triple threats. The most common forms of hybrid dictatorships are personalist/single-party hybrids and personalist/military hybrids.

Examples:

Personalist/Single-party

- Cuba: 1959–present, Fidel Castro/Communist Party of Cuba (PCC)
- North Korea: 1948–present, Kim Il-sung and Kim Jong-il/Workers' Party of Korea (WPK)

Personalist/Military

- Chile: 1973–1989, Augusto Pinochet
- Pakistan: 1977–1988, Muhammad Zia-ul-Haq

Single-party/Military

- Burundi: 1966–1987, National Progress and Unity Party (UPRONA)
- El Salvador: 1948–1984, Revolutionary Party of Democratic Unification (PRUD)

Triple Threat

- Egypt: 1952–present, Gamal Abdel Nasser, Anwar Sadat, and Hosni Mubarak/ National Democratic Party (NDP)
- Syria: 1963–present, multiple leaders, Ba'ath Party

Summary and Conclusion

Without meaningful ways of classifying authoritarian regimes, it is impossible to answer key questions about authoritarian politics. Typologies are important because they drive the way that we think about how dictatorships work. In this chapter, we summarized the key typologies in the authoritarian politics literature, grouping them according to whether they are continuous or categorical in nature.

As we have shown, categorizations of dictatorship have evolved considerably since the early studies on totalitarianism. In contemporary work, the discussion does not center on *whether* to disaggregate dictatorships, but rather *how* to do so. That authoritarian regimes are no longer viewed as a residual category marks a major advancement in our understanding of the authoritarian world.

In the following chapter, we examine the causes of authoritarianism. We then turn to discussing the strategies that dictators and dictatorships pursue to ensure their political survival, before examining how differences across dictatorships influence political outcomes. We close this study by offering in-depth analyses of single-party, military, personalist, monarchic, and hybrid dictatorships and, in doing so, offer a colorful glimpse inside the world of dictatorships and the leaders who rule them.

Review Questions

- Why do scholars develop typologies of dictatorships? Why are they important?
- What is totalitarianism?

- How do authoritarian and totalitarian regimes differ from each another?
- How does Huntington distinguish single-party states?
- What are the different types of military rules according to Perlmutter?
- What are the strengths and weaknesses of using continuous typologies to categorize authoritarian regimes?
- In what ways are competitive authoritarian regimes distinct from both authoritarian regimes and democracies?
- What are the strengths and weaknesses of using categorical typologies of dictatorships?
- How do strategy-based typologies of dictatorship differ from structure-based typologies?
- What is the "dictator's dilemma"?

Key Points

- Early scholarship on dictatorships emphasized totalitarianism.
- The work that followed distinguished totalitarianism from authoritarianism.
- Emphasis on the different institutions under dictatorships began with research on rule by a single party or the military.
- The contemporary literature classifies dictatorships using either continuous measures or categorical measures.
- Continuous typologies of dictatorships place regimes on a linear scale based on how authoritarian they are.
- Categorical typologies of dictatorships distinguish regimes based on either the strategies used by the dictator to stay in power or the structure of the dictatorship.

Notes

1. Linz, *Totalitarian and Authoritarian Regimes* (1975, p. 255).
2. Huntington, *The Third Wave* (1991).
3. Acemoglu and Robinson, *Economic Origins of Dictatorship* (2006, p. 17).
4. Ibid. (p. 18).
5. Brooker, *Non-Democratic Regimes* (2000, p. 3).
6. Przeworski et al., *Democracy and Development* (2000, p. 15).
7. Ibid., (p. 18).
8. Brooker, *Non-Democratic Regimes* (2000, p. 2).
9. Huntington, *The Third Wave* (1991).
10. Arendt, *The Origins of Totalitarianism* (1951).
11. Ibid. (p. 323).
12. Ibid. (p. 326).

13. Friedrich and Brzezinski, *Totalitarian Dictatorship and Autocracy* (1956).

14. Brzezinski, *Ideology and Power* (1962).

15. Brzezinski, "*Totalitarianism and Rationality*" (1956, p. 755).

16. Linz, *Totalitarian and Authoritarian Regimes* (1975).

17. Huntington and Moore, *Authoritarian Politics in Modern* (1970, p. 4).

18. Ibid., (p. 23).

19. The revolutionary one-party system is a variant of what previous writers labeled a "totalitarian, mobilization, or movement regime" (Purcell 1973, 304).

20. Ibid. (pp. 40–41).

21. Perlmutter, *The Praetorian State* (1969); *The Military and Politics* (1977).

22. Perlmutter, *The Military and Politics* (1977, pp. 104–114).

23. Ibid.

24. Perlmutter, *The Praetorian State* (1969).

25. Perlmutter, *The Military and Politics* (1977, p. 105).

26. Perlmutter, *The Praetorian State* (1969, p. 392).

27. Diamond, *Developing Democracy toward Consolidation* (1999, pp. 15–16); Coller and Levitsky, *Democracy with Adjectives* (1997); Carothers, *End of the Transition* (2002, p. 10).

28. Diamond, *Thinking about Hybrid Regimes* (2002).

29. Diamond uses the term "hybrid" to refer to these grey zone regimes. Whereas Diamond views hybrid regimes as regimes falling in the grey zone between dictatorship and democracy, we view them as mixes of single-party, military, and/or personalist regimes. Because we conceptualize the concept of hybridism differently than Diamond, we omit the usage of the term "hybrid" in this section to avoid confusion.

30. Ibid. (p. 24)

31. Ibid. (p. 22).

32. Levitsky and Way, *Rise of Competitive* (2002).

33. Ibid. (p. 52).

34. Ibid. (p. 53).

35. Ibid. (p. 54).

36. Ibid. (p. 56).

37. Schedler, *Elections without Democracy* (2002).

38. Ibid. (p. 37).

39. Ibid.

40. Ibid. (p. 8).

41. Hadenius and Teorell, *Pathways from Authoritarianism* (2007, p. 144).

42. Wintrobe, *Political Economy of Dictatorship* (1998); *Dictatorship: Analytical Approaches* (2007).

43. Ibid. (1998).

44. Wintrobe, *Political Economy of Dictatorship* (1998, pp. 43–47); *Dictatorship: Analytical Approaches* (2007, pp. 365–370).

45. Haber, *Authoritarian Government* (2006).

46. Ibid. (p. 701).
47. Ibid. (p. 702).
48. Geddes, *Minimum-Winning Coalitions* (2004).
49. Geddes, *Paradigms and Sand Castles* (2003).
50. Regimes that combine characteristics of all three are classified as triple threats.
51. Hadenius and Teorell, *Pathways from Authoritarianism* (2007).
52. Ibid.
53. Bruce Bueno de Mesquita et al., *Logic of Political Survival* (2003).
54. See Haber (2006) and Magaloni (2008) for a further critique of the selectorate theory. For a discussion of the quantitative methods used in the test of the theory, see Clarke and Stone (2008). The authors find that when the appropriate methods are implemented, the results fail to support the predictions of the theory.
55. Lai and Slater, *Institutions of the Offensive* (2006).
56. Ibid. (p. 113).
57. Ibid. (p. 114).
58. Gandhi and Przeworski, *Authoritarian Institutions* (2007).
59. Ibid. (p. 1284).
60. Ibid. (p. 1283).
61. Geddes, *Paradigms and Sand Castles* (2003).
62. Ibid.
63. The regime classifications used in this study come from Geddes (1999), as used in Peceny, Beer, Sanchez-Terry (2002), accessed via http://www.uvm.edu/~cbeer/geddes/Geddes.html. For regimes in existence after 1999, we estimated their end dates. We also estimated the beginning and end dates for monarchies discussed in this study. We should note that the precise beginning and end dates of many regimes are often debatable. The dates provided in this study should be viewed as approximate.
64. Geddes, *Paradigms and Sand Castles* (2003).
65. Ibid. (p. 52).
66. Ibid.
67. Hadenius and Teorell, *Pathways from Authoritarianism* (2007, p. 146).
68. Hybrid monarchic regimes are rare.

The Causes of Dictatorship

2

Authoritarian government has been the norm for most of the history. Despite waves of democratization in the post World War II era,[1] authoritarian regimes still dot much of today's political landscape. In fact, by a modest estimate, nearly one in three countries in the world is ruled by dictatorship.[2] The Chinese communist regime alone rules nearly a quarter of the world's population.[3]

Given the perseverance of authoritarian government, it is important to gain an understanding of its origin. In this chapter, we present and examine in detail the various theories proposed to account for why dictatorships emerge as opposed to democracies. We then explore the subset of theories dedicated to explaining the emergence of particular *types* of authoritarian government, namely those that we concentrate on in this book: personalist, military, single-party, and monarchic regimes. In doing so, we highlight the particular regions where these types of dictatorships have been more common and point to potential explanations for these regional correlations.

Explaining the Emergence of Authoritarian Government

What explains why dictatorships emerge in some countries but not in others? What types of conditions are breeding grounds for authoritarianism? Initial scholarship in this area explored the foundations of totalitarianism. The literature that followed concentrated on obstacles to democratization and the factors that pave the way for democratic consolidation. In the sections that follow, we present and examine this literature.

Foundations of Totalitarianism

The early work in this field has as its focus the origins of totalitarian and fascist forms of dictatorship. Central to this literature is an emphasis on the masses. According to Hannah Arendt,[4] the rigors of extreme levels of individualism in capitalist societies attract people to totalitarianism as a form of government. Similarly, Juan Linz[5] argues that totalitarianism emerges as a result of class and ideological conflict. In response to the spread of capitalism, fascist movements form as a means of incorporating the masses into the political process and, as such, help to create totalitarian states.

In Linz's view, the increased salience of nationalism also contributes to totalitarianism, by creating conflicts within societies. As dominant ethnic groups seek to integrate ethnic and cultural minorities into society—and minorities in response claim their rights to self-determination—the dominant group will often push for an authoritarian state as a means of maintaining order. This corresponds with the role hyper-nationalism played in the rise of fascist regimes in Germany under Adolf Hitler and Italy under Benito Mussolini.

Factors Conducive to Democratization

As totalitarianism waned following World War II, scholars began to shift their focus from the causes of totalitarianism to the conditions favorable to democratization. Though some of the studies in this research strain look explicitly at the causes of dictatorship, most center on the factors conducive to the emergence of democracy.

Institutional Factors

In Samuel Huntington's[6] view, modernization and mobilization, coupled with a lag in the development of political institutions, are problematic for stability and democracy. The *type* of government is less important in this regard than the *degree* of government, or *level of institutionalization*. Governments with low levels of institutionalization are in states of political decay, characterized by high levels of corruption, the blurring of private and public in government, lack of civil associations, and an absence of political consensus. Such scenarios lead to "ungovernability" and the unfeasibility of democracy. Huntington argues that the intersection of modernization and mobilization with political decay impinges on political development and makes democracy unlikely, a situation typical of much of the developing world. George Kahin, Guy Pauker, and Lucian Pye[7] identify similar factors that inhibit democratization. These include charismatic leadership, lack of formally organized interests, and "a tendency for unorganized and generally inarticulate segments of society, such as peasants and urban masses, to involve themselves in politics in a discontinuous, sudden, erratic and often violent way."[8]

Economic Factors

For Seymour Martin Lipset,[9] economic and demographic factors explain why some countries are democratic and others are not. In particular, urbanization, industrialization, education, and healthy populations all lead to pressures within a country to democratize. "Modernization" of society makes democracy more likely by leading to a change in the mentality of citizens. Absent such societal characteristics, dictatorship will persist.

Adam Przeworski et al.[10] also explore how economic factors influence the rise of dictatorship vs. democracy. They show that the proportion of democracies is indeed larger in rich countries than in poor (see **Figure 2.1**). In contrast to Lipset, however, the authors find that economic development (or modernization, as Lipset puts it) does not *cause* democratization. Though the consolidation of democracy is more likely when countries are rich, so is the consolidation of dictatorship. Wealth leads to political stability, whether in the form of long-lasting democracy or long-lasting dictatorship. Poverty, by contrast, leads to political instability, whether in the form of short-lived democracies or short-lived dictatorships. Countries that are very poor may

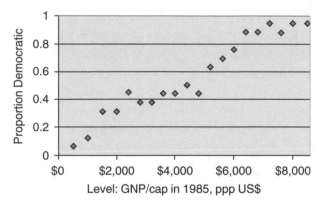

Figure 2.1 Level of Development and Incidence of Democratic Regimes. *Source*: Przeworski and Limongi (1997)

democratize, but they are likely to fall apart soon after. Though economic development does not directly explain the cause of dictatorship, it does play an important role in understanding the durability of authoritarian government more generally.

Natural resource wealth is also posited to influence regime type. Michael Ross[11] shows that authoritarianism is highly correlated with the abundance of oil and other natural resources. Access to natural resource rents (or profits) provides incentives for political actors to behave in ways conducive to dictatorship. Such rents facilitate the ability of political actors to please supporters via the doling out of patronage rather than the implementation of political reforms. This argument has been used to explain why so many natural resource-rich Middle Eastern states are governed by dictatorship. **Figure 2.2** shows the relationship between wealth and regime type among a selection of major oil and gas producing countries (as of 2003).[12] The bulk of wealthy, resource-rich countries are non-democratic. Though the presence of abundant natural resources is not a necessary condition for dictatorship (in that many resource-poor countries are authoritarian also), it does appear to cause dictatorship to emerge.

Class Factors

Barrington Moore[13] highlights how the presence of a large middle class is favorable to democratization. He points to the critical role of the established,

	Wealthy	Poor
Democratic	USA UK Norway Venezuela	Nigeria
Non-Democratic	Kuwait Qatar UAE Oman Saudi Arabia Bahrain Libya Brunei	Angola Turkmenistan Uzbekistan

Figure 2.2 Major Oil/Gas Producing Countries. *Source*: World Bank (2003), Polity IV (2008)

landed upper class and the peasantry during countries' transitions from agrarian to industrial societies in determining the type of political system that takes shape. Democracy is most likely to emerge where there are groups in society that have independent economic bases, i.e. where there is a *middle class*. As Moore puts it, "no bourgeois, no democracy."[14]

In countries where landowners are able to secure their own political power and commercialize agriculture so that the peasants who work the land face minimal repression, democracy will result. By contrast, in countries where landowners are allied with the state and can use its tools to repress the peasantry, dictatorship will result. This can happen for two reasons: either the peasantry stages a revolution against the non-commercial landowning class, as in the Soviet Union, or the landowning class uses the state to impose its will on the peasantry, as in Japan.

The presence of a middle class, central to Moore's argument, is indicative of a society in which wealth is relatively evenly distributed. In this same vein, Daron Acemoglu and James Robinson[15] argue that inequality is an impediment to democratization, as unequal societies can be highly explosive making the prospects of democracy very threatening to political elites.[16]

In Dieter Rueschemeyer et al.'s[17] view, the consolidation of democracy is linked closely to capitalist development, as capitalism limits the power of landholders and strengthens popular classes. Key to this process is the mobilization of the working and middle classes. These classes are able to organize themselves better where there is greater urbanization, factory production, and new forms of communication and transportation. Unlike Moore, however, Rueschemeyer et al. state that the existence of a bourgeoisie is not enough to spark pressures to democratize, as the bourgeoisie has historically been hostile to democratization when its interests have been threatened.[18] Where *organized labor*, along with other professional groups and associations, can challenge the state, the power balance is most conducive to democracy.

The Role of Ethnicity

A handful of scholars have sought to disentangle the role of ethnicity in determining regime type. Donald Horowitz[19] claims that ethnic cleavages and diversity are obstacles for countries attempting to democratize. He writes, "Democracy has progressed furthest in those East European countries that have the fewest serious ethnic cleavages and progressed more slowly or not at all in those that are deeply divided."[20] Huntington[21] concurs, arguing that states that are ethnically diverse are more likely to be dictatorships. Greater ethnic-political diversity makes states more prone to conflict, making it more difficult for them to implement democratic procedures. In such societies, political competition emerges along ethnic lines, causing instability and making democratization unlikely.[22] Along the same lines, Adrian Karatnycky[23] views ethnic diversity as an impediment to democratic consolidation. He states that "democracy has been significantly more successful in monoethnic societies than in ethnically divided and multiethnic societies."[24]

Other scholars argue, however, that ethnicity is not a driving force in the emergence of dictatorship. M. Steven Fish and Robin Brooks,[25] for example, find that ethnic diversity does not adversely affect the prospect of democracy. Indeed, there are many ethnically diverse states that have managed to temper societal polarization via power-sharing mechanisms, which ensure political stability. In such states, democracy may actually be a means by which to channel and address ethnic grievances and alleviate conflict.[26]

Culture and Democracy

The Civic Culture (1963), by Gabriel Almond and Sidney Verba, is a foundational piece in the field of comparative politics. In this study, Almond and Verba examine mass values and citizen attitudes in five nations and look at their impact on political development and association with democracy. The authors argue that a country's political culture plays a key role in democratic consolidation. Three types of political cultures are identified: participant, subject, and parochial. Almond and Verba write:

> A participant is assumed to be aware of and informed about the political system in both its governmental and political aspects. A subject tends to be cognitively oriented primarily to the output side of government: the executive, bureaucracy, and judiciary. The parochial tends to be unaware, or only dimly aware, of the political system in all its aspects.
>
> (p. 79)

Parochial cultures are theorized to be an impediment to democratization, since they are characterized by low levels of trust and social capital. The political culture most amenable to democratic consolidation is a "balanced political culture," which combines involvement and activity, as well as some passivity (pp. 31–32). Overall, a democratic political culture is one that consists of "beliefs, attitudes, and norms" that support participation (p. 178).

Studies in comparative politics that have examined the role of culture in democratic consolidation are often criticized for ethnocentrism, since Western political cultures are typically posited as the most conducive to stable democracy. Looking at the impact of culture on democratic consolidation is also discouraged on the grounds that culture is an amorphous concept and difficult to measure or define. Culture is often a residual category that scholars emphasize only after "we have ruled out some structural and institutional explanations" (Elkins and Simeon 1979, p. 130; see also Lane 1992).

Explaining the Type of Dictatorship

As emphasized throughout this study, dictatorships often differ from one another as much as they do from democracies. Therefore, understanding the causes of different *types* of dictatorships is an important endeavor.

As Barbara Geddes[27] shows, most dictatorships begin following an illegal seizure of power—or coup—carried out by military officers (or, less frequently, members of revolutionary parties). The type of dictatorship that takes shape afterward, however, is the result of a complex set of factors. Once the coup has occurred, its leader will nearly always seek to maximize his/her power. The leader's co-conspirators in the coup will typically try to contain the leader's ambitions. Their ability to do so, however, will depend on their organizational strength. Tightly organized militaries and parties are usually better able to unify and limit the leader's efforts to consolidate power than are weakly assembled groups. In other words, the more well-established the military or party is prior to the seizure of power, the more likely its members will be following it to resist the leader's attempts to personalize the regime. This argument implies that when a professionalized military seizes power, military dictatorship is likely to result; when a professionalized party seizes power, single-party dictatorship is likely to result; and when weakly organized groups seize power, personalist dictatorships are likely to result.

Though we have a theoretical understanding of how these regimes form, few systematic tests of this relationship have been carried out to our knowledge. Many questions remain about the conditions under which militaries or parties are likely to be organizationally strong, and the factors that lead to militaries, as opposed to revolutionary parties seizing power. Though few studies have examined the conditions that account for the heterogeneity of dictatorships, scholars have identified the factors that underlie the emergence of each type of dictatorship.

In the sections that follow, we present this research and highlight the key conditions conducive to the formation of the types of dictatorships explored in this study: personalist, military, single-party, and monarchic. In doing so, we discuss in detail the correlation between region and regime type, delineating the causal pathways through which each type of dictatorship has dominated the landscapes of particular regions of the world. Central to each of these discussions is an analysis of a series of historical, geo-political, and ideological forces that give way to each type of regime.

Foundations of Military Dictatorships

Nearly all military dictatorships begin with the military executing (or threatening to execute) a coup d'état.[28] The military is involved in staging coups because of its "advantageous qualifications for staging them."[29] Though coups do not always lead to military dictatorship (as discussed above), the military's decision to enter politics via coup is a key foundational moment in the establishment of any military dictatorship. When militaries choose to stage coups, they do not always do so with the intention to stay in power.

According to Samuel Finer,[30] two factors dictate whether the military will rise to power: disposition and opportunity. Militaries are motivated to intervene when their corporate interests are threatened.[31] Interventions are also likely when the civilian government lacks legitimacy or has been discredited. In such scenarios, the military views its own intervention as key to the country's (and its own) survival.[32] Others concur that, corporate grievances of the military, can serve as a motive for intervention.[33]

Military influence in politics is often a function of its professionalism.[34] Military centrality theory posits that resourceful and cohesive militaries are more likely to intervene.[35] In newly independent states, the military is frequently the "most modern institution, having professionally trained leaders, access to advanced technology, organizational resources, and a strong esprit de corps among its officers."[36] Huntington further argues that low levels of institutionalization coupled with high levels of modernization can lead to military interventions. He writes that the military is the most professionalized institution in newly established nations and because of this, the military thinks that it is best suited to rule.[37]

Economic conditions can also affect the rise of the military. Martin Needler writes that "a successful coup or revolt is less likely when economic conditions are improving."[38] Moreover, military coups are more likely to occur when the civilian government lacks legitimacy or has been discredited. In such scenarios, the military views its own intervention as key to the country's (and its own) survival.[39]

Economic inequality (or polarization) can contribute to both disposition and opportunity. Inequality can generate societal unrest, prompting the military to intervene to restore stability. It can also lead to societal groups allying with the military to protect and further their economic interests. Severe economic inequalities (in the early days of a country's formation) can engender pushes by the upper classes for the establishment of strong militaries. Such strong militaries, in turn, are more likely to helm successful coups that launch them in power. As Huntington[40] points out, military regimes tend to emerge in bifurcated and polarized societies.

Others argue that military regimes are more likely to arise in states that have had experience with military coups, which is known as the coup trap (see **Chapter 5**).[41] John Londegran and Keith Poole write that a "successful coup continues to elevate the propensity for yet another coup."[42] Finer claims that this is because the political culture of a country is deeply affected by the coup, breaking the ice for more coups to take place.[43]

Military Dictatorship in Latin America

Latin America has been home to many of the world's military dictatorships. Since World War II, the majority of Latin American countries have experienced some form of military dictatorship. Many scholars have made note of this relationship. As Eric Nordlinger writes, "the recurring pattern of military coups and governments is strikingly evidenced among the Latin American countries."[44] Similarly, Howard Wiarda states that the "incidence of Latin American coups has been so constant over a such a long period of time that they could be considered a normal or regular part of the political process . . . there appears to be no diminution in the numbers of coups over time; indeed the strong presence of the military in national political life seems to be constant, ongoing and ubiquitous."[45] Peter Mayer adds that "in no part of the developing world has the influence of the military been more profound than in Latin America. Political intervention and rule by the military have been almost the norm and not the regrettable exception."[46]

Many explanations of the pervasiveness of military dictatorships in Latin America emphasize the region's close proximity to the United States. For geo-political reasons, Latin American countries received substantial military aid during the Cold War, along with military training. The US government was disinclined to pressure military governments in Latin America to democratize at this time, so long as they were anti-Communist. The United States even worked to prop up some Latin American military dictatorships in order to ensure a regional anti-Communist front and thwart the ambitions of leftist guerilla movements. Such efforts intensified following the success of the Cuban revolution in 1959 and the subsequent formation of leftist guerilla offshoots.

Many militaries in Latin America were externally well funded and endowed with disproportionate amount of power. This often afforded officers the capacity to stage coups and to set up their own rules.[47] External military funding was particularly aggressive when military dictatorships were at war with leftist groups. In Nicaragua, Guatemala, and El Salvador, for example, arms imports increased dramatically between 1979 and 1985, accounting for some of the most rapid military buildups in the history of the region. In the region as a whole, arms imports increased 159 percent during this time.

Cold War considerations are linked closely to the emergence of military dictatorships in Latin America. John Duncan Powell argues, for example, that the US Military Assistance Program, which endorsed the military taking a more direct role in politics, was a "contributory cause of militarism" in Latin America.[48] Similarly, Eric Nordlinger[49] claims that external funding and training in Latin America strengthened the political position and role of the military in its relationship with other groups. As Beatriz Magaloni writes, the Cold War period was particularly amenable to military dictatorship "because there was sharper ideological polarization between left and right that interacted with poverty and economic instability to generate propitious structural conditions for the armed forces to intervene."[50]

Economic inequality also helps to explain the prevalence of military dictatorships in Latin America. At the time of the Cold War, economic polarization persisted throughout much of Latin America, with high levels of social and economic inequality common to many countries in the region. Under such circumstances, strong militaries were important in defending the interests of the elite and thwarting societal unrest.

Because Latin American military elites typically espoused conservative values, they were desirable candidates in the eyes of the upper classes and foreign powers, to implement those policies civilian politicians had proven incapable (or unwilling) to promote.[51] As such, these actors all had coinciding interests in maintaining the status quo, so as to prevent the lower classes from making potentially threatening demands for increased political participation and deterring the advancement of leftist political interests.[52] Military coups were often supported by civilian elites[53] and calls for military intervention were widely publicized.[54] As a result of the strengthening and increased power of the military, society as a whole became militarized in many Latin American countries, blurring the boundaries between the military and civilian spheres.[55]

In Latin America the military has always played a prominent political role compared to the East, where the military has been subservient to the Communist party. Civil military relations in Eastern Europe have been much different than in Latin America. In contrast to Latin America, in Eastern Europe there has been a "long tradition of civilian control over the military."[56] Valerie Bunce argues that this tradition goes far back in Russian history after the Bolshevik Revolution. Eastern European regimes have had domestic control of the military and the secret police almost entirely after 1968.

Political elites in Latin America always had "indirect and uneven control over a capitalist economy, which in comparison, to Eastern Europe necessitated a military to defend its interests."[57] In Latin America, the military gained strength vis-à-vis civilian forces. According to José Nun, the military has intervened on behalf of the incapacitated middle and upper classes, acting as the protector of their interests. Nun claims that the middle classes aspired to the values of the economic elite and were willing to abandon the idea of democratization because they perceived democracy as a threat to their well-being. Nun writes that the military compensated for the middle classes' "inability to establish itself as a well integrated hegemonic group."[58] Elites and the middle classes cultivated military alliances, and with the tacit and sometimes overt support of these classes, the military emerged as the most legitimate institution to run the country. After the military gained power, it remained strong enough to rule on its own since elites were never powerful enough to establish clear hegemony over it.

Guatemala and El Salvador, for example, have each experienced significant periods of military rule. Their militaries were created by oligarchs and other elites as a means of ensuring that the poor remained suppressed. In turn, their societies were characterized by high levels of economic polarization. Strong militaries became an essential means of maintaining political control.

By contrast, Costa Rica—one of the only countries in Latin America where the military has played a small role in politics—is a relatively equal society. According to Acemoglu et al.,[59] the military in Costa Rica never needed to be developed due to the structure of the economy. Unlike its regional counterparts, Costa Rica was not dominated in its early days, by predatory caudillos who influenced political and economic life. At the time of colonization, Costa Rica was characterized by a small indigenous population (preventing the formation of major plantations) and few exploitable natural resources (like gold). These factors reduced the chances for social conflicts to emerge that would necessitate the establishment of a strong military.

In fact, by 1949, Costa Rica's military was demobilized and disbanded after a brief period of dictatorship. Costa Rica has experienced virtually no external or internal conflicts during its history, further limiting the military's role in politics.[60] As a result, Costa Rica's military has never been very powerful nor required high levels of professionalization to ensure societal control.

Bureaucratic Authoritarianism

Though not synonymous with military dictatorship, Guillermo O'Donnell (1973) provides an in depth analysis of bureaucratic authoritarian regimes, which he identifies as a new kind of militarized state endemic to Latin America. In O'Donnell's conceptualization, bureaucratic authoritarianism takes shape when the military and the technocratic class ally to form a dictatorship in a society that is modernized. Modernized societies are those in which the masses are urbanized and politically activated and technocrats are powerful and politically entrenched. When societies undergo modernization, poor economic conditions will inevitably result, such as high inflation and foreign exchange shortages. Such economic turmoil, coupled with mass pressure to find a solution, make authoritarianism a means by which the country can implement the politically unpopular policies necessary to stabilize the economy. As O'Donnell sees it, bureaucratic authoritarianism is part of the process by which modernized states move from the "easy" stages of industrialization to more capital-intensive industrial economies. A strong military state can suppress the masses sufficiently to enable the country to move forward in its development. In turn, intervention is appealing to the military as it is the means by which threats to economic growth and development can be deterred.

Foundations of Single-party Dictatorships

Single-party dictatorships arise under a variety of circumstances. According to Huntington,[61] single-party dictatorships emerge when the incumbent state power has been weakened, a war of liberation or revolution has occurred, or during the process of decolonization. Some take shape via revolutionary movements, while others evolve out of democratic systems, through—at times subtle—electoral manipulation. Such manipulation can be in the form of electoral fraud, clever electoral engineering, buying off citizens for votes, or co-optation of the opposition.[62] The motivation underlying the party's decision to dominate the political process at the expense of other political actors can be nationalistic or ideological, or simply out of corporate self-interests.[63]

It should be noted that the alliance of a political party with the leadership of the regime does not constitute single-party rule. It is common for dictators to create political parties upon their assumption to power, if they do not already belong to one.[64] Political parties enhance the survival of the dictator by providing the dictator with a means by which to mobilize supporters and distribute the spoils of office to those who are most loyal. In many dictatorships, parties are merely tools of the dictator. In single-party dictatorships, they are institutions that penetrate all levels of society and influence policy.

Single-party Dictatorship in Eastern Europe and Asia

Eastern Europe and Asia (primarily East and Southeast Asia) have experienced many years of single-party rule. Though some argue that single-party dictatorships have been common to parts of Asia due to Asian values that emphasize consensus and consultation, this argument does not account for their dominance in much of Eastern Europe. Rather than values, a set of historical circumstances account for much of the regional groupings of single-party dictatorships, most notably the factors surrounding the Cold War, as both regions were of strategic importance to world powers at the time. We first discuss the reasons posited to explain the prevalence of single-party dictatorships in Eastern Europe, before turning to Asia.

In Eastern Europe, single-party states were implemented with the (at times forceful) assistance of the Soviet Union. Following the destruction suffered in World War II, the Soviet Union sought to create proximal buffer states, to potentially shield it from another German invasion or infiltration from the West. These satellite states were required to implement a communist political system and command economy, all of which necessitated, "monolithic party-state political structures."[65] In order to ensure the strength of the communist party, coalitions were formed with other parties and mass organizations that would eventually become "communist controlled puppets."[66] As Ivan Berend writes, Eastern European countries were basically "forced to copy the Soviet model;"[67] the system was introduced from a blueprint and "transplanted from the pages of textbooks."[68]

To maintain these regimes, the Soviet Union provided generous subsidies, in particular to Czechoslovakia and East Germany. Deviation from the Soviet system was costly for Eastern European states. The Soviet Union displayed its zero tolerance policy via invasions of Hungary and Czechoslovakia in 1956 and 1968, respectively. In essence, Soviet military power created the Communist states of Eastern Europe[69] as these states "were not born of revolution but of Soviet military liberation and occupation."[70] Brooker writes that in particular, the communist regimes in Mongolia, Poland, East Germany, Hungary, Bulgaria, Romania and North Korea were installed by the Soviets by force.[71]

It was not just Eastern Europe that was vital to the superpowers during the Cold War. Asia was also of strategic importance to both the United States and the Soviet Union. In Asia, communist parties took power in China, Vietnam, North Korea, and briefly in Cambodia. Single-party dictatorships also emerged in Taiwan, Malaysia, and Singapore. The parties that dominated them, however, were not communist. Malaysia's United Malays National Organization (UMNO) came to power amidst colonial rule, foreign occupation, and a war of insurgency; Taiwan's Nationalist/Kuomintang party (KMT) seized power, while fleeing the Communists; and Singapore's People's Action Party (PAP) rose to power following its independence and split from Malaysia.

The spread of dominant party systems in East and Southeast Asia, as elsewhere, was in many ways the result of Cold War-related geo-political considerations. According to Richard Stubbs, the insecure geo-political environment in East and Southeast Asia has had a "profound effect on the institutional states and economies of the region."[72] The establishment of dominant party systems was a means by which these states could achieve stability given the chaotic environment they were a part of.

As in Latin America, the US played a role in shaping the type of dictatorship that emerged. The US was concerned with creating strong states that were economically prosperous enough to defend themselves against communism. During the Cold War, many US policymakers believed that the promotion of "capitalism, anti-communism, and security could 'hang together.'"[73] Large amounts of US aid, the prosperity from the Korean and Vietnam Wars and the opening of the US markets to Asian exports led to the development of strong states.[74] Government capacity grew due to the need to "mobilize and coordinate financial, manpower, and other resources to meet the military threat posed by Communist neighbors and insurgents.[75] For example, in Taiwan the U.S. did everything possible to strengthen the Taiwanese economy to counter the threat from China. Between 1949 and the mid 1960s the U.S. gave Taiwan $1.7 billion in economic aid.[76] Singapore benefited from its proximity to Vietnam and Indonesia. US foreign direct investment and the influx of US dollars strengthened state capacity and gave the PAP government revenues to become more powerful.[77, 78]

Overall, the level of institutionalization in Eastern Europe and East and Southeast Asia has been comparatively higher than in Africa, Latin America and the Middle East. Strong governments and economies were in large part viewed as a necessity in order to fend off the spread of communism and capitalism during the Cold War. In addition, the one-party states in East and Southeast Asia and Eastern Europe have not had such wide disparities between rich and poor. Moreover, the absence of rich and powerful landed elites precluded the necessity of having military rule to defend its interests against the poor.

Hegemonic Party Systems

Hegemonic party systems are essentially a subset of single-party dictatorships. Magaloni (2006) provides a thorough examination of the origins of hegemonic party systems and the strategies they employ. Hegemonic party dictatorships are those in which "one political party remains in office uninterruptedly under semi-authoritarian conditions while holding regular multiparty elections" (p. 32). Hegemonic party systems form when a single party is able to maintain a super-majority in the legislature. With such an oversized coalition, the party can change the constitution to favor it and maintain its grip over electoral laws. For a hegemonic party system to take shape, the party must be able to access critical state resources such that it can distribute material rewards and government offices to party supporters.

Huntington (1970) points to three explanations for why such dictatorships emerge. First, "party systems reflect the class structure of societies, and in a society where there are no pronounced differences among social and economic classes, there is no social basis for more than one party" (p. 10). Second, "justification of the single-party is found in the need to counterbalance the fissiparous tendencies of a heterogeneous society" (Ibid.). Lastly, Huntington writes that a "one-party system is, in effect, the product of the efforts of a political elite to organize and legitimate rule by one social force over another in a bifurcated society. The bifurcation may be between socio-economic groups or between racial, religious, or ethnic ones" (p. 11).

Foundations of Personalist Dictatorships

Personalist dictatorships typically emerge following seizures of power in which the co-conspirators are not tightly organized, enabling the leader to maximize power, as discussed above. Personalist dictatorships can also take shape in other scenarios, however, such as when democratically-elected leaders implement constitutional changes enabling them to stay in power indefinitely. Such changes are possible, primarily because the leader does not face a tightly organized group that is capable of resisting him.

In essence, personalist dictatorships are more likely to sprout in poorly institutionalized societies. These types of underdeveloped circumstances are often characteristic of states negatively affected by colonialism and extreme poverty.

Personalist Dictatorship in Sub-Saharan Africa

The weak institutional environment conducive to the formation of personalist dictatorship is typical of much of sub-Saharan Africa, helping to explain why personalist dictatorships have been so prevalent there. Indeed, nearly every country in sub-Saharan Africa has experienced personalist dictatorship at some point since World War II. As Michael Bratton and Nicolas van de Walle point out, the "big man and his extended retinue defines African politics, from the highest reaches of the presidential palace to the humblest village assembly."[79] In many sub-Saharan African countries, those political institutions that exist are neo-patrimonial and largely based on patron-client ties.

Personalism in many sub-Saharan African dictatorships has been possible because of the weakness of political parties and the military there. Political parties and militaries in the region are often poorly organized, making them susceptible to personalized control.[80]

Part of the reason the military is weak in many sub-Saharan African countries is that, the infrequency of inter-state war (as opposed to civil war) has not necessitated the military to be professionalized and strong.[81] The armed forces are often mediocre at best and not oriented towards combat.[82] Foreign powers frequently used their own militaries to deal with conflicts in the region, giving sub-Saharan African leaders few reasons to develop robust militaries. For example, under mutual-aid pacts, French troops are "allowed to intervene in the internal affairs of their formal colonies to ensure that domestic discontent does not lead to instability."[83]

Militaries in sub-Saharan Africa have further been undermined by constant political reassignments to thwart coups, forced retirements of officers with expertise, and rapid turnover, all of which have done little to encourage discipline or an esprit de corps.[84] As Samuel Decalo[85] writes, sub-Saharan African militaries possess low levels of organizational unity; any politicization has quickly led to cleavages, and the erosion of the military's professionalism. Though many sub-Saharan African dictators have military roots, the military as an institution has often been too weak to provide any formidable challenge to their rule.[86] Even though the leader of the regime wears a military uniform, such scenarios are really just cases of personalist rule.

In addition to weak militaries, political parties in sub-Saharan Africa have also been fairly weak.[87] Many of the political parties, that formed in the region, were created as part of independence movements. These parties often lacked platforms beyond calls for independence, and weakened in strength once independence was attained.

Many also did not survive past the death of the party leader. Indeed, the leader of the party is often what keeps the party together in sub-Saharan Africa. Many political parties in the region lack national organization and are tied to the area where the individuals who lead them originate. Many are used primarily as tools by which their leaders can consolidate control.[88] The structure of the party is often altered to further the leader's interests, and support for the party is based on the leader's charisma and capacity to distribute patronage. Thus, when the leader goes, so too does the party.[89]

The negative consequences of colonialism also played a role in the emergence of personalist dictatorships in sub-Saharan Africa. After gaining independence, predominately in the latter half of the 20th century, sub-Saharan African leaders inherited from their colonial predecessors highly pluralistic societies with weak central bureaucracies and widespread government inefficiencies.[90] These conditions made it easier for a strongman to rule by decree and declare himself president for life if he saw fit. The institutions that existed were nominal in nature and did little to check the power of the leader.[91]

The colonial history of many sub-Saharan African countries left them poorly equipped to face their post-independence realities. With the previous means of administering order eradicated, fast-paced urbanization placed pressures on governments before they were ready to accommodate societal demands. By the time these countries achieved independence, they were poorly institutionalized and the colonial institutions that remained were inappropriate to fit the needs of the population. Because of the weak legitimacy of the state inherited by post-independence leaders, political contestation led to high levels of instability. As a result, elites in sub-Saharan Africa were more likely to resort to personalized and authoritarian rule.[92]

The strategies used by colonial governments to create and exacerbate ethnic divisions among their sub-Saharan African subjects had long-lasting effects in the region, leading to overemphasis on ethnicity as a political dimension. After independence, sub-Saharan African leaders often mimicked these strategies, favoring one ethnic group over another and using ethnicity as a means to consolidate their power.

The colonial experience was also extremely violent, socializing future sub-Saharan African leaders. As Robert Fatton, Jr. writes, "The colonial state was not only conceived in violence, but it was maintained by the free use of it."[93] What emerged after independence were various "forms of personal rule that achieved varied degrees of successes with varied degrees of coercion."[94] In essence, governance in sub-Saharan Africa was shaped by the individual ruler, rather than by effective political institutions and the rule of law.

International factors have also contributed to the prevalence of personalist rule in sub-Saharan Africa. In the Cold War era, sub-Saharan African states were often pawns in the hands of world powers, serving as important playgrounds for carrying out proxy wars. The promotion of democracy often took a back seat to geo-political considerations. Sub-Saharan African states that allied with and supported world powers often received steep payments in return, regardless of their human rights records or competency. For many years, France supplied Emperor Jean-Bédel Bokassa of the Central African Republic with half of his budget; money that went directly to the pockets of Bokassa and his cronies.[95] Such policies worked to sustain many sub-Saharan African strongmen in power.

Pressure for reform did not truly take place until the late 1980s with the end of the Cold War. The altered geo-political landscape afforded international donors and rich Western countries the flexibility to link resources to democratic reform and good governance.[96]

Joseph Mobutu of Zaire (today's Democratic Republic of Congo), for example, received backing from the United States for decades because he could be counted on as anti-communist during the Cold War. Though pressures mounted for him to democratize, Mobutu toyed with the West and told donors that the country was on the road to reform. In reality, Mobutu's actions domestically made a mockery of the democratic process.[97] It was not until the United States suspended aid to Mobutu in 1992 following the Cold War, that Mobutu's power was weakened.[98]

Sultanism

Sultanistic regimes, which in many ways capture what we mean by personalist dictatorship are examined in detail by Juan Linz and H.E. Chehabi (1998). Sultanistic regimes are those in which the "ruler exercises his power without restraint, at his own discretion and above all unencumbered by rules or by any commitment to an ideology or value system" (p. 7). According to Linz and Chehabi, the rise of sultanism is more likely to occur where the masses are relatively isolated (i.e. rural societies), where the educational system is less developed, and where there are high levels of poverty.

Such conditions often bring with them clientelistic and paternalistic socio-political structures and, in turn, weak institutions. Lacking well-formed institutions, clientelistic relationships will dominate politics and personal relationships and connections will be the key means by which to influence policy.

Foundations of Monarchies

Monarchies differ from other forms of dictatorship in that they involve institutionalized hereditary rule, often rooted in the historical legacies of family bloodlines. The leadership pool is comprised of the royal family, rather than a military or party institution. Though the origins of monarchies are in many ways less understood than the origins of other types of dictatorships, monarchs must be able to establish the legitimacy of their familial dynasty in the eyes of the citizenry in order to justify their rule. Their ability to do so is often a function of historical factors, such as the family's prior dominance in the state's political affairs.

Monarchy in the Middle East

Monarchies have dotted the political landscapes of much of the Middle East, including Bahrain, Kuwait, Oman, Qatar, Saudi Arabia, and the United Arab Emirates. The ruling families in these monarchic regimes have held power for substantial periods of time, in some cases for centuries. These monarchies are often referred to as absolute monarchies, as the monarch wields ultimate power and is not merely a ceremonial figurehead.

Though much of the region had at some point been ruled by dynastic groups, such groups did not have absolute control over the state. Rather, families ruled their own domains, and power was dispersed. The formation of absolute monarchies was seen as an important way by which to build the state. As Michael Herb writes, monarchies "took root because there was an affinity between monarchy as a regime type and nation building."[99]

In addition, many of the countries in the Middle East were modernizing, resulting in the need for a strong hand to govern them, ideally one with links to the past. To combat the disruption of modernization, monarchic government provided a means by which to revive the country's past heritage and links to traditional legitimacy.[100]

Modernization also served to open up Middle Eastern economies to imperial penetration. As Lisa Anderson[101] writes, the dominance of monarchies in the Middle East is in many ways a reflection of European imperial policy. Indeed, though royal families have historically ruled much of the Middle East, it was not until European (primarily British) colonization that absolute monarchies were officially established. European states did not necessarily want to rule countries in the Middle East directly. Rather, they sought to put in power rulers who were likely to be cooperative and help them achieve their objectives in the Gulf.[102] The establishment of monarchies throughout the region was a means of ensuring regional stability in an area of geographic importance for European powers (particularly the United Kingdom) as they sought monopolistic access to regional resources, such as oil.[103]

European powers also sought to exert influence in the Middle East as a means of thwarting foreign threats. The United Kingdom, for example, was particularly worried about Russian encroachment in Iran. To strengthen Iran, the British engineered a military coup to topple the old regime led by the Qajar dynasty, which had a weak—but constitutional—government. In its place, the British gave support for strongman Reza Khan (signing the Anglo-Persian Agreement in 1919 as he was rising to power), even though he had no royal lineage.

For European states, there were many reasons why the encouragement of monarchic rule in the region was desirable. For one, the presence of dynastic families made the Middle East congenial to the establishment of absolute monarchies. European powers also believed that cultural characteristics and traditions of the region made it suitable for monarchic rule (though many of these "traditions" were actually western imports).[104] One such tradition was the institution of hereditary succession, imported into the Middle East by European powers.[105] The establishment of clear rules for succession was important to European states, as it was a means of ensuring that transfers of power would not have violent consequences and lead to regional instability.

The choice of implementing a monarchy or a republic was also affected by the strength of religious groups. In Iran, having witnessed the secular politics of the republic under Atatürk in Turkey, the religious community (Shiite clergy) pushed for the former when the Reza Khan rose to power in 1925.[106] It was also thought that Iranians would be upset by the idea of a republic after years of rule under the Qajar dynasty.[107]

For some of the ruling families in the region, the idea of kingship was appealing, especially after more than a century of contact with European counterparts.[108] King Hussein bin Ali claimed to be a direct descendant of the Prophet Mohammad, and his family ruled the Hijaz on behalf of the Ottoman Sultan. Hussein bin Ali declared himself King of the Hijaz in what is now Jordan in 1917. King Fuad I was the 9th ruler of the Mohammad Ali dynasty and proclaimed himself King of Egypt and Sudan in 1922. King Mohammed V was a member of the Alaouite Dynasty and declared himself King of Morocco in 1957.

Table 2.1 Explaining the Emergence of Types of Dictatorships

Monarchies in the Middle East	*Possible Internal Factors*	*Possible External Factors*
	Idea of kingship appealing to ruling families	British influence
	Religious groups preferred monarchies over republics	Stability needed due to the importance of oil; rules for succession guaranteed stability
	Monarchies viewed as important to state building	
	Cultural characteristics and traditions in Middle East viewed to be compatible with monarchies	
Military regimes in Latin America	*Possible Internal Factors*	*Possible External Factors*
	Militaries were well funded	Enormous military aid from the US
	Large levels of economic inequality	Intense ideological polarization during Cold War

(Continued)

Military regimes in Latin America	*Possible Internal Factors*	*Possible External Factors*
	Military elites defended and represented the upper and middle classes	US encouraged military to become involved in politics
	Coups were supported by upper and middle classes	
	Military not subservient to the party; weak political parties	
Single-Party Regimes in Asia and Eastern Europe	*Possible Internal Factors*	*Possible External Factors*
	Military subservient to the party	Role of the USSR
	Less levels of economic inequality	Role of the US
	Government capacity strengthened	Economic aid given to fight capitalism/communism
	Strong party needed to promote economic program	Chaotic environment and high security threats necessitated a strong state to confront communism/capitalism
Personalist Regimes in Africa	*Possible Internal Factors*	*Possible External Factors*
	Ethnic diversity	Role of colonialism
	Weak militaries	Few inter-state threats
	Weak political parties	Cold War donors and patrons looked the other way and helped prop up the support of personalist dictators
	Low levels of institutionalization	
	Fragmented; no cohesive group; no middle class	

Summary and Conclusion

This chapter explored the various theories proposed to understand the emergence of authoritarian government. Initial research in this area primarily focused on the causes of totalitarianism. The work that followed has discussed the factors conducive to democracy and the causes of dictatorship, more generally. Poverty and economic inequalities are posited as central to the formation of dictatorships, but, so are historical and geo-political considerations.

Though the literature on the causes of authoritarianism is quite rich, many questions still remain. What conditions explain the emergence of one form of dictatorship instead of another? Why do military dictatorships sprout as opposed to single-party dictatorships? Are there systematic factors that account for the formation of monarchies? As we seek to improve our understanding of the authoritarian political universe, answering such questions remains as important as ever.

Review Questions

- What factors explain the emergence of totalitarian regimes?
- What are some of the obstacles to democratization pointed out by scholars? What conditions are conducive to democratic consolidation?
- What two factors according to Finer account for why the military chooses to intervene in politics?
- What is military centrality theory and how does it explain military interventions?
- What does O'Donnell mean by bureaucratic authoritarian regimes and how does modernization affect their rise to power?
- Why have military dictatorships been common in Latin America?
- What reasons explain the prevalence of single-party regimes in East and Southeast Asia and Eastern Europe?
- What factors account for the pervasiveness of personalist dictatorships in sub-Saharan America?
- What are the causes behind the frequency of monarchic rule in the Middle East?

Key Points

- The literature on authoritarian regimes has focused on the causes of totalitarianism and obstacles to democratization.
- Though most military dictatorships start with military coups, coups staged by the military can lead to different forms of dictatorship. A complex configuration of structural, geo-political, and historical factors has led to the emergence of different types of authoritarian rule.
- A correlation exists between the *type* of dictatorship and its regional distribution. Latin America has had a propensity toward military regimes, sub-Saharan Africa toward personalist regimes, Eastern Europe and East and Southeast Asia towards single-party regimes, and the Middle East towards monarchies.

Notes

1. Huntington, *The Third Wave*, (1991).
2. See "Combined Average Ratings: Independent Countries 2009," Freedom House, http://freedomhouse.org/template.cfm?page=475&year=2009 (accessed December 29, 2009).
3. Brooker, *Non-Democratic Regimes*, (2000, p. 1).
4. Arendt, *The Origins of Totalitarianism* (1951); *The Origins of Totalitarianism*, (1953).
5. Linz, *Totalitarian and Authoritarian Regimes*, (2000).
6. Huntington, *Political Order*, (1968).
7. Kahin, Pauker and Pye, *Comparative Politics*, (1955).
8. Ibid., (p. 1026).
9. Lipset, *Some Social Requisites*, (1959).
10. Przeworski et al., *Democracy and Development*, (2000).
11. Ross, *Does Oil Hinder Democracy?*(2001).
12. Countries are classified as democratic if they received a score of 5 or better on the Polity IV democracy variable (Polity IV Project 2008).
13. Moore, *Social Origins of Dictatorship*, (1968).
14. Ibid., (p. 418).
15. Acemoglu and Robinson, *Economic Origins of Dictatorship*, (2006).
16. Egalitarianism, as in Singapore, can also impede democratization, however, since the non-democratic status quo is stable (Acemoglu and Robisnon 2006).
17. Rueschemeyer et al., *Capitalist Development and Democracy*, (1992).
18. Ibid., (pp. 76–78).
19. Horowitz, *Democracy in Divided Societies*, (1993).
20. Ibid., (p. 19).
21. Huntington, *Democracy for the Long*, (1997).
22. This corresponds with J. Craig Jenkins and Augustine J. Kposowa's (1990) argument that ethnic diversity is one of the main explanations for the prevalence of military coups (an indicator of political instability) in Africa.
23. Karatnycky, *2001 Freedom House Survey*, (2002).
24. Ibid., (p. 107).
25. Fish and Brooks, *Does Diversity Hurt Democracy?* (2004).
26. Rummel, *Democracy, Power, Genocide*, (1995).
27. Geddes, *Minimum Winning Coalitions*, (2004; 2007).
28. Finer, *The Man on Horseback*, (1962); Luttwak, (1969).
29. O'Kane, *Military Regimes: Power*, (1989, p. 335).
30. Finer, *The Man on Horseback*, (1962).
31. Nordlinger, *Soldiers in Politics*, (1977).

32. Geddes, *Paradigms and Sand Castles*, (2003).

33. see Thompson (1975).

34. Huntington, *Political Order*, (1968).

35. Andreski (1968); Janowitz (1977); Finer (1988); see also Acemoglu, Ticchi and Vindigni, (2009).

36. Kposowa and Jenkins, *Structural Sources of Military*, (1993, p. 130).

37. Huntington, *Political Order*, (1968).

38. Needler, *Political Development*, (1966, p. 617).

39. Geddes, *What Do We Know*, (1999).

40. Huntington, *Political Order*, (1968).

41. McGowan and Johnson; see also Hibbs, (1973).

42. Londegran and Poole, *Poverty, the Coup Trap*, (1990, p. 152).

43. Finer, *The Man on Horseback*, (1962); McGowan and Johnson; (O'Kane 1983).

44. Nordlinger, *Soldiers in Politics*, (1977, p. 207).

45. Wiarda, *Critical Elections*, (1978, p. 43).

46. Mayer, *Militarism and Development*, (1999, p. 434).

47. Acemoglu et al., *Theory of Military Dictatorships*, (2009, p. 46).

48. Powell, *Military Assistance and Militarism*, (1965, pp. 383–386).

49. Nordlinger, *Soldiers in Mufti*, (1970).

50. Magaloni, *Credible Power-Sharing*, (2008, p. 726).

51. Baines, *U.S. Military Assistance*, (1972); Fitch, *Armed Force and Democracy*, (1998).

52. Carranza, *Review Essay: Military Coups*, (1983).

53. Valenzuela, *Latin American Presidencies Interrupted*, (2004).

54. Fitch, *Armed Force and Democracy*, (1998).

55. Karl, *Hybrid Regimes of Central*, (1995).

56. Bunce, *Rethinking Recent Democratization*, (2003, p. 175).

57. Bunce, *Comparing East and South*, (1995, p. 89).

58. Nun, *Middle Class Military Coup* (1967, p. 112).

59. Acemoglu et al., *Theory of Military Dictatorships*, (2009).

60. Ibid.

61. Huntington, *Political Order*, (1968).

62. Brooker, *Non-Democratic Regimes*, (2000).

63. Ibid.

64. Magaloni, *Comparative Autocracy*, (2007; Geddes 2007).

65. Berend, *Central and Eastern Europe*, (1999, p. 39).

66. Brooker, *Non-Democratic Regimes*, (2000, p. 83).

67. Berend, *Central and Eastern Europe*, (1999, p. 79).

68. Ibid., (p. 39).

69. Johnson, *The Warsaw Pact*, (1981, p. 1).

70. Ibid., (p. 2).

71. Brooker, *Non-Democratic Regimes*, (2000).

72. Stubbs, *War and Economic Development*, (1999, p. 351).

73. Packenham (1973, p. 111); Meernik, Krueger, Poe, (1998, p. 67).

74. Stubbs, *War and Economic Development*, (1999 p. 342, 350).

75. Ibid. (p. 341).

76. Ibid. (p. 345).

77. Ibid., (p. 346).

78. Stubbs writes that in 1967 alone U.S. servicemen spent U.S. $108 million in Singapore (1999, p. 346).

79. Bratton and van de Walle, *Neo-patrimonial Regimes*, (1994, p. 459).

80. Goldsmith, *Donors, Dictators and Democrats*, (2001).

81. Bienen, *Armies and Parties*, (1978a).

82. Howe, *Military Forces in African*, (2004).

83. Monga, *Eight Problems with African*, (1997, p. 168).

84. Howe, *Military Forces in African*, (2004).

85. Decalo, *African Personal Dictatorships*, (1985).

86. Ikpe, *Patrimonialism and Military Regimes*, (2000).

87. Monga, *Eight Problems with African*, (1997; Tordoff 2002).

88. Monga, *Eight Problems with African*, (1997; Tordoff 2002).

89. Monga, *Eight Problems with African*, (1997).

90. Decalo, *African Personal Dictatorships*, (1985).

91. Bratton and van de Walle, *Neo-patrimonial Regimes*, (1994).

92. Englebert, *Pre-Colonial Institutions*, (2000).

93. Fatton, *Liberal Democracy in Africa*, (1990, p. 457).

94. Ibid., (p. 457).

95. Rubin, *Modern Dictators* (1987).

96. Goldsmith, *Donors, Dictators and Democrats*, (2001).

97. Bratton and van de Walle, *Neo-patrimonial Regimes*, (1994).

98. Goldsmith, *Donors, Dictators and Democrats*, (2001).

99. Herb, *All in the Family*, (1999, p. 3).

100. Binder, *Iran: Political Development*, (1962).

101. Anderson, *Absolutism and the Resilience*, (1991).

102. Ibid., (pp. 3–4).

103. Kamrava, *Revolution in Iran*, (2005).

104. Anderson, *Absolutism and the Resilience*, (1991, p. 9).

105. Ibid.

106. Kamrava, *Revolution in Iran*, (2005).

107. Graham, *Iran: The Illusion*, (1979).

108. Anderson, *Absolutism and the Resilience*, (1991).

3 The Survival of Authoritarian Regimes: Strategies and Trends

Some dictatorships are remarkably long-lasting, while others are surprisingly short-lived. The Communist Party of the Soviet Union, for example, ruled for more than 70 years, whereas the Turkish Armed Forces in the 1980s only held onto power in Turkey for three years. What factors account for these vast differences in the vulnerability of dictatorships? Are some *types* of dictatorships more likely to be enduring than others? What are the different strategies that dictatorships pursue to maintain their hold on power?

This chapter examines these complex questions. We begin by discussing the factors that influence the survival of dictatorships. In particular, we look at how and why durability varies across categories of dictatorship, offering data on regime longevity in the post-World War II era. We then explore how dictatorships fall and provide analyses of the different modes of exit for dictatorships. Lastly, we examine in detail the role of elections and political parties in dictatorships as tools to enhance survival.

Factors that Influence the Survival of Dictatorships

In this section, we examine the array of factors that affect the longevity of authoritarian regimes. Before doing so, however, it is first useful to define what constitutes a *regime*.

A regime is the "set of formal and informal rules and procedures for selection of national leaders and policies."[1] Fleeting periods during which a group takes power and leaves a few days later do not qualify as a regime, just as brief interludes of political instability do not always mean the regime has fallen. Regimes are *authoritarian* when "opposition parties have been banned or subjected to serious harassment or institutional disadvantage, or if the ruling party has never lost control of the executive and has controlled at least two-thirds of legislative seats in all elections."[2]

A plethora of scholars have tackled the question of why some authoritarian regimes seem to last forever, while others only rule for a few years. Their analyses have incorporated a range of factors, such as the importance of mass support and the value of a fragile opposition. We first discuss the *critical factors* that regimes require to stay in power, before turning to the *structural factors* that influence longevity.

Critical Factors

Mass Support

All authoritarian regimes require the support of a subset of the populace to maintain power. Though the size of this subset of the population varies across dictatorships, some mass support is necessary in all dictatorships for the regime to maintain its grip over society. As Beatriz Magaloni argues, authoritarian regimes can only survive as long as they are able to mobilize citizens in their favor, regardless of, whether citizens sincerely support the regime or are merely responding to coercion.[3] Lack of mass support for the regime can help opposition movements gain traction.

Yet, why would any citizens support a dictatorship? Wouldn't most prefer a democracy? Though these answers are complicated, at the most basic level citizens support dictatorships as long as they have incentives to do so. Incentives can range from financial, like the distribution of government spoils, to security, like the belief that life is more secure with the dictatorship in power given that violence would likely erupt if the regime fell. Repression is also used in many dictatorships as a disincentive for withdrawing support for the regime.

In order to engender and maintain the support of this critical subset of the masses, leaders, and elites in dictatorships work to ensure that such incentives exist. They must distribute benefits to regime supporters, while withholding benefits from (or otherwise punishing) regime opponents. Benefits include subsidies, cash transfers, public goods, housing and health services, and jobs. The particular mixture of incentives that dictatorships will rely on typically depends on the particular resources the regime has at its disposal. It is very difficult, for example, to maintain support via financial incentives during periods of economic crisis, just as it is difficult to use repression without a well-developed and entrenched security apparatus.

A Fractured and Weak Opposition

In all dictatorships, there exist individuals who do not support the regime. Key to the regime's survival is, ensuring that these individuals do not unify, and become so organizationally robust, that they threaten the regime's hold on power.

Opposition groups in dictatorships can come in a variety of forms, ranging from civil society organizations to political parties to armed revolutionary groups. The mere existence of these groups is not always damaging to the regime, so long as they are divided and not too large in size. A unified and sizeable opposition group is very threatening to the regime, as it easily steamrolls into a mass movement calling for regime change. Well-organized opposition groups can weaken the regime in a number of ways, such as mobilizing the public to turn out to vote in elections or organizing mass protests, both of which can erode public support away from the incumbent regime.

As such, dictatorships engage in a variety of strategies to keep opposition groups fractured and weak. These strategies include repression (arresting or otherwise threatening members of the opposition), co-optation (offering members of the opposition reasons to support the regime), and manipulation of electoral institutions (keeping opposition members from legally gaining political posts).

Paradoxically, the opposition is less likely to present a formidable challenge to the regime when it is co-opted into the regime apparatus, according to Ellen Lust-Okar.[4] When members of the opposition are given opportunities to participate in the system (primarily via political posts), they have fewer incentives to coalesce and challenge the regime. Regimes can further ensure their stability by selectively co-opting the opposition, choosing a particular grouping of opposition members to participate so that the opposition as a whole is divided.

Opposition Movement in Saudi Arabia

Is there an opposition movement in Saudi Arabia? Though it is perhaps surprising that a regime as tightly controlled as the Saudi Arabian monarchy would have groups that would dare to challenge it, an opposition movement does exist. It is mainly comprised of religious groups and pro-democracy groups. These groups voice their opposition through either intellectual non-violent criticism, non-violent political activism, or violent political activism (Cordesman 2003). The Saudi government has responded to the opposition movement using everything from "bribes, co-optation and divide and conquer strategies to repression" (Ibid., p. 179). The divide and conquer strategies in particular have been effective at preventing the various religious groups from cooperating with one another. Pro-democracy groups are also kept fractured, disorganized and weak.

One of the more prominent and well-organized opposition groups in Saudi Arabia is the Committee for the Defense of Legitimate Rights (CDLR). The CDLR broke up in the mid-1990s and split into two groups due to discrepancies between its two principle figures, Muhammad al-Mas'ari and Saad al-Fagih. Disagreements arose over what the group stood for and how its campaign should operate. Mas'ari now heads the CDLR, though the group has become largely ineffective; Fagih formed a new organization, the London-based Islamic Reform Movement, which is distinct from the CDLR and has modified aims (Ibid., p. 188).

Elite Loyalty

Authoritarian regimes also require the continued support of regime elites—those individuals who participate in policy making, are central to the distribution of patronage, and sanction the use of repressive security forces. As Magaloni[5] writes, elites perform important services for the regime, such as mobilizing voters, rigging elections, threatening opposition members, and spying on the public. As with the masses, continued elite support is contingent in many ways on a cost-benefit analysis. Elites must perceive that the benefits of supporting the regime outweigh the costs of defection.

The benefits of support typically involve policy influence, access to economic rents, and political posts, while the costs of defection range from loss of employment to execution. The cost-benefit analysis of elites can alter under a variety of circumstances, such as when the regime loses the ability to dole out economic perks due to a faltering economy or when the opposition movement intensifies such that elites suddenly have high confidence that opposition efforts will be successful.

Mexico, under the Institutional Revolutionary Party (PRI) provides a good example of the role of each of these critical factors. According to Magaloni, though some electoral fraud was used by the PRI to maintain its dominance in elections, the party was legitimately popular among key segments of the masses. This was due to the PRI's extensive patronage network and ability to identify and track who its key supporters were. The opposition movement in Mexico faced an uphill battle typical of many dictatorships. The two opposition parties, National Action Party (PAN) and Party of the Democratic Revolution (PRD), lied on opposite ends of the ideological spectrum and were consistently portrayed in an unflattering manner by the PRI. They received scant media coverage and had little access to public financing. In comparison, the PRI was an electoral machine, spending large amounts of government revenues to run campaigns, both legally and illegally. In the 1990s, politicians sensed that the PRI was losing steam after years of domination, as the incentives to remain inside the party apparatus started to crumble. Key elite defections from the party during this time period provided an opening for the PAN to gain mass and elite support. The PAN eventually took over the executive branch with the wins of Vicente Fox in 2000 and Felipe Calderón in 2006.

Structural Factors

Structural factors are also important to understanding the survival of dictatorships. They help explain why some authoritarian regimes are simply less vulnerable to collapse than others. As Barbara Geddes[6] shows, dictatorships differ systematically in their survival rates: military dictatorships are the most fragile, followed by personalist dictatorships, and lastly single-party dictatorships.[7] Differences in the institutional settings of dictatorships lead to different incentives for leaders and elites, in turn affecting the longevity of regimes.

Geddes focuses on the propensity for divisions within the elite corps to destabilize dictatorships. Her argument emphasizes the importance of elite defections in provoking the collapse of the regime. Geddes groups regime elites into two main factions: the majority faction (comprised of the leader and the leader's supporters) and the rival faction (comprised of potential rivals to the leader and their supporters). Whether dictatorships are governed by a single-party, a professionalized military, or neither influences the preferences and strategies of the members of these two factions.

Military Dictatorships

In military dictatorships, military elites hold political power. However, unlike civilian politicians who value attaining and holding on to office above all else, the "survival and efficacy of the military itself" is what professional soldiers value most.[8] Because of this, the greatest threat to military elites is not the fall of the regime, but rather, the military splitting and civil war breaking out.

In military dictatorships, if elite splits intensify, most officers prefer to return to the barracks than risk the disunity of the military. Any rivalries within the elite corps or factionalization within the regime can prompt the military to leave power on its own volition. Because most members of the regime can return to the barracks with their careers relatively intact, leaving office does not carry with it negative repercussions. As a result, military dictatorships carry within them "the seeds of their own destruction."[9] The slightest internal division can cause the military to leave power voluntarily. For these reasons, military dictatorships are the most short-lived type of dictatorship, ruling only for an average of nine years.[10] They are also very vulnerable to economic crises (due to the internal pressures such crises can precipitate) and are the most likely type of dictatorship to leave power through a negotiated, orderly transition.

Sources of Instability in Military Dictatorships:

- Propensity for internal splits and factionalism
  - The practice of governing can lead to disagreements among members of the military
  - The military needs to be insulated from society to remain united
- Greater incentives to leave office
  - The military prefers to return to the barracks than to stay in power as a factionalized force
  - There is life after military rule for most members of the regime

Single-party Dictatorships

The interests of elites in single-party dictatorships are quite simple. As with democratic politicians, party elites primarily want to hold office; staying in power is what they value most. Geddes shows that all factions within the party elite corps, and even the main rivals of the leader, are better off if the party remains in power. If the party falls out of power, elites—including those who oppose the leadership—have "fewer opportunities to exercise influence or line pockets."[11]

As a result, factions can form in single-party dictatorships, but they do not destabilize the regime. Factions do not benefit from ruling alone, as all factions are better able to further their goals with the party in power. In essence, party splits are undesirable for all actors. Leadership struggles may emerge, but they do not seriously threaten the regime.

Because party elites have incentives to cooperate with one another and maintain the party in power, single-party dictatorships are extremely durable, lasting on average for 23 years. They can withstand succession issues (and therefore the death of the leader) and are fairly resilient to economic downturns. Rarely do single-party regimes fall; when they do it is due to an array of factors, ranging from international or external pressures to democratize, severe economic crises, or irreconcilable elite splits.

Sources of Instability in Single-party Dictatorships:

- International or external pressures to democratize
- Severe economic crises that affect state control over economic rents and the regime's coercive capabilities
- Irreconcilable factional infighting that leads to permanent elite splits

Personalist Dictatorships

In personalist dictatorships, a single individual dominates the political apparatus. Though factions form, "during normal times they have strong reasons to continue supporting the regime and leader."[12]

Though in many ways the behavior of elites in personalist dictatorships mirrors that of elites in single-party dictatorships, Geddes[13] identifies three ways in which they differ, each of which make personalist dictatorships more vulnerable than single-party dictatorships. The first is that personalist dictatorships rarely withstand the death of the dictator. This is because personalist dictators often marginalize their closest rivals (as they face fewer institutional constraints to such behavior lacking the presence of a professionalized party or military in government). The second is that personalist dictatorships typically have narrower bases of support than single-party dictatorships because elites are usually friends or family members of the dictator. This means that the size of the group who can challenge the regime is large. Lastly, because personalist dictators typically use material rewards to satisfy their supporters (rather than political posts), personalist dictatorships are more easily destabilized by economic crises.

For these reasons, personalist dictatorships are more durable than military dictatorships, but less durable than single-party dictatorships. They rule on average for 15 years. When they do fall from power, it is likely to occur through violent means, such as coup, insurgency, or assassination; when the dictators dies, they are unlikely to survive, as there are few institutionalized methods for dealing with crises over succession.

Sources of Instability for Personalist Dictatorships:

- Exogenous shocks, such as an economic crisis or the loss of foreign aid, preventing the dictator from distributing patronage to supporters
- Revolution or foreign intervention
- The death of the dictator

How Dictatorships Fall

In this section we examine how dictatorships fall from power. We should note that when dictatorships collapse, this by no means is an indicator of an impending transition to democracy. Though some dictatorships do democratize upon dissolution, many are replaced shortly afterward with yet another dictatorship. We discuss four key ways in which dictatorships fall:

- **Military Coup**: Overthrow by force or threat of force. The military overthrows the civilian leadership or, in cases of military dictatorships, a disgruntled set of junior officers ousts the ruling junta.
- **Foreign Intervention**: Overthrow via overt foreign interference. A foreign power forces the regime out, either through a direct invasion, or through the transfer of military support to key sectors of the populace.

- **Negotiated settlement**: Peaceful exit. The regime voluntarily leaves power; leader and elites negotiate the terms of their departure.
- **Revolution**: Overthrow by force or threat of force. The masses rise up to uproot the regime, sometimes with the covert backing of a foreign power.

According to Geddes,[14] military dictatorships are more likely to leave power via negotiated settlement, and less likely to leave through military coup, or revolution. Military dictatorships are also more likely to be followed by democratic rule, however lasting. Personalist dictatorships, by contrast, are more likely to collapse upon the death of the dictator. They are also more likely to end through violence (coup, revolution, or foreign intervention) than negotiation. Personalist dictatorships are unlikely to be succeeded by a democratic regime. Single-party dictatorships, like military dictatorships, are more likely to end through negotiation and result in democracy (even if brief), particularly when party elites are able to participate in the democratic regime that follows and contest elections. Though monarchies are less well studied than military, personalist, or single-party dictatorships, anecdotal evidence suggests that they are more likely to fall via violent means (as with personalist dictatorships), particularly revolution (e.g. Egypt 1952, Afghanistan 1973, Iraq 1958, Libya 1969, Nepal 2006, Ethiopia 1974, Iran 1979).

Transitions from Military Rule:

- Negotiated exits that are usually not that violent
- Democracy often follows (even if short-lived)

Transitions from Single-party Rule:

- Negotiated and peaceful transitions
- Democracy may follow (however briefly), particularly when party elites can participate in elections

Transitions from Personalist Rule:

- Dictator is likely to cling to power; violent transitions typical (often by way of assassination, coup, revolution, or foreign intervention)
- Transitions to democracy highly unlikely

Military coups

As stated in **Chapter 2**, military coups are driven by motive and opportunity.[15] The 2005 overthrow of the Mauritanian personalist dictatorship under Maaouiya Ould Taya illustrates this. The motive for the coup was rooted in the perception among segments of the military that Ould Taya was threatening military institutions and harassing certain tribes and their allies. Ould Taya had also insulted several senior officers and reduced their access to the regime's financial spoils.[16] The opportunity for the coup arose as Ould Taya loosened his grip on Mauritania in a bid to appease the United States during the "War on Terror." Ould Taya left the country in August 2005, which he did only on rare occasions, providing his nephew and a few other disgruntled members of the military with the chance to depose him in a non-violent coup.

Perhaps surprisingly, many military coups have widespread public support. In many cases, the military stages a coup on behalf of the masses. Public perception that the civilian government is inept and incapable of solving the country's problems often provides the motive for the military to seize power. Such coups are precipitated by public dissatisfaction with the incumbent regime, its lack of political legitimacy, and its alienation of key societal groups.

Often, military coups are undertaken after public signals surface— like protests or demonstrations—of underlying societal unrest. In Latin America, many civilian dictatorships (as well as democracies) have been ousted via military coup due to public discontent with the incumbent regime. The dictatorship of Juan Perón in Argentina, for example, courted the organized labor movement at the expense of key sectors of Argentine society, namely the middle class, the elite, and the Catholic Church.[17] Perón had also empowered the secret police, leading to dissatisfaction within the military. Because of these factors, many Argentines supported the military coup that toppled the Peronist regime in 1955. The personalist/military dictatorships of Colombia and Venezuela were also removed via military coup. In Colombia, when the regime's leader, Gustavo Rojas Pinilla, tried to extend his rule for another four years, a series of street demonstrations broke out prompting the military to stage a coup in May 1957. The regime of Marcos Pérez Jiménez of Venezuela was also ousted after mass protests sparked a military coup. Pérez Jiménez had alienated many civilian groups, including the business community, and was deposed via coup in January 1958.

Foreign Intervention

Foreign interventions to remove unfavorable dictatorships can occur directly and indirectly. Direct foreign interventions to topple rogue regimes typically involve the deployment of foreign troops. The United States, for example, has directly overthrown dictatorships on multiple occasions. It ousted the personalist dictatorship of Saddam Hussein in Iraq in 2003 through Operation Iraqi Freedom. Similarly, it deposed the personalist/ military dictatorship of Manuel Noriega in Panama in 1989 through Operation Just Cause. With direct foreign interventions, the head of the regime is usually arrested (or executed), as are other leading regime officials.

With indirect foreign interventions, the foreign power intervenes in the country's affairs in a variety of ways, all with the intention of taking down the regime. It does so by working with elements of the regime and the masses that can be easily swayed to join the opposition, while simultaneously strengthening the capacity of the opposition movement.[18] This entails a range of activities, such as supplying military and economic aid to these groups and providing them with logistical assistance to stage a coup. If the regime holds elections, the foreign power can try to undermine the regime by supporting the opposition during these elections. It can also try to push the regime out through the threat of interventions, sanctions, the withdrawal of military and economic aid, and diplomatic pressure. The overthrow of the personalist dictator Joseph Mobutu of Zaire (today's Democratic Republic of Congo), provides an example of an indirect foreign intervention. Laurent Kabila and his troops ousted Mobutu, but only with strong military support from Rwanda, Burundi, and Uganda, each of which had long wanted Mobutu out of power due to his treatment of ethnic Tutsis.

According to Geddes, several factors account for transition via foreign intervention: "being in the US sphere of influence, weakness combined with the territorial ambitions of neighbors, [and] the economic crisis of the late eighties and early nineties, which gave international financial institutions unusual leverage."[19]

Negotiated Settlement

A negotiated settlement occurs when the regime leaves power peacefully and voluntarily, regardless of whether the threat of military coup, revolution, or foreign invasion prompts such a departure. Negotiated settlements usually take place when leaders and elites deem the likelihood of their continued rule to be low, given societal unrest and political tensions. They are often a starting point for democratic transitions, even though the democratic regime replacing the dictatorship can be short-lived.

Negotiated settlements are sometimes referred to as "pacted transitions," which are essentially compromises between the regime and the democratic opposition.[20] In pacted transitions, regime elites reach an agreement with the opposition that typically allows them to leave power under favorable conditions. Elites are often able to negotiate terms for themselves that enable them to contend for power in democratic elections; they are generally not expelled from politics.

Multiple factors can account for the regime's decision to leave power via negotiated settlement. First, the opposition may grow so large that its efforts to push for democratic reform can no longer go unnoticed by the regime. Second, the opposition may become unruly—and its threats to use violence become more credible—giving elites little choice but to step down. Third, the regime may leave power due to legitimacy issues, when rulers feel that the regime has lost credibility in the eyes of the citizenry.

The fall of Francisco Franco's personalist dictatorship in Spain in the 1970s is an example of a negotiated settlement. Following Franco's death, King Juan Carlos was appointed the ruler of Spain (as stipulated by Franco prior to his passing). Though the dictatorship could have continued under King Juan Carlos, efforts were instead undertaken to reach a settlement between regime elites and other key sectors to transition to democracy. As Kerstin Hamann writes:

> It was actors representing the Franco regime who guided the regime change, while state actors—noticeably the military—explicitly or implicitly posed a constant threat to the democratization process. The transition took place in a context of interdependence and strategic interaction between regime and state actors, whose interests had to be satisfied at least minimally in order to safeguard the transition.[21]

A negotiated settlement was possible in Spain because of widespread elite and mass support for democratic rule.

Revolutions

Revolutions occur when the masses work from below to oust a regime. The regime that is overthrown is sometimes democratic, but usually authoritarian. The political system that results following a revolution is typically significantly different than its predecessor, both in terms of ideology and institutions. Revolutions are often very violent, though violence is not integral to their definition.[22] Though revolutions receive widespread international attention when they take place, they have occurred infrequently in the post-World War II era.

Revolutions are so rare because they are difficult to carry out. The masses typically lack access to the weaponry required to forcibly remove a regime out of power. For a revolution to take place, the opposition movement must be so large in size that it becomes unfeasible for the regime to use violence to suppress it, or elements of the regime's security forces must, in significant numbers, refuse to use force against citizens and/or defect and offer their support to the opposition. According to Theda Skocpol and Jeff Goodwin,[23] revolutionary movements are more likely to gain traction and be successful when they are able to capture the support of a cross-section of the public, in both urban and rural areas, and among different social classes and ethnic groupings.

Though revolutions are rare, monarchies have been particularly susceptible to them. In some of these cases, little violence was needed to unseat the monarchy, while others were marked by widespread bloodshed. Following a revolution, leaders and elites in the monarchy are usually forced into exile or killed.

In Iraq in 1958, for example, the Hashemite dynasty was overthrown via a military coup that quickly erupted into a revolution, with King Faisal II and other members of the ruling family massacred. Prime Minister Nuri as-Said was also killed and his body paraded around the streets of Baghdad by violent mobs. A new constitution was passed 13 days after the takeover, Iraq was declared a republic, and Islam was announced as the state religion.

In the 1979 Iranian revolution that deposed the Shah, Mohammad Reza Pahlavi, the regular army was never disloyal to the regime, but it refused to fire on civilian revolutionaries. Key officers within the Iranian military believed that it was better to concede to the movement than fight, as the Islamic revolutionaries were certain to win. This perception was enhanced by the unity of the opposition movement and the steamroll of public calls to oust the Shah. Those security forces that had not dropped their arms were unable to contend with the sheer size of the protest movement, and the Shah and his family were forced into exile.

Elections, Parties, and the Survival of Authoritarian Regimes

Elections and political parties are institutions that exist in a variety of dictatorships. Research in this field, though nascent, has revealed new ways in which dictatorships use these institutions and why they do so. The overarching theme in this literature is that elections and political parties serve as institutional tools by which dictatorships can lessen their vulnerability and enhance their survival in power. In this section, we look at the role that elections and political parties play in authoritarian regimes and present the various theoretical arguments scholars have proposed to account for their existence.

Elections under Dictatorship

Though elections are typically associated with democracies, they are actually quite common in dictatorships. About three-quarters of all post-World War II dictatorships have held elections, half of them on a regular basis.[24] Most single-party dictatorships hold elections, as do about half of personalist dictatorships, and nearly a quarter of military dictatorships. Though elections under dictatorship occasionally are a means by which the populace can select those who will rule them, predominantly they serve as a means by which to strengthen the regime, which we discuss in more detail below.

Types of Elections
Not surprisingly, nearly all elections that are held in dictatorships are viewed as uncompetitive by international standards. That being said, elections in dictatorships are not homogenous. In many dictatorships they bear no

resemblance to democratic elections, while in others they are only slightly dissimilar. Elections in dictatorships differ in their competitiveness, frequency, and inclusiveness.

Some dictatorships hold elections that are entirely predetermined and manufactured by the regime. In such elections, the regime's candidate always receives 100 percent of the vote, regardless of whether anyone actually turned out to vote. The regime decides who will appear on the ballot and voters are limited to a single choice. In other dictatorships, however, multiple candidates are allowed to compete in the election, even individuals from opposition political parties.

Elections held in Iraq under Saddam Hussein and in Malaysia under the United Malays National Organization (UMNO) help illustrate the extent of electoral heterogeneity across dictatorships. In 2002, during the personalist dictatorship of Hussein, Iraqis were called to the polls to participate in a referendum regarding whether Hussein should rule for seven additional years. Out of the 11,445,638 eligible voters, every single one of them voted in support of the referendum, according to official reports. Hussein was the only candidate.[25]

Elections in Malaysia under the single-party dictatorship led by the UMNO, the party in control of Malaysian politics since 1957, present a markedly different picture. In the 1999 general elections, the UMNO's share of the vote was only 54 percent. The UMNO won only 102 out of 144 potential legislative seats. Though members of the opposition alleged that there was vote rigging, the election was clearly somewhat competitive; opposition candidates were able to compete in the election and even were allowed to win seats.

The Purpose of Elections

Though dictatorships have multiple tools to ensure that their preferred candidates win elections, there is always the possibility (even slight) that they could lose. Elections are also fairly costly, as the regime must pay for ballots, campaigns, and electoral officials to monitor them. As Gary Cox writes, "The Soviets put literally millions of people to work in their elections, exerting real effort to attain near-100 percent turnout and approval figures."[26] Why, then, do so many dictatorships hold elections?

For one, dictatorships that hold elections, last longer than those that do not.[27] Simply put, dictatorships hold elections because they help them sustain power. Elections enhance the durability of the regime.

Elections also serve the purpose of ensuring that, should the regime fall, a violent transition will be unlikely. They provide a peaceful means by which the regime can leave power, should it choose to do so, eliminating the need for the opposition to resort to more violent alternatives.[28]

Primarily, elections are tools by which dictatorships can discourage and co-opt the opposition, manage elites, enhance regime legitimacy, acquire foreign support, and gain information about the strength of the opposition movement. All of these factors, which we discuss in more detail below, are keys to ensure the survival of the regime.

Discouraging and Co-opting the Opposition

One effect of elections in dictatorships is that they can discourage the opposition by providing evidence of support for the regime. As Andreas Schedler writes, "To the extent that they [elections] serve to legitimate the system and demonstrate the power and popularity of the ruling party as well as the weakness of its opponents, elections tend to demoralize and demobilize opposition forces."[29] Electoral landslides in support of regime candidates are signals to those elites who might potentially join the opposition that doing so is essentially an exercise in futility.

Holding elections allows dictatorships to set the rules for who can compete and who cannot, according to Ellen Lust-Okar. This creates "divided structures of contestation" where there are outsiders and insiders.[30] It can engender divisions within the opposition, between those who choose to compete in elections (and thus participate in the system), and those who choose to boycott them.

Elections are also tools, dictatorships can use to co-opt the opposition.[31] By participating in elections, the opposition is directing its energies for dissent within the system, as opposed to outside of it. When, members of the opposition, have something at stake in the maintenance of the current system (because they hold positions within it), they, will be less likely to seek its overthrow.

Managing Elites

Elections give the regime the opportunity to monitor the behavior of elites. Elections serve a number of important purposes in terms of elite management.[32] In dictatorships, elites engage in a constant competition over political posts, and access to the spoils of office, a potential source of internal conflict. Elections help mitigate this conflict by providing an institutional arena through which elites (and lower-level officials) can compete for power. They are an important venue for competition over the distribution of state resources.[33] Having consistency in the rules of the game also, works to manage the expectations of elites, and deter them from defecting.

Elections also force elites to mobilize their constituent groups and vie for the loyalty of the public. As such, they serve to strengthen the ties between elites and the masses. Elites must attune their campaigns to the preferences of their supporters, ensuring that the regime is in touch with mass sentiments.

Lastly, elections enable the regime to monitor the loyalty of elites and lower-level officials. They provide information to the regime about which individuals are the most loyal, while, simultaneously giving these individuals something at stake in the regime's survival.[34] Elections serve as a natural way of ensuring that the most competent, popular, and loyal members of the regime are promoted.[35]

Enhancing Regime Legitimacy

Another purpose of elections is that they enhance the regime's legitimacy. Elections are commonly used in dictatorships to mask that the regime is authoritarian.[36] They enable regimes "to reap the fruits of electoral legitimacy without running the risks of democratic uncertainty."[37] Elections are a tool the regime can use to project an image of democracy. In Mexico, under the Institutional Revolutionary Party (PRI), for example, the party used elections to convey that the regime was democratically legitimate to avoid characterization as a one-party dictatorship.[38] The regime sought to maintain nominally democratic institutions, like elections, to enhance its legitimacy in the eyes of the public.

In some cases, of course, elections are so closely controlled by the regime and fraudulent that any legitimacy the regime achieves is far from genuine. As Lisa Wedeen argues, in the case of Syria, elections exist but no one believes in them; they are simply symbolic "mechanisms of coercion."[39]

Acquiring Foreign Support

Elections are also used by regimes to satisfy foreign interests. They are a means by which dictatorships can claim that democratization has taken place to improve the regime's credentials in the eyes of foreign powers and international donors. With regular elections in place, these groups are more likely to give aid to the regime, which in many cases is necessary for the regime to maintain its complex rings of patronage.[40] Thus, elections provide dictatorships with an easy means of pleasing international actors without having to actually undergo a democratic transition.

Gaining Information about the Strength of the Opposition Movement

Elections also serve the purpose of providing the regime with information about its popularity and the strength of any opposition to it. They make it easier for the regime to identify who its supporters and opponents are. In the case of the PRI in Mexico, for example, elections were used to inform the party about the geographical distribution of the opposition and the location of opposition strongholds.[41] The regime could then, in turn, withdraw resources from these areas and transfer them instead to "swing" districts, where it needed to sway voters most. Elections give the regime the opportunity to measure the strength of its support and identify those sectors of the populace in which this support is strongest.

Winning Elections

Dictatorships have many tools at their disposal to ensure that regime candidates win elections. That being said, victory is by no means guaranteed. Though a handful of losses are tolerable (in some dictatorships), too many can precipitate the fall of the regime. Dictatorships—particularly those that hold elections that are somewhat competitive—must use all of their resources to ensure that the regime lands on top. In this section, we discuss the methods dictatorships use to win elections.

Electoral Fraud

The most obvious way in which dictatorships ensure that their candidates win elections is through electoral fraud. Electoral fraud includes ballot stuffing, illegal voter registration, and the intimidation of voters at the polls. The extent to which dictatorships engage in such fraudulent activity varies from regime to regime, as well as from one election to the next.

Some dictatorships (or regime candidates) are legitimately popular among the citizenry, lessening the need for fraud. Though the People's Action Party (PAP) in Singapore has been challenged by the opposition in past elections, voters do not actually want "to displace the PAP from power."[42]

PAP co-founder, Lee Kwan-Yew, the former Prime Minister of Singapore for 31 years, has historically enjoyed high levels of public support.

Harassment

Authoritarian regimes can use various forms of harassment to ensure that they are victorious in elections. The targets of such harassment are typically opposition candidates and the voters who might potentially support them. Harassment can include surveillance, blacklisting, denial of employment or university entrance, as well as low-profile activities, like using "tax, regulatory, or other state agencies to investigate and prosecute opponents."[43] Voters in Zimbabwe who have supported opposition parties have reported cases of harassment by Robert Mugabe's ZANU-PF led regime.[44] Opposition news outlets in Kenya were also harassed during elections by the dominant KANU party and opposition parties were forbidden from meeting or holding rallies (from 1992–1997) to prevent them from gaining any organizational traction.[45]

Campaigning Advantages

Dictatorships have enormous advantages during election campaigns. They can pour state resources into campaigns, monopolizing media outlets with campaign advertising for regime candidates, while preventing opposition candidates from doing the same. Such campaign advantages are often used by single-party dictatorships in elections, as is true of the UMNO in Malaysia and the PAP in Singapore. Well-funded political campaigns—coupled with the inundation of pro-regime messages in the media—are simple means by which to favor the regime in elections.

Manipulation of Electoral Laws

Dictatorships can alter the electoral system to the regime's advantage. For example, they can dictate that certain seats are appointed by the regime, rather than up for contestation. In South Korea, for example, the military dictatorship of Park Chung Hee put in place two-member electoral districts, where the top two highest vote getters per district were awarded a seat.[46] Though this stipulation seemed good on paper, in practice at least a third of the legislative seats were appointed by Park himself. For the remaining two thirds of seats in the legislature, regime candidates only needed to come in second in each district to gain a seat. As long as Park's candidates gained some nominal support, his party was ensured to dominate the legislature. Similarly, in Mexico, the PRI implemented a "governability clause" to ensure that the party maintained power even when candidates fared poorly at the polls. The PRI gerrymandered the districts in such a way that even when the party received only a third of the vote, it still maintained a majority in the legislature.[47]

High Barriers to Entry

Another tool at the disposal of dictatorships is the implementation of high barriers to entry for opposition parties or candidates. Opposition parties may be banned, disabling them from competing in elections, or their candidates may be vetted by regime institutions. The dictatorships of the Ivory Coast, Kenya, and Zambia, for example, had nationality clauses that prevented opposition parties from running in elections, while many dictatorships in the Middle East have banned Islamic parties from competing.[48] In Iran, the regime implements a strict vetting process via the Guardian Council to ensure that threatening candidates are ineligible to run. The candidacies of pro-reform supporters are often rejected prior to parliamentary and presidential elections.

Disenfranchisement

The ruling government can assure its victory in elections by eliminating certain groups of society from voting altogether. Sectors of the populace viewed threatening to the regime, like the poor or youth, may be disenfranchised via literacy or age requirements, keeping them from voting for opposition candidates. Similarly, certain ethnic groups may be banned from voting, or subject to harsh registration methods or identification requirements. In Brazil, for example, up until the military left power in 1985, illiterates were not granted the right to vote.[49]

Manipulation of the Economy

Another method of ensuring that the regime comes out on top in elections is to manipulate the economy. This strategy has been used effectively in Egypt (a triple threat dictatorship), luring voters into believing that the regime has given them economic prosperity.[50] Such economic manipulation can take the form of altering the exchange rate prior to the election so that domestic products are cheaper, or heavily subsidizing certain goods (such as bread or fuel) to make them more affordable—however temporarily—for voters. Pre-electoral economic manipulation was also commonplace in Mexico under the PRI.[51] According to Steven Block,[52] economic tinkering was common prior to elections held under the personalist dictator, Jerry Rawlings of Ghana. During the 1992 election year, domestic spending soared and inflation dropped as a means of wooing voters.

Vote Buying

Another strategy dictatorships use is to simply buy votes. This was done successfully in Taiwan, under the Nationalist/Kuomintang (KMT) party, in Mexico under the PRI, and in the personalist dictatorship of Ferdinand Marcos in the Philippines. In the case of Taiwan, little red envelopes filled with cash were delivered to voters' doorsteps encouraging them to go to the polls and vote for KMT candidates. Buying votes is particularly effective with poor voters who can be easily enticed to turn out at the polls if there are financial incentives to do so.

Political Parties under Dictatorship

Though some dictatorships ban or repress political parties, many dictatorships forge close alliances with political parties. In fact, political parties are quite common in dictatorships. Some of these parties predate the regime (or were formed to help launch it into power); while others are manufactured by the regime after power has been seized.

Though political parties are typically associated with single-party dictatorship, they are actually common in *all* forms of dictatorship. What differs across regimes is the extent to which the party plays a dominant role in governing. In single-party dictatorships, the party truly controls policy, while in other regimes the party has marginal de facto political power.

As with elections, parties help enhance the durability of a regime; they are institutions that prolong the regime's survival. As Geddes[53] shows, regimes that rely on parties last at least twice as long in power as those that do not. Alliance with a political party is strongly correlated with more durable regimes.

Scholars have pointed to multiple reasons why parties are useful for dictatorships. We discuss this research in the section that follows.

The Purpose of Parties

Co-opting Politicians

One purpose of political parties is that they provide a means through which dictatorships can co-opt politicians.[54] Political parties in dictatorships give those individuals with a vocation for politics the opportunity to participate in the political system, rather than concentrate their political energies underground (as when parties are repressed or banned).[55] They help elites think about their long term interests, which are usually best served by binding themselves to the party.[56]

Alliance with a political party is an inexpensive way for dictatorships to co-opt large number of politicians in ways that give them a vested interest in the longevity of the regime. If the regime falls, so too do the privileges, that come with party membership. Parties enable dictatorships to incorporate politicians into the regime, while offering them little control over policy.[57] As Geddes writes, "regardless of whether parties provide any benefits to ordinary party members, improve the quality of life for ordinary citizens, or persuade them to agree with regime views ... they provide their officials and volunteer activists with benefits that give them a stake in the regime."[58]

Reducing the Risk of Coups

Political parties can also work to lower the risk of a coup in dictatorships. According to Geddes, "mass parties capable of mobilizing 'the street' on behalf of the revolution, national sovereignty, Christian values, or Islamic opposition to western decadence can help to protect authoritarian leaders from coups by disaffected military factions."[59] The protective effect of parties occurs because of the following confluence of factors. Factions within the military are less likely to attempt a coup if they believe that it will divide the military or be unpopular among the masses. Political parties provide a vehicle for mobilizing the masses into street protests in support of the regime whenever it is threatened. Such protests pressure coup plotters to decide whether to use force against civilian demonstrators, which some soldiers may refuse to do, while also providing a display of public support for the regime.

Managing Elite Conflict

Like elections, political parties are also tools for managing elite conflict.[60] When elite disagreements surface, political parties are institutions that can regulate this conflict and handle disputes. Regimes can use parties as vehicles for patronage distribution to ensure elite satisfaction. Such perks give elites incentives to maintain the status quo, even in the midst of factional disputes.[61]

Parties also mitigate elite conflict by helping to manage issues that might arise over leadership succession. Succession issues in dictatorships can be extremely destabilizing, as factional tensions over succession can erupt into violence and even civil war. The stronger and more institutionalized the party, the better it will be able to provide institutional guidance regarding who will succeed the leader.

Winning Elections

Political parties also help dictatorships win elections. Though some dictatorships hold elections without political parties, alliance with a political party is an effective way for dictatorships to mobilize voters in support of the regime. This can occur through "large-scale clienteles, campaigning, public rallies, and other means."[62] According to Jason Brownlee, parties also help dictatorships carry out electoral fraud. Fraudulent activities, like ballot stuffing, require "coordination and discipline,"[63] which mass organizations like political parties are able to provide.

Elections and Parties in Monarchies

Monarchic regimes typically place great emphasis on dynastic association as a means of political legitimacy. Because bloodlines are the key sources of political power in monarchies, elections are rarely—if ever—used to determine the leader of the regime. Though elections in monarchies are quite common, they are largely restricted to the parliamentary and local level. For example, in the monarchies of Kuwait and Jordan, parliamentary elections are regularly held, but the position of ruler of the regime is not up for grabs. In personalist dictatorships, by contrast, elections deciding who will lead the regime are frequently held, even if there is only one candidate on the ballot.

Monarchies are also less likely to ally themselves with a political party than other types of dictatorships. Though political parties are allowed to exist in some monarchies, the regime itself is not typically associated with a political party. In five of the seven monarchic dictatorships (with more than one million inhabitants) in existence in 2009, for example, political parties are banned entirely. Though little research has been done exploring why monarchies are less likely to align with a political party, it is likely that this is due to the centrality of heredity in the justification of monarchic rule.

Summary and Conclusion

Authoritarian regimes differ markedly in their longevity and in the tools that they use for survival. In this chapter, we explored the factors that underlie the durability of dictatorships and how they vary with regime type. We also looked at the ways in which dictatorships fall and the methods of ouster that correlate with regime type. Lastly, we examined the role that elections and political parties play in dictatorships and how they work to strengthen the regime.

In doing so, this chapter has sought to reduce some of the complexities that shroud the authoritarian world. Though dictatorships are extremely heterogeneous, similarities among them can be identified. Illuminating trends in the institutional mechanics of dictatorships yields important insights regarding their behavior.

Authoritarian regimes differ from one another in systematic ways. As we have shown, these differences have dramatic consequences for the survival of these regimes and for the strategies that they employ to stay in power.

Review Questions

- What are the critical factors that influence the survival of dictatorships?
  - o What is the role of the masses?
  - o How do dictatorships ensure that the opposition remains weak?
  - o How do dictatorships ensure that elites remain loyal to the regime?
- Why are military regimes the most short-lived type of dictatorships? How do the preferences of military elites differ from those of their civilian counterparts?
- Why are single-party dictatorships so durable? Why do factions pose little threat to the survival of single-party dictatorships?
- What are the key ways that dictatorships collapse?
- What type of dictatorship is least likely to transition to a democracy? Why is this, the case?

- Why are elections held under dictatorships? What tools do regimes use to ensure electoral victories?
- What is the purpose of political parties in dictatorships? What role do they serve for regime survival?

Key Points

- Critical factors required for the survival of dictatorships include some level of mass support, a fractured opposition, and elite loyalty.
- The institutional structure of dictatorships affects their longevity. Military dictatorships last the shortest and single-party dictatorships the longest.
- There are four primary modes by which dictatorships collapse: military coup, foreign intervention, negotiated pact, and revolution.
- Many dictatorships hold elections and allow political parties to exist. Both institutions play key roles in prolonging the survival of the regime.

Notes

1. Geddes, *Paradigms and Sand Castles* (2003, p. 70).
2. Ibid., (p. 71).
3. Macaroni, *Comparative Autocracy* (2007, p. 23).
4. Lust-Okra, *Divided They Rule* (2004).
5. Macaroni, *Comparative Autocracy* (2007).
6. Geddes, *Paradigms and Sand Castles* (2003).
7. We should note that because no study, to our knowledge, has empirically examined the longevity of monarchies in comparison to other forms of dictatorship, we do not discuss them in this section.
8. Geddes, *Paradigms and Sand Castles* (2003, p. 126).
9. Ibid. (p. 131).
10. Ibid.
11. Geddes, *Paradigms and Sand Castles* (2003, p. 129).
12. Geddes, *Paradigms and Sand Castles* (2003, p. 130).
13. Ibid.
14. Geddes, *What Do We Know* (1999)?
15. Finer, *The Man on Horseback* (1962).
16. N'Diaye, *Mauritania, August 2005* (2006).
17. Dix, *The Breakdown of Authoritarian* (1982).
18. Snyder, *Explaining Transitions from Neo-patrimonial* (1992).

19. Geddes, *What Do We Know* (1999, p. 26).

20. O'Donnell, Schmitter and Whitehead, Transitions from Authoritarian Rule (1986).

21. Hamman, *The Pacted Transition* (1997, p. 115).

22. Fairbanks, *Revolution Reconsidered* (2007).

23. Goodwin and Skocpol, *Explaining Revolutions* (1989).

24. Geddes, *The Role of Elections* (2005). These statistics exclude monarchies, which Geddes omits from her analysis.

25. Source: *Saddam 'wins 100 percent of vote'*, BBC News (October 16, 2002), http://news.bbc. co.uk/2/hi/2331951.stm (accessed January 17, 2010).

26. Cox, Authoritarian Elections and Leadership (2009, p. 3).

27. Geddes, *The Role of Elections* (2005). We should note that dictatorships will most likely not choose to hold elections if they do not believe they will win them. As Barbara Geddes points out, differences in the survival rates of dictatorships that hold elections and those that do not "probably reflect the tenuousness of some dictatorships that choose not to hold elections" (2005, 2007).

28. Cox, *Authoritarian Elections and Leadership* (2009, p. 4).

29. Schedler, *Electoral Authoritarianism* (2006, p. 410).

30. Lust-Okar, *Structuring Conflict* (2005, p. 6).

31. Boix and Svolik (2008); Magaloni (2006); Gandhi & Przeworski (2006); Gandhi (2008); Gandhi and Lust-Okar (2009).

32. Geddes, *The Role of Elections* (2005); Blaydes, *Authoritarian Elections* (2008).

33. Lust-Okar, *Elections under Authoritarianism* (2006).

34. Magaloni, *Comparative Logic* (2006); Blaydes, *Authoritarian Elections* (2008).

35. Blaydes, *Authoritarian Elections* (2008).

36. Schedler, *Elections without Democracy* (2002); Crespo, *Party Competition in Mexico* (2004).

37. Schedler, *Elections without Democracy* (2002, p. 37).

38. Crespo, *Party Competition in Mexico* (2004).

39. Wedeen, *Acting As If* (1998, p. 519).

40. Gandhi and Lust-Okar, *Elections under Authoritarianism* (2009).

41. Magaloni, *Comparative Logic* (2006, p. 9).

42. Means, *Soft Authoritarianism in Malaysia* (1996, p. 108).

43. Geddes, *Why Parties and Elections* (2005).

44. Laakso, *Why Are Elections* (1997).

45. Brown, *Authoritarian Leaders and Multiparty* (2001).

46. This system was employed during the Yushin Constitution of 1972.

47. Schedler, *Elections without Democracy* (2002).

48. Schedler, *Elections without Democracy* (2002).

49. Dore and Ribeiro, *Political Citizenship* (2009).

50. Blaydes, *Electoral Budget Cycles* (2006).

51. Magaloni, *Demise of Mexico's One-Party* (2005). The 1994 Mexican Peso crisis is an often-cited example of an incumbent regime waiting until after an election to correct an overvaluation of currency (Stein and Streb 2004).

52. Block, *Political Business Cycles* (2002).

53. Geddes, *The Role of Elections* (2005).

54. Magaloni, *Comparative Autocracy* (2007).

55. Geddes and Frantz, *Legacy of Dictatorship* (2007).

56. Brownlee, *Authoritarianism in an Age* (2007).

57. Gandhi, *Dictatorial Institutions* (2003).

58. Geddes, *The Role of Elections* (2005, p. 3).

59. Ibid. (p. 14).

60. Geddes, *The Role of Elections* (2005); Brownlee (2007).

61. Magaloni, *Comparative Autocracy* (2007).

62. Way, *Pigs, Wolves* (2005, p. 16).

63. Brownlee, *Authoritarianism in an Age* (2007, p. 56).

The Survival of Authoritarian Leaders: Strategies and Trends

4

Though the survival of *dictatorships* and the survival of *dictators* are often viewed as one and the same, the mechanisms that underlie each of these processes are actually quite distinct. As this study emphasizes, authoritarian regimes are not synonymous with the leaders who rule them; conflating the two can lead to fundamental misunderstandings of authoritarian politics.

Whereas regime longevity involves a complex and system-wide effort to ensure the satisfaction of elites and the regime's mass constituents, leadership longevity centers on the ability of leaders to please their elite constituents and deter elite defections. The masses, though integral to the survival of many dictatorships, play a minimal role in the survival of most dictators. In fact, most dictators are ousted by elites. The greatest threat to authoritarian leaders comes from within the regime.

This chapter gives an overview of how and why dictators fall from power. First, we discuss the role of elites in the survival of dictators. We then turn to the strategies that dictators pursue to ensure their survival and, in turn, the structural factors that influence it. We explore the conditions under which leadership turnovers are likely to occur, as well as how turnover patterns vary across regime types. Lastly, we detail the key ways in which leaders are removed from power and offer insights into how the type of ouster is affected by the domestic institutional environment.

We should note that in personalist dictatorships, the lines between the dictator and the dictatorship are often blurred. Though transfers of power from one leader to the next do occur *within* personalist dictatorships, they are much less likely than in other forms of dictatorships. That being said, even personalist dictatorships can last well beyond the tenure of an individual leader, as demonstrated by Nicaragua under the Somoza family and Haiti under the Duvaliers.

The Role of Elites

All political leaders require the support of *some* individuals in order to maintain their command. As Paul H. Lewis writes:

> Regardless of how powerful dictators are, the complexities of modern society and government make it impossible for them to rule alone. They may dominate their respective systems, but some of their authority must be delegated, which means that a government elite stratum is formed just below them.[1]

While the nature and method of selection of their supporting group may vary across regimes, no leader rules entirely alone. Individuals agree to support the leader in return for benefits. These individuals constitute the elite tier of dictatorships.[2]

Paradoxically, the dictator's elite supporters pose the primary challenge to the dictator's power. Perhaps surprisingly, the vast majority of dictators are ousted by internal coups rather than by popular uprisings.[3] In fact, nearly 80 percent of the time dictators are removed from power by government insiders.[4] It is the dictator's elite supporters who are most frequently to blame for the dictator's dismissal. As King Sesostris of Egypt was rumored to have warned future kings in 1965 BCE, "Be on your guard against all subordinates, because you cannot be sure who is plotting against you."[5] The importance of the dictator's elite supporters, often highlighted in scholarship on regime transitions,[6] has recently surfaced in research on the survival of dictators.[7]

Examples of elite-led overthrows of dictators abound. In Nigeria in 1975, for example, the leader of the military dictatorship, General Yakubu Gowon, was ousted by his colleagues because they thought that he was too indecisive and did not consult enough with members of the Supreme Military Council. In Argentina, the regime's leader, Roberto Viola, was overthrown in 1981 by the military junta because its members were frustrated that he had included civilians in the cabinet and engaged in talks with the union leadership. In Ghana, Ignatius Kutu Acheampong was arrested in 1981 by his chief of staff, Frederick Akuffo, who later became head of state and Ghana's leader.[8] As Jean-Bédel Bokassa of the Central African Republic knew well, the greatest threat to his rule came from his own entourage.[9]

Elites serve as the dictator's main political rivals. As such, their support is critical for the dictator's survival. In single-party dictatorships, this elite group is typically the central committee or politburo. In military dictatorships, it is usually the military junta. In personalist dictatorships, it is often comprised of friends or family members of the dictator, while in monarchies it is the ruling family.

Strategies for Survival

Much of the research done on political survival in modern dictatorial regimes has emphasized the various strategies dictators employ to stay in power.[10] In Mancur Olson's[11] conceptualization, for example, dictators come to power as stationary bandits who monopolize and rationalize theft in the form of taxes. The time horizons of dictators influence the extent to which they will provide a peaceful order and other public goods that increase the productivity of their subjects. Olson's story, however, assumes that dictators do not face any threats to their survival once in power. Ronald Wintrobe's[12] argument emphasizes this point. Dictators are inherently insecure because they never know whether their subjects are their allies or their rivals. They face the constant threat of popular rebellion.[13] To deter this threat, dictators have a variety of tools at their disposal, such as repressing some part of the population while nurturing the loyalty of others[14] and incorporating potential opposition forces into the regime via partisan legislatures.[15]

This emphasis on the threat of popular uprising, however, is somewhat misguided. Empirically, the *primary* threat to the leader's tenure is not popular rebellion or revolution. As the Malawian personalist dictator Hastings

Banda was aware, "danger to [his] rule comes not from any likely popular uprising, but from a 'palace coup' within his own ruling party."[16] The threat of revolution does exist, but dictators are ousted far more frequently by members of their own inner circle than by members of opposition groups, as discussed above.

Various scholars acknowledge this and look specifically at the strategies dictators engage in to mitigate threats from within their elite support group.[17] Beatriz Magaloni, for example, argues that dictators must establish "power-sharing agreements with their ruling coalitions, which are often not credible" in order to survive in office.[18] Because there is nothing to ensure that dictators will follow through with their commitments to members of their support group, potential rivals have reasons to rebel or conspire. To alleviate this commitment problem, dictators opt to distribute some of their power to coalition members, mainly through the vehicles of political parties and elections.

This study posits that all dictators seek to increase their power and will pursue those strategies that will maximize the likelihood of their survival in office. In the section that follows, we discuss the structural factors that influence their ability to do so.

Structural Factors that Influence Leadership Survival

Structural factors play a key role in explaining why some dictators seem to rule forever, while others are easily overthrown. In this section, we examine how regime type influences leadership survival in dictatorships.

We emphasize the ability of elites to *forcibly* remove leaders from power. The threat of a coup simply carries greater weight than the threat of impeachment.[19] This does not mean that the use of force is always necessary for dictators to leave power. During Uruguay's military dictatorship, for example, elites demanded that President Juan María Bordaberry resign in 1976 due to his inability to adequately deal with the country's economic troubles. He adhered to their demands and power was transferred peacefully to the next leader.[20] Leaders follow orders to leave office when they are backed by a credible threat of forcible removal.

The institutional structure of the dictatorship—whether the regime is governed by a professionalized military or party or neither—plays a strong role in determining the risks dictators face of being ousted.[21] Two key factors affect the ability of *elites* to overthrow dictators: 1) whether elites share membership in a unifying institution, and 2) whether elites have access to troops and weaponry. Due to these factors, military dictators face the greatest risk of being overthrown by their elite supporters, followed by single-party dictators, and lastly personalist dictators.[22]

Elite Membership in a Unifying Institution

The first factor that is important to identify is whether elites share membership in a unifying institution, like a military or party.[23] Such membership affects whether elites bargain with the dictator individually or collectively.[24] The behavior of elites in single-party and military regimes is analogous to that of workers in a union. They are bound together by an institution that unites them and makes it possible for them to bargain with the dictator as a unit rather than as individuals who can easily be replaced by others. Just as membership to a union makes it easier for workers to coordinate to strike, in single-party and military regimes membership in the party or military, makes it easier for elites to coordinate to stage a coup.

In contrast, in personalist dictatorships there are no strong institutions that unite elites. Though parties and militaries exist, they tend to be weak, riven by factions, and often based on ethnicity.[25] Elites must overcome a greater coordination barrier in order to unseat the leader in personalist dictatorships because they do not share membership in a unifying institution.

Elite Access to Troops and Weaponry

The second factor that is important to highlight is the extent to which elites have control over the armed and security forces.[26] Most coups are carried out by military forces.[27] The leader's position is more vulnerable, the more direct control elites have over these forces. Though all countries have militaries and individuals capable of carrying out coups, this is particularly true in military dictatorships. Elites in military dictatorships are typically military commanders of various forces and, as such, tend to have greater control over the security apparatus than elites in personalist or single-party regimes.

In single-party and personalist dictatorships, elites generally do not have direct control over troops and weaponry. Leaders in personalist dictatorships often come from the military themselves and have full control over the armed forces, as well as private paramilitary forces. In single-party dictatorships, the military is secondary to the party. Soldiers are often indoctrinated in the party ideology and party functionaries are placed within the military to ensure that it is loyal. These differences make the execution of a coup more difficult.

Leadership Vulnerability

Because of these two factors, it is easier for military elites to oust dictators, followed by single-party elites, and lastly personalist elites. To summarize:

- *Military Dictatorships:* Elites have access to troops and weaponry and belong to a unifying institution (the military), making it easier for them to successfully stage a coup.
- *Single-party Dictatorships:* Elites do not have access to the material forces required to stage a coup, but do belong to a unifying institution (the party), making it somewhat difficult for them to successfully stage a coup.
- *Personalist Dictatorships:* Elites do not have access to troops and weaponry nor do they share membership in a unifying institution, making it very difficult for them to successfully stage a coup.

For these reasons, the risk leaders face of being ousted by elites varies markedly across regime categories (see **Figure 4.1** and **Figure 4.2**). Military dictators face the greatest risk of being overthrown by elites in any given year and only rule on average for around three years.[28] Personalist dictators, by contrast, face the lowest risk of being removed from power by elites, and rule on average for around ten years. Single-party dictators are slightly more vulnerable than personalist dictators but less so than military dictators; they rule on average for around eight years.

How Dictators are Ousted

The *way* in which dictators are removed from power varies dramatically in intensity; in some cases the overthrow is violent, while in others power is

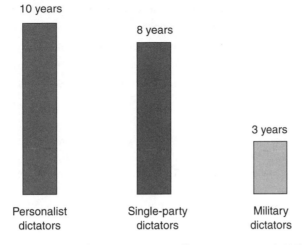

Figure 4.1 Average Number of Years Dictators in Office. *Source:* Frantz (2007)

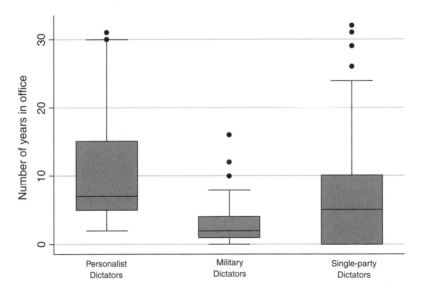

Figure 4.2 Survival Rates of Authoritarian Leaders. *Source:* Frantz (2007)

peacefully transferred. Though dictators rarely step down from power on their own volition, this does occur on occasion. In most cases, however, dictators are forced to leave office, either through a coup or through institutionalized procedures the leader must adhere to (or risk forced removal). In this section, we detail the four primary modes of exit for dictators.[29] They include:

- **Expulsion:** The dictator is forcibly removed from power by the ruling elite or their allies (either through the threat or staging of a coup).
- **Institutionalized turnover:** The leader steps down from power due to institutionalized rules for leadership succession, like term limits.
- **Assassination:** The dictator is assassinated, either by an individual within the regime, a disgruntled citizen, an opposition group, or a foreign force.
- **Resignation:** The leader voluntarily leaves power on account of personal or legitimacy reasons.

Sometimes dictators fall from power simply because the regime has fallen from power. These modes of exit (revolution, coups by low-level officers, etc.) are discussed in **Chapter 3**. In turn, dictators occasionally fall from power and precipitate the regime's downfall. This can happen when elites oust the dictator and underestimate the destabilizing effect this will have on the regime. The modes of exit most likely to give rise to the fall of the dictator are mentioned below.

Expulsion

Expulsion occurs when members of the ruling elite forcibly remove the leader from power. Expulsions typically entail the threat or staging of a coup. They can be bloodless or quite violent. When elites oust dictators in this manner, their intentions are usually not to engender the fall of the regime, but rather to get rid of a leader who has fallen out of their favor.

The reasons why elites choose to forcibly remove dictators from power do not vary noticeably from the reasons why democrats are voted out of power by voters. Slow economic growth, inflation, high unemployment, and costly foreign policy are all potential causes of elite dissatisfaction with dictators. Such dissatisfaction is heightened when it is accompanied by reduced elite access to the material spoils of the regime.

Expulsions are the typical mode of exit for leaders in military dictatorships,[30] primarily because it is so easy for military elites to stage coups. Though less common than in military regimes, expulsions also occur in single-party dictatorships. Party elites forced Nikita Khrushchev out of power in the Soviet Union; the same is true of Matyas Rakosi in Hungary and Vulko Chervenkov in Bulgaria. Even monarchic leaders have faced expulsion by elites, albeit on rare occasions. King Talal I of Jordan was forced to abdicate (due to mental health problems), while Said bin Taimur of Oman was ousted by his son Qaboos bin Said al Said.

Personalist dictatorships appear to be the exception, however. When leadership turnovers occur *within* personalist dictatorships, they are nearly always preceded by the death or resignation of the dictator. The forceful removal of a personalist dictator from power (whether by elites or regime outsiders), is nearly always accompanied by the fall of the regime.

Institutionalized Turnover

Some dictatorships have institutionalized rules dictating leadership turnover. Such turnovers can occur via elections or through guidelines established by the regime, like term limits. For example, in Mexico under the Institutional Revolutionary Party (PRI), presidential term limits of six years were strictly adhered to. In Argentina as well, prior to the coup that overthrew the Peronist government in 1955, the military junta established a ruling formula, stipulating the rotation of the presidency and the dispersion of power among the services. These measures were implemented as a means of keeping any single individual from gaining too much power.[31] The coup plotters of the military regimes that followed agreed to the following rules:

> Service rivalry must be minimized and there must be no *caudillos*—no military chief would be allowed to try to convert himself into a popular political leader. . . . The chiefs agreed that the commanders' junta—they themselves—would serve as the source of state power. Jobs and authority would be divided in three so that no service would predominate.[32]

Though institutionalized turnovers are less common in dictatorships than other modes of exit, they typically provide for a smooth transition of power.

Assassination

An assassination is when a person of interest or a public figure is deliberately targeted and killed in a planned and premeditated manner. In dictatorships, the assassination of the leader can be carried out by a variety of individuals or groups. Empirically, members of the elite, disgruntled citizens, members of the opposition, and foreign forces have all assassinated authoritarian leaders.

Assassinations often occur from within the regime. The assassination of Park Chung Hee, a personalist/military[33] dictator in South Korea, provides an example of how assassinations from within the regime take place. Park was killed in October 1979 by a member of his own elite, Kim Jaegyu, the director of South Korea's intelligence agency and one of Park's closest friends. The regime executed Kim seven months later and installed General Chun Doo-hwan at the helm.

Assassinations only require a single individual. Because simply killing the dictator entails less coordination than staging a coup, assassinations are easier to carry out. They are, however, more risky endeavors, as the consequences for failing in such an effort can be grave.

Most assassinations of dictators have occurred in personalist dictatorships or hybrids of them (see **Table 4.1**). There are a variety of reasons that could account for this. For one, it is very difficult for personalist elites to forcibly remove the dictator from power and few (if any) personalist dictatorships have institutionalized methods for turning over power. This leaves elite with little means to remove the dictator from power barring assassination. In turn, the masses (and opposition groups) are largely excluded from the political process in personalist dictatorships, potentially leading to situations in which an individual's frustrations reach a boiling point. Lastly, foreign powers often lose their patience with personalist dictators, particularly given that they are so long-lasting, making assassination an appealing alternative to waiting for the natural death or resignation of the dictator.

The Dominican Republic under Rafael Trujillo offers an example of an assassination sanctioned by foreign powers. Trujillo managed to stay in power for over 30 years, but his rule became increasingly repressive and abusive. By 1960, the United States, which had historically backed the Trujillo regime, became dissatisfied with Trujillo's performance in office.

Table 4.1 Assassinations of Post-World War II Dictators

Date	Leader	Country	Regime Type
Africa:			
1987	Thomas Sankara	Burkina Faso	Personalist
1993	Melchior Ndadaye	Burundi	Military
1975	Francois Tombalbaye	Chad	Personalist/Single-party
1977	Marien Ngouabi	Congo	Single-party/Military
2001	Laurent Kabila	DRC	Personalist
1990	Samuel Doe	Liberia	Personalist
1975	Richard Ratsimandrava	Madagascar	Military
1976	Murtala Ramat Mohammed	Nigeria	Military
1994	Juvenal Habyarimana	Rwanda	Single-party/Personalist
Latin America:			
1961	Rafael Trujillo	Dominican Republic	Personalist
1957	Carlos Castillo Armas	Guatemala	Personalist
1956	Anastasio Somoza Garcia	Nicaragua	Personalist
1950	Carlos Delgado Chalbaud	Venezuela	Personalist/Military
Middle East			
1978	Mohammed Daoud Khan	Afghanistan	Personalist
1992	Mohamed Boudiaf	Algeria	Military
1981	Anwar Sadat	Egypt	Triple Threat
1958	Faisal II	Iraq	Monarchy
1951	Abdullah I	Jordan	Monarchy
1975	Faisal	Saudi Arabia	Monarchy
1948	Imam Yahya	Yemen	Monarchy
1978	Ibrahim al-Hamadi	North Yemen	Military
Asia			
1981	Ziaur Rahman	Bangladesh	Personalist
2001	Biendra	Nepal	Monarchy
1988	Muhammad Zia-ul-Haq	Pakistan	Personalist/Military
1979	Park Chung Hee	South Korea	Military
1963	Ngo Dinh Diem	South Vietnam	Personalist

The United States began to see Trujillo as meddling and dangerous, especially after he tried to have Venezuelan President Rómulo Betancourt killed in 1960. Trujillo was assassinated on May 30, 1961 by a small group of men from the Dominican Republic. The assassination was most likely coordinated with the assistance of US intelligence agencies.[34] As with most personalist dictatorships, Trujillo's death signaled the end of the regime.

Resignation

Though many leaders hold on to power for as long as they can, leaders do on occasion step down from power voluntarily. Resignations can occur for many reasons, such as old age or mental illness. Leaders may also resign because they sense that they are highly unpopular among elites and other regime constituents.

Resignations typically do not lead to regime change. For example, Lee Kwan-Yew of Singapore stepped down from power voluntarily in 1990 after serving as Prime Minister since 1959. Lee's resignation was planned carefully by the regime to ensure a smooth transition. Goh Chok Tong succeeded Lee and the transfer of power was peaceful.[35] Julius Nyerere also retired from power as leader of Tanzania's single-party regime in 1985 on his own accord. The regime remained intact afterward and there is little evidence that the resignation was forced.

Resignation of Castro

On February 19, 2008, the long-time leader of Cuba, Fidel Castro, resigned from power ending nearly fifty years of dictatorial rule. Castro remained in power longer than any other head of government, having ruled Cuba (a personalist/single-party dictatorship) since 1959. At the age of 81, however, Castro felt the time had come for him to pass the torch to his younger brother, 76-year old Raul Castro. Though it cannot be verified, Raul Castro may have began serving as acting president as early as July 2006. The elder Castro had experienced a series of health problems that required surgery. He stated that though he wished to be in charge until his last breath, "it would be a betrayal to my conscience to accept a responsibility requiring more mobility and dedication than I am physically able to offer." ("Fidel Castro Resigns Cuban Presidency After Half-Century in Power," Associated Press, February 19, 2008, http://www.foxnews.com/story/0,2933,331149,00.html, accessed March 21, 2010). Upon Fidel Castro's announcement, the transition was seamless; power transferred peacefully to Raul Castro.

Summary and Conclusion

In this chapter, we explored the key causes of leadership survival in dictatorships. We discussed not only the major threats that dictators face, but also where these threats originate and what dictators do to deter them. In doing so, we illustrate that the vulnerability of dictators differs systematically across regime types. Institutional differences in the structure of authoritarian regimes have a strong influence on the survival rates of dictators and how easy or hard it is for elites to oust them.

Dictators face a constant threat of removal from power. Surprisingly, this threat comes primarily from their elite inner circle. As such, elites serve as the dictator's main rivals. Because of the persistent threat posed by elites, dictators must engage in a variety of strategies to stay in power, ranging from repression to co-optation. Independent of these strategies, structural factors play a key role in the vulnerabilities dictators face on their leadership. Personalist dictators are the least vulnerable to overthrow, followed by single-party dictators, and lastly military dictators.

Though the literature on leadership survival is quite rich, this chapter points to a significant hole in this research area. Relatively little is known about the survival rates of monarchic leaders as compared to other types of dictators and the factors that influence their survival. Further research on the vulnerability of leaders in monarchies is critical to advancing our understanding of the dynamics of leadership survival in the authoritarian world.

Review Questions

- What are the strategies dictators use to stay in power?
- Why should dictators be more concerned with their elite supporters than the masses?
- What are the two factors that affect the ability of elites to overthrow dictators?
- How do dictatorships differ in the longevity rates of their leaders?
- What are the four methods by which dictators are ousted? Which methods are more common in each type of regime? Why is this, the case?

Key Points

- Dictators are more in danger of being ousted by elites than by the masses.
- Elite access to troops and weaponry, coupled with shared membership in a unifying institution, increase the ability of elites to overthrow dictators.
- Expulsion is a common mode of exit for both military dictators and single-party dictators.
- Institutionalized turnover occurs in both military and single-party dictatorships, but is essentially unobserved in personalist dictatorships.

- Assassinations occur most often in personalist dictatorships because there are few (if any) other means by which to remove personalist dictators from power.
- Resignations are rare in dictatorships, and typically do not lead to, regime change.

Notes

1. Lewis, *Salazar's Ministerial Elite*, (1978, p. 622).
2. Though factions within the elite are common in authoritarian regimes, the leader does not need the backing of each and every elite to maintain power. Most elites support the dictator, but there may be some who do not. The exact number of elites required to keep the dictator in power is unknown and varies from regime to regime.
3. Tullock, *Autocracy*, (1987).
4. Svolik, *Power Sharing and Leadership*, (2007).
5. Rindova and Starbuck, *Distrust in Dependence*, (1997).
6. Higley and Burton (1989); Kugler and Feng (1999); and Haggard and Kaufman (1995).
7. Svolik (2009); Gallego and Pitchik (2004); Gandhi and Przeworski (2007).
8. Source: *Background Note: Ghana*, United States Department of State, June 2008, http://www.state.gov/r/pa/ei/bgn/2860.htm (accessed January 18, 2009).
9. Titley, Dark Age, (1997).
10. Friedrich and Brzezinski (1956); Arendt (1951); Tullock (1987).
11. Olson, *Power and Prosperity*, (2000).
12. Wintrobe, *Political Economy of Dictatorship*, (1998).
13. Acemoglu and Robinson (2001); Boix (2003); Sanhueza (1999).
14. Wintrobe, *Political Economy of Dictatorship*, (1998).
15. Gandhi and Przeworski, *Authoritarian Institutions*, (2007).
16. Legum, *Africa Contemporary Record*, (1975–1976, p. B268).
17. Svolik (2007); Gallego and Pitchik (2004); Egorov and Sonin (2005).
18. Magaloni, *Credible Power Sharing*, (2008, p. 715).
19. Frantz, *Tying the Dictator's Hands*, (2008).
20. Klieman, *Confined to Barracks*, (1980).
21. Frantz, *Tying the Dictator's Hands*, (2008).
22. Frantz (2008) does not include monarchies in her analysis.
23. Frantz, *Tying the Dictator's Hands*, (2008).
24. Geddes, *Minimum Winning Coalitions*, (2004).
25. Geddes, *What Do We Know?* (1999).
26. Frantz, *Tying the Dictator's Hands*, (2008).
27. Kebschull, *Operation 'Just Missed'*, (1994).
28. Frantz, *Tying the Dictator's Hands*, (2008).

29. Though dictators often die in office from natural causes, we do not discuss these cases here.

30. Frantz, *Tying the Dictator's Hands*, (2007).

31. Remmer, *Military Rule in Latin America*, (1991).

32. Gugliotta, *Inner Workings of Dictatorship*, (1986, p. 1).

33. Geddes categorizes his regime as purely military but a significant amount of power was concentrated in his hands and he was personally responsible for much of the implementation of a series of five-year plans. The creation of the Yushin Constitution in 1972 cemented most of his personal power.

34. Wiarda, *Review: The United States*, (1980).

35. Though Lee resigned, he still has some political influence via his position as Minister Mentor.

5 Coups

Illegal seizures of power by armed forces, or coup d'états, play a key role in authoritarian politics. As mentioned in the preceding chapters, coups are often pivotal in the rise and fall of authoritarian regimes, as well as in the removal of authoritarian leaders. Coups can signal the downfall of dictatorships and, in turn, precipitate the start of new ones. They are an omnipresent threat in the minds of authoritarian leaders. As such, they are central to authoritarian politics. Because coups affect so many key aspects of the authoritarian world, we devote this chapter to coups.

Definition of a Coup

A coup consists of the "infiltration of a small but critical segment of the state apparatus, which is then used to displace the government from its control of the remainder."[1] As the definition indicates, coups are carried out by individuals who are part of the state; these individuals are nearly always members of the military forces. Civilian politicians or actors may back or sponsor a coup effort, but they are typically not involved in its execution. Armed takeovers by revolutionary or separatist groups are not usually considered coups. Coups do not always require elite support to be undertaken (even in military dictatorships); they are often carried out by junior officers within the military.

Coups differ from assassinations in multiple ways: 1) killing the dictator is required for assassinations, but not for coups; 2) killing the dictator in no way assures a coup's success; 3) assassinations can be carried out by a single individual, while coups require multiple actors; and 4) the goal of the assassin is to kill the leader, whereas the goal of coup plotters is to seize power. Coups are more ambitious endeavors than assassinations. They entail coordination among multiple actors because no one can seize power alone.

Though coups bring with them images of violence and bloodshed, this is not always required for their success. Indeed, 80 percent of all coups are non-violent.[2] While violence is not integral to the success of a coup, the credible threat that force will be used if necessary, must always underlie it.

At the most basic level, coups signify a forced change in leadership. This change is not always permanent, however. Deposed leaders are occasionally able to maneuver back into power shortly afterward. Though coups can precipitate regime change, they are by no means an indicator of it. Coups often occur within an authoritarian regime, similar to votes of no confidence in parliamentary systems. This is particularly true in military dictatorships, where intra-regime coups are quite common.

Types of Coups

The goals of coup plotters vary markedly. In some cases, coup conspirers merely seek to remove an unfavorable leader, while in others their ambitions are to fundamentally transform the political system. Some coups represent interventions by the military on behalf of a disgruntled population; others are motivated by the preferences of a small faction within the military.

Coups can be categorized into three groups based on the goals of those undertaking them: reform coups, veto coups, and guardian coups.[3] Reform coups occur when members of the military overthrow an oligarchic regime.

These coups are typically led by lower-level officers who seek the fundamental transformation of the system. In particular, these officers aim to implement social and economic reforms, and create, a new bureaucratic, and ruling elite. In reform coups, the military plays a progressive role, challenging the oligarchy and extending political participation. Examples include the 1952 Egyptian coup in which army officers overthrew the monarchy led by King Farouk I and when Colonel Abdul Salam Arif ousted the Hashemite monarchy in Iraq in July 1958.[4]

A veto coup is when members of the military stage a coup so as to limit the public's participation in politics. It is often a by-product of modernization. Veto coups typically occur in democracies in response to members of the military feeling threatened by mass mobilization and involvement in politics, as was the case of Brazil in 1964. The military may also intervene when a civilian government has begun to promote radical policies or "appeal to groups that the military wishes to exclude from power."[5] According to Samuel Huntington, veto coups often lead to dictatorships with high levels of repression, as was the case in the 1973 Chilean coup that launched the dictatorship of Augusto Pinochet into power. These coups are also more prone to violence.

Lastly, a guardian (or government) coup takes place when members of the military seize power as a means of achieving order and restoring efficiency to government, usually on behalf of the middle class. Huntington writes that the intervention is prompted by the "corruption, stagnation, stalemate, anarchy, and subversion of the existing system."[6] With guardian coups, the coup stagers typically portray themselves as temporary custodians; few fundamental changes in the power structure are undertaken. The military aims to purify the existing order and does not attempt to create a new one. With guardian coups, the coup stagers are usually older officers, and their motives are believed to be genuine by the public. These types of coups tend to be less violent. The 1980 Turkish coup is an example of a guardian coup. The military seized control of the government as a means of restoring order to Turkey and stepped out of power three years later.

Staging a Coup

Successful coups involve proper training and coordination. An established hierarchy and clear chain of command is necessary so that instructions

Types of Coups (Huntington)

Reform

- Aim of military: extend political participation, create a new social order, and implement progressive reforms
- Rank of the officers staging the coup: low-level officers
- Length of rule: indefinite
- Role of the public: military acts on behalf of the masses
- Level of violence: high

Veto

- Aim of military: limit political participation of the lower classes in order to prevent the implementation of radical policies that would threaten both the military and the middle and upper classes
- Rank of the officers staging the coup: higher-level officers
- Length of rule: indefinite
- Role of the public: military acts on behalf of the middle and upper classes
- Level of violence: high

Guardian

- Aim of military: restore order and efficiency and reduce corruption; clean up the mess of an incompetent civilian regime
- Rank of the officers staging the coup: high-level officers
- Length of rule: temporary
- Role of the public: acts on behalf of the public
- Level of violence: low

can be closely adhered to. Given these requirements, the military is best suited to stage coups.[7] In addition to its organizational strengths, the military possesses the critical means for executing a coup: trained troops and weaponry.[8]

Coups typically occur very quickly. One or more teams usually work as independent units designating key targets as swiftly and discreetly as possible. Quick seizures are required, as any delays could be viewed as signs of weakness.[9] In addition, the rapid acceptance of the new regime by the remaining parts of the government and the public is critical to the coup's success.[10]

Coup plotters need not gain control over every part of the country, just selected points of power.[11] Key areas must be taken over by coup plotters to signal to the rest of the military corps—and to the population at large—that an intervention has taken place. These areas typically include: the presidential palace, garrisons in and around the capital, the main airport, and the radio and television stations.[12]

For example, in the September 1980 coup in Turkey, armored tanks rolled into the major cities and set up barricades at major intersections. The military police searched for people of interest, and a curfew was announced on the radio communicating to the public that the armed forces had taken power. The National Assembly was dissolved, the Prime Minister was taken into custody, his cohorts were arrested, martial law was declared, and the Constitution was suspended. This all took place rapidly in the early morning hours.[13]

Coups do not necessarily require large numbers of military forces, but they do require at least a handful. The actual number of individuals needed to stage a coup varies depending on the political and logistical circumstances at play. The fewer people involved, the easier it is to keep plans of the seizure under wraps. Yet, greater numbers of coup conspirers make coups easier to execute and give them greater legitimacy. A high likelihood of success, in turn, can induce other officers to follow suit and go along with the plot.[14] Coup plotters must weigh all of these considerations when recruiting co-conspirers.

Lastly, one of the most critical factors in staging a coup is simply finding the right opportunity to do so,[15] as discussed in **Chapter 3**. For this reason, many coups take place when a leader has left the country. The leader's departure makes it more difficult for the leader to organize a counter-coup force and respond quickly to the events taking place.

Factors that Increase the Likelihood of Coups

There are many factors that underlie the decision of coup plotters to seize power; this literature is extensive and varied. Some scholars emphasize military centrality as a key determinant of coups,[16] while others look at the role of arms transfer in encouraging coups.[17] Though this literature is heterogeneous, we concentrate on three key factors posited to increase the likelihood of coups: economic conditions, personal ambitions, and threats to the military as an institution. We also discuss the phenomenon of the "coup trap."

Economic Conditions

Poverty

According to Edward Luttwak[18] and Samuel E. Finer,[19] economic backwardness is essentially a necessary condition for coups. Coups are nearly 21 times more likely to occur in the poorest countries than in the richest.[20] As John B. Londregan and Keith Poole write, "coups are virtually non-existent in developed countries."[21] By contrast, between 1945 and 1985, about half of all third world countries experienced a coup of some sort.[22]

Coup Ceiling

According to Samuel Huntington (1995), there is a "coup ceiling," in that a country's per capita income can predict the probability a coup attempt will occur and whether it will be successful. He writes:

> There is a coup-attempt ceiling and there is a coup-success ceiling, both of which can be defined more or less in terms of per-capita GNP. Countries with per-capita GNPs of $1,000 or more do not have successful coups; countries with per-capita GNPs of $3,000 or more do not have coup attempts. The area between $1,000 and $3,000 per-capita GNP is where unsuccessful coups occur, while successful coups in Nigeria, Sudan, and Haiti were in countries with per-capita GNPs under $500.
>
> (p. 15)

This concept of a "coup ceiling" helps to explain the higher incidence of coups in the developing than in the developed world.

One reason to account for the relationship between poverty and coups is that poor countries are more likely to be politically unstable.[23] Political instability provides an opportunity for military forces to seize power. Governments in less developed countries also lack the material resources required to maintain the support of the military (and other sectors of the populace). Such deprivations can easily mobilize members of the military to protest their dissatisfaction via coup.

Poor Economic Growth

Like poverty, poor economic growth is an excellent predictor of coups.[24] There are several reasons for this. According to Claude E. Welch and Arther

K. Smith,[25] economic slumps can lead to social displacement due to labor unrest and strikes. Such conditions can, in turn, spark a coup. By destabilizing the political environment, slow economic growth forces the military to stage a coup as a means of restoring order.

In addition, economic upheaval can be a signal of the incompetence of civilian government in the eyes of the military. The military may see itself as better equipped to handle the economy and opt to intervene, a central motivation for the coup that toppled Salvador Allende's government in Chile in 1973. The failure of civilian governments to create economic growth can provide the military with incentives to carry out a coup.

Faltering economies can also cause coups aimed at leadership change. In democracies, incumbents with poor economic performance records are frequently defeated in elections. Coups, like elections, are opportunities for state actors to punish leaders for their economic performance.

Export Dependence

States that are dependent on a single export are more likely to experience coups, according to Rosemary O'Kane.[26] The reason for this is that export dependent countries, which typically rely on primary products, often have coercive labor systems in place in order to keep labor in check.[27] According to Augustine J. Kposowa and J. Craig Jenkins[28] export dependence is related to coups because it creates the need for a strong military. Strong militaries, in turn, are more likely to have the organizational capacity and resources to carry out a coup.

Personal Ambitions

Coups often occur due to the ambitions of the individuals engineering them, according to Samuel Decalo.[29] The stated goal of the coup may be to restore order or end corruption, but really it is motivated by a lust for power.

There are several examples of this. In Dahomey (today's Benin) in 1963, Colonel Christophe Soglo staged a coup after being publicly humiliated by Dahomey Unity Party leader Justin Ahomadégbé. Soglo's actions stemmed from anger and damaged pride.[30]

Similarly, in the Central African Republic, personal ambitions drove Colonel Jean-Bedel Bokassa to topple his cousin, David Dacko, in a coup. Though initially Dacko found Bokassa's ambitions amusing, members of his cabinet were aware early on of the threat posed by Bokassa. In 1965, as a means of curbing Bokassa's power, Dacko tried to reduce the budget accorded to Bokassa's army and increase the budget of other groups within the military. These efforts did not deter Bokassa, however, and Dacko was ousted later that year.

In Uganda, as well, personal motivations triggered Idi Amin's coup toppling Milton Obote in 1971. The relationship between Obote and Amin was thorny, and Amin worried that Obote would soon remove him from his post as Commander in Chief of the Army. The Amin-led coup is a "classic example of a personalized takeover caused by a General's own fears and ambitions, within the context of a widespread civic malaise and a fissiparous fratricidal army rife with corporate grievances."[31]

Threats to the Military as an Institution

Many scholars have highlighted how threats to the military as an institution can provoke it to stage a coup.[32] As stated in **Chapter 2**, military coups often occur to protect or advance the needs of the military and safeguard the military's interests.[33] According to Eric Nordlinger, the defense of the military's corporate interests is "easily the most important interventionist motive."[34] Threats to the military as an institution can take the form of budget reductions, interference in military affairs by government entities, the creation of rival military forces, and governmental tampering with military promotions, benefits, housing facilities, and salary scales.[35]

The military places high value on the maintenance of its budget. Well-endowed budgets enable it to acquire advanced weapons, crucial to both the prestige and professionalization of the military as an organization. Military budgets also ensure that officers are well-paid. Economic downturns can invoke fears within the military that its budget will be reduced and spark a coup.[36] This is exemplified by the case of Ghana. Following the government of Kofi Busia's decision to cut the military budget by ten percent, Colonel Ignatius Acheampong led a coup to topple it in 1972.[37]

The establishment of rival armed forces can also prompt a military intervention. Equipping parallel forces is very threatening to the military, as it reduces the military's power. Guatemala under Jacobo Arbenz provides a good example of this. When Arbenz organized and equipped a new military force, the military's loyalty toward him waned. As a result, in the face of invading forces led by Carlos Castillo Armas in 1954, the military refused to defend Arbenz and his government.[38]

Threats to the corporate interests of the military can make intervention an urgent necessity.[39] When militaries feel that their futures are insecure and their power potentially diminished, they typically respond by staging a coup.

Coup Trap

Scholars have identified that past coups are good predictors of future coups.[40] As stated in **Chapter 2**, the probability of a coup in many ways depends on a country's recent experience with coups. This is referred to as the "coup trap." When a coup occurs, the risk of another one occurring in the future, increases significantly.

In such circumstances, a political culture develops in the country where military coups are the norm.[41] With coups, "once the ice is broken, more coups follow."[42] As T. Y. Wang points out, "a number of African countries have experienced a succession of coups and attempted coups following an initial event."[43] The aftereffects of coups can last for up to six years.[44]

Thailand and the Coup Trap

The phenomenon of the coup trap is particularly evident in Thailand. Few countries in Asia have seen the military play a more prominent political role than Thailand. The Thai military has had a long history of intervening in politics, having staged at least eighteen coups. Coups are the primary means by which the military exercises power in Thailand and communicates its displeasure with proposed policies and/or government decisions.[45] As Sukhumbhand Paribatra writes, coups in Thailand have become an "institutionalized means for political leaders to alternate in power and at the same time keep popular participation and political institutions under control."[46]

Military leaders have repeatedly staged a coup, changed the constitution, reintroduced participatory institutions, and then neglected to adequately develop or monitor these institutions. Shortly afterwards, the military, then stages yet another coup to avoid a renewed political crisis. This creates a vicious cycle where instability and military interference beget more instability and military interference.

In fact, military interventions have led to 15 changes in the constitution.[47] Such constitutional changes are a means for the military to ensure that the state acts to protect its interests. Many of changes to the Thai constitution were carried out so that the military could maintain its legitimacy rather than having to rely on force to remain in power.[48]

During those times that the military has not directly ruled Thailand, it has exercised power behind the scenes, using coups as a way to exert its will. By threatening the civilian leadership that it will stage a coup if it does not abide by its wishes, the military is able to influence the political process even when it is not in charge.[49] The Thai military's use of coups as a means of shaping politics is reflected in the actions of the Class Seven military clique, a group of influential military leaders in the late 1970s and 1980s. In 1977, the Class Seven officers forced the Thai Prime Minister, Tanin Kraivixien, to resign because they did not approve of his economic policies.[50] Such military interferences in Thailand are typically sparked by perceived threats to the military as an institution. This can occur for a variety of reasons, such as, when civilian governments decrease military budgets, or when they become too involved in military promotions.[51]

When civilian politicians have tried to rein in the military's power, they have been ousted; no strong political or societal organizations exist that can protect them.[52] Such organizations have failed to develop because of the pervasiveness of military interventions. In the 20th century only four parliaments since 1932 were completed; the rest were interrupted by military coups.[53] As a result, politicians have lacked the power to make do on promises made, causing the public to have little trust in them.

Though multiple military coups have occurred in Thailand, it should not be assumed that the same military actors have led them. The Thai military has historically been plagued by "rivalry within its own ranks."[54] Most coups have entailed one military faction replacing another,[55] with alterations of the constitution simply reflecting a redistribution of the balance of power among factions.[56] After the military took over in 1932, for example, its attempt at united rule was hampered by the presence of four factions competing for power, led by Phraya Manopakorn Nititada, Phraya Phahon, Luang Phibunsongkhram (Phibun) and Pridi Phanomyong. Each of these individuals eventually became prime minister of Thailand.[57]

Regional Coup Trends

Coups have been fairly common in the developing world. In many parts of the world, absent democratic institutions, the coup has become the "institutionalized method for succession."[58]

The African continent has been particularly ridden with coups. Studies of coups in sub-Saharan Africa indicate that 41 out of 48 states (85 percent) have experienced a coup or coup attempt.[59] Between 1956 and 1984, half of all coups and a third of all attempted coups took place in Africa.[60] In 2009 alone, coups occurred in Madagascar, Guinea Bissau, and Mauritania. Poverty and poor economic performance, coupled with the coup trap, help to explain the pervasiveness of coups in Africa.

Though Latin America has experienced many years of military dictatorship, and in turn many military coups, coups have become far less frequent as the region has democratized. The fact that the 2009 Honduran coup shocked many observers of Latin American politics, points to the rarity of coups in the region.

In Asia, coups have been uncommon, with the exception of Thailand. The same is true of Eastern Europe, where they are very rare occurrences. The frequency of coups in the Middle East is also comparatively low, though coups have occurred on multiple occasions in Iraq and Turkey.

Failed Coups

Coups are risky precisely because they do not always succeed. Indeed, coups often fail. In Venezuela, for example, a coup attempting to overthrow Hugo Chavez failed in 2002. The coup attempt lasted 47 hours, during which Chavez was detained, the National Assembly dissolved, and the constitution declared void.[61] Pedro Carmona was declared the interim president. The coup failed however, because key factions within the military and the opposition did not back Carmona. The Chavez-supported Presidential Guard regained control over the presidential palace and Chavez was reinstalled as president soon after.

Coups are challenging to carry out and, as a result, provide a variety of opportunities for things to go wrong. H.G. Kebschull highlights a number of reasons why coups fail.[62] One of the coup plotters may be a traitor and undermine or reveal coup efforts to government authorities. A communication accident may occur that is intercepted by government forces. A key coup team may not reach its target on time. Even the weather can affect the coup's success by taking a turn for the worst at a critical moment.

Coups can also fail because conspirators overestimate the likelihood that their efforts will be supported by key segments of society. In Argentina in 1990 and in the Soviet Union in 1991, for example, coup plotters fundamentally misunderstood the current political context in which they operated. As Kebschull writes, "conspirators failed to understand how much military and civilian attitudes had changed over the years about, respectively, the military's role in Argentina, and the acceptance of democracy in the USSR. As a result of the misreading, anticipated support for the coups did not appear, and both were crushed."[63]

Scholars differ in their definitions of what constitutes the success of a coup.[64] For some, the coup plotters must stay in power for a week or so for the coup to be considered a success; for others, sustained control of power for a month or more is required.

Though there are disagreements over how successful coups are conceptualized, they are far easier to identify than failed coups. It is often difficult to know with any accuracy whether coup plots that failed have actually occurred. For example, a government may announce that it has "discovered" a coup plot, "even if the claim is deliberately contrived nonsense, put forward to serve the regime's purpose of initiating emergency rule, suppressing a particular group, or justifying other actions sought by the regime."[65] The reverse can also occur. Governments may choose not to acknowledge coup plots that have failed so as to give the impression that the regime is stable and legitimate. These factors make failed coups particularly tricky to study.

Table 5.1 Sample List of Coups and Coup Attempts

MIDDLE EAST	Successful	Failed
Afghanistan	1973, 1992	1990
Algeria	1965, 1992	
Egypt	1952	
Iran	1953	
Iraq	1958, 1963, 1968	
Libya	1969	
Syria	1949,1951, 1954, 1961, 1962, 1966	1963
Turkey	1960, 1971, 1980	

Sub-Saharan Africa

AFRICA	Successful	Failed
Angola		1977
Benin	1963, 1965 (Nov.), (Dec.), 1968, 1972	1972, 1992
Burkina Faso	1966, 1974	
Burundi	1965, 1966, 1996	1993 (Jul.), (Nov.), 1994

(Continued)

Table 5.1 Cont'd

AFRICA	Successful	Failed
Central African Republic	1966, 1981, 2002	1996, 2001
Cameroon		1975
Chad	1975, 1990	1991, 2004, 2006
Comoros	1978, 1989	1985, 1987, 1992, 1995
Congo	1968	
Cote d'Ivoire	1999	2001, 2007
Djibouti		1991
DRC	1960, 1965	1963, 1992, 2004 (Mar.), (Jun.)
Equatorial Guinea	1979	2004
Ethiopia	1974	1960, 1990
Gabon		1964
Gambia	1994	1981
Ghana	1966, 1972, 1979, 1981	1964
Guinea	1984, 2008	1970
Guinea-Bissau	1980, 2003	
Kenya		1982
Lesotho	1986, 1991	
Liberia	1980	1994
Madagascar	1972, 2009	1990, 1992, 2006
Mali	1968	
Mauritania	1978, 2005, 2008	2003
Mozambique		1975
Niger	1974, 1996	
Nigeria	1966, 1983, 1993	1990
Rwanda	1973	
Sao Tome and Principe	2003	1995
Senegal		1962
Seychelles	1977	
Sierra Leone	1967, 1992, 1997	1971, 1987, 1996, 2000
Somalia	1969, 1991	1961
Sudan	1958, 1985, 1989	1966, 1990
Swaziland	1973	1984
Tanzania		1964
Togo	1963, 1967, 2005	1991(Oct. 1), (Oct. 7), (Nov.), (Dec. 3), (Dec. 15)
Uganda	1971, 1980, 1985	1988
Zambia		1989, 1990, 1997
Zimbabwe		1982

Latin America and the Caribbean

LATIN AMERICA	Successful	Failed
Argentina	1943, 1955, 1966, 1970, 1976	1990
Bolivia	1964, 1969, 1970, 1971, 1978, 1979, 1980, 1981	

(Continued)

LATIN AMERICA	Successful	Failed
Brazil	1964	
Chile	1973	
Colombia	1953	
Cuba	1952	
Dominican Republic	1963, 1965	
Ecuador	1935, 1943, 1961, 1963, 1972, 1976, 2000, 2005	
El Salvador	1931, 1979	
Grenada	1979	
Guatemala	1963, 1970, 1982, 1983	
Haiti	1950, 1991 (Sept.)	1991 (Jan.)
Honduras	1963, 1972, 1975, 1978, 1988, 1991, 2009	
Nicaragua	1936	
Panama	1968, 1982, 1989	1990 (Oct.), (Dec.)
Paraguay	1954	
Peru	1948, 1962, 1968, 1975, 1992	
Suriname	1980, 1989	
Trinidad and Tobago		1990
Uruguay	1973	
Venezuela	1948, 1958	1992, 2002

East, South and Central Asia

ASIA	Successful	Failed
Bangladesh	1975, 1982	1996
Burma	1958, 1962	
Cambodia	1970	1990
Fiji	1987, 2006	2000
Nepal		2005
Pakistan	1958, 1969, 1977, 1999	1949, 1980, 1999
Philippines		1990, 2006
South Korea	1961	
South Vietnam	1963	
Sri Lanka		1962, 1966
Tajikistan		1992
Thailand	1933, 1938, 1947, 1957, 1958, 1959, 1963, 1971, 1976, 1977, 1980, 1991, 1992, 2006	

EUROPE	Successful	Failed
Georgia	1992	
Greece	1935, 1967	1933
Portugal	1974	
Soviet Union		1991
Spain		1981

*This list of coups and coup attempts is not meant to be exhaustive. (See Turunç 2003; McGowan 2003; BBC news)

Summary and Conclusion

Coups play an unquestionably central role in authoritarian politics. They are one of the most common modes of exit for authoritarian leaders. Dictators (and occasionally democrats) face the constant threat of a coup. They must act at all times to deter coups from occurring. Coups are also one of the main ways in which dictatorships rise and fall. In many dictatorships, illegal seizures of power are pivotal in the regime's consolidation (or deterioration) of power.

For these reasons, coups warrant special attention. In this chapter, we examined what coups mean, how they are carried out, and the factors that propel them. We also looked at why coups fail. By improving our understanding of coups, this chapter has sought to sharpen our grasp of the very real threats confronted by dictatorships and the leaders who rule them.

Review Questions

- How do coups differ from assassinations?
- What are the different types of coups?
- What factors explain why coups occur?
- What is the coup trap?
- What parts of the world are more prone to coups and why?

Key Points

- Coups require complex, planning, coordination, and training. They are risky endeavors.
- Poor countries are more likely to experience coups and coup attempts.
- Countries that have experienced coups in the past are more likely to experience coups in the future.
- Coups have been most common in Africa and Latin America, though their frequency in Latin America has declined.
- When coup plots are unsuccessful, it is difficult to know with any certainty whether they have actually occurred.

Notes

1. Luttwak, *Coup d'Etat* (1968, pp. 26–27).
2. Zimmerman, *Toward a Causal Model* (1979, p. 435).

3. Huntington, *Political Order* (1968).

4. Ibid. (p. 202). The Iraqi coup of 1958 is sometimes referred to as a revolution.

5. Huntington, *Political Order* (1968, pp. 223–224).

6. Ibid. (p. 226).

7. Luttwak, *Coup d'Etat* (1968).

8. O'Kane, *Military Regimes: Power* (1989).

9. Luttwak, *Coup d'Etat,* (1968).

10. Quinlivan, *Coup-Proofing: Its Practice* (1999).

11. Luttwak, *Coup d'Etat* (1968).

12. Geddes, *What Do We Know?* (1999).

13. Paul, *The Coup, Turkey* (1981).

14. Geddes, *What Do We Know?* (1999).

15. Finer, *Man on Horseback* (1962).

16. Kposowa et al., *Structural Sources of Military* (1993); Janowitz (1977); Finer (1962).

17. Wang, *Arms Transfers and Coups* (1998).

18. Luttwak, *Coup d'Etat* (1968).

19. Finer, *Man on Horseback* (1962).

20. Londregan and Poole, *Poverty, the Coup Trap* (1990).

21. Ibid. (p. 151).

22. Belkin and Schofer, *Toward a Structural Understanding* (2003).

23. Przeworski et al., *Democracy and Development* (2000).

24. Londregan and Poole, *Poverty, the Coup Trap* (1990).

25. Welch and Smith, *Military Role and Rule* (1974).

26. O'Kane, *Toward an Examination* (1983).

27. Paige (1975); Hechte (1978); Wallerstein (1979).

28. Kposowa and Jenkins, *Structural Sources of Military* (1993).

29. Decalo, *Military Coups and Military* (1973).

30. Ibid. (p. 110).

31. Ibid. (p. 112).

32. Bienen (1974); Welch (1972); Zimmerman (1979).

33. Needler, *Military Motivations* (1975).

34. Nordlinger, *Soldiers in Politics* (1977, p. 65).

35. Needler, "*Military Motivations*" (1975); Nordlinger, *Soldiers in Politics* (1977).

36. Wang, *Arms Transfers and Coups* (1998).

37. Nordlinger, *Soldiers in Politics* (1977).

38. Needler, *Military Motivations* (1975).

39. Nordlinger, *Soldiers in Politics* (1977).

40. Londregan and Poole, *Poverty, the Coup Trap* (1990); Przeworski et al. (1996).

41. Londegran and Poole, *Poverty, the Coup Trap* (1990).

42. Ibid. (p. 152).

43. Wang, *Arms Transfers and Coups* (1998, p. 664).

44. Londregan and Poole, *Poverty, the Coup Trap* (1990).

45. Tamada, *Coups in Thailand* (1995).

46. Paribatra, *State and Society in Thailand* (1993, p. 880).

47. Dalpino, *Thailand's Search for Political* (1991); LoGerfo and King (1996).

48. Mezey, *1971 Coup in Thailand* (1971).

49. Neher, *Political Succession in Thailand* (1992).

50. Tamada, *Coups in Thailand* (1995).

51. Bunbongkarn, *Thailand in 1991* (1992).

52. LoGerfo and King, *Thailand: Toward Democratic Stability* (1996).

53. Paribatra, *State and Society in Thailand* (1993).

54. Girling, *Thailand in Gramscian Perspective* (1984, p. 390).

55. Dalpino, *Thailiand's Search for Political* (1991).

56. Neher, *Constitutionalism and Elections* (1970).

57. Dalpino, *Thailand's Search for Political* (1991); Aphornsuvan, *Search for Order* (2004).

58. Jenkins and Kposowa, *Explaining Military Coups* (1990, p. 861) from Young (1988, p. 57).

59. McGowan, *African Military Coups* (2003).

60. Agyeman-Duah, *Military Coups, Regime Change* (1998); McGowan and Johnson, *Sixty Coups in Thirty* (1986).

61. Source: *Interim Venezuelan president sworn in*, BBC News (April 13, 2002), http://news.bbc.co.uk/2/hi/americas/1927322.stm (accessed January 23, 2010).

62. Kebschull, *Operation 'Just Missed'* (1994).

63. Ibid. (p. 571).

64. see Kebschull, *Operation 'Just Missed'* (1994).

65. Ibid. (p. 568).

Dictatorships and Political Gridlock

6

Chapter Outline

Policy making in dictatorships often occurs inside a black box. The considerations underlying policy decisions are typically obscure to outside observers. Some regimes are so closed off that basic information about them, like poverty levels, literacy, and inflation, is impossible to estimate. Though these factors can make it difficult to study policy making in dictatorships, their institutional structures can provide insights into this black box.

In this chapter, we explore how the type of dictatorship affects the extent to which they are characterized by political gridlock. Political gridlock—or policy stability—occurs when policy makers share divergent policy preferences and cannot agree to policy changes. When policy makers conflict substantially with respect to their policy goals, large changes in policy will be impossible to implement.[1] As Witold J. Henisz writes, policy makers who are constrained "will be less able to craft a change in a given policy that is amenable to all veto players and the status quo policy will be likely to persist even in the face of a substantial shift in the macroeconomic environment."[2] By contrast, when policy makers share similar political views, it is easy for them to agree to significant changes in policy.

In dictatorships, policies essentially require the tacit support of two actors: the dictator and the dictator's elite support group.[3] Elites support the dictator in exchange for political and economic benefits, as discussed in **Chapter 4**. Just as prime ministers require the approval of parliament to stay in power in parliamentary regimes, leaders in dictatorships require the support of elites. Dictators must take into account the policy preferences of their elite support group or risk being deposed. Elites sustain the leader in power so long as they endorse the dictator's policies. When elites disapprove of the dictator's policies, they can "veto" them by credibly threatening to oust the dictator.

In the sections that follow, we examine how regime type influences the constraints dictators face when implementing significant changes in policies. In particular, we discuss how the policy preferences of elites, and consequently political gridlock, vary across dictatorships.

Regime Type, Elite Policy Preferences, and Political Gridlock

Because elites in personalist dictatorships do not belong to a unifying institution like military or party (see **Chapter 4**), the leader has greater control over elite recruitment in personalist dictatorships than in other types of dictatorships.[4] Personalist dictators do not have to adhere to party or military guidelines for elite promotions; they can select those elite supporters who are most likely to agree with them. Because of this, elites in personalist dictatorships tend to have policy preferences that mirror those of the dictator. Personalist leaders can also dismiss those elites who disagree with them, as there is no autonomous party or military that can collectively challenge such an action. Elites are more likely to agree with the dictator in order to stay in the dictator's good favor. As a result, elite policy preferences are essentially the leader's policy preferences. With no one to "veto" the dictator's policy choices, significant changes in policy are possible at any moment according to the whims of the leader.

Leaders in single-party and military dictatorships, by contrast, cannot handpick their elite support group. Elites must work their way up the party or military hierarchy to attain their positions, and leaders have less control over individual promotions. This means that elites in single-party and military regimes do not share the exact policy preferences of the leader, as in personalist dictatorships. Policy changes will be more difficult to agree to.

Governance by a party or military, however, also influences the heterogeneity of elite preferences in these regimes. Elites in military dictatorships tend to be much more united in their policy preferences than elites in single-party dictatorships. There are many interrelated reasons for this, such as the military's emphasis on unity, the military's aversion to factionalism, and the fact that military elites do not typically represent citizen constituent bases that would force them to adopt more varied policy positions. This internal cohesiveness means that it will be easier for policy makers in military dictatorships to agree to large changes in policy than in single-party dictatorships.

In sum:

- Policy changes are the easiest to agree to in personalist dictatorships. Elites are handpicked by the leader and share the leader's preferences.
- Policy changes are easier to agree to in military dictatorships than in single-party dictatorships, but more difficult to agree to than in personalist dictatorships. Though elites' preferences do not mirror those of the leader, the military's elite corps is relatively monolithic.
- Policy changes are the most difficult to agree to in single-party dictatorships. Party elites do not share the same preferences as the leader, and the preferences of the elite corps are heterogeneous.[5]

This means that significant swings in policy are most possible in personalist dictatorships and least possible in single-party dictatorships. Personalist dictatorships are characterized by the least political gridlock and single-party dictatorship by the most. This is illustrated in **Figure 6.1**.

Instances of the ease with which personalist dictators can dramatically change policies abound. As an extreme example, Jean-Bédel Bokassa of the Central Africa Republic changed the country from a capitalist state, to a socialist state, to an Islamic Republic, to an empire, all between 1976 and 1977. Bokassa's policy choices were often unpredictable and impulsive,[6] primarily due to his "excessive vanity, flights of fancy, and whimsical vacillations."[7] Similarly, the Philippines under Ferdinand Marcos was characterized by an "unpredictability and inconsistency" in state policies as "personal whims triumphed."[8] Because personalist dictators face little opposition

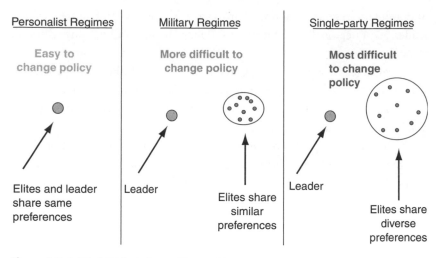

Figure 6.1 Political Gridlock Across Dictatorships

to their policies, changes in policy are relatively easy to realize. As Muammar al-Gaddafi's son, Saif al-Islam al-Gaddafi, said in an interview, "the moment we sit together and decided to solve the issue, we solved it in a couple of days.... It's very easy to reform the economy, to modernize our country."[9]

Single-party dictatorships lie at the other end of the spectrum. A few scholars have highlighted the slow policy process characteristic of single-party regimes. Phillip G. Roeder,[10] for example argues that, in the Soviet Union, leaders attempted to implement changes, but their efforts were defeated by institutional resistance, to reform. As the need for reform grew, stability became a fatal flaw. Single-party regimes have even been characterized as having "policy paralysis."[11] In Vietnam, for example, elites do not always agree on policy, and gridlock is common.[12] Because of internal disagreements "economic policy will muddle through the middle of the road," and the leader has no choice but to proceed cautiously.[13] The diversity of policy preferences in single-party dictatorships helps to generate alternative policy recommendations, but this also means that changes tend to be incremental.[14] As Valerie Bunce and John M. Echols show, annual budgetary changes in communist party systems are "small and relatively insignificant" and "no more dramatic than in democracies," because of elite conflict in "a political culture of bargaining and accommodation."[15]

In what follows, we examine in greater detail how the structure of dictatorships affects the heterogeneity of elite policy preferences and, consequently, the likelihood for political gridlock.

Elite Preferences in Personalist Dictatorships

In personalist dictatorships, the preferences of elites typically mirror those of the dictator. This occurs because personalist dictators largely control who will comprise their elite support group, as they do not have to contend with a powerful party or military. There is no institution in personalist dictatorships that could enforce any guidelines for elite promotions. Personalist dictators are able to hire and fire elites as they choose. In the Philippines, for example, Marcos chose to only surround himself with those who posed no challenge to his rule. He "skillfully wove together a broad political coalition that was loyal to him personally" and "used military repression and legal harassment against those who opposed him."[16] They find individuals to support them who are agreeable to their policy choices. Those who oppose them are easily replaced.

Elite Purges

In personalist dictatorships, purges of the elite corps are quite common. Such purges are indicative of the power of the dictator to control elite promotions. Iraq under Saddam Hussein provides a good example of this. Hussein executed most members of his elite support group in 1979, replacing them with new supporters. Of those executed, many "had been among Saddam Hussein's most intimate associates . . . even those closest to him could fall suddenly and fatally from favor."[17] Individuals who disagree with personalist dictators often face a violent fate. As a result, elites frequently communicate to the dictator what it is the dictator wants to hear, out of fears of replacement. Bokassa, for example, treated his aides ruthlessly; those who he deemed to be untrustworthy were often sent to "face firing squads in distant garrisons."[18] Purges, such as these, reflect the ability of personalist dictators to control the selection of their support groups.

Concentration of Power

Because personalist dictators stack the elite tier with those who support them (and purge those who do not), policy making power is essentially in the hands of a single individual. Many scholars have highlighted the concentration of power characteristic of personalist dictatorships.[19] In Portugal under Antonio Salazar, for example, there were no independent political institutions or entities that could challenge his policies.[20] The relationship between Salazar and his ministers "[was] one of the concentration of decision-making power in the person of the dictator and of the reduction of the independence of both the ministers and of the president of the republic."[21] Salazar went over every single piece of legislation, refusing to "allow advisers anything but the smallest margin for autonomous decision-making."[22] Salazar was completely "intolerant of those who did not share his views," discouraging Portugal's talented youth from pursuing a job with the government.[23]

Because of this concentration of power, personalist dictatorships can change policy on a whim. There are no actors that can potentially "veto" their dictator's proposed policies. Libya under Gaddafi provides an example of how the extreme concentration of power typical of personalist dictatorships can lead to capricious policies. There are few who can challenge Gaddafi in Libya, leaving him free to implement the policies of his choosing, regardless of their prudence. In 1977, Gaddafi decided that all Libyan families had to raise chickens in their homes, as a means for Libya to achieve self-sufficiency. Though this was not difficult for those living in the countryside, it was all but impossible for Libya's city dwellers.[24]

Elite Preferences in Single-party Dictatorships

Single-party leaders cannot handpick their elite subordinates, as individuals must work their way up the party apparatus to gain elite status. Leaders and elites do not share exactly the same policy preferences, as they do in personalist dictatorships. For reasons we discuss below, elites in single-party regimes are more divided ideologically than in other dictatorships.

Internal Heterogeneity

Elites in single-party dictatorships are less internally united than their counterparts in military dictatorships. As Rounaq Jahan states, "Due to the rigorous discipline and the value placed upon cohesiveness, the military is less divided than are political elites."[25] In Zambia, for example, the United National Independence Party (UNIP) was so divided that party leader

Kenneth Kaunda had to use his "personal legitimacy to curb intra-party disagreements," even threatening to resign "in an effort to prevent open schism."[26] In Kenya, as well, the Kenya African National Union (KANU) at the parliamentary level was loosely organized and characterized by a lack of discipline. Backbenchers often criticized the government in speeches and on occasion voted against it.[27] As Samuel E. Finer[28] writes, political parties simply do not share the same internal unity as the armed forces do.

Party Factionalism

In single-party dictatorships, the lack of inter-party competition means that varied interests that would normally be represented by other political parties often emerge in the form of factions.[29] The abolition of inter-party competition, "frees factions to compete vigorously with each other because they no longer fear the loss of the party's supremacy."[30] Enduring factionalism have been characteristic of a wide variety of long-lasting, single-party, dictatorship. In Mexico under the Institutional Revolutionary Party (PRI), for example, factions functioned as *corrientes* or political groups within the ruling coalition.[31] In Tunisia, as well, "dissent took the form of competing tendencies inside the party"[32]; disputes over policy "have always been fought inside the [party] by ever-shifting factions of party officials."[33] The same is true of Taiwan, where Kuomintang (KMT) sessions were marked by furious debate over the direction of the country, and factions competed for power and policy influence.[34] Indeed, factionalism was so rife in Botswana that the Botswana Democratic Party (BDP) was unable to elect a Central Committee in 1997.[35] BDP party leaders "are like ducks in a pond: calm on the surface but peddling furiously underneath."[36]

Factionalist tensions are often mitigated by the broad sharing of power recognizing the claims of each group.[37] As Tun-jen Cheng and Stephan Haggard point out, "pervasive factionalism within the ruling party provides further protection for Caesarian rule," allowing for the "representation of diverse social interests.[38] In Tunisia, for example, factions are a key means by which disgruntled elites can express dissent.[39] Factions in single-party regimes serve the purpose of approximating the type of competition of ideas that occur in democracies without threatening the survival of the party.[40] Factionalism is often tolerated in single-party regimes, at times institutionalized, and, some have argued, may help prolong the life of the regime.[41]

Factions

Factions are "informal networks of interdependent personal relationships" (Baum 1996, p. 9). They are also defined as "political conflict groups that are not corporate and whose members are recruited by a leader on diverse principles" (Bosco 1992, p. 157). Though factions occasionally have permanent names, well-developed policy platforms, and a stable leadership, they are inherently informal groups. If a faction "develops the functional specialization and structure of a bureaucracy, then it ceases to be a faction" (Ibid.). More often, factions are fluid, ideologically flexible bodies that do not have fixed membership. They are usually built around personal loyalties and are malleable in the face of changing political alignments (Baum 1996).

Representation of Constituencies

Elites in single-party regimes generally represent constituencies, leading to a greater diversity of preferences within the elite coalition. As Douglas Pike writes with respect to Vietnam, "Each member [of the Politburo] has a constituency he runs but which also constrains him and often determines his policy position on a particular issue before the Politburo."[42] In Kenya, as well, party elites represent subgroups and bring them into factional alliances through their ties to the national network.[43] The same is true of China, where official ideology is pragmatic and has allowed "informal groups to make a plausible case that their policy preferences correspond to the public interest."[44] The preferences of single-party elites are varied because elites serve as the "representatives" of a variety of groups in the citizenry.

Elite Preferences in Military Dictatorships

As in single-party dictatorships, military leaders cannot personally control who will comprise their elite support group, as promotions are dictated by military guidelines. This means that elites and leaders in military dictatorships do not share the same policy preferences, as in personalist dictatorships. Nonetheless, elites share much more in common in military dictatorships than in single-party dictatorships. There are several reasons for this, which we discuss below.

Internal Unity

The military, as an institution, tends to place great emphasis on internal unity.[45] "Professional status, internal unity, and discipline" are a top priority among military officers.[46] Armies are typically more organized and united than civilian bodies are.[47] Organizational features of the military include a centralized command, unity and solidarity, and insulation and separation from society.[48] The respect of rank is important, in further unifying the organization, and "direct orders are always to be obeyed."[49]

Common background and training serves to increase internal unity within the military. Members of the military typically share a common socialization, with values often instilled in officers from a young age. The common socialization typical of military elites is not always shared by single-party elites.[50] In Algeria, for example, military leaders "grew up in an ethos of unity that denies factionalism"; a certain solidarity and respect of rank operated at all times.[51] The military's emphasis on internal unity is reflected in the training process potential members undergo, where the goal is to "replace the inductee's individual or civilian identity with a corporate spirit."[52] This type of indoctrination occurs within a sheltered learning environment, so that soldiers are protected from the potentially divisive influences of the civilian world.[53]

The Brazilian military dictatorship provides a good example of the military's emphasis on internal unity. As Wilfred A. Bacchus highlights, the military leadership "needed to present a unified front in facing national issues, simply to carry out policies in such a way that public approval might create some de facto legitimacy. The unity requirement went far beyond mere avoidance of threats of a coup d'état or disruptive violence; it was necessary for major accomplishments."[54] Organizational unity was central to the regime, and allowed the military to further its political interests, without being bogged down by divisions from within.[55] Consensus within the military was highly valued[56] and elites were internally unified.[57]

Aversion to Factionalism

Another reason military elites tend to be unified is that factionalized militaries often do not survive in office. As Brian Lai and Dan Slater[58] note, what defines a military regime in institutional terms is not the personal background of its leadership, but the absence of any effective party institutions to help manage elite factionalism and curb mass dissent. Factionalism over policy has particularly destabilizing effects in military dictatorships and often leads to a return to the barracks.[59] This is because most officers prefer to leave office than stay in power as a factionalized military force.[60] This preference is unique to military regimes. As Barbara Geddes writes, "the officer corps will not go along with disintegration of the military into openly competing factions . . . most professional soldiers place a higher value on the survival and efficacy of the military itself than on anything else."[61] Issues which might split the armed forces internally are usually avoided.[62]

Lack of Constituencies

Another reason military elites are ideologically cohesive is that they generally do not represent a constituency. Elites in military dictatorships tend to insulate themselves from the diversity of policy preferences represented in the public. They often have "an aversion to legitimating a constituency base of politics because it threatens corporate cohesion and unity."[63] As one cabinet member in the military dictatorship of Nigeria stated, "In the military regime there is no constituency whatsoever."[64] Rather than having a civilian constituency, military elites aim to please the lower-level members of the military. In Turkey, for example, the military government implemented policies aimed at improving the standard of living of the officer corps, in order to secure elites' positions relative to their "internal constituency."[65] Compared to politicians, the military is typically "less tied to localized interests and therefore more cohesive and relatively isolated from civil cleavages."[66]

The Consequences of Political Gridlock

Because it is easy for personalist dictatorships to agree to big policy changes, the policy environment in these regimes is more volatile. Policies from one moment to the next can change rapidly. The opposite is true of single-party dictatorships. The variety of political preferences among party elites means that changes are often incremental, and the policy environment, as a consequence, is relatively stable. In military dictatorships, policies are less volatile than in personalist dictatorships, but they are more likely to change from one year to the next than in single-party dictatorships.

Due to these institutional differences, there is greater political gridlock in single-party dictatorships, followed by military dictatorships, and lastly personalist dictatorships. Such political gridlock—in itself—has a number of policy consequences, which we discuss below.

For one, it is easier for personalist dictatorships to respond quickly to an exogenous price shock.[67] Personalist regimes do not have to deal with a bevy of divergent political opinions held by policy makers to make a quick decision. Single-party dictatorships, by contrast, have more difficulty responding to external price shocks. The heterogeneity of preferences makes it hard for policy makers to agree to the correct responses.

In addition, monetary policy fluctuates the most from year to year among personalist dictatorships, followed by military dictatorships, and lastly single-party dictatorships.[68] Similarly, inflation rates are the most stable in single-party dictatorships, and the least stable in personalist dictatorships.[69]

Because single-party dictatorships have a more predictable policy environment, they are also more attractive to foreign investors, as there is less concern that policy could change dramatically on a whim. The opposite is true of personalist dictatorships. Single-party dictatorships attract the greatest levels of foreign direct investment and personalist dictatorships the least, with military dictatorships lying in between.[70] Volatility in policy has also been shown to negatively impact long-term growth rates.[71]

Summary and Conclusion

In this chapter, we examined how the institutional structure of dictatorships influences policy making and, in particular, political gridlock. In personalist dictatorships, members of the dictator's elite support group generally share the dictator's preferences, because the dictator can largely control who comprises it. This is not the case in single-party or military dictatorships. Though dictators have less control over the selection of elites in these regimes, governance by a military or party does influence the heterogeneity of elite preferences. Elites in military dictatorships tend to share more similar preferences than elites in single-party dictatorships. Policy changes are easiest to agree to in personalist dictatorships and most difficult to agree to in single-party dictatorships.

Structural differences across dictatorships largely impact how easy or difficult it is to change policies. Political gridlock is the most intense in single-party dictatorships, followed by military dictatorships, and lastly personalist dictatorships. This gridlock has both positive and negative ramifications. On the one hand, policy stability is desirable to investors and increases foreign direct investment. According to Antonio Fatas and Ilian Mihov, "increases in the political constraints on the executive serve as a disciplinary device to limit unnecessary and possibly harmful changes in economic policy."[72] But on the other hand, leaders are more constrained in their ability to respond quickly to exogenous price shocks, which can easily precipitate an economic crisis. As we showed here, the ability of regimes to enact large changes in policy—and break the standstill of political gridlock—has important implications for a range of political and economic outcomes.

Review Questions

- In which types of dictatorships do elites belong to a unifying institution?
- Why is it easier for personalist dictators to select the members of their elite support group?
- Why do elites in single party dictatorships have more heterogeneous policy preferences than elites in military dictatorships?
- Why are single-party dictatorships most prone to political gridlock?
- Why are personalist dictatorships most prone to large swings in policy?
- What are the policy implications of political gridlock for dictatorships?

Key Points

- Dictators are sustained in power by an elite support group; this support group can "veto" the dictator's proposed policies that it disapproves of.
- It is easiest for the leader and elites to agree to policy changes in personalist dictatorships. It is most difficult for them to do so in single-party dictatorships. Elites and the leader tend to share the same policy preferences.
- Political gridlock is most rampant in single-party dictatorships, followed by military dictatorships, and lastly personalist dictatorships.

Notes

1. Tsebelis, *Veto Players* (2002).
2. Henisz, *Political Institutions and Policy* (2004, p. 7).
3. Frantz, *Tying the Dictator's Hands* (2008).
4. Frantz, *Tying the Dictator's Hands* (2008).

5. Frantz (2008) does not examine monarchies in her study.

6. Titely, *Dark Age* (1997).

7. Decalo, *African Personal Dictatorships* (1985, p. 227).

8. Hutchcroft, *Review: Oligarchs and Cronies* (1991, p. 446).

9. Source: *A Happy Ending: Gaddafi son hails nurses accord*, Reuters (July 30, 2007), http://africa.reuters.com/wire/news/usnL30136235.html (accessed January 14, 2010).

10. Roeder, *Red Sunset* (1993).

11. Ibid.

12. Koh, *Politics of a Divided* (2001).

13. Ibid. (p. 543).

14. Dominguez, *Leadership Changes, Factionalism* (1989, p. 130).

15. Bunce and Echols, *Power and Policy* (1978, pp. 930–932).

16. Hawes, *Philippine State* (1987, p. 14).

17. Farouk-Sluglett and Sluglett, *Iraq Since 1958* (2001, p. 209).

18. Decalo, *African Personal Dictatorships* (1985, p. 223).

19. Hartlyn (1998); Farouk-Slugett and Slugett (2001); Decalo (1989).

20. Pinto, *Elites, Single Parties* (2002).

21. Ibid. (p. 432).

22. Ibid.

23. Egorov and Sonin, *Dictators and their Viziers* (2005, p 5).

24. Black, *Deterring Libya* (2000).

25. Jahan, *Ten Years of Ayub* (1970, p. 279).

26. Gertzel, *Dynamics of the One-Party* (1984, p. 12).

27. Bienen, *Armies and Parties* (1978a, p. 84).

28. Finer, *Man on Horseback* (1962).

29. Taras, *Leadership Change in Communist* (1989); Linden and Rockman, *Elite Studies and Communist* (1984).

30. Dominguez, *Leadership Changes, Factionalism* (1989, p. 136).

31. Langston, *Breaking Out Is Hard* (2002, p. 77).

32. Penner Angrist, *Expression of Political Dissent* (1999, p. 753).

33. Ibid. (p. 756).

34. Lee, *Political Logic of Institutional*, 2000; Bosco, *Faction versus Ideology* (1994).

35. Makgala, 'So Far So Good'? (2003).

36. Molomo, *Understanding Government and Opposition* (2000, p. 79).

37. Teiwes, *Politics at Mao's Court* (1990).

38. Cheng and Haggard, *Taiwan in Transition* (1990, p. 72).

39. Penner Angrist, *Expression of Political Dissent* (1999).

40. Dominguez, *Leadership Changes, Factionalism* (1989).

41. Taras, *Leadership Change in Communist* (1989); Bienen, *Armies and Parties* (1978a).

42. Pike, *Origins of Leadership change* (1989, p. 120).

43. Bienen, *Armies and Parties* (1978a).

44. Dittmer and Wu, *"Modernization of Factionalism"* (1995, p. 493).

45. Nordlinger (1977); Bienen (1978a); Remmer (1991); Harbeson (1987).

46. Remmer, *Military Rule in Latin* (1991, p. 33).

47. Finer, *Man on Horseback* (1962).

48. Ibid.

49. Nordlinger, *Soldiers in Politics* (1977, p. 46).

50. In the Chinese regime, for example, party leaders "have often spanned different geographic and bureaucratic units . . . their ties, when most successful, have crossed more than one power network" (Cheng and White 2003, p. 587).

51. Harbeson, *Military in African Politics* (1987, p. 23).

52. Kier, *Imagining War* (1997, p. 29).

53. Pion-Berlin, *Military Autonomy and Emerging* (1992).

54. Bacchus, *Mission in Mufti* (1990, p. 43).

55. Hunter, *Eroding Military Influence* (1997).

56. Barros, *Constitutionalism and Dictatorship* (2002).

57. Bienen and Gersovitz, *Economic Stabilization, Conditionality* (1985).

58. Lai and Slater, *Institutions of the Offensive* (2006).

59. Haggard and Kaufman (1995); Finer (1975); Decalo (1976); Kennedy (1974); Geddes (2003).

60. Finer (1962); Bienen (1978a); Decalo (1976); Kennedy (1974); Van Doorn (1968); Geddes (2003).

61. Geddes, *Paradigms and Sand Castles* (2003, p. 226).

62. Bienen, *Armies and Parties* (1978a).

63. Bienen, *Armies and Parties* (1978a, p. 203).

64. Bienen, *Military Rule and Political* (1978b, p. 202).

65. Jacoby, *For the People*, (2003 p. 677).

66. Pye , *Armies in the Process* (1962, pp. 82–84).

67. Frantz, *Tying the Dictator's Hands* (2008).

68. Ibid.

69. Ibid.

70. Ibid.

71. Fatas and Mihov, *Policy Volatility, Institutions* (2005, p. 3).

72. Ibid. (2005, p. 22).

Dictatorships and the Economy

Politics and the economy are in many ways inextricable. Political leaders typically control economic decisions and make choices that drive economic outcomes, while economic conditions strongly influence the political choices available to leaders and the types of decisions they will make. In this chapter, we examine the complex relationship between domestic political institutions and the economy. First, we discuss the literature on democracy, dictatorship, and economic performance. Next, we look at how regime type impacts the way that dictators use foreign aid. Lastly, we explore the incidence of corruption across dictatorships and the phenomenon of predatory states.

Regime Type and the Economy

The relationship between regime type and the economy has been of fundamental interest to scholars for decades. Is dictatorship more conducive to economic prosperity than democracy? Does wealth lead to internal pressures for democratization? How do economic considerations, in turn, influence the decisions that leaders make? These questions are important for many reasons. Poverty is often accompanied by high infant mortality, low literacy rates, and low life expectancy. Economic development directly affects the livelihood and wellbeing of citizens. Understanding if and how regime type influences the economy is of central interest to political scientists, investors, international donors, and policy makers alike. In this section, we unravel this relationship and look at how democracies and dictatorships differ in their economic trends.

Regime Type and Economic Development

Scholars have long observed the coincidence of democracy and wealth. Wealthy countries are nearly always democratic, with the oil-rich autocracies in the Middle East being the exception. **Figure 7.1** illustrates this relationship clearly.[1] Does this mean that democracy causes countries to grow richer or is it that wealth causes democratization?

	Wealthy			Poor		
Democratic	Argentina Belgium Canada Croatia Estonia Germany Iceland Italy Luxembourg New Zealand Portugal Spain U.K.	Australia Botswana Chile Czech Republic Finland Greece Ireland Japan Mexico Norway Slovenia Sweden U.S.	Austria Brazil Costa Rica Denmark France Hungary Israel S. Korea Netherlands Poland S. Africa Switzerland Uruguay	Armenia Ghana Kenya Mali Nicaragua	Bangladesh Honduras Madagascar Moldova Senegal	Benin India Malawi Mozambique
Non-Democratic	Bahrain Malaysia Singapore	Gabon Oman U.A.E	Kuwait Saudi Arabia	Angola Burkina Faso Cameroon Comoros Rep. Congo Ethiopia Guines Kyrgyz Rep. Mauritania Nigeria Sierra Leone Tanzania Uzbekistan Zambia	Azerbaijan Burundi C.African Rep. Dem .Rep. Djibouti Gambia Guinea-Bissau Lao PDR Nepal Pakistan Sudan Togo Vietnam Zimbabwe	Bhutan Cambodia Chad Congo Eritrea Georgia Haiti Liberia Niger Rwanda Tajikistan Uganda Yemen

Figure 7.1 Countries in Top and Bottom Third of Wealth, 2000. *Source*: World Bank (2003); Polity IV (2008)

Adam Przeworski et al.[2] disentangle the relationship between economic development and regime type. As discussed in **Chapter 2**, they find that economic development does not cause democracy, but that democratic regimes are more likely to survive in rich societies. In other words, wealthy countries are democratic not because wealth spurs democratization, but because democracies are more likely to survive in developed countries.

Perhaps surprisingly, the same is true of dictatorships. Dictatorships are less likely to survive in poor countries. They are more likely to be stable in rich countries, helping to explain the anomalous incidence of long-lasting oil-rich autocracies in the Middle East.

Poverty has a destabilizing effect on all regimes. Wealth enhances the survival of regimes, regardless of whether they are democratic or dictatorial.

Regime Type and Economic Growth

Equally complex is the relationship between regime type and economic growth. Are dictatorships better able to implement policies conducive to growth than democracies? This fundamentally important question has long baffled scholars. If authoritarian rule is necessary to the growth of a country's economy, then pressures for democratization from the international community should perhaps be moderated.

The impetus for this debate was the phenomenal growth records of a handful of autocratic governments from the 1960s to the 1990s. Most notably, dictatorial regimes in Taiwan, South Korea, and Singapore (referred to as the East Asian tigers) experienced rapid growth, while their democratic counterparts floundered. The argument is that the policies that are conducive to economic growth are often politically unpopular.[3] They also take time to bear results. Democratic governments are incapable of implementing such policies because they will be voted out of office too quickly by frustrated citizens. Because authoritarian governments cannot be voted out of office easily, they can persist with politically unpopular policies sufficiently long enough for them to reap the desired results. In addition, dictatorships can more easily clamp down on mass opposition to economic reforms and can ban strikes by labor unions. In post-war Latin America, for example, elected politicians had more difficulty curing rapid inflation, increasing foreign exchange earnings, while also achieving growth in the short term.[4] Any elected government that implemented economic reforms undermined its own political position.

Though it is true that democratic governments often face difficulties reforming their economies without getting removed from office, dictatorship does not necessarily lead to high economic growth. Emphasis on the positive records of the East Asian tigers neglected the multitude of dictatorships with terrible records during the same period. Przeworksi et al.[5] find, for example, that regime type has no impact on the growth of national incomes. On average, dictatorships and democracies have the same growth rates.

These average growth rates, however, may conceal heterogeneous behavior within the category of dictatorship. Dictatorships have greater freedoms to implement the policies of their choice. They can enact policies that are painful for citizens in the short term but beneficial for the country in the long term without facing the wrath of voters. At the same time, just because dictatorships have the freedom to pursue policies that will lead to growth does not mean that they will do so. Some dictatorships experienced outstanding growth rates in the past few decades, while other dictatorships had dismal records. Przeworski et al.'s[6] compilation of economic miracles and disasters, help illustrate this. Listed in **Table 7.1** are the fastest- and slowest-growing regimes, over periods of at least ten years.

Interestingly, all of the miracles and disasters were authoritarian during the time indicated, with the exception of Peru.[7] To our knowledge, little research has been done on whether the variance in the growth rates of democracies and dictatorships differs systematically. It may be that there is less potential for miracles *or* disasters in democracies, because leaders face checks and balances (preventing truly terrible policies) and are held accountable for their actions by citizens (preventing unpopular but beneficial policies).

Table 7.1 Economic Miracles and Disasters

Economic Miracles (growth > 8.5%)	Economic Disasters (growth < .5%)
Botswana, from 1960 to 1990	**Mozambique, from 1975 to 1991**
Nigeria, from 1966 to 1979	**Angola, from 1975 to 1990**
Yemen, from 1970 to 1990	**Guyana, from 1966 to 1991**
Singapore, from 1965 to 1991	**Uruguay, from 1973 to 1985**
South Korea, from 1961 to 1988	*Peru, from 1980 to 1990*

Dictatorships are in bold; democracies are in italics. *Source*: Przeworski et al. (2000).

Dictatorships, by contrast, may be capable of miracles *and* disasters. With the right leadership, authoritarian regimes can implement the tough policies required for long-term economic prosperity. With the wrong leadership, however, they can squander the country's economic resources and bring growth to a halt. Some dictatorships are like Singapore under the People's Action Party (PAP), while others are like Zaire (today's Democratic Republic of Congo) under Joseph Mobutu. Government spending in Zaire went from 17 percent in the 1970s to two percent twenty years later;[8] while the president's share of the budget increased from 30 percent to 95 percent.[9] The potential for disastrous leadership in dictatorships seems remarkably high. Further research is necessary to explore this possibility.

Foreign Aid in Dictatorships

Foreign aid is predominantly distributed to authoritarian regimes: between 1960 and 2002, the majority of aid recipients were dictatorships.[10] In this section, we look at how regime type influences the way in which dictators use foreign aid.

This relationship is examined in detail by Joseph Wright.[11] He focuses on the concept of "time horizons." Time horizons refer, to how long leaders perceive that they will be in power. When leaders feel secure in their positions and have high certainty that they will rule for a long period of time, they are more likely to implement policies that will benefit the country in the long term, like investment in public goods and protection of property rights.[12] When leaders feel insecure about their futures, they are more likely to pursue policies aimed at deterring the threat posed by their rivals and consume or abuse state resources as a means of surviving in power.

Wright finds that foreign aid is often wasted when dictators face short time horizons. Dictators with short time horizons are more likely to abuse aid and have poor economic growth. By contrast, aid is more likely to be used in line with donor goals when dictators face long time horizons. Dictators with long time horizons are more likely to use aid effectively and enact policies conducive to growth.

Though the length of time horizons does not translate perfectly into regime type, a few trends can be pointed out. According to Wright, regimes that have institutionalized rules for succession are more likely to have long time horizons, as their leaders have greater assurances that they will stay in power for multiple years. Without such rules dictating succession, leaders have no way of guaranteeing that they will not be forcibly removed from power at any given moment in time. When leadership turnover is institutionalized, leaders "have a weaker incentive to steal as a form of insurance against being ousted by irregular means."[13]

Though further research is necessary to explore in greater detail the relationship between authoritarian regime type and leadership type horizons, such rules are more likely to be in place in single-party, monarchic, and military dictatorships than in personalist regimes. Wright shows that personalist dictators, particularly in the last years of their rule, are more likely to have short time horizons. They have no means of assuring that they will not be overthrown by their rivals in the near future. Personalist dictators who are insecure about their political futures are more likely to steal from the state and enact wasteful economic policies, which we discuss in more detail below.

Dictatorships and Corruption

Beyond reducing government efficiency, corruption negatively impacts the economy. Understanding how authoritarian domestic institutions influence corruption is important, given corruption's harmful effect on economic growth.[14] In this section, we discuss the current data on corruption across dictatorships, explore the ties between authoritarianism and corruption, and provide an in depth analysis of the phenomenon of predatory states.

Corruption Trends across Dictatorships

The literature on authoritarian regime type and the propensity for corruption is somewhat underdeveloped. Most studies in this area are largely observational in nature. Miriam Golden and Eric Chang[15] are the exception to this. The authors examine how dictatorships differ with respect to their levels of corruption. They find that personalist and personalist-hybrid dictatorships are more prone to corruption than single-party or military regimes.

Indeed the raw data on corruption supports this finding. Listed in **Table 7.2** are the corruption rankings of existing dictatorships (as of 2009),

Table 7.2 Corruption and Authoritarian Regime Type (2009)

Personalist Dictatorships	Military Dictatorships	Single-party Dictatorships	Monarchic Dictatorships	Hybrid Dictatorships
Avg. ranking=142	Avg. ranking= 114.5	Avg. ranking=101	Avg. ranking=59	Avg. ranking= 111.5
Armenia #120	Algeria #111	Angola #162	Jordan #49	*Triple Threat*
Azerbaijan #143	Myanmar #178	Botswana #37	Kuwait #66	Egypt #111
Belarus #139		Cambodia #158	Morocco #89	Syria #126
Burkina Faso #79		China #79	Oman #39	
Cameroon #146		Ethiopia #120	Saudi Arabia #63	*Single-party/ Military Hybrids*
Central Africa Republic #158		Laos #158	United Arab Emirates #30	
Chad #175		Malaysia #56	Swaziland #79	Rwanda #89
Congo #162		Mozambique #130		*Personalist/Single-Party Hybrids*
DRC #162		Namibia #56		
Gambia #106		Singapore #3		Cuba #61
Guinea #168		Tanzania #126		Eritrea #126
Ivory Coast #154		Vietnam #120		Gabon #106
Kazakhstan #120		Tunisia #65		Turkmenistan #168
Kyrgyzstan #162		Zambia #99		Uzbekistan #174
Libya #130		Zimbabwe #146		
Mauritania #130				
Russia #146				
Sudan #176				
Tajikistan #158				
Togo #111				
Uganda #130				
Yemen #154				

Source: Transparency International (2009).

divided according to regime categories.[16] Countries are evaluated based on how corrupt they are perceived to be, as determined by Transparency International. Higher rankings correspond with states that are relatively free of corruption, while lower rankings are given to states that have high levels of corruption.

Though the sample size is small, the data support Golden and Chang's finding. Personalist and personalist-hybrid regimes have higher average corruption rankings than do other forms of dictatorship, including monarchies. Golden and Chang posit that their results help to explain why corruption is typically so rampant in sub-Saharan Africa. Personalist dictatorships are the most prevalent regime type in sub-Saharan Africa, helping to account for the pervasiveness of observed corruption in the region.

Personalist Rule and Corruption

What accounts for the coincidence of personalist rule and high levels of corruption? Bruce Bueno de Mesquita et al.[17] argue that corruption is highest when the ratio between the size of the *winning coalition* and the *selectorate* is small. As mentioned in **Chapter 1**, the winning coalition is the minimal set of people whose support the incumbents need in order to remain in power; and the selectorate is the set of people who have a say in choosing leaders. Because the size of the winning coalition is small, rulers maintain the support of coalition members through patronage and private goods, as opposed to public goods. According to Golden and Chang,[18] corruption may be higher in personalist dictatorships, because the ratio between the size of their winning coalitions and selectorates, is typically small.

Others argue that personalist dictatorships are more corrupt because they lack the institutions that could potentially provide leaders with more security regarding the duration of their time in office. Without institutionalized provisions for succession—characteristic of some military, single-party, and monarchic dictatorships—leaders in personalist dictatorships face greater uncertainty regarding their political futures. This may make them more likely to steal from the state, as it will satisfy their short-term needs, even if the long-term economic consequences of doing so are dire.

The institutional environment in personalist dictatorships also means that there are few checks on the behavior of their leaders.[19] Resting at the top of the political system, personalist dictators are free to "dispense favors, money and resources to gain loyalty, obedience and submission."[20] Leaders have complete discretionary control over public life and maintain a regular flow of resources to elite loyalists and other strategic coalition groups.

As in other regimes, corruption is used by leaders in personalist dictatorships as a means by which to: 1) distribute perks to supporters, and 2) pad their personal bank accounts.

Distributing Perks to Supporters

Corruption provides an opportunity for leaders to increase the amount of material goods at their disposal to distribute to supporters. As Michael

Bratton and Nicolas van de Walle[21] point out, at the most basic level, personalist dictatorships differ from other forms of dictatorships in their dependence on the transfer of material rewards in exchange for political support. Wright[22] echoes this view, arguing that personalist dictators sustain formal political institutions (that have little de facto function) primarily as a means of strengthening patron-client networks. In personalist dictatorships, "resources are distributed on the basis of clientelism and patronage ties without institutional oversight, which in turn provides a breeding ground for corruption."[23]

Increasing Personal Wealth

Corruption also enables personalist dictators to increase their own personal wealth. As Robert Jackson and Carl Rosberg write, "corruption constitutes an important means by which individual wants and needs in a personal regime can be satisfied; it is a black market mode of conduct quite consistent with personally appropriated government yet fundamentally at odds with state rules and regulations, whose violation or evasion corrupt conduct entails."[24] It has been estimated that Ferdinand Marcos of the Philippines and Sani Abacha of Nigeria each stole over $5 billion while in power. Alberto Fujimori of Peru reportedly robbed Peru of $600 million, while the Duvaliers took around $800 million for themselves while in power in Haiti.[25]

Predatory States

Predatory states are a unique subset of personalist dictatorships. They are, by definition, highly corrupt states. In predatory states, a single ruler has near total control over state resources, which the leader uses to maximize personal wealth.[26] The ruler's insatiable appetite for wealth means that society functions primarily as a means by which to enrich the ruler at the expense of citizens. Jean-Bédel Bokassa of the Central African Republic, for example, plundered the country's resources with reckless abandon, even though most citizens lived in severe poverty.[27] In predatory states, everything is for sale, ranging from material goods to policies and laws.

Because leaders in predatory states prioritize personal wealth maximization, public goods are rarely provided for citizens. In predatory states, "entire sectors have been built up to feast upon public systems built originally for public purposes."[28] Predatory states are characterized by low state investment in infrastructure, health care, education, and other social services. Not surprisingly, levels of inequality in predatory states are typically very high.

Predatory rulers act in ways that erode incentives for growth and harm the economy. Such actions include excessive taxation, exchange rate manipulation, and heavy import licensing. In predatory states, "economic stagnation, political malaise, and moral cynicism" are commonplace.[29] We provide a few examples of predatory states below.

Predatory States (Some key characteristics)

- Goals are to maximize its own take
- Does not provide basic needs such as infrastructure, health and education
- No rule of law and corruption, no predictability
- No coherent bureaucratic apparatus
- Squeezes out the formal sector
- Promotes the informal economy only to ensure stability
- Rules and decisions are commodities
- Wastefully consumes
- Disorganizes civil society

Mobutu's Zaire (1965–1997)

Zaire (today's Democratic Republic of Congo) under Mobutu is a classic example of a predatory state. Mobutu was Zaire's head of state, commander in chief of the armed forces and police, and minister of defense. He ruled Zaire unchecked for over 30 years, allowing him to amass astonishing amounts of wealth, while simultaneously destroying Zaire's economy. Mobutu was considered one of the richest people in the world, with personal wealth said to be greater than $5 billion.[30] In the early 1990s, while civil servants went unpaid, Mobutu flew the Concorde to Paris to go on shopping sprees.[31] There are even reports that Mobutu had Zaire's national currency, which was printed in Germany, flown directly to his yacht.[32] Mobutu accrued these riches by capitalizing on Zaire's abundant natural resources, including minerals, diamonds, gold, and some oil. His actions were not without economic consequences for Zaire, of course. Under Mobutu's rule, GNP declined two percent a year, and by 1992 GDP per capita was less than half its value at independence over thirty years earlier.[33]

The Duvaliers' Haiti (1957–1986)

In Haiti under the Duvaliers, kleptocracy (rule by thieves)[34] ran in the family. François Duvalier (known as Papa Doc) and his son and successor Jean-Claude Duvalier (known as Baby Doc) each turned Haiti into a predatory state. James Ferguson writes that "Duvalier's predatory state did not merely siphon off foreign aid, but also perpetuated the internal corruption which Papa Doc had practiced."[35]

Baby Doc reportedly embezzled somewhere between $300 and $800 million (or upwards of 4.5percent of Haiti's GDP) during his tenure, in a country that was at the time one of the poorest in the Western hemisphere.[36] Neither Baby Doc nor Papa Doc formulated a coherent economic policy for Haiti; their goals instead appeared to be to recklessly enjoy the fruits of office.[37] For example, in 1980 Baby Doc's government was given $22 million by the International Monetary Fund (IMF). Within weeks $20 million of this sum was mysteriously withdrawn from the government's account.[38]

Despite the seriousness of Haitian poverty, Baby Doc spent over $7 million on his wedding.[39] His wife was given a salary of $100,000 a year, which diplomats reported went to "her impressive collection of mink coats."[40] Former Haitian Minister of Finance and World Bank official Marc Bazin determined that at least "36% of government revenue in Haiti was embezzled" under Baby Doc, declaring the country the "most mismanaged in the region."[41] Real economic growth in Haiti decreased by 2.5 percent a year from 1980 to 1985, and unemployment reached 30 percent.[42] Under the Duvaliers, corruption—"in the form of government rake-offs of industries, bribery, extortion of domestic businesses, and stolen government funds"— enriched the family and its closest supporters.[43]

Marcos' Philippines (1972–1986)

Marcos' reign over the Philippines led to great personal wealth for Marcos and his inner circle and economic disaster for everyone else in the country. As Belinda Aquino[44] points out, corruption became an epidemic during the Marcos years. Marcos established business monopolies that were dominated by his cronies, made sure that he was personally connected to all directorates of companies, and nationalized public enterprises so that he could control them.[45] Under Marcos, the entire business sector was concentrated in the hands of 81 families.[46] Government spending increased by 92 percent,[47] and the number of state-owned enterprises tripled, consuming 30 percent of public expenditures.[48] Gary Hawes writes that the government owned "numerous banks, finance corporations, hotels, and mines," in addition to construction companies and shipping lines.[49]

While the Philippines' neighbors were able to attract the attention of foreign investors, by the end of Marcos' tenure, both net and gross foreign direct investment were close to zero.[50] External debt increased 214 percent from 1970 to 1975 alone.[51] Any attempts to increase government revenue were hampered by tax incentives granted to Marcos' associates.[52] Control over the budget was entirely in Marcos' hands and state monopolies were used for "private ends."[53] Surplus from the government owned sugar industry went to "the personal and political needs of the First Family."[54] For example, ten percent of all ministerial budgets went to the First Lady's "special projects."[55] By 1975, the Marcos regime "came to be characterized almost exclusively by patronage networks and cronyism."[56] The government of the Philippines now estimates that Marcos and his wife owe the country upwards of $500 billion.[57]

Summary and Conclusion

This chapter has sought to unpack some of the complexity surrounding the relationship between domestic institutions and the economy. We presented key developments in this literature with respect to a wide variety of economic factors. We first discussed how regime type affects economic development and growth by presenting major findings in the literature on democracy, dictatorship, and the economy. Next, we examined how dictatorships use foreign aid and the conditions under which aid is likely to be efficiently used. Lastly, we looked at corruption in dictatorships and the concept of predatory states.

There are multiple avenues available for future research in this area. In particular, scholars have yet to tackle how different types of dictatorship vary in their levels of development and in their growth records. Personalist dictatorships appear more likely than other forms of dictatorships to sprout in poor countries (as mentioned in **Chapter 2**), but little systematic work has been done examining the relationship between level of development and categories of dictatorship. We also know very little about whether economic growth is influenced by the kind of dictatorship in power.

Many questions remain unanswered regarding authoritarianism and corruption, as well. There are indications that personalist forms of dictatorships are prone to corruption, yet the reasons underlying this trend warrant greater exploration. While personalist dictatorships are, on average, more corrupt than are other types of dictatorships, why is it that some personalist dictatorships are not corrupt? Similarly, why do some personalist dictatorships devolve into predatory states, but not others?

Pursuing these varied research avenues is an important task, one that would greatly enhance our knowledge of how and in what ways authoritarian institutions impact key economic outcomes.

Review Questions

- How does wealth affect both democratic and authoritarian regimes?
- Are there differences in the growth rates of democratic and authoritarian regimes?
- What are "time horizons"? How do they affect how leaders use foreign aid?
- What types of dictatorships are most prone to corruption and why?
- Why are personalist dictatorships most likely to engage in predatory behavior?
- In what ways was the behavior of Mobutu, the Duvaliers, and Marcos predatory?

Key Points

- Wealth leads to political stability, both for democracies and for dictatorships. Poverty leads to political instability, making it more likely that regimes (of all kinds) will break down.
- Average economic growth rates of dictatorships and democracies are comparable. These averages, however, may conceal heterogeneous performance among dictatorships.
- Personalist dictators have fewer checks on their power than other dictators do. This may explain why they are more prone to corruption.
- Predatory states are a subset of personalist dictatorships. They are characterized by high levels of corruption, as leaders steal from the state to pad their bank accounts.

Notes

1. Countries are classified as democratic if they received a score of 5 or better on the Polity IV democracy variable (Polity IV Project 2008). Countries are included if they were in the top/bottom thirtieth percentile with respect to GDP per capita (World Bank 2003).

2. Przeworski et al., *Democracy and Development* (2000).

3. O'Donnell, *Modernization and Bureaucratic-Authoritarianism* (1973).

4. Skidmore, *Politics of Economic Stabilization* (1977).

5. Przeworksi et al., *Democracy and Development* (2000).

6. Przeworski et al., *Democracy and Development* (2000, p. 177).

7. The determination of regime type (whether countries are dictatorships or democracies) is based on Przeworski et al.'s (2000) classification. .

8. Reno (1997).

9. Wright, *To Invest or Insure?* (2007).

10. Ibid.

11. Ibid. (2007; 2008).

12. Ibid. (2007, p. 3).

13. Ibid. (p. 7).

14. Mauro, *Corruption and Growth* (1995).

15. Golden and Change, *Corruption and Authoritarian Regimes* (2006).

16. Those countries for which data are not available are excluded.

17. Bueno de Mesquita et al., *Logic of Political Survival* (2003).

18. Golden and Chang, *Corruption and Authoritarian Regimes* (2006).

19. Frantz, *Tying the Dictator's Hands* (2008).

20. Fatton, *Liberal Democracy in Africa* (1990, p. 461).

21. Bratton and van de Walle, *Neo-patrimonial Regimes and Political* (1997).

22. Wright, *Do Authoritarian Institutions Constrain?* (2008).

23. Golden and Chang, *Corruption and Authoritarian Regimes* (2006, p. 10).

24. Jackson and Rosberg, *Personal Rule in Black* (1982, p. 5).

25. Estimates come from *Transparency International* and Wright (2007).

26. Jeffries, *State, Structural Adjustment* (1993); Mosell, *Model of a Predatory State* (2001).

27. Decalo, *African Personal Dictatorships* (1985).

28. Galbraith, *Predatory State* (2008, p. 146).

29. Fatton, *Liberal Democracy in Africa* (1990, p. 462).

30. Source: Howard W. French, *Mobutu Sese Seko, 66, Longtime Dictator of Zaire*, The New York Times, September 8, 1997, http://partners.nytimes.com/library/world/090897obit-mobutu.html (accessed March 21, 2010).

31. Hertz, I.O.U.: *The Debt Threat* (2004); Bratton and van de Walle, *Neo-patrimonial Regimes and Political* (1994).

32. Bratton and van de Walle, *Neo-patrimonial Regimes and Political* (1994).

33. Acemoglu et al., *Kleptocracy and Divide* (2004).

34. Kleptocracy is defined as a government that increases the personal wealth and political power of the ruling class and government officials at the expense of the public. See Acemoglu et al. (2004).

35. Ferguson, *Papa Doc, Baby Doc* (1987, p. 70.)

36. Source: Country Studies, *Jean-Claude Duvalier, 1971–1986*, United States Library of Congress (December 1989).

37. Ibid.

38. Ibid.

39. Ibid.

40. Ibid. (p. 73).

41. Source: Country Studies, *Jean-Claude Duvalier, 1971–1986*, United States Library of Congress (December 1989).

42. Source: Country Studies, *Jean-Claude Duvalier, 1971–1986*, United States Library of Congress (December 1989).

43. Source: Country Studies, *Francois Duvalier, 1957–1971*, United States Library of Congress (December 1989).

44. Aquino, *Politics of Plunder* (1997).

45. Celoza, *Ferdinand Marcos* (1997).

46. Ibid.

47. Hawes, *Marcos, His Cronies* (1995).

48. Haggard, *Philippines: Picking up* (1988).

49. Hawes, *Philippine State* (1987, p. 138).

50. Kind, *Philippines: The Sick Man* (2000).

51. Hawes, *Marcos, His Cronies* (1995).

52. Montes (1988), from Hutchcroft, *Oligarchs and Cronies* (1991).

53. Hawes, *Philippine State* (1987).

54. Ibid. (p. 128).

55. Montes (1988, p. 108), from Hutchcroft, *Oligarchs and Cronies* (1991).

56. Smith, *Life of the Party* (2005, p. 447).

57. Source: Keith Morgan, *Estrada embarrassed by proof of Marcos billions*, World Socialist Web Site, July 20, 1999, http://www.wsws.org/articles/1999/jul1999/phil-j20.shtml (accessed January 28, 2010).

8 Dictatorships and International Conflict

Inter-state conflict is nearly always a costly endeavor. Beyond the raw economic costs, conflict can damage infrastructure, deter foreign investment, and lower dramatically the quality of life of citizens. For these reasons and more, understanding the conflict behavior of states is an important task. What are the causes behind a state's decision to engage in conflict with another state? What factors explain why conflict escalates in some situations, but not in others? Are some states simply more violent and conflict prone than others?

In this chapter, we look at the relationship between domestic institutions and international conflict. In particular, we examine how dictatorship influences states' conflict patterns. First, we present the literature on the conflict behavior of dictatorships. We then discuss how dictatorships vary with respect to their ability to signal their resolve during disputes. Next, we probe the factors that motivate the foreign policy choices of dictatorships. Lastly, we explore how the quality of military intelligence differs across regimes and influences the likelihood that they will make foreign policy errors.

The Conflict Behavior of Dictatorships

The literature on the conflict behavior of dictatorships has blossomed in recent years. Scholars have begun to disaggregate the category of dictatorship, revealing interesting differences in the patterns of their behavior. In this section, we present this literature.

Dictatorial Peace

Much of scholarly attention has focused on "democratic peace theory," which posits that democratic regimes are unlikely to fight one another. But is there a "dictatorial peace"? In their study, Mark Peceny, Caroline Beer, and Shannon Sanchez-Terry[1] (referred to as Peceny et al.) find that some types of dictatorships are more peaceful toward one another than others. They show that no two personalist dictatorships or two military dictatorships have ever gone to war since 1945. Single-party regimes are the only homogenous dyad in the study to have gone to war. Still, single-party dictatorships are less violent toward one another than are mixed dyads (comprised of a democracy and a dictatorship). Though the authors find little empirical support for a dictatorial peace, they do find that pure forms of dictatorship exhibit more peaceful behavior toward one another than do mixed dyads.

Personalist dictatorships are more likely to engage in military disputes with democracies than are other forms of regime, according to Peceny et al. The authors assert that this finding is due to varying war-fighting capabilities. Personalist dictatorships have the worst war-fighting capabilities of any regime type because efforts by the personalist dictator to stay in power render military institutions weak. Democracies, on the other hand, have the highest war-fighting capabilities due to professionalized armies and the subordination of the military to civilian authorities. Peceny et al. argue that democracies and personalist dictatorships have an increased likelihood of conflict because strong and capable democracies pick weak personalist regimes as targets. It is possible, however, that war-fighting capabilities do not account for this finding. Democracies could be more effective in war, for example, because of higher GDP per capita, larger winning coalitions,[2] or higher domestic audience costs.[3] It is also debatable whether personalist dictatorships have the lowest war-fighting capabilities, as there are many cases of personalist dictatorships with substantial war-fighting capabilities (i.e. Adolf Hitler's Germany).

Conflict Propensity

Dan Reiter and Allan C. Stam[4] examine Peceny et al.'s findings in greater detail by looking at the direction of disputes (in other words, which state provoked the other). They find that though democracies and personalist dictatorships are more conflict prone, it is not because democracies are more likely to target personalist dictatorships. Rather, this is due to the fact that personalist dictatorships are more likely to challenge democracies. In a similar fashion, military dictatorships and single-party dictatorships are also more likely to provoke democracies than vice versa. Reiter and Stam also find some evidence that personalist dictatorships fight wars poorly. From 1946 to 1992, there were 19 personalist dictatorships that fought wars. None of them won.

Democracies are less aggressive than dictatorships due to institutional constraints, according to Reiter and Stam. Because democratic leaders are elected, they have to avoid unpopular and costly policies, deterring them from instigating risky military ventures. Dictators, by contrast, are aware that they are unlikely to face punishment for costly actions and can act without restraint.[5] This helps to explain the aggressiveness of dictatorships. As Reiter and Stam write, "dictators more than other state types use military force short of war as a means to try to push democracies into making substantial concessions over some issue. If war does come, dictators hope to win by simply outlasting their cost-averse democratic opponents."[6]

Peceny and Christopher Butler[7] build on this analysis and examine in depth the propensity of dictatorships to initiate or be targets of disputes. They find that, compared to other forms of dictatorship, single-party regimes are less likely to initiate disputes and less likely to be targeted. Personalist dictatorships, by contrast, are more likely to initiate disputes and more likely to be targeted. They argue that this is because single-party dictatorships have large winning coalitions, whereas personalist dictatorships have small winning coalitions.[8]

Leaders with large winning coalitions must be less risky in their international ventures because they face a higher risk of being removed from office should their efforts be unsuccessful. In turn, once they are embroiled in conflict they are more likely to fight harder as a means of avoiding the costs of defeat, helping to explain why they are targeted less frequently. Though this argument is plausible, it does not account for the fact that the size of the winning coalition may not vary systematically across regime type. While some single-party dictatorships are characterized by large winning coalitions, as in Mexico under the Institutional Revolutionary Party (PRI), others are characterized by small winning coalitions, as in Laos under the Lao People's Revolutionary Party.

The conflict propensity of dictatorships is also examined by Brian Lai and Dan Slater.[9] They de-emphasize the importance of the personalization or institutionalization of decision-making procedures in dictatorships and instead look at the types of institutions dictatorships maintain "to enhance social control and secure political incumbency."[10] According to Lai and Slater, single-party dictatorships are more capable than military dictatorships of fostering these types of institutions, making them less likely to turn to the use of force as a means of deterring domestic challenges to their power. In single-party dictatorships, the party organization is more likely to provide the leader with security because parties are effective tools for deterring elite defections and mobilizing the masses. Military dictatorships, on the other hand, lack such tools. Leaders have little assurance that elites or the masses do not pose a threat to their tenure and, as such, are more likely to initiate disputes as a means of unifying society.

Military dictatorships are more likely than single-party dictatorships to instigate conflict with other states, regardless of whether they are highly personalized or not, according to Lai and Slater. Their findings highlight the need to focus on "the institutional basis for an authoritarian government's control over potential opponents," as opposed to whether the regime is ruled by a single individual or many.[11] Though Lai and Slater's emphasis on the relationship between the risks leaders face of ouster and the regime's conflict behavior is valuable, their argument ignores the extent to which the *lack* of institutions in dictatorships exacerbates this. In personalist dictatorships, there are no provisions for succession, making leaders significantly more anxious about their hold on power. Though it is likely that party institutions are more effective than military institutions at providing leaders with job security, in regimes lacking either of these institutions leaders are the most insecure of all.

Domestic Institutions and Signaling

The factors underlying a state's decision to escalate conflict with another state is one of the key questions of international relations. Much of the literature in this field has centered on the distinction between democratic and non-democratic regimes. The observation that democracies rarely go to war with one another is well known and documented. Yet, why are some regime types more likely than others to engage in inter-state disputes?

A multitude of explanations have been set forth to explain this puzzle. In the rationalist framework, inter-state conflicts result due to lack of perfect information between states. Disputes escalate because states have uncertainty regarding the intentions of potential adversaries.[12] As James Fearon writes, "international crises occur precisely because state leaders *cannot* anticipate the outcome, owing to the fact that adversaries have private information about their willingness to fight over foreign policy interests and the incentive to misrepresent it."[13] There would be no conflict if all states perfectly knew the intentions of other states. Conflicts are avoided when states are able to convey to their adversaries that their threats are serious and more than just "cheap talk."

Domestic institutions are key to a state's ability to convey such signals. Inter-state disputes between democracies are rare because democracies have institutions that make it easier for them to signal that they mean what they say.[14]

Audience Costs

Exactly how democratic institutions decrease the uncertainty surrounding an aggressor state's resolve during crises is also debated.[15] One theory that helps to explain this is Fearon's[16] audience cost theory. According to the theory, domestic audiences play an important role in determining whether a state is making a credible threat. When leaders publicly issue threats and then renege on them, their domestic audiences punish them for having done so. By issuing their threats in the public arena, leaders create *audience costs* that they will suffer from if they fail to follow through with them.[17]

Audience costs are the domestic costs that leaders pay for backing down on their commitments during international crises. When leaders face high costs for reneging on their threats, they are better able to signal their resolve and their adversaries are more likely to take them seriously. Leaders are better able to signal their commitment during crises when they face high domestic audience costs for backing down on their threats.

Fearon's Theory

Fearon models an international crisis as a political "war of attrition."[18] This formulation is grounded in the empirical claim that crises are public events carried out in front of domestic political audiences; this fact is crucial to understanding why they occur and how they unfold. The basic premise of the theory is that: 1) states at every moment can choose to attack, back down, or escalate the crisis further, and 2) if a state backs down, its leaders suffer audience costs that increase as the crisis escalates. As Fearon puts it, "these costs arise from the action of domestic audiences concerned with whether the leadership is successful or unsuccessful at foreign policy."[19] International crises are a response to the dilemma posed by two characteristics of international politics: 1) whether a state leader's willingness to use force is private information, and 2) in order to get a better deal, state leaders have incentives to misrepresent this information. Because of this, in order to learn whether a state is really willing to attack, one must look at what makes escalating and backing down worse for a leader than simply conceding at the outset.

According to Fearon, domestic audiences play an important role in determining whether a state is making a credible threat; they are crucial in generating the costs that enable states to learn. When leaders make a public threat and then back down, it is assumed that their domestic audience will punish them for having done so. Domestic audiences typically understand the significance of threats and the deployment of troops to "engage the national honor." These actions expose leaders to potential criticism or even loss of authority if leaders are perceived to have performed poorly by these audiences. Thus states with the greatest audience costs are better able to signal their commitment and resolve to carry out threats because they have the greatest price to pay if they do not follow through with their commitments.

Fearon claims that democracies are better able to generate audience costs than autocracies are. In democracies, elections are a means for citizens to hold leaders accountable for their past actions. Democratic leaders endanger their electoral futures by making bold public statements during international disputes. This is not the case in dictatorships. In dictatorships, there are no ways for citizens to punish leaders for poor choices, as elections are not free and fair. Short of revolution, it is nearly impossible for citizens to hold leaders accountable. Authoritarian leaders can make bold and provocative statements without paying domestic costs for backing down at the last minute.[20]

Because democratic leaders are able to generate higher audience costs when they make public threats than authoritarian leaders are, they are better able to communicate their intentions to their adversaries. In Fearon's view, the concept of audience costs helps to explain why democracies rarely go to war with one another: democracies are able to moderate the security dilemma between them because they can more clearly signal their ambitions. Crises are averted when there is complete information about resolve. The outcome can be anticipated ahead of time, and the state that would eventually be defeated backs down.

Multiple studies have corroborated Fearon's claim.[21] When democracies initiate disputes, their targets often back down and conflict is avoided. When dictatorships initiate disputes, their targets often reciprocate the aggressive action and conflict escalates.

Dictatorships and Audience Costs

Scholars have only recently begun to explore how the residual category, dictatorships, behaves. As this study emphasizes, dictatorships vary from one another in striking ways. They have different institutional arrangements, decision-making procedures, methods of dealing with succession, and ways of reacting to opposition. They also differ with respect to the costs imposed upon leaders for poor policy choices.[22] The international conflict behavior of dictatorships varies markedly from one regime category to the next. Aggregating dictatorships into one category conceals important variations in the ability of these regimes to generate audience costs. Some may be more capable than others of communicating their intentions during international disputes. We explore this possibility in this section.

The audience costs theory depends on the assumption that citizens can punish leaders for poor policy decisions. In dictatorships, there is no routine and easy way for citizens to punish leaders for poor choices. This does not mean, however, that dictators rule without accountability.[23] Just as voters can punish leaders for reneging on their commitments in democracies, so can members of the elite corps in dictatorships.

The "domestic audience" in dictatorships is comprised of the elite tier: the select group of individuals the leader relies on to stay in power.[24] Since ordinary citizens cannot routinely oust dictators, the ability of dictatorships to generate audience costs depends on how well elites can credibly threaten to overthrow the dictator for poor foreign policy choices.

Some dictatorships are more capable of signaling their commitment during inter-state disputes than others. In dictatorships, audience cost levels are a function of the elite corps' ability to oust the dictator.[25] As mentioned in **Chapter 4**, elites are more capable of unseating dictators in military regimes, followed by single-party regimes, and lastly personalist regimes. Therefore military dictatorships should be the most capable of generating audience costs and personalist dictatorships the least.

There is positive support for this argument. Among dictatorships, threats issued by military dictatorships tend to be seen as the most credible and threats issued by personalist dictatorships tend to be seen as the least credible.[26] Crises are more likely to escalate when personalist dictatorships initiate them, followed by single party dictatorships, and lastly military dictatorships.

This concept is also explored by Jessica Weeks.[27] Weeks argues that scholars underestimate the extent to which dictators can be held accountable by domestic actors and, in turn, generate audience costs. She highlights three key factors that influence a dictatorship's ability to generate audience costs: "whether domestic groups can and will coordinate to punish the leader; whether the audience views backing down negatively; and whether outsiders can observe the possibility of domestic sanctions for backing down."[28] In Weeks' view, democracies have no signaling advantages over dictatorships when elites can solve the coordination dilemma entailed in trying to punish the leader, and when this possibility of coordination is viewable to other states.

Most dictatorships are able to generate audience costs on a level similar to democracies, according to Weeks. She finds that democracies have a signaling advantage only when compared to personalist forms of dictatorship.[29] The ability of dictatorships to signal that they mean what they say, varies systematically across regime types.

Foreign Policy in Dictatorships

Key to understanding the behavior of dictatorships in the international arena is identifying who it is that dictators aim to please with their policies. As we underscore throughout this study, elites serve as dictators' primary constituents. Dictators must take into account the preferences of elites or risk being deposed. The dynamics of elite-leader relations in dictatorships provide critical insights into the factors that underlie the foreign policy decisions of autocratic leaders.

Authoritarian regimes vary markedly in this regard. The domestic political structure in dictatorships largely influences the relationship between dictators and elites and, as a consequence, their foreign policy behavior. In this section, we examine how dictatorships differ with respect to foreign policy decision making. In doing so, we rely heavily on Brandon Kinne's[30] research in this field, which applies poliheuristic theory of decision making to the world of dictatorships.

Poliheuristic Theory

In essence, poliheuristic theory bridges the two dominant strains of thought in the international relations literature: rational choice and cognitive psychology. Integrating the two schools enables "more realistic and productive assessments of the nature of foreign policy decision making."[31] In the poliheuristic field, leaders filter through layers of complex information when making decisions using shortcuts, or heuristics.[32] Leaders must resort to such strategies because they are often provided with overwhelming amounts of information prior to making difficult decisions.

A particularly effective shortcut is the "non-compensatory" decision rule, where leaders rule out those options that are likely to yield negative outcomes on a single dimension of concern.[33] In other words, even if other decisions will produce very positive outcomes for leaders, they are more likely to opt for the decision that avoids producing a negative outcome.

In the poliheuristic literature, the political dimension is always non-compensatory in the foreign policy sphere.[34] As Kinne writes, "leaders measure their success in political units, such as public approval ratings, and they are only able to turn their attention to other dimensions—e.g., economic or diplomatic concerns—after their political concerns have been satisfied."[35]

To apply poliheuristic theory to dictatorships, Kinne relies on three assumptions: 1) the political dimension in foreign policy making is defined in terms of a leader's interest in staying in power, which is typical of all leaders; 2) all leaders are accountable to a group of individuals, who can collectively control the leader's fate; and 3) the types of individuals and mechanisms that make up the political dimension varies systematically across regimes. According to Kinne, in single-party dictatorships, the dynamic between the leader and the party dominates the political dimension. In a similar vein, the relationship between the leader and the military takes precedence in military dictatorships. In personalist dictatorships, by contrast, the leader's key concern is relative status among peers, whether they be military leaders, members of rival factions, regional actors, or the mass public. The dictator's status is the key way that personalist leaders assess their chances of remaining in office. Leaders in dictatorships will make foreign policy choices to deter those individuals who can oust them from doing so, minimizing the likelihood of a negative outcome.

Kinne offers three case studies to illustrate how these differences impact foreign policy decisions across dictatorships, which we summarize below.

Personalist Dictatorship: Iraq's Decision to Stay in Kuwait

Why did Saddam Hussein choose to stay in Kuwait despite the imminence of a US invasion in 1991? Many observers argue that this decision was essentially that of a madman. Yet, as Kinne shows, poliheuristic insights can help explain this choice.

In 1990, Hussein began to suspect that Kuwait, along with the United Arab Emirates, was colluding with the United States by overproducing oil, which would hurt Arab interests. This concern (coupled with a number of other grievances) prompted Hussein to place troops along the Kuwaiti border in July 1990.

Though this gesture caught the attention of the United States, the US did not convey to Iraq in any clear way the extent to which it would act to defend Kuwait. In fact, the US ambassador at the time, April Glaspie, told Hussien, "We have no opinion on the Arab-Arab conflicts, like your border disagreement with Kuwait."[36] Given such a statement, it is well within the realm of possibility that Hussein did not believe that his actions toward Kuwait would elicit a US military response. According to Kinne, "Saddam's (mis)perception of American intentions is important in showing that he did not purposely make a foreign policy decision that put his political status in peril."[37] Hussein only began to feel threatened when US President George H. W. Bush issued an ultimatum urging Iraq to retreat.

Despite this signal, Hussein chose to stand firm and withstand the massive military and economic aftereffects. Why? Because backing down would have significantly hurt Hussein's status among his peers in the Arab world, who would have viewed such an action as giving in to the West and to Israeli interests. Hussein's political power depended on his status relative to his peers. In giving in to Western demands, Hussein would have been viewed as cowardly and inept at pushing for Arab interests, which in turn would elicit threats to his power from a range of other actors. Hussein's decision to stay in Kuwait despite the prospect of US military action can be understood in light of his need to maintain his status as a means of political survival.

Military Dictatorship: Pakistan's Choice Not to Send Military Forces to Iraq

After the September 11, 2001 terrorist attacks on the United States, US President George W. Bush was actively seeking the support of other countries to fight worldwide terrorism. Pakistan chose to side with the US, such that Bush referred to Pakistan as the most pivotal ally of the US in the fight against terrorism. Yet, despite US pressure, Pakistan refused to send troops to assist US efforts in Iraq.

In making this decision, it is clear that Pakistani leader Pervez Musharraf was not seeking to please the public, as previous polls and surveys indicated that public opinion did not influence him. Indeed, Pakistanis vehemently opposed the US-led "war on terror," perhaps more so than any other country.[38] As Kinne points out, Musharraf could ignore the masses because they played no role in his survival in office. What explains this decision, then?

In Kinne's view, the relationship between Musharraf and the Pakistani military junta is the key to answering this question. The military had long played a dominant role in Pakistan and depended a great deal on the aid from the US, which used such aid as a means of securing Pakistani support. From 2001 to mid-2003 alone, the US gave over $350 million in aid to Pakistan's military.[39]

Rather than the masses, it was the military that Musharraf was aiming to please. Many Islamist hardliners exist within the Pakistani military elite.

One of the top-ranking military elites, for example, was Lieutenant General Mohammad Aziz Khan, a noted religious hardliner.[40] Though Musharraf attempted to eliminate extremists from the military hierarchy,[41] many hardliners remained. Such hardliners did not oppose the military's acquisition of military aid from the US, but found Pakistani assistance in US war efforts totally intolerable. As Kinne writes, "Thus, regardless of Musharraf's personal intentions, sending troops to Iraq would create unrest among important factions of the Pakistani military, which would certainly raise potential threats to Musharraf's political survival."[42]

Single-party Dictatorship: Dramatic Changes in Foreign Policy under Gorbachev

The foreign policy of the Soviet Union underwent dramatic changes during the 1980s. Such changes are often accredited to Mikhail Gorbachev. Examples include "pursuing rapprochement with China, failing to decisively intervene in East European revolutions, and generally taking a more conciliatory stance toward the West."[43] Why did Gorbachev embark on such a new path rather than follow in the traditional steps of his predecessors?

According to Kinne, though Gorbachev was an influential figure in Soviet politics, the major shift in foreign policy was really due to the central ideological interests of the Communist Party. As with his predecessors, Gorbachev had to ensure that his policies were condoned by the Communist Party machine. Though many things account for the Soviet Union's alteration of its foreign policy during the 1980s—such as economic, security, and geopolitical issues—political factors also exerted a major influence.

At the time, the Soviet Union was in the throes of a policy vacuum. As Douglas W. Blum writes:

> The realization emerged that the prevailing [Soviet] worldview was itself an obstacle to the pursuit of true Soviet national interests, and was in fact, inherently linked to a dangerous and unproductive foreign policy. The emergence of this realization, as it spread throughout the elite in the late-1970s and early-1980s, powerfully delegitimized the belief system and provided an impetus for intellectual reformers to fashion a new one.[44]

Within the party, the ideology the regime had thus far relied on began to be questioned seriously, such that fresh ideas became a key means for establishing alliances within the party elite. Traditionalists were slowly excluded from decision making, opening up an opportunity for new voices to shape the party's foreign policy agenda.

As Kinne points out, "regardless of Gorbachev's personal inclinations, poliheuristic theory tells us that he simply could not have reverted to established Soviet tradition; such an action would likely have incited an unfavorable response from the party leaders."[45]

These cases illustrate that dictators do not formulate their foreign policy decisions in a black hole. Even seemingly irrational decisions can be better understood by examining leaders' political realities. All leaders—even dictators—must act in ways to please their constituents. The nature of this constituent group varies systematically across regime types. Identifying who this group is and what its needs and concerns are provides enormous leverage for understanding the foreign policy choices of dictators.

Military Intelligence in Dictatorships

High quality military intelligence is critical to a state's ability to formulate sound foreign policy. Without accurate information about the activities of other states, successful foreign policy ventures are unlikely. To make good foreign policy choices, states must be able to gauge the intentions and capabilities of their adversaries, as well as what their own capabilities are. In this section, we examine the quality of military intelligence across dictatorships. We show how the domestic institutions influence the caliber of information channels and, in turn, the likelihood for dictatorships to make foreign policy errors. Before doing so, we provide some background information on military intelligence more generally.

Military Intelligence

Multiple types of intelligence are important for maintaining security. Intelligence officers must collect and analyze information with respect to covert action, counter intelligence, strategic intelligence, tactical intelligence, and actionable intelligence (Kruys 2006). Covert action is used to directly influence political events in a foreign state. It is more subtle than war, but more aggressive than diplomacy. Counter intelligence is geared toward protecting one's own intelligence apparatus

⇨

from foreign threats or penetration (Ibid., p. 67). Strategic intelligence is concerned with the "policies, cultural tendencies, thinking processes, and domestic vulnerabilities" of foreign states (or other international organizations, like terrorist groups) (Ibid., pp. 67–68). It is used to assess the types of foreign policies that are likely to be effective in influencing the behavior of these actors. Tactical intelligence pertains to the "capabilities, limitations, vulnerabilities or reactions of a hostile force—either air or surface"—required to carry out tactical operations (Ibid.). Finally, actionable intelligence entails "awareness of the target, timing, and type of attacks being planned by an enemy" (Ibid.).

Background on Military Intelligence

Following the September 11, 2001 terrorist attacks on the United States, the importance of high-quality military intelligence gained prominence in policy circles. A weak intelligence apparatus can be very costly for states. To monitor imminent threats from enemy states or groups, states must ensure that their intelligence apparatus is internally well organized with effective lines of communication, and that, intelligence officers are highly skilled. Most importantly, accurate information about the intentions of a state's adversaries must be passed on to the state's leader, who must ultimately determine the appropriate course of action. Without high quality intelligence—both in terms of the thoroughness of information and how well it is analyzed—leaders will be likely to commit foreign policy errors. The consequences of these errors range from exposing the state to a domestic attack to expending state resources unnecessarily in ill-advised acts of aggression overseas.

The process of acquiring accurate intelligence is contingent upon good communication between intelligence officers and policymakers. As Richard K. Betts writes, "Collected information must pass through numerous bottlenecks. It must be screened at low levels to raise initial suspicion; it must be transmitted to higher levels of the intelligence bureaucracy to be compared with data from other sources; it then has to be passed to policymakers who must judge whether the evidence warrants action."[46] Problems can easily arise at multiple levels. Important, but seemingly benign, information may not get passed on to top officials. The information that is passed on may not be properly communicated. Moreover, power struggles among different agencies or groups may lead to impeded coordination or dangerously limit the sharing of information.

A key problem for decision makers, which we discuss in more detail below, is that subordinates often distort the truth in order to please them. As Betts points out, subordinates tend "to bias messages so as to minimize distress to their superiors."[47] Individuals often favor reassuring data rather than negative information, which typically have to pass through vigorous tests to be believed. The information that is transferred is usually interpreted in ways so that it corresponds with what superiors are expecting to hear. In addition, intelligence personnel are often "goaded into supplying intelligence" that suits particular policies and ignoring intelligence that does not.[48]

Given the range of threats that states face on any given day, gathering accurate intelligence is an extraordinarily complex process that requires efficiency at multiple levels, from low-level intelligence operatives to the leader's top security advisers. In what follows, we discuss how this process differs given the institutional arrangement of the dictatorship.

The Quality of Intelligence in Dictatorships

In dictatorships, leaders receive sensitive information from the same group that can overthrow them: members of their elite advisory group.[49] These advisers are the dictator's primary source of information for domestic and international security concerns. Though other information channels exist, dictators rely most heavily upon their elite advisory group for sensitive matters as it is made up of their most trusted individuals. Even if the rest of the intelligence apparatus is highly trained and well organized, if the dictator's advisers do not pass on accurate information to the dictator, the dictator will be incapable of making sensible foreign policy choices. The likelihood that elites will do so varies systematically across dictatorships.

The quality of military intelligence dictators receive is directly related to the extent to which leaders control who will comprise their elite advisory group.[50] Greater control over elite selection lowers the caliber of intelligence provided to dictators. This is true for two reasons: 1) when dictators are given the choice, they will choose to surround themselves with low-skilled individuals who, though less likely to overthrow them, are also less competent; and 2) when elites know that the dictator can easily fire them, they will only pass on to the dictator information that he wants to hear, out of fear of reprisal. When dictators control the selection of their elite advisers, "they are more likely to end up surrounded by 'yes men': individuals who say whatever the dictator wants to hear in order to stay in his good favor."[51]

As we mentioned in **Chapter 6**, personalist dictators have a greater say in the selection of their elite advisory group than single-party or military dictators do. In personalist dictatorships, leaders do not have to abide by institutional provisions for elite promotions. Elites do not share membership in a party or military. As such, they are less capable of bargaining over hiring and firing as a group, which lowers their bargaining power vis-à-vis the dictator. Just as labor unions can protect workers from being fired on a whim, so can military and party institutions. Because personalist dictators have greater control over membership to their elite advisory group than their counterparts in single-party and military dictatorships, they are more likely to receive low quality intelligence and commit foreign policy errors.[52] We discuss elite selection across dictatorships in more detail below.

Valuing Loyalty over Competence in Personalist Dictatorships

When dictators are given the choice, they will select elites to their support group who are unlikely to overthrow them; loyalty is valued over competence.[53] Advisers who are competent are undesirable as they serve as potential rivals to the dictator. In personalist dictatorships, leaders usually fire those advisers who they distrust and promote those individuals who are least likely to oust them.

Examples of personalist dictators choosing loyalty over competence in their selection of elites abound. As Brian Titley[54] writes, in the Central African Republic, Jean-Bédel Bokassa's choice of advisers was typically based on loyalty not merit. For instance, in 1966 when Commander Martin Lingoupou proved to be too skilled and well-liked, Bokassa fired him and he disappeared soon after.[55] Bokassa felt threatened by more qualified personnel; he craved "adulation and constant glorification."[56] As a result his military was poorly trained and "morale, discipline and esprit de corps were rapidly undermined."[57]

Similarly, Idi Amin of Uganda often chose illiterate advisers, as he resented any individuals who were better educated.[58] At one point, Amin even complained that some of his aides were "too competent."[59] For Amin, an individual's qualifications were unimportant; sycophants were preferred. The following example illustrates this well:

> Fickle appointments characterize all of his relationships such as the brief career of Toro Princess Elizabeth Bagaya who was a former fashion model who became Amin's Foreign Minister. She debuted at the UN General Assembly in a tightly fitted gold gown. Her downfall was due to Amin's accusation that she had made love to an unknown European in a toilet. She escaped after being detained under house arrest in 1975.[60]

Loyalty trumped competence for Rafael Trujillo of the Dominican Republic, as well. Trujillo appointed Jacinto Bienvenido Peynado as Vice President "due to his loyalty and the fact that he preferred leisure to power."[61] Similarly, General José Estrella's loyalty was said to be "of a kind not often encountered except among four-legged animals. His mentality was rude and rustic, totally unsophisticated."[62] It also helped to be related to Trujillo. Though most of his family members embarrassed him, he chose to make his son a colonel at the age of four and a brigadier general at the age of nine.[63]

Muammar al-Gaddafi's inner circle is also made up of cronies and family members, rather than individuals with proven expertise. To deter any one individual from getting too powerful, Gaddafi created a chain of command that was intentionally confusing. Ranks and titles had little meaning and it was unclear what each individual's responsibilities were. Captains, for example, occasionally reported to individuals with no rank.[64] The goal of this setup is to ensure that "ambitious underlings" are kept in check by being played off one another.[65] As Craig Black writes, "No one outside Libya—and perhaps even inside— knows for sure who controls exactly what. The vagueness and obscurity of this system is said to be of Gaddafi's own design, intended to confuse potential competitors within the regime."[66] Family connections also help advance one's political career under Gaddafi. His cousin, Hassan Ishkal, was put in charge of domestic security, though as soon as he was viewed as disloyal he was gunned down.[67] As these cases illustrate, when leaders have the choice, they will surround themselves with loyal, yet incompetent, advisers.

The Threat of Purges in Personalist Dictatorships

Dictators who control the selection of elites also control their fates. Individuals deemed disloyal are typically purged out of the elite corps; some are even killed. Indeed, purges are quite common in personalist dictatorships, as discussed in **Chapter 6**. The threat of being purged induces elites to only relay to the dictator information that the dictator wants to hear. Telling the truth, if it is unpleasant, is often unwise.

In the Philippines under Ferdinand Marcos, for example, few members of the cabinet would express concerns to him about his excesses; "loyalty dictated that they would not state anything to contradict Marcos or say anything to protest his interference."[68] In Uganda, anyone who doubted Amin's facts was personally beat up.[69] A Minister of Finance made the mistake of reporting, correctly, that cotton production had declined by 60 percent. The minister disappeared soon after.[70] The Central African Republic's Bokassa surrounded himself with individuals who worshipped him and were willing to "nurture his delusions of grandeur."[71] Being part of his support group was a dangerous endeavor, however. The consequences of displeasing Bokassa included torture, amputation, and death.[72] For elites in personalist dictatorships, the threat of being purged is omnipresent, making them unlikely to tell the dictator information the dictator does not want to hear.

Poor Intelligence in Personalist Dictatorships

In comparison to military and single-party dictatorships, personalist dictators have near total control of who will comprise their elite advisory group. Greater control, however, has negative consequences for intelligence. When, dictators have greater control over the selection of their elite advisory group, like in personalist regimes, "elites are more likely to be incompetent and less likely to report to the dictator, unfavorable information, decreasing the quality of intelligence that the dictator receives."[73]

Personalist dictators are often isolated from reality, forcing them to make foreign policy decisions in a vacuum. Those who surround them give them endless flattery and positive feedback, such that personalist dictators "frequently engage in self-delusional fantasies—that the intervention will not really occur, that some third force will halt the standoff before it runs to its logical conclusion, or that their own military forces will somehow deter the enemy."[74]

Because personalist dictators receive poor quality intelligence, they are more likely to make foreign policy errors. Such errors can prove extremely costly. Below, we provide a few examples of this.

Amin of Uganda

In Uganda, Amin got rid of advisory bodies and formal meetings to avoid feeling uncomfortable, as he had difficulty understanding complex matters.[75] His trusted advisers, instead, were his drinking buddies and cronies who were incapable of helping him create sound policies or astute military strategy. In the end, Amin used his instincts to make tough choices, which eventually got him into a costly war with Tanzania.

Amin's downfall came not long after the Kagera invasion of Tanzania in 1978. Amin saw the invasion as a means to placate some of his troops that were problematic to his control, like the Chui and Simba battalions, by giving them the opportunity to pillage and plunder opponents. Amin also wanted to neutralize his enemies in Tanzania who had been supported by Julius Nyerere, the Tanzanian president at the time.[76]

Amin had goaded Tanzania for years. In 1978, however, Amin took it a step further by invading and occupying part of the Kagera region and declaring it a new province.[77] In doing so, Amin made multiple miscalculations. First and foremost, he had trouble gauging the resolve and capabilities of Tanzania. Soon after the invasion, Nyerere dispatched over 40,000 troops, which cost over $500 million.[78] Amin also did not anticipate that Ugandan anti-Amin forces living in Tanzania would be given free reign by Nyerere to counterattack, nor that they would work closely with Tanzanian units. These forces, known as the Ugandan National Liberation Front were too much for Amin's disgruntled and divided troops to bear. Because of this venture, opposition to Amin mounted and he was forced to flee Uganda on April 11, 1979.

Mobutu of Zaire

Joseph Mobutu of Zaire (today's Democratic Republic of Congo) was particularly threatened by his elite advisers, such that he set in place a number of provisions to ensure that their competence was limited. Crawford Young and Thomas Turner write that the military under Mobutu had "legendary indiscipline" and demonstrated a "repeated incapacity" to "defeat even small and poorly armed foes."[79] In the military, promotions in the upper ranks were highly politicized, rather than based on merit or experience. Officers were rotated frequently and encouraged to report any rumors of insubordination directly to Mobutu.[80]

The consequence of these actions was that Mobutu was never given accurate information regarding his own capabilities nor those of his enemies.[81] Though Mobutu had complete supremacy over the command structure of the military, he did little to establish a professionalized military with a hierarchical command.[82] As evidence of this, in 1978 and 1979, Zairian troops were unable to fight off a small group of around 1,500 mercenaries from Angola. Given that, Mobutu was supported by millions of dollars in military aid and training during this time, his army should have performed better. Because of the poor information channels in Zaire, however, Mobutu was unaware of the extent to which his troops were unprepared.

Lacking a competent advisory group that could tell him (without facing punishment) when his proposed foreign policy choices were unwise, Mobutu pursued multiple reckless military ventures, such as invading Angola in 1975 and supporting Hutu perpetrators of the Rwandan genocide in 1994. The latter case of rash behavior eventually led to his downfall.

Mobutu's attack on the Tutsis led to the formation of a coalition helmed by Laurent-Desire Kabila known as the Alliance of Democratic Forces for the Liberation of the Congo (Alliance des Forces Démocratiques pour la Libération du Congo-Zaïre) (AFDL). The main goal of the AFDL was to oust Mobutu, a feat that was eventually accomplished in May 1997. Nevertheless, even while confined to a military camp in Kinshasa, Mobutu and his cronies projected a "false air of infallibility," never ready to believe that his reign had come to an end.[83]

Poor intelligence can have dire consequences for personalist dictators. Without accurate information about the intentions, resolve, and capabilities of enemy states (and often misinformed about their own capabilities), personalist dictators are more likely to make foreign policy mistakes. The evidence indicates that this is true.[84] Compared to single-party dictatorships, military dictatorships, and democracies, personalist dictatorships are the most likely to exhibit uncertainty in their responses to threats and commit foreign policy errors.

Summary and Conclusion

International relations scholars have long emphasized the tight relationship between domestic institutions and conflict behavior. As Robert Putnam[85] highlights, the international relations of states is often best understood as a two-level game: leaders' decisions in the international arena are intricately tied to the domestic constraints that they face at home. Grasping this relationship is fundamental to understanding the dynamics of inter-state relations, the foreign policy choices of regimes, and when conflicts are likely to escalate.

In this chapter, we explored the tie between institutions in dictatorships and international conflict. We looked at how the international conflict patterns of dictatorships vary given regime type, as well as the ability of different types of dictatorships to signal their resolve during inter-state disputes. We also examined the factors that underlie the foreign policy decisions of dictators and how this is affected by the institutional structure of the dictatorship. Lastly, we discussed how the quality of military intelligence differs across dictatorships and the effect that this has on the likelihood that dictators will make foreign policy errors.

This chapter provided insights into the behavior of dictatorships with respect to a wide array of sub-issues in the field of international relations. In bridging the worlds of comparative politics and international relations, this chapter has shown that institutional arrangements in dictatorships have predictable foreign policy consequences. Greater analytical leverage for understanding the actions of dictatorships in the international sphere can be gained by adopting a perspective that differentiates authoritarian regime structures.

Review Questions

- Is there a "dictatorial peace"?
- What trends have emerged regarding the conflict propensity of dictatorships?
- What are audience costs? How do dictatorships differ in their ability to generate audience costs and why?
- What does poliheuristic theory predict about the foreign policy decisions of dictators? What factors motivate leaders' foreign policy choices?
- Why is it difficult to gain accurate military intelligence in general?
- How and why do dictatorships differ in the quality of their military intelligence?

Key Points

- Some dictatorships are more peaceful towards one another than others.
- Dictatorships differ in their ability to generate audience costs. Personalist dictatorships are the least capable of generating audience costs, making them more likely to be participants in escalatory inter-state conflicts.

- The foreign policy decisions of dictators are often driven by the groups that leaders are trying to please.
- The quality of military intelligence varies across dictatorships. It is poorer in personalist dictatorships, making them more prone to foreign policy errors.

Notes

1. Peceny, Beer, and Sanchez-Terry, *Dictatorial Peace?* (2002).
2. Bueno de Mesquita et al., *Institutional Explanation* (1999).
3. Fearon, *Domestic Political Audiences* (1994a).
4. Reiter and Stam, *Identifying the Culprit* (2003).
5. Goemans, *Fighting for Survival* (2000).
6. Reiter and Stam, *Identifying the Culprit* (2003, p. 336).
7. Peceny and Butler, *Conflict Behavior of Authoritarian* (2004).
8. Ibid. See **Chapter 1** for a discussion of the terms winning coalition and selectorate.
9. Lai and Slater, *Institutions of the Offensive* (2006).
10. Ibid. (p. 113).
11. Ibid. (p. 123).
12. Herz (1950); Jervis (1978); Waltz (1959).
13. Fearon, *Domestic Political Audiences* (1994a, p. 583).
14. Schultz, *Domestic Opposition and Signaling* (1998); Siegel, *I Know that You* (1997).
15. Schultz, *Do Domestic Institutions Constrain* (1999).
16. Fearon, Domestic Political Audiences (1994a).
17. Fearon (1994, 1997); Schultz (1998, 2001), Ramsay (2004); Smith (1998).
18. Fearon, *Domestic Political Audiences*, (1994a p. 577).
19. Fearon, *Signaling Versus the Balance*, (1994b p. 241).
20. The price of failure can be more severe for autocratic leaders, however, such as execution. Nondemocratic leaders potentially face much greater and/or fatal "audience costs" in the face of a coup than do democratic leaders (Gowa 1995; Goemans 1995).
21. Eyerman and Hart (1996); Schultz (1999); Partell and Palmer (1999); Gelpi and Griesdorf (2001).
22. Kinne, *Decision Making in Autocratic* (2005); Weeks, *Autocratic Audience Costs* (2008).
23. Weeks, *Autocratic Audience Costs* (2008).
24. Frantz, *Tying the Dictator's Hands* (2008).
25. Ibid.
26. Ibid.
27. Weeks, *Autocratic Audience Costs* (2008).
28. Ibid. (p. 35).
29. Weeks' findings differ slightly from Erica Frantz's (2008). Whereas Frantz finds that only military dictatorships have signaling advantages comparable to democracies, Weeks finds that this is true for military *and* single-party dictatorships, as well as for most hybrids. The differences

between the results of the two studies are largely due to the inclusion of two key control variables in Frantz's study: whether the dispute involves a naval seizure and the number of days the dyads have been at peace.

30. Kinne, *Decision Making in Autocratic* (2005).

31. Ibid. (p. 115).

32. Mintz and Geva (1997); Mintz et al. (1997); Mintz, *How Do Leaders Make* (2004).

33. Mintz, *Decision to Attack Iraq* (1993).

34. Mintz and Geva, *Poliheuristic Theory of Foreign* (1997); Mintz, *How Do Leaders Make* (2004).

35. Kinne, *Decision Making in Autocratic* (2005, p. 115).

36. Ibid. (p. 123).

37. Ibid. (p. 124).

38. Hadar, *Pakistan in America's War* (2003).

39. Harrison, *Bush Needs to Attach* (2003).

40. Bearak, *Pakistan Is* (2003).

41. Shah, *Democracy on Hold* (2002).

42. Kinne, *Decision Making in Autocratic* (2005, p. 124).

43. Ibid. (p. 125).

44. Blum, *Soviet Foreign Policy Belief* (1993, p. 386).

45. Kinne, *Decision Making in Autocratic* (2005, p. 126).

46. Betts, *Surprise Despite Warning* (1980–1981, p. 555).

47. Ibid.

48. Kruys, *Intelligence Failures: Causes* (2006, p. 73).

49. Frantz and Ezrow, *Institutions, Intelligence Apparatuses* (2009).

50. Ibid.

51. Ibid. (p. 3).

52. Ibid. Frantz and Ezrow (2009) do not include monarchies in their study.

53. Egorov and Sonin, *Dictators and their Viziers,* They point out that "while incompetent ministers are not completely unusual in democratic countries, most historians and political scientists would agree that dictatorships are especially marred by incompetence" (2006, p. 2).

54. Titley, *Dark Age* (1997).

55. Ibid.

56. Decalo, *African Personal Dictatorships* (1985, p. 222).

57. Titley, *Dark Age* (1997, p. 44).

58. Ravenhill, *Military Rule in Uganda* (1974).

59. Basajabka et al., *Social Origins of Violence* (1994, p. 122).

60. Legum, *Behind the Clown's Mask* (1997, p. 257).

61. Crassweller, *Trujillo: The Life,* 1966 (p. 167).

62. Ibid. (p. 185).

63. Egorov and Sonin, *Dictators and their Viziers* (2006).

64. Black, *Deterring Libya* (2000).

65. Ibid. (p. 10).

66. Ibid.

67. Ibid.

68. Hawes, *Marcos, His Cronies*, (1995 p. 158).

69. Decalo, *African Personal Dictatorships* (1985).

70. Source: *Fall of Idi Amin, Economic and Political Weekly* (May 26, 1979, pp. 907–910.)

71. Titley, *Dark Age* (1997, p. 44).

72. Decalo, *African Personal Dictatorships* (1985); Titley, *Dark Age* (1997).

73. Frantz and Ezrow, *Institutions, Intelligence Apparatuses* (2009, p. 8).

74. Carothers, *Why Dictators Aren't Dominoes* (2003, p. 59).

75. Decalo, *African Personal Dictatorships* (1985).

76. Valeriano and Gibler, *Steps to Interstate War* (2006); Brett, *Neutralising the Use* (1995).

77. Aluko, *African Response* (1981).

78. Ibid.

79. Young and Turner, *Rise and Decline* (1988, p. 248).

80. Afoaku, *Politics of Democratic Transition* (1999).

81. Ibid.

82. Ibid.

83. Ibid. (p. 12).

84. Frantz and Ezrow, Institutions, Intelligence Apparatuses (2009).

85. Putnam, Diplomacy and Domestic Politics (1988).

9 Military Dictatorships in Latin America and Beyond

The second half of this study provides an in-depth exploration of individual types of dictatorship. This chapter is devoted to military dictatorships. We begin by presenting the theoretical literature on military rule, before offering a selection of case studies that highlight how politics works under military dictatorships.

What is Military Rule?

Military dictatorships are regimes in which control over policy and the security forces is in the hands of the military. The leader of the regime is typically a current or former military officer; in some cases a junta—or group of military officers—holds power. Though occasionally when the military seizes power coup plotters install a civilian chief executive (as in Uruguay in 1976), true power lies in the hands of the junta.

The organization of military dictatorships tends to mirror that of the military itself. Just as most militaries are cohesive and disciplined units that are tightly organized,[1] military dictatorships have a clear and respected hierarchical structure. Some even have institutionalized formulas for the rotation of power.[2]

In military dictatorships, the military has a monopoly over the state security forces and government institutions.[3] Policy is directed and implemented by the professional military and its structure is transferred to the political sphere.[4] As Samuel E. Finer writes, the distinguishing feature of military regimes is that the individuals working in the executive branch are members of the military who have been installed as a result of a military coup.[5] The precise role of the military in terms of policy making varies across regimes, as does the relative power of the leader vis-à-vis the junta.

Definition of Military Dictatorship

- Professional military force in power, led by a military officer; power is not concentrated exclusively in the leader's hands
- Group of officers (military junta) determines who is in charge and directs policy
- Military hierarchy is clear and respected
- Military has a monopoly over the use of force
- Cohesive, disciplined governing unit with efficient lines of communication
- Policy implemented by the military, which maintains most government institutions

Theoretical Analyses of Military Dictatorships

Scholars have long been fascinated with military rule. This is reflected in the expansive literature examining how politics works in military dictatorships, ranging from the factors that motivate the military's decision to intervene in politics to the causes of its eventual departure. In this section, we provide the key highlights of this literature.

Types of Military Rule

Structural Forms of Military Rule

Finer[6] disaggregates regimes according to the role, goals, and composition of the military. According to Finer, there are several structural forms of military rule: indirect limited, indirect complete, dual, direct, and quasi-civilized. Indirect limited rule occurs when the military exerts control over the government intermittently, and only as a means of securing limited objectives. Under indirect complete rule, the military rules continuously and calls the shots of a nominally civilian government. With dual military rule, the leader of the regime develops a political party or organized civilian group to act as a civilian counterweight to the views and the influence of the military. Such regimes are particularly prone to evolving into personalist dictatorships. With direct rule, as the name suggests, the military overtly determines the policy agenda, and members of a military junta hold key government posts. Lastly, quasi-civilized rule occurs when the military incorporates some civilian elements into the regime, in order to appear more legitimate.

Moderator, Guardian, and Ruler Types

Eric Nordlinger[7] divides military dictatorships into three categories based on the military's goals: moderator, guardian, and ruler. Moderator types seek to rule the country behind the scenes. The military does not overtly take power and exercises veto power over policies privately. The main goal of the military in this model is to maintain political order and stability. Guardian types take this a step further: the military displaces civilian politicians and overtly controls the government, but its goals are similar in scope to those of the moderator types. The ruler type is the most ambitious of all. It seeks to implement significant political and economic changes to the system and rule indefinitely.

Moderator, Guardian, and Ruler Types of Military Dictatorships (Nordlinger)

Moderator

- Type of rule: indirect
- Goals: preserve the status quo and ensure political order, replace a civilian government with one more amenable to the military

⇨

- Length of rule: short term
- Level of repression: likely to be moderate

Guardian

- Type of rule: direct
- Goals: correct problems of civilian rule, revamp the government, make it more efficient, rid it of corruption
- Length of rule: short term
- Level of repression: likely to be moderate

Ruler

- Type of rule: direct
- Goals: change the political, economic, and social system
- Length of rule: indefinite
- Level of repression: likely to be high

Professional vs. Praetorian Military Dictatorships

Military dictatorships can also be divided based on the professionalization of the military. In professional military dictatorships, the military is experienced, well-organized, cohesive, and concerned with maintaining corporate unity.[8]

In praetorian military dictatorships, by contrast, the military is poorly funded, with soldiers lacking in experience and education. Because soldiers are not well trained, praetorian military dictatorships are ill prepared for dealing with external enemies.[9] Praetorian military regimes are characterized by high levels of corruption, little respect for hierarchy, and rampant factionalism. The praetorian military's motivation for seizing power is typically to gain access to the spoils of office. Because of this, they frequently intervene in politics, as they see doing so as a means to increase their riches. Praetorian military dictatorships are highly unstable and short-lived, as they usually lack the organizational strength necessary to govern and maintain power.

Pratetorian Militaries

- High levels of corruption
- Little respect for hierarchy; junior officers are ambitious and resent senior officers

⇨

> ## Pratetorian Militaries—Cont'd
>
> - Little cohesion; unconcerned with corporate unity; may be divided by ethnic cleavages, generation gaps, differences in rank and education, and ideological commitment
> - Aim to rule so as to take advantage of the spoils of office; enormous wealth accrued by military generals
> - Unconcerned with legitimacy
> - Little respect for civilian governments
> - Highly unstable; intervene in politics repeatedly
> - Poorly equipped and trained; not well prepared to combat an external foe

The Structure of Military Dictatorships

The structure of military dictatorships looks very similar to the structure of the military. Military regimes have a centralized command with a pyramid style of authority that is highly stratified. As Finer writes, the greatest strength of the military is its ability to be "well organized, disciplined, and efficient."[10] This hierarchy is important to fighting as a unit.[11]

Members of the military are socialized to be united as a group and are often insulated from society. Potential members typically undergo a selection process that places great emphasis on indoctrination. The goal of this process is to "replace the inductee's individual or civilian identity with a corporate spirit."[12] Indoctrination, education, and discipline help create the conformist nature of the military institution.[13]

Critical to the military is internal cohesiveness (as discussed in **Chapter 6**). According to Guy L. Siebold, such cohesion requires "trust among group members together with the capacity for teamwork."[14] This trust can diminish when the military is placed in more public settings and when team building efforts, such as collective drills, are not practiced. As Anthony King[15] points out, military unity is adversely affected when the military is not engaged in coordinated action. For the military to successfully govern in the absence of warfare, it is critical that it remains engaged in some type of mission. When objectives become blurred or confused, factions will emerge or resurface.[16]

Key Attributes of Military Dictatorships

- Centralized command structure
- Clearly defined internal hierarchy
- Internal organization that mirrors that of the military
- Shared socialization among regime members via indoctrination during training
- Internal cohesiveness; emphasis on internal unity

The Durability of Military Dictatorships

Many scholars have highlighted the internal fragility of military dictatorships. As discussed in **Chapter 3**, among dictatorships, military regimes are the most short-lived. They are far less durable than other types of dictatorships.[17] There are several reasons why military dictatorships are prone to breakdowns, which we discuss in detail below.

The Preferences of Military Elites

Military elites differ from their counterparts in other forms of dictatorships in one key way: they value the survival of the military over staying in political office. In contrast to elites in other types of dictatorships, military elites do not always want to stay in power.[18] Rather, the most important goal of the military is to ensure that its corporate interests are secured. Corporate unity is necessary so that the military remains capable of defending the country in the face of threats to national security and order.

Because military elites value the survival of the military above all else, they are more likely to voluntarily step down from power when threatened. As Claude Welch writes, military disengagement from politics is often due to "a belief that military unity and effectiveness would be further impaired by remaining in power."[19] If the military were to fail in its mission, its legitimacy would be tarnished in the eyes of the masses, as well as internally. Most officers "prefer to remain in the barracks if their objectives, particularly the defense or enhancement of the military's corporate interests, could have been realized from that vantage point."[20]

The Destabilizing Effect of Factionalism

Entrance into politics can pose many challenges to the military's unity. By taking on a public political role, the military as an organization loses its insulation from society. The longer that it stays in power, the more likely its cohesion will be destroyed by being politicized.[21] The military's commitment to govern directly conflicts with its commitment to survive as a hierarchical and united institution.[22]

When the military intervenes in the political sphere, it is also forced to formulate policy, a potentially divisive endeavor. When disputes over policy arise, this can easily prompt a return to the barracks. Junta members may conflict over the types of policies to pursue, how to respond to a crisis, and how to draw up budgets.[23] Factional divisions in the military dictatorships of Argentina, for example, opened the doors for civil society to initiate the process of regime transition.[24]

Military unity can also be threatened by competition over the distribution of the perks of office. As elites struggle with one another to gain access to economic rents, conflicts can arise among them, and their various military branches, and within the military's hierarchical ladder. This was the case in the military dictatorships of Nigeria, where retired soldiers became millionaires causing resentment among junior officers.[25]

Internal divisions are particularly likely to arise in the face of crises. Militaries often seize power due to the poor economic performance of civilian governments; yet few military officers are trained to bring an economy out of a crisis. According to Nordlinger,[26] any economic growth that occurs in military dictatorships happens in spite of the military, not because of it. Domestic and international crises caused the downfall of the Argentine military dictatorship in 1983. Economic turmoil, coupled with the military's disastrous defeat in the Falklands War, became too much for the military to withstand.[27] As Barbara Geddes writes, military dictatorships are "more vulnerable to economic downturns than are other authoritarian regimes because poor economic performance is likely to precipitate or worsen splits in the officer corps."[28]

Commitment to Temporary Rule

Militaries often come to power promising to the public that their rule will be temporary. Nigeria's first military dictatorship (1966–1979) exemplifies this. Upon assuming power, the military made clear that its rule would be short-lived. General Johnson Aguiyi-Ironsi claimed that "the military government has no political affiliation or ambition; it has no desire to prolong its interim administration of government longer than necessary for the orderly transition of the country to the type of government desired by the people."[29] In 1970, General Yakubu Gowon promised to transfer power to civilians by 1976. Yet, by 1974 little progress had been made in this area and Gowon declared that the country was not yet ready for civilian rule. Gowon's inability to fulfill his promise to return power to a civilian government provided the justification for a faction within the military to unseat him in 1975.[30] Soon after, General Murtala Mohammed declared that "the present military leadership does not intend to stay in office a day longer than is necessary, and certainly not beyond this date."[31] Such repeated proclamations can damage the legitimacy of the military and eventually cause it to actually step down.[32]

Having publicly stated that its rule will be short-lived, the longer the military remains in power, the more its legitimacy erodes in the eyes of the public. William Graf summarizes this well:

> The paradox of the current military regime (and every military regime since independence) is that it derives much of its popularity and legitimacy from a self-proclaimed 'corrective' mission; yet with the passage of time the popular consciousness grows impatient with the ossification, corruption and lack of measurable change which the military—as merely one faction of the elite— is incapable of transforming, once its limited corrective aims have been asserted.[33]

Public commitments to temporary rule can cause the military to leave power, either because it accomplished its stated objectives on its initial seizure of power or because it has lost all legitimacy in the eyes of the public through continued rule.[34]

Sensitivity to Pressures for Democratization

Because the military is quick to leave power in the face of problems, it is particularly sensitive to mass pressures for democratization. As George Klay Kieh and Pita Ogaba Agbese[35] emphasize, the military may step down from power because of calls by organized political groups such as labor unions, student groups, and professional organizations for it to do so. Henry J. Barkey argues, for example, that "increased civil disobedience, broad-based opposition, foreign pressures, and lack of business confidence, which in turn lead to economic difficulties, if not a crisis, and divisions in the military, may propel the military to relinquish power."[36] Whether the military will remain in power amid civilian pressures to leave depends on its ability to destroy other sources of political power.[37] When the costs of holding on to power become too high, the military will disengage.

The military dictatorships of South America provide an example of this. Most of these regimes were greatly assisted by US military aid. As Cold War tensions thawed, however, aid to these regimes decreased. The United States Congress began to apply greater pressure on them to democratize given widespread reports of egregious human rights violations. In the case of Chile's military dictatorship, international human rights organizations helped fund and support domestic opposition groups to push for democratization. The regime agreed to step down from power in 1988 after losing a public vote on its political future.

Case Studies

In this section, we offer a selection of case studies of military dictatorships to provide insights into how these regimes actually work. As mentioned in **Chapter 2**, military dictatorships have been most prominent in Latin America, for a variety of geo-political reasons. Because of this regional relationship, we provide a handful of case studies of Latin American military dictatorships. To show how military dictatorships function in other regions, we also present case studies of military dictatorships in Turkey, Thailand, and Nigeria. Weaved throughout, each of these case studies are elements of the themes presented earlier in this chapter. See table 9.1 for sample military dictators and Dictatorships.

Destabilizing Factionalism in Argentina (1976–1983)

Argentina has been particularly prone to military rule. Military dictatorships governed Argentina on four different occasions in the 20th century, each only ruling for somewhere between three and seven years. In this case study, we discuss the problem of destabilizing factionalism in Argentina's most recent military dictatorship that ruled from 1976 to 1983. As with other Argentine military regimes, this dictatorship was a professionalized military regime; in that, the military apparatus was well-organized and

Table 9.1 Sample of Military Dictators/Dictatorships

Argentina

1943–1946	Pedro Pablo Ramírez (June 1943–February 1944)
	Edelmiro Julián Farrell (February 1944–June 1946)
1955–1958	General Pedro Eugenio Aramburu (November, 1955–May, 1958)
1966–1973	Juan Carlos Onganía (June, 1966–June, 1970)
	Roberto Marcelo Levingston (June 1970–March 1971)
	Alejandro Agustin Lanusse (March 1971–May 1973)
1976–1983	Jorge Videla (March 1976–March 1980)
	Roberto Viola (March 1980–December 1981)
	Leopoldo Galtieri (December 1981–July 1982)
	Reynaldo Bignone (July 1982–December 1983)

Brazil

1964–1985	Humberto Castelo Branco (April 15, 1964–March 15, 1967)
	Artur Costa e Silva (March 15, 1967–August 31, 1969)
	Emilio Medici (October 30, 1969–March 15, 1974)
	Ernesto Geisel (March 15, 1974–March 15, 1979)
	Joao Figueiredo (March 15, 1979–March 15, 1985)

Guatemala

1963–1966	Alfredo Enrique Peralta Azurdia (March 1963–July 1966)
1970–1985	Carlos Manuel Arana Osorio (July 1970–July 1974)
	Kjell Eugenio Laugerud García (July 1974–July 1978)
	Fernando Romeo Lucas García (July 1978–March 1982)
	Military coup breaks off from National Liberation Movement
	José Efraín Ríos Montt (March 1982–August 1983) 2 years
	Óscar Humberto Mejía Victores (August 1983–January 1986) 3 years

Turkey

1960–1961	Cemal Gürsel (May 27, 1960–March 28, 1966)*
1980–1983	Kenan Evren (September 12, 1980–November 9, 1989)*
	Though a military general was still in power as president, the military technically stepped down in 1961 and 1983 respectively

Nigeria

1966–1979	General J.T.U. Aguiyi-Ironsi (January–July 1966)
	Yakubu Gowon (August 1, 1966–July 29, 1975)
	Murtala Mohammed (July 29, 1975–February 14, 1976) *assassinated
	Olusegun Obasanjo (February 13, 1976–October 1, 1979)
1983–1993	Muhammadu Buhari (December 31, 1983–August 27, 1985)
	Ibrahim Babangida (August 27, 1985–August 27, 1993)
	unless otherwise noted, military leaders were overthrown

---

highly trained. This case highlights the problems that can accompany power-sharing at the top echelons.

When the Argentine military staged a coup in 1976, it represented the close of a "counterrevolutionary cycle in the Southern Cone of Latin America," starting with Brazil in 1964, Bolivia in 1971, and Uruguay and Chile in 1973.[38] The decision to intervene was driven by the disastrous performance of Isabel Perón, the wife and successor of Juan Perón, who had died in office in 1974. Under Isabel Perón's tenure, the economy deteriorated rapidly. Societal discontent soon escalated into violence, with leftist guerilla groups and rightist paramilitary groups undertaking armed confrontations. Given the state of political chaos in Argentina, the military chose to take over the government.

The military junta that took power in 1976 was unified in its decision to oust the civilian government as a means of protecting Argentina from the threat of leftist insurgencies. Upon its assumption to power, the military was united in its belief that state terror was an effective tool for ensuring national security (its tenure is often referred to as the Dirty War due to the massive human rights violations committed by the military during this period). The military also agreed that rules should be implemented in the new regime that would prevent any individual from becoming too powerful (so as to minimize the likelihood of elite rivalry, which had led to the downfall of past military governments).[39] When the junta assumed power, it agreed to divide responsibilities among the three key coup plotters. This was to ensure that no single actor could evolve into the regime's prominent leader.[40]

The junta's plan initially worked. Soon after, however, self-defeating behavior on the part of the leadership surfaced and eventually contributed to the regime's unraveling. This occurred because no members of the junta possessed the capacity to manage internal dissent and intra-elite conflicts. These divisions at the elite level ultimately led to the downfall of the regime.

Beyond the items mentioned above, junta members shared few areas of common ground with respect to policy. At the time, the Argentine economy was in bad shape. Under the junta's first leader, Jorge Videla (1976–1981), the regime had trouble deciding what the proper course of action should be to bring the economy into recovery. In such an environment, policy divisions were many. Part of the problem was that the military junta lost faith in its own programs.[41] Videla personally supported a liberal economic agenda, but his military colleagues disagreed. Internal dissent was so strong over this issue that Videla eventually stepped down from power. Doing so was preferable to pursuing his economic program without the consensus of the rest of the military elite. If Videla were to have implemented such a program without the junta's support, he risked going against proper procedure, which would in turn compound the military's internal divisions.[42] Thus "corporate interests of the military were placed above the desire of the economics ministry to complete its liberal mission."[43]

Breakdown of the Regime

Though Videla made an effort to cover up the problems within the regime, there was little he could do to curb the emergence of deeper divisions. The leadership that followed him made the fatal mistake of exposing the internal weakness of the regime to the public, as well as to lower-level members of the military, compounding the regime's fragility. For example, the leadership issued several public statements that were contradictory and easily identifiable to different competing factions within the military.[44] While Videla's successor, Roberto Viola (March 1981-December 1981) was in power, junta member, Leopoldo Galtieri released statements to the public in opposition to those of Viola. This was in sharp contrast to protocol under Videla, where public discourse that could raise questions about the regime's unity was avoided.[45] These top-level divisions, limited the military's ability to govern, as officers became more interested in pursuing ideological or personal ends. Such actions threatened the military as an institution by diminishing the value of corporate responsibilities and eventually led to its decision to leave power.

Though the primary sources of the Argentine military dictatorship's instability were endogenous, the nail on the coffin was its disastrous performance in the 1982 Falkland Islands war. The war, which lasted 72 days, not only led to the humiliating defeat of the Argentine military, but also elevated Argentina's already soaring levels of inflation and foreign debt. The defeat was the catalyst for the military's departure from power. In 1983, the military stepped down following presidential elections and the victor, Raúl Alfonsín, assumed power shortly later.

Corporate Unity in Brazil (1964–1985)

The Brazilian military dictatorship is classified as a professionalized military regime, as the military was well trained, highly experienced, and institutionally strong. In many ways, this dictatorship is anomalous. Compared to other

Latin American military regimes, Brazil's was long-lasting, holding onto power for almost twenty years. It held regular elections and even allowed multiple political parties to compete in them.[46] In this case study, we describe the factors that contributed to the Brazilian military dictatorship's longevity, primarily its corporate unity.

Prior to seizing power, the Brazilian military had been strategizing over what its role in politics should be for some time. Brazil's military officers had contemplated the military's proper place in government since their days at the Superior War College between 1954 and 1960.[47] Undergoing comparable and sophisticated training socialized officers into developing a similar belief with respect to what the goals of the military should be.[48] Military officers were united in their support for a single national security doctrine, which guided military rhetoric and decision making. The consensus among military elites was that national security depended on the development of a strong capitalist economy, which could only be achieved through suppression of demands for popular mobilization.[49] As a result, when the military junta took power, it was cohesive with no prominent factions.[50] This ideological unity enabled it to pursue its political and corporate interests without being undermined by internal opposition.

Junta members were also aware that internal divisions had weakened the military in the past. Unity had been threatened by ideological factions, defiance of discipline, a lack of respected hierarchy, and the politicized character of promotions and appointments.[51] Cognizant of the need to maintain its internal strength, the regime enacted many regulations to encourage corporate unity. Numerous rules were implemented stipulating that factionalism or other forms of disobedience would not be tolerated, and those who spoke out against the regime or defied the military's hierarchy would be disciplined accordingly.[52] Laws were also created prohibiting retired officers from issuing public statements that were damaging to the military's values, such as respect for hierarchy and discipline.[53] The regime stipulated that the president could not hold the rank of commander in chief of the army simultaneously, further dividing power among elites.[54] All of these institutional mechanisms helped to enhance the regime's longevity.

The regime's first leader, Humberto de Alencar Castello Branco (1964–1967), also used his powers to eradicate competition within the military that could potentially threaten its ability to govern effectively.[55] He instituted rules and promoted norms of behavior that discouraged individualism. This ensured that an individual's authority in the regime was derived not from "charismatic appeal or personal followings" but through institutional positions.[56] In addition to such efforts to preserve the military's corporate unity, the policy choices of the regime were considered successful, further suppressing the emergence of potentially destabilizing factions.[57]

Breakdown of the Regime

For many years under the military dictatorship, the Brazilian economy was robust. The regime had legitimacy in the eyes of the public because of its strong economic performance.[58] As in other parts of the region, however, by 1980 economic stagnation hit Brazil. Thomas Skidmore[59] points out that by 1981, Brazil entered its worst recession in 30 years. Brazil's GDP declined for the first time since 1942, and (because of population growth) its GDP per capita hit –4.3percent. The deficit also rose as capital inflows dropped significantly. This economic crisis led to disagreements within the regime as to how to properly fix the problem. Internal conflicts emerged in multiple economic areas, even over wages.[60] In addition, the economic crisis led to a decline in military budgets. Due to budgetary constraints, the military was forced to pull out of potentially lucrative ventures and operate with out-moded equipment.[61] Strained relations developed within the ruling government over which economic policies to pursue, weakening the regime.[62]

The regime also began to disagree over the pace of political reform. Some factions wanted to open the regime to greater political competition, while others wanted to keep it closed.[63] The regime's goals started to diverge, as some members of the military increasingly became concerned with the use of greater societal repression.[64] As time passed, the regime eventually "became politicized and subject to internal divisions."[65]

In the end, the military chose to step down from power after nearly twenty years at the helm of the Brazilian government. Some segments of the military had always envisioned a return to civilian rule, in line with their Western values. Indeed, during its tenure, the regime aligned with a political party, consistently held elections, and allowed other parties to compete in them.[66] For others, the timing was ripe, as the military still enjoyed some legitimacy in society. As the Cold War ended, it had become more difficult for the military to justify its rule under the national security doctrine, which emphasized protecting the country from the threat of communism and mass movements. Because there was no longer a visible enemy, the Brazilian military could no longer defend its hold on power in such terms.[67]

The Brazilian military left power at a time when it was still moderately cohesive. Because of this, it was able to negotiate an exit that was beneficial to its interests. After it stepped down, the military assigned 13 officers to work full time as advisers to the military and to lobby on its behalf in the Brazilian Congress.[68] These officers attended every hearing held that was relevant to the military, including those on national security. Thus, upon its departure, the military transformed itself into one of the most well-organized lobbying groups in Brazil, such that early on in the democratization process, the Brazilian Congress was incapable of exercising much control over military affairs.[69]

Institutional Weakness in Guatemala (1970–1985)

The military in Guatemala has intervened in politics, numerous times; often based on its belief, that the civilian government was corrupt and/or incompetent.[70] Most of the post-World War II military interventions in Guatemala have been short-lived, with the exception of the military dictatorship that ruled from 1970 to 1985. Under this regime, military rule was long-lasting not because of the professionalization of the military, but, because of the comparable weakness and disorganization of civilian actors. Because of the military's institutional underdevelopment and lack of order, this regime is viewed as a praetorian military dictatorship.[71] In this case study, we examine the problem of institutional weakness in the 1970–1985 Guatemalan military dictatorship.

The Guatemalan military's ascension to power in 1970 did not come out of nowhere; it was preceded by significant efforts on the part of the military to exert political influence. As James Mahoney writes, "by 1970, the question of executive transfer had been standardized through the use of elections every four years in which fraud and repression ensured that officers representing the official military party controlled the presidency."[72] The military's ability to consolidate its power in the Guatemalan government was in many ways heightened by its use of counterinsurgency campaigns against leftist groups, such as peasant movements calling for more equitable land distribution. As Jennifer Schirmer points out, "The counterinsurgency campaigns of the 1970s permitted the military to deepen its control over state and civilian institutions, and to strengthen and make permanent its presence in the western highlands, where it had traditionally been weak or absent."[73]

Though the Guatemalan military was strong enough as an institution to take over and govern Guatemala, overall, it was institutionally weak. Poor organization had been characteristic of the Guatemalan military for much of its history. Lacking a well-established and well-respected internal hierarchy, officers frequently felt slighted. These recurring divisions were present throughout the 1950s, 1960s, and 1970s, but were particularly acute during the 1980s. The military's prior organizational problems carried over into the 1970–1985 military dictatorship.

A recurring theme of this regime was that junior officers rarely obeyed the rules of hierarchy, believing that they were more capable of serving the country than the older military elite.[74] Older officers, in turn, felt marginalized when junior officers received promotions and resented the fact that junior officers frequently disregarded the command structure.[75] Though senior officers regained some control when Minister of Defense, Óscar Humberto Mejía staged a coup in 1983, ousting the regime's leader, Efraín Ríos Montt, such an action was too little too late.[76]

Despite the institutional weakness of the regime, it managed to hold on to power for fifteen years. Part of the reason for this is that civilian actors that could have pressured the military to step down from power also lacked organizational strength.[77]

Breakdown of the Regime

Ironically, as the military extended its control over Guatemalan society, this only deepened the divisions and factions within the institution itself.[78] As the military expanded its counter-insurgency campaigns, segments within it began to question the brutality of the tactics used. Disagreements surfaced over how to proceed with the campaigns, and many believed that current methods were ineffective. Arbitrary killings, kidnappings, and forced disappearances became counterproductive in maintaining the military's corporate order.[79]

Such human rights violations also led to serious reductions in military aid from the United States under the Carter administration.[80] The US' approach toward Latin America began to place greater emphasis on human rights. Sustaining prior levels of military aid to Guatemala became impossible as evidence of gross human rights violations emerged. Cuts in US military aid further weakened the Guatemalan military dictatorship.

As with the rest of Latin America, the economic crisis of the 1980s hit Guatemala hard. It created new challenges for the military, as competition over the spoils of office intensified. The crisis also meant that the military was less capable of paying off its civilian allies. Some sectors of the military even began to openly expose the regime's corrupt activities.[81] In 1981 for example, accusations surfaced that "$250 million of Guatemala's $425 million arms budget had been siphoned off to bank accounts in the Cayman Islands of five top military generals."[82]

The culmination of all of these factors made an exit from power begin to look desirable in the eyes of regime elites. Forcing civilian politicians to deal with the political mess would allow the military to escape greater blame while keeping the door open for a return to power once the situation improved.[83] The military held elections in 1984 for a Constituent Assembly that would draft a new version of the Guatemalan constitution. Once the draft of the constitution was finalized in May 1985, presidential elections were scheduled for the end of the year. Civilian politician Vinicio Cerezo was elected president and the military stepped down from power soon after.

Restoring Stability in Turkey (1980–1983)

For the past 200 years, the military has been prominent in Turkey.[84] It has been a source of pride for the country and played an important role in Turkey's development. Compared to many of the world's militaries, the Turkish military is a professionalized and modernized force. The military has intervened occasionally in Turkish politics, but has usually only stayed in power long enough to restore order to society before returning to the barracks.[85] The Turkish military would essentially intervene "whenever it came to the conclusion that the civilians" could not protect the country from internal and external threats.[86] In this case study, we show how this process played out in the 1980–1983 Turkish military dictatorship, during which the military entered power as a means of restoring order to Turkey before stepping down a few years later.

Beginning in the mid-1940s, the Turkish military frequently desired to intervene in politics, but refrained from doing so because of resistance from the military's upper echelon. Though soldiers supported staging a coup on multiple occasions, they were unable to do so due to lack of support among the military's senior officers.[87] Eventually, as conditions worsened the military staged a coup in 1960, though its tenure in power was brief. It threatened to stage a coup in 1971, but did not actually have to do so, as the civilian government acceded to its wishes.

As the 1970s progressed, however, Turkish politics became increasingly volatile. The military staged a coup in September 1980, heralding the first sustained military dictatorship in Turkey in the post-World War II era.

The decision to intervene was prompted by a number of factors. Violence from both left- and right-wing sectarian groups began to challenge Turkey's secular state, and rampant guerilla-style terrorism led to concerns of the state's impending collapse.[88] The conflict with Cyprus also intensified the state's political polarization, as did the decision over whether to join the European Community. Deep economic problems only exacerbated the political crisis, as unemployment, inflation, and debt all continued to rise. The state became subject to paralysis, as political parties faced difficulties forming a viable government coalition. Moreover, the Grand National Assembly could not elect a president for six months.

The confluence of such developments ultimately precipitated the military's decision to take over the government. In the military's view, the prestige of the state had deteriorated markedly, and Turkey's national unity was in jeopardy. The coup was headed by the Chief of the General Staff, General Kenan Evren. Unlike the previous coup of 1960, the military had full control over the lower ranks.[89] Most officers agreed that significant changes needed to be made to the Constitution to prevent the political stalemate that had plagued Turkish politics during the 1970s. The military's intervention was well received by many sectors of the public, as they saw the military as the sole institution that could restore order to Turkey. The military, through a National Security Council, would rule for the next three years.

Breakdown of the Regime

Upon entering power, the military enacted economic reforms to try to repair the Turkish economy and worked to clamp down on the political violence. Though the military achieved its goal of restoring order, its internal discipline began to deteriorate and it gradually became vulnerable to corruption. Evren soon addressed this concern, stating "We are exerting every effort to prevent those below our echelon from getting involved with these affairs."[90] As problems worsened, Evren eventually handed legislative power over to the Motherland Party (Anavatan Partisi) via general elections in 1983.[91]

A primary factor motivating the military's decision to step down was its decreasing popularity. Having already restored order in Turkey, the longer it remained in power, the more it undermined its own effectiveness and esprit de corps and lost legitimacy among the masses.[92] The Turkish military saw itself as the sole organization that could defend the national interests of Turkey and was committed to maintaining its dignity and professionalism. Leaving power became the primary means by which to do so.

Military Strength in Nigeria (1966–1979, 1983–1993)

Nigeria is one of the few countries in Africa to have experienced military dictatorships lasting a decade or longer. Part of the reason for the longevity of Nigeria's military dictatorships is the military's strength. As a powerful organization, the military has frequently operated in Nigeria independent from the direction or interference of civilian actors. It has been able to secure itself large budgets and weapons arsenals, along with access to other state perks. In this case study, we discuss the strength of the Nigerian military and how this contributed to the durability of Nigeria's first (1966–1979) and second (1983–1993) military dictatorships.

The Nigerian military is one of the largest in sub-Saharan Africa. Its strength and power is reflected in its ability to stage coups. Since independence, there have been at least five successful military coups in Nigeria. Though some of these coups occurred within the two military dictatorships discussed here, others were the result of the military's decision to unseat civilian governments that it perceived as corrupt, since it had little trust in the abilities of civilian forces to uphold the "disciplinary standards necessary for effective governance."[93] Occasionally the motivation for the coup was political, but other times coups were staged so that officers could gain greater pay and/or weapons.[94]

The power of the Nigerian military only increased once it took over the state. The Nigerian military first seized control of the government in a coup in 1966, bringing General Gowon to power. Under Gowon's tenure, the strength of the Nigerian military amplified. Already a sizeable force, the

Nigerian military grew even larger during the Biafran War from 1967 to 1970. The army alone went from a light infantry force of 6,000 to a force of over a quarter million.[95] Because of the war, the military also became better equipped, with access to expensive weapons and air and naval power.[96]

In addition, control over the government provided the military with opportunities to engage in corruption given its seemingly unlimited access to economic perks and kickbacks.[97] Military weapons purchases were particularly profitable for the Nigerian military. In the 1970s, for example, the regime received $3.6 million from the Lockheed Corporation for buying six Hercules C-130 transport planes that were valued at $45 million.[98] Other purchases included "fifty T-55 main battle tanks, MiG and Alpha fighter jets, and Roland surface-to-air missiles."[99] Though none of these purchases were necessary for security purposes (as no neighboring countries possessed an army of any significance), the corrupt procurement practices enabled officers to pad their pockets and supplement their incomes.[100]

The stability of the first and second Nigerian military dictatorships was further enhanced by their ability to buy off key civilian elites and officers within the military. Generous incentives for supporting the dictatorship were offered: cooperative and loyal officers benefited from access to housing, cars, and cash. Many officers also used their power to bribe civilians, believing that they were entitled to all of the fruits of the state.[101] Soldiers who served in political (rather than purely military) roles could use their positions of power to gain control over various economic sectors, such as "shipping, airlines, retail, and manufacturing."[102] Both military dictatorships also profited from embezzling profits from the lucrative Nigerian oil industry.[103] With select patronage networks flowing, Nigeria's military dictatorships faced little challenges to their rule.

Breakdown of the Regimes

The strength of the Nigerian military should not be conflated with professionalism. Though the military was large in size and economically powerful, officers had little experience in combat, and military hierarchy was often ignored. The lack of any real domestic or international threats to security meant that there were no incentives for the Nigerian military to professionalize.[104] At the same time, the constant threat of a coup led to a large number of forced retirements at the senior officer rank, sapping the military of those individuals with the most expertise and training.[105] Promotions were not typically based on merit, but instead hinged on loyalty, ethnicity, and personal connections.[106]

Despite this lack of professionalism, both Nigerian military dictatorships were remarkably long-lasting. This is primarily due to the sheer size and economic might of the Nigerian military during this period. The military's strength made it difficult for civilian actors or groups to counter it and easy for the regimes to pay off potential (internal or external) challengers.

No regimes are invincible, of course. After 13 years in control, the first Nigerian military dictatorship stepped down in line with the military's stated roadmap for transferring power back into civilian hands. Following general elections in 1979, the regime and its leader, General Olusegun Obasanjo, voluntarily left power, a mode of exit typical of many military dictatorships.

The second Nigerian military dictatorship fell on account of the decision of General Ibrahim Babangida (the head of the regime at the time) to annul democratic elections held in 1992 because the results did not suit him. The annulment exacerbated internal tensions within the regime, as a segment of the military genuinely supported restoring democracy.[107] In response to the annulment, widespread civil unrest erupted and a cohort of colonels and brigadiers retired from the military in protest.[108] The situation became so unstable that Babangida resigned and the military stepped down from power in 1993.

Summary and Conclusion

Military dictatorships are often a fleeting phenomenon. When the military does consolidate its hold on power, it is usually for short periods of time. The reason behind the impermanence of military dictatorships is that the preferences of military elites are usually distinct from those of typical civilian politicians. As this study has discussed, military actors generally value the preservation of the military above all else, including political power. Consequently, when threats to the military as an institution surface, it can prompt the military to resort to drastic measures, ranging from staging a coup and ousting a civilian government to voluntarily stepping down from power.

In this way, military dictatorships are unique. Though they are by no means homogenous as the case studies illustrate, general trends in their behavior quickly surface. As with all political regimes, military dictatorships are prone to factionalization; factionalism, however, is particularly destabilizing and can prompt the military's departure from power. The military typically seizes power because it believes that it is the sole institution that can save the nation from political crises and restore stability. Seizures of power are nearly always accompanied by statements in which the military promises that its rule will be temporary. In addition, military dictatorships are extremely cognizant of their public legitimacy and sensitive to mass movements calling for the restoration of democracy.

As this chapter has shown, institutions under dictatorship have important consequences for their behavior. Governance by the military profoundly shapes the types of policies that a government will pursue and the motivations that underlie such choices.

Review Questions

- How does Finer classify military rule? How do his classifications differ from Nordlinger's?
- How do praetorian militaries differ from professional militaries?
- Why does entering politics destabilize the military?
- For what reasons did the Argentine military fall apart in 1983?
- How was the Brazilian military able to stay in power for almost 20 years?
- Why is the Guatemalan military dictatorships considered to be praetorian? Why was it able to stay in power for so long in spite of this?
- Why was the Turkish military dictatorship so short-lived?
- Why has Nigeria experienced so many military interventions? Why has the military been able to stay in power for long periods of time despite its lack of professionalism?

Key Points

- Military dictatorships are regimes in which the military governs, controls policy, and runs the security forces.
- Military regimes can be categorized according to their levels of professionalism and objectives.
- Military regimes are short-lived because members of the military would rather return to the barracks than rule as a factionalized force. Any threats to the military's internal unity can prompt it to step down from power.

Notes

1. Jenkins and Kposowa, *Political Origins of African* (1992).

2. Geddes, *What Do We Know* (1999).

3. Bratton and van de Walle, *Neo-patrimonial Regimes and* Political (1994); Heeger, *Politics in the Post-Military* (1977).

4. Bratton and van de Walle, *Neo-patrimonial Regimes and Political* (1994).

5. Finer, *Man on Horseback*(1962, p. 150).

6. Finer, *Man on Horseback* (1962).

7. Nordlinger, *Soldiers in Politics* (1977).

8. Finer, *Man on Horseback* (1962); Huntington, *Solider and the State* (1959).

9. Perlmutter, *Praetorian State* (1969).

10. Finer, *Man on Horseback* (1962, p. 8).

11. Feit, *Pen, Sword and People* (1973).

12. Lee, *Military Cohesion and Regime* (2005, p. 86).

13. Pion-Berlin, *Military Autonomy and Emerging* (1992).

14. Siebold, *Essence of Military* (2007, p. 288).

15. King, *World of Command: Communication* (2006).

16. Janowitz, *Military Institutions and Coercion* (1974).

17. Geddes, *Paradigms and Sand Castles* (2003).

18. Geddes, *What Do We Know* (1999).

19. Welch, *Soldier and State* (1970, p. 55).

20. Nordlinger, *Soldiers in Politics* (1977, p. 142).

21. Perlmutter, *Praetorian State* (1969); Kieh and Agbese (1993).

22. Gillespie, *Negotiating Democracy* (1991).

23. Geddes, *What Do We Know* (1999).

24. Pion-Berlin, *Fall of Military Rule* (1985).

25. Kieh and Agbese, *From Politics Back* (1993).

26. Nordlinger, *Soldiers in Mufti* (1970).

27. Pion-Berlin, *Fall of Military Rule* (1985); *Maniruzzaman* (1987).

28. Geddes, *What Do We Know* (1999, p. 135).

29. Duke, *Revolutionary Potentials* (1987, p. 71), From Kieh and Agbese, *From Politics and Back* (1993).

30. Obasanjo (1990); Kieh and Agbese, *From Politics Back* (1993).

31. Kieh and Agbese, *From Politics Back* (1993, p. 415).

32. Barkey, *Why Military Regimes Fail* (1990).

33. Graf, *Nigerian State: Political Economy* (1988, pp. 157–158).

34. Kieh and Agbese, *From Politics Back* (1993).

35. Ibid.

36. Barkey, *Why Military Regimes Fail* (1990, p. 171).

37. Kieh and Agbese, *From Politics Back* (1993).

38. Munck, `*Modern*' *Military Dictatorship* (1985, p. 41).

39. Geddes, *What Do We Know* (1999).

40. Gugliotta, *Inner Workings of Dictatorship* (1986).

41. Pion-Berlin, *Fall of Military Rule* (1985).

42. Ibid.

43. Ibid. (p. 62).

44. Pion-Berlin, *Fall of Military Rule* (1985).

45. Ibid. (. 65).

46. This corresponds with the arguments presented in **Chapter 3** emphasizing the ability of elections to prolong the survival of regimes.

47. Gillespie, *Negotiating Democracy* (1991).

48. Hunter, *Eroding Military Influence* (1997).

49. Ibid.

50. Bienen and Gersovitz, *Economic Stabilization, Conditionality* (1985).

51. Hunter, *Eroding Military Influence* (1997).

52. Ibid.

53. Ibid.

54. Barros, *Brazilian Military: Professional Socialization* (1978).

55. Skidmore, *Politics of Military Rule* (1990).

56. Hunter, *Eroding Military Influence* (1997, p. 27).

57. Hunter, *Eroding Military Influence* (1997).

58. Mainwaring, *Transition to Democracy* (1986).

59. Skidmore, *Politics of Military Rule* (1990).

60. Mainwaring, *Transition to Democracy* (1986).

61. Skidmore, *Politics of Military Rule* (1990).

62. Mainwaring, *Transition to Democracy* (1986).

63. Ibid.

64. Skidmore, *Politics of Military Rule* (1990).

65. Mainwaring, *Transition to Democracy* (1986, p. 153).

66. Ibid.

67. Ibid.

68. Stepan, *Rethinking Military Politics* (1988).

69. Ibid.

70. Schirmer, *Guatemalan Politic-Military Project* (1999).

71. Berrios, *Civil Military Relations* (1998).

72. Mahoney, *Legacies of Liberalism* (2001, p. 239).

73. Schirmer, *Guatemalan Military Project* (1998, p. 18).

74. Loveman and Davies, *Politics of Anti-Politics* (1997).

75. Schirmer, *Guatemalan Military Project* (1998).

76. Ibid.

77. McClearly, *Dictating Democracy: Guatemala* (1999).

78. Handy, *Resurgent Democracy* (1986).

79. Schirmer, *Guatemalan Military Project* (1998).

80. Ibid.

81. Schirmer, *Guatemalan Military Project* (1998).

82. Handy, *Resurgent Democracy* (1986).

83. Ibid.

84. Tachau and Heper, *State, Politics*(1983).

85. Heper and Shifrinson, *Civil-military Relations* (2005).

86. Ibid. (p. 241).

87. Maniruzzaman, *Arms Transfers, Military Coups* (1992).

88. Hale, *Turkish Politics* (1994).

89. Ibid.

90. Ibid. (p. 250).

91. Maniruzzaman, *Arms Transfers, Military Coups* (1992).

92. Heper and Guney, *Military and the Consolidation* (2000).

93. Amadife, *Liberalization and Democratization* (1999, p. 628).

94. Bienen, *Military Rule and Political* (1978b).

95. Butts and Metz, *Armies and Democracy* (1996).

96. Ibid.

97. Kieh and Agbese, *From Politics Back* (1993).

98. Howe, *Military Forces in African* (2004, p. 41).

99. Ibid.

100. Howe, *Military Forces in African* (2004).

101. Ikbe, *Patrimonialism and Military Regimes* (2000).

102. Kieh and Agbese, *From Politics Back* (1993, p. 417).

103. Lewis, *Endgame in Nigeria?* (1994).

104. Butts and Merz, *Armies and Democracy* (1996).

105. Howe, *Military Forces in African* (2004).

106. Ibid.

107. Lewis, *Endgame in Nigeria?* (1994).

108. Butts and Merz, *Armies and Democracy* (1996).

Single-party Dictatorships in Eastern Europe, Asia, and Beyond

10

Chapter Outline

Though often associated with communism, single-party dictatorships are actually quite heterogeneous. While some single-party dictatorships place great emphasis on a political ideology, there are many others that do not. In this chapter, we examine single-party dictatorships in detail. We begin by providing an in-depth definition of single-party rule and how it is structured, and then present the theoretical literature devoted to it. We close this chapter by offering a selection of case studies on single-party dictatorships in Eastern Europe and Asia (where they have been more common) and in Mexico, which has hosted one of the world's longest lasting single-party regimes.

What is Single-party Dictatorship?

Single-party dictatorships are regimes in which policy making control and political offices are in the hands of a single party.[1] Other parties may be allowed to operate, compete in elections, and hold political posts, but their hold on power is minimal. The leader of the regime is typically the head of the party, who is selected to this post by the party's central committee or politburo or via some sort of electoral process controlled by the party.

The power of the leader with respect to the party elite varies across single-party dictatorships, just as in democracies. Some party leaders are extremely powerful (like many democratic presidents), while others are subject to constant party monitoring (like many democratic prime ministers). The one feature that is characteristic of all single-party dictatorships (and differentiates them from personalist dictatorships) is that the party is well-organized and "autonomous to prevent the leader from taking personal control over policy decisions and the selection of regime personnel."[2]

In single-party dictatorships, the party usually controls nearly all state institutions and dominates most aspects of the political sphere, such as local government, civil society, and the media. Even the military is subordinate to the party. Party officials typically formulate and determine policy, either through mandates and decrees or through a legislative process. Legislatures, which are common in single-party dictatorships, are nearly always stacked (or entirely filled) with party supporters.

Single-party dictatorships can appear quite similar to democracies, as most have elections and legislatures and most emphasize the importance of public participation in the political process. Some even impose term limits on leaders and elites and have rules that dictate how key political posts are filled. Single-party dictatorships differ from democracies, however, in that opposition parties (if they are not banned) face institutional disadvantages and/or constant threats and harassment. Moreover, unlike democracies, in single-party dictatorships there is no alternation in power from one party to the next. Rather than determining who will rule, elections in single-party dictatorships serve the purpose of conveying to the masses and elites the party's strength via its impressive (and often fraudulent) electoral victories.

Definition of Single-party Dictatorship

- One party controls politics; power is not exclusively in the hands of a single individual
- Central committee or politburo dictates who is in charge and formulates policy

⇨

- Opposition parties are occasionally allowed to exist and compete in elections
- The party controls most state institutions, including the media
- The military is subordinate to the party
- Elections are common and designed to favor the party
- Legislatures are common and filled with party supporters

Theoretical Analyses of Single-party Dictatorships

In this section, we present central features of the literature dedicated to single-party rule. In particular, we put forth the different types of single-party dictatorships that scholars have identified, along with the various strategies employed by dominant parties to stay in power. We also discuss the factors that make single-party dictatorships vulnerable, as well as those that contribute to their longevity.

Types of Single-party Dictatorships

Weak and Strong Single-party Systems

Single-party dictatorships can be categorized according to whether they are weak or strong, according to Samuel Huntington and Clement Henry Moore.[3] These categorizations are primarily based on the party's concentration of power and how it came into power.

In weak single-party systems, one or more actors eclipse the role of the party. According to Huntington and Moore, these systems are more common in Africa. In strong single-party systems, by contrast, the party plays a dominant role. The authors argue that the strength of the party depends on the intensity and duration of its struggle to gain power. When parties have revolutionary origins, for example, they are more likely to evolve into strong single-party systems once they ascend to power.

Within the category of strong single-party systems there are three variants: revolutionary, exclusionary, and established. These variants are distinguished by the goals of the party in power. Revolutionary one-party systems are characterized by "social dynamism, autocratic and charismatic leadership, a disciplined party, a highly developed ideology, stress on propaganda and mass mobilization, combined with coercion and terror."[4] In these systems, the party's goal is to subordinate the social divisions in a "bifurcated society" and eliminate the capitalist class.

In exclusionary single-party systems, the party works to repress or suppress the political activity of non-party members. Whereas revolutionary parties may seek to rid society of those who oppose them, exclusionary parties merely seek to marginalize the opposition.

Lastly, established single-party systems are typified by low levels of mobilization, limited pluralism, and pragmatic (rather than ideological) goals. These systems can evolve out of revolutionary single-party systems, once the party has consolidated power and reduced societal bifurcation.[5] In established single-party systems, the party has more of an administrative rather than revolutionary function, and the political leadership is less "personalist, charismatic, and autocratic" and more "oligarchical, bureaucratic, and institutionalized."[6]

Hegemonic Party Systems

Hegemonic party systems are a type of single-party dictatorship that has received substantial attention in the literature. In hegemonic party systems, a single political party holds power even though multi-party elections are regularly held.[7] Giovanni Sartori defines hegemonic party systems as follows:

> The hegemonic party neither allows for a formal nor a de facto competition for power. Other parties are permitted to exist, but as second class, licensed parties; for they are not permitted to compete with the hegemonic party in antagonistic terms and on an equal basis. Not only does alternation not occur in fact; it *cannot* occur, since the possibility of a rotation in power is not even envisaged. The implication is that the hegemonic party will remain in power whether it is liked or not.[8]

Hegemonic party systems prefer to mask that they are authoritarian by incorporating seemingly democratic institutions into the political system, like elections.[9] Though electoral fraud is often used, it is only one of many tools at the disposal of the regime and not always the most vital.[10]

According to Beatriz Magaloni,[11] hegemonic party systems maintain their hold on power by winning legislative supermajorities, enabling them to change the rules of the game continuously in the party's favor. Supermajorities also help deter intra-party elite splits because they convey an image of party invincibility. Elites are less likely to defect from the party when they believe that the party is extremely powerful.

Hegemonic party systems differ from other types of single-party dictatorships in that they rely less on repression. As Magaloni puts it, "hegemonic-party autocracies are a more benign form of dictatorship."[12] Repression is used, but it is typically the last resort.[13]

Hegemonic Party Systems

- Role of ideology is less important; party ideology does not penetrate society
- Rely less on repression
- Other parties may exist, but there is no rotation in power
- Electoral fraud and other tools help maintain the party in power

Ideological One-Party States

Another type of single-party dictatorship is the ideological one-party state. As the name suggests, ideological one-party states are characterized by: (1) a single political party holding power, and (2) the reliance on an official state ideology. The official ideology that is used varies in terms of its ideals and goals, as does the political structure of the dominant party.[14]

Ideological one-party states aptly describe many 20th century dictatorships, according to Paul Brooker,[15] ranging from Italy under Benito Mussolini to Germany under Adolf Hitler.[16] Another classic example of an ideological one-party state is the Soviet Union under the Communist Party. The regime emerged following the October 1917 Russian revolution. The Marxist-Leninist ideology it promoted, "espoused not only socialism but also 'leadership' by the Communist Party over state and society."[17]

In ideological one-party states, other parties are typically banned and public criticism of the party (or the state ideology) is illegal. The use of repression is often high, so that members of the opposition are forced to operate underground.

Leaders in these regimes are usually charismatic individuals who can draw popular support for the official ideology, which pervades all levels of society. Indoctrination campaigns are common in the educational system and nationalistic themes are omnipresent. Some ideological one-party states enforce a strict vetting process for party membership, while others mandate that party membership is required of all citizens.

Ideological One-party States

- Led by charismatic individuals
- Indoctrination campaigns are common
- Official ideology pervades all levels of society
- High levels of repression
- No room for other parties to compete

The Structure of Single-party Dictatorships

The structure of single-party dictatorships is typically a reflection of the structure of the dominant party. This means that how single-party dictatorships are organized can vary markedly from regime to regime.

The internal organization of the party is usually not very different from that of parties in democratic regimes; it is dictated by party rules. At the helm is the leader of the regime, who operates under a variety of titles, ranging from president to prime minister to party chairman. In the tier below the leader, sit the party elite. These individuals often hold a position with the party as well as an official political post. Party elites are usually career politicians—as opposed to friends or family members of the leader or members of the military—who have worked their way up the party ladder.

The tenets of the party vary significantly across single-party dictatorships. As mentioned above, in some, the ideology of the party permeates society, establishing set rules of behavior for citizens and clear policy guidelines for how society should progress. In others, the ideology of the party is comparable to the ideology of parties in democracies, resembling more of a party platform than a vision of society. Some dominant parties are leftist or liberal, while others are right-wing or conservative.

> ## Key Attributes of Single-party Dictatorships
>
> - Internal organization mimics that of the dominant party
> - Hierarchical structure determined by party rules
> - Party elites are career politicians
> - Heterogeneity across regimes in the role of ideology and the type of ideology espoused

The Durability of Single-party Dictatorships

Single-party dictatorships are a remarkably robust regime type and the most long-lasting form of dictatorship, as mentioned in **Chapter 3**. Single-party dictatorships are more durable than other dictatorships because they are better able to "co-opt potential opposition, respond to a crisis by granting modest increases in political participation, increase opposition representation and grant some opposition demands."[18] We discuss factors, such as these, that increase the longevity of single-party dictatorships below.

The Preferences of Party Elites

Like politicians in democracies, the primary goal of elites in single-party dictatorships is staying in office. Party elites value holding and maintaining political power above all else and will act in ways to ensure that their preferences are met. In single-party dictatorships, political actors work to "maximize their individual self-interest, and therefore, compete and cooperate under the formal and informal rules."[19] Elites are better off if the dominant party is in power than if it is not.[20] This gives them incentives to cooperate with one another—even when they strongly disagree—to help prolong the survival of the regime.

For elites in single-party dictatorships, allying with the regime is superior to the alternative. Defection brings with it an uncertain future, giving elites "strong reasons to continue supporting the regime and leader."[21] Because party elites will do what it takes for them to stay in office, they have a vested interest in maintaining the status quo. With the party in power, elites have policy-making influence and political power, along with access to other perks of office.[22] As such, the benefits of cooperating with rivals are high, reducing the likelihood that elites will leave the regime and helping prolong its longevity.[23]

The Strategy of Co-optation

In single-party dictatorships, those with a vocation for politics are typically incorporated in the regime, lowering the likelihood that such individuals will seek to overthrow it. Because elites in single-party dictatorships value staying in power above all else (as discussed above), they would rather include potential members of the opposition in the system than marginalize them and risk overthrow. Single-party dictatorships rely heavily on the strategy of co-optation to prolong the life of the regime.[24]

In China, for example, the party co-opts elites and creates channels of participation for the public as a means of enhancing the regime's legitimacy. The public is given the opportunity to vote, help candidates in local-level elections, and lobby on behalf of certain leaders. Andrew Nathan refers to these as "input institutions" because they allow individuals to believe that they are influencing policy decisions.[25] By allowing the public to participate in the political process (albeit in an extremely controlled and moderated fashion), the regime instills in individuals a sense of political efficacy and the belief that they can make an impact on the political system.[26]

Co-optation can take many forms. At the most basic level, it involves giving large numbers of individuals a vested interest in the survival of the regime. This can include doling out high-level political positions to key opponents, distributing state jobs to supporters, and even giving tax credits to loyal political districts. When individuals are better off with the party in power than without it, they are more likely to support the regime and less likely to try to push for regime change. This strategy of co-optation helps to explain why some single-party dictatorships are genuinely popular among large sectors of the masses.

Allowing opposition parties to exist and run in elections is also a form of co-optation. By permitting the opposition to participate in the political process, single-party dictatorships ensure that the opposition's political activity takes place within the boundaries of the regime. Doing so redirects the focus of the opposition from trying to overthrow the regime to trying to win elections, making the regime less vulnerable to ouster by underground political groups. Many single-party dictatorships have allowed opposition parties to run in elections, such as Botswana, Mexico, Taiwan, Tanzania, Angola, and Mozambique.

Resistance to Factionalism

In contrast to many other types of regimes, factions are not a source of instability in single-party dictatorships. Party factions are better off if they cooperate with one another, even when they disagree on policy. Unlike military dictatorships, internal splits are less likely to cause the downfall of single-party dictatorships.

Factionalism in single-party dictatorships is quite common, even in those regimes that have been long-lasting. In Vietnam, for example, factional infighting is so prevalent, that it serves as the means to carry out political competition.[27] Fundamental differences within the party on economic policy have even led to party stalemates.[28] In Kenya, while the center of decision-making power resided with Jomo Kenyatta, policies were often subject to "heated debates among contending groups" before officially being announced.[29] The same is true of Mexico and the Institutional Revolutionary Party (PRI), where factions compete for power. Party factionalism in Mexico was common and characterized by "protracted leadership competition" with "major rounds of bargaining."[30]

This is not to say that single-party dictatorships openly tolerate the emergence of intra-party factions. In fact, most work to hide any appearance of internal splits from the public eye so as to project an aura of party invulnerability. As we discussed in **Chapter 6**, though factions may be interpreted as a sign of internal weakness, they often help the party address and deal with conflicts better.

The example of Botswana helps illustrate this. Factional disputes in Botswana have been so prevalent that observers from time to time have predicted that the Botswana Democratic Party (BDP) would fall apart. The BDP is divided into two main factions, known as the Kwelagobe and Merafhe factions, led by Daniel Kwelagobe and Moptai Merafhe, respectively.[31] These two factions differ over many factors, ranging from party strategy and tactics to leadership styles.[32] Despite this, the BDP has remained sufficiently well organized to maintain power. No splinter groups have broken off from the party, indicating that most party members have shared (up to this point) the ultimate objective of being in power.[33]

Survival beyond the Tenure of a Single Leader

Single-party dictatorships often have agreed-upon rules for guiding the process of succession.[34] Because of this, they are frequently able to survive beyond the tenure of any single leader. While the death or resignation of the leader can be particularly destabilizing for personalist dictatorships, single-party dictatorships are usually able to withstand such crises. Because rules for succession are often in place, there is less uncertainty over who is going to take power, making destabilizing power struggles less likely to arise.[35] In Tanzania, for example, the Chama Cha Mapinduzi (CCM) party (previously known as the Tanganyika African National Union) survived the departure of party founder and regime leader Julius Nyeyere in 1985. Leadership struggles in single-party regimes do not usually result in transitions or signal the demise of the party; rather, "most ordinary cadres just keep their heads down and wait to see who wins."[36]

Case Studies

This section provides an assortment of case studies to help illustrate the internal mechanics, dynamics, and behavior of single-party dictatorships. Because these regimes have been more common in Eastern Europe and Asia, we devote most of this section to cases from these two regions. We close with an examination of Mexico under the PRI. Integrated throughout, where possible, are the thematic messages emphasized in prior sections of this chapter and in those that precede it.

Intra-Regime Leadership Change in Eastern Europe

The Eastern European cases that we discuss below demonstrate the ability of single-party dictatorships to withstand the departure of any individual leader. Intra-regime leadership turnovers occur in many single-party dictatorships and often do not destabilize the regime. The cases below also show the ability of the party apparatus to check the power of the leader of the regime; even those who appear to be omnipotent. Though many of the leaders of Eastern European dictatorships remained in power for long stretches of time, their power was continuously kept in line by the party and the various factions within it.

We should note that all three of the regimes that we discuss were, for much of their time in power, maintained by the Soviet Union. Staying in the good favor of the Soviet Politburo was in essence a requirement for survival in office. Because of this, many of the actions taken by party elites that we highlight should be viewed as extensions of the preferences of the Soviet Communist Party leadership.

Hungary (1949–1990)

The Hungarian single-party dictatorship, experienced (and withstood) many changes in the regime's leadership. Leaders in Hungary were rarely able to outmatch the strength of the party and were frequently removed if they displeased the party elite.

The reign of Matyas Rakosi is a case in point. Rakosi was appointed as General Secretary of the Hungarian Communist Party in 1945 and was known as "Stalin's best pupil."[37] Rakosi sought to exert the regime's dominance over the population through brutality: intellectuals were purged and around 1.5 million people were persecuted.[38] Rakosi's brutality, however, was not favored by some of the party elite. His actions exposed him to criticism that he was too bossy and power hungry. Party officials also complained that Rakosi was trying to foster a cult of personality.[39] Within the party, anti-Rakosi opposition grew more vocal and in November 1956 Rakosi was forced to step down from power.

His successor, Janos Kadar, by contrast, sought to operate under the radar so as to avoid inciting criticism from party elites. Kadar took the middle road ideologically while an intense struggle played out within the party from the left and right wings.[40] Though he purged the Rakosi elements from the party once he assumed power, Kadar in many ways allowed and encouraged intra-party debate.[41]

Nevertheless, Kadar faced many threats from other party elites with extensive support bases. Karoly Grosz was one of them. Grosz was the First Secretary of the Budapest Committee of the party and wanted to challenge Kadar for the party's leadership.[42] Kadar assigned Grosz to the post of prime minister, with hopes that this would cut off Grosz's power base and put him in the unenviable position of dealing with the problematic economy. This tactic backfired for Kadar, however, as Grosz used his new position to garner additional support for his rule outside the party apparatus.[43] Grosz eventually replaced Kadar as General Secretary in May 1988.

Czechoslovakia (1948–1990)

When Antonin Novotny took over as president of Czechoslovakia in 1957, he engaged in various efforts to exert total control over the party. At the time, the party was highly divided, as some elements within it wanted the party to be more internally democratic.[44] In addition to dealing with contending factions, Novotny faced many internal challenges to his power. In the early 1960s, for example, Novotny had to contend with the ambitions of Rudolph Barak, the minister of Home Affairs and a member of the Politburo. Barak was popular among a selection of party members and had his own following; it was no secret that he wanted to replace Novotny.[45]

Though Novotny was able to withstand Barak's challenge, dissatisfaction with his rule intensified among party elites.[46] Novotny's unpopularity stemmed from his efforts to purge those who disagreed with him from the party, prompting many of his colleagues to voice concerns that he was concentrating too much power in his own hands. By the end of 1967, a number of high-ranking party members supported ousting Novotny, as he had proven incapable of healing the party.[47] In January 1968, he was forced out of power and a handful of disgraced party members, including two of Novotny's eventual successors, Ludvik Svoboda and Gustav Husak, were allowed to return.[48] The regime survived the change in leadership unscathed.

East Germany (1945–1990)

The fall of Walter Ulbricht of East Germany in 1970 also illustrates that leadership transitions in single-party dictatorships are often relatively smooth and seamless. Though Ulbricht was a brilliant politician who excelled at finessing his way out of difficult situations, the Socialist Unity Party of Germany (SED) in the end proved capable of reining in his power and preventing him from acquiring sole control of the regime.[49]

When Ulbricht first took power in the early 1950s, he tried to expand his power by gaining control over the security forces. The first Minister of State Security, Wilhelm Zaisser, was removed in 1953. He was replaced by Ernst Wolweber, who in turn was deposed in favor of Erich Mielke in 1957.[50] Ulbricht's efforts, however, were in vain. Mielke proved loyal to the party, supporting its goals and the need to maintain a climate of fear and anxiety.[51]

Many elites within the SED disliked Ulbricht and his style of leadership. Zaisser and Rudolf Herrnstadt, for example, both alleged that Ulbricht was developing a leadership cult. They advocated a more collective style of leadership, one that relied on greater consultation.[52] Opposition to Ulbricht steadily grew due to his willingness to cooperate with the West in exchange for economic aid. The opportunity to unseat Ulbricht was seized upon by a faction within the Politburo led by his former protégé, Erich Honecker.

Honecker quickly assembled a group of party elites who supported ousting Ulbricht. This group included Willi Stoph (Chairman of the Council of Ministers), Hermann Axen (Ulbricht's foreign affairs specialist), and Gunter Mittag (Ulbricht's economic affairs specialist). Even though creating an opposition faction was considered a serious party crime, Honecker pressed forward with his efforts through a subtle campaign. His campaign was met with success, and Ulbricht officially retired due to "poor health" in May 1971. Honecker quickly took over the regime, which survived in power for nearly twenty more years, and Ulbricht was given the ceremonial title of Chairman of the SED.[53]

Breakdown of the Regimes

As many observers have highlighted, the fall of the single-party dictatorships in Eastern Europe were in many ways due to the fall of the Soviet Union. The Soviet Union's withdrawal of support (as it dealt with its own domestic problems) undermined the coercive capabilities of the Eastern Bloc regimes in the face of growing public discontent. By 1990, most of them had collapsed. Party leaders came to believe that their best shot of survival was through negotiating the terms of reform. Most of their exit negotiations involved power sharing and attempts to reconcile past divisions. Compromises and alliances were made, allowing the Communist administrations to "save face."[54] The fall of the Eastern European single-party dictatorships were for the most part non-violent and paved the way for the emergence of stable, multi-party democracies, a fate characteristic of various single-party dictatorships.

Factionalism in Asia

The cases from Asia that we examine below demonstrate the pervasiveness of factionalism in single-party dictatorships and, more importantly, the ability of these regimes to withstand it. Whereas in military dictatorships the emergence of factions can be extremely destabilizing, in single-party dictatorships factionalism can help extend the life of the regime by enabling a variety of political preferences to be represented within a single dominant party. Though factionalism is rarely embraced by the dominant party, in many ways it helps it survive in office. Indeed, each of the Asian single-party dictatorships we discuss below have ruled for at least 45 years and all of them are still in power today.[55]

China (1949–present)

The Chinese Communist Party (CCP) has ruled China for over sixty years. Though the party seeks to project an image of unity, it has always been subject to factionalization. The emergence of varied viewpoints in single-party dictatorships like China's may seem paradoxical given that their legitimacy is in many ways based on a well-defined ideology. A strong party ideology, however, does not necessarily provide guidance for the best policies to pursue to achieve ideological goals, nor does it prevent struggles for power from emerging. In this case study, we discuss the healthy role that factionalism has played in the Chinese single-party regime.

Internal divisions within the party elite have been typical of the CCP even in the days of Mao Zedong. Mao ruled the Chinese communist regime from its inception in 1949 until his death in 1976. Mao was not only father of the nation, but was also lauded for his brilliance as a military strategist. This gave him respect among his peers and the public, since China had constantly been threatened by outside powers throughout its history. As such, Mao achieved almost cult-like status in China.

Though Mao was an extremely powerful force in Chinese politics, this did not mean that the party elite always supported his decisions. Factions were common in the early days of the regime; they were both ideologically and personally defined.[56] Even though party ideology was strong during Mao's era, the party could neither homogenize the viewpoints of elites nor "prevent internal strife."[57]

In many ways, Mao was less dominant than he seemed, as factions within the CCP were a key constraint on his power.[58] Though Mao tried to marginalize those who disagreed with him, he was often unable to do so because his opponents had built their own personal followings as a means of challenging him. Such challenges provided a way for the party to prevent the "the accretion of power in Mao's hands."[59] Despite Mao's personal grip over the regime, he was ultimately "dependent upon the Party for the means of wielding" power.[60]

Factionalism was also rife during Deng Xiaoping's tenure from the late 1970s through the late 1980s. In contrast to Mao, Deng spent very few years officially in power, preferring to exercise his influence behind the scenes. The factionalization of the CCP forced Deng to contend with intra-party divisions. To achieve his desired policies, Deng had to skillfully push for what he wanted, with the outcome not always in line with his ideas.[61]

During this period, factions were predominately organized around policy lines and bureaucratic interests;[62] they were contentious nonetheless. Deng maneuvered by trying to fill the CCP's Central Committee, Politburo, Standing Committee, and the National People's Congress with like-minded party members. He could not control the party's middle and lower ranks, however, and, though he wanted to oust leftists, he was forced to strategically moderate the scope of his purges.[63] Deng's survival in this factional environment was in many ways due to his adept negotiating skills and ability to get select factions to side with him as necessary.[64]

Factionalism has led to stability in China, as it has provided a way for politicians who oppose one another to remain within the party apparatus. Rather than defecting from the party and joining the opposition, factions provide an outlet for dissatisfied politicians.

Factionalism in China in many ways serves to balance power in the regime. All sides must negotiate with one another, elevating the importance of consensus building. Factions are increasingly interdependent, which suggests a dispersion of influence in the political system.[65] That many Chinese factions are cross-cutting also mitigates tensions, as close allies may have once been bitter enemies.[66] Successful politicians in China now have networks that cross varied bureaucratic and geographic units, creating incentives for coalition building. As Li Cheng and Lynn White write, "no individual, no faction, no institution, and no region can now dominate China."[67]

Factions also enable a variety of political preferences to inform policy choices in China. Within the umbrella of the CCP, a diversity of preferences is held among party officials. This goes hand in hand with the fact that the CCP's ideology was not intended to be an exclusive ideology that could only appeal to one particular ethnic group, but was supposed to cut across cleavages.[68] Because factions have alternated in power, there is a continuous feedback process that enables the CCP to adjust older policies and create new ones as necessary.[69] The result of all of this factional negotiation is that most policy outcomes have been pragmatic and stable, as decisions are arrived at slowly and with great difficulty.[70] Factionalism means that policies in China emerge out of disputes, and "stability is maintained through endless struggles."[71]

Malaysia (1957–present)

Since Malaysia's independence, it has been ruled by the United Malays National Organization (UMNO) party. Though the UMNO joined the National Front (Barisan Nasional) coalition in 1973, it remains the dominant political force in Malaysian politics. The party was formed in 1946 as a nationalist party. In Malaysia's first post-independence general elections, the UMNO won an absolute majority of seats in the parliament; it has held power in Malaysia ever since.

As with other single-party dictatorships, the UMNO has dealt with its share of factionalism.[72] Factionalization has only intensified as the party has incorporated new recruits. The influx of a younger generation of party officials in the UMNO created a class of individuals ready to question and criticize the choices of party leaders.[73] Because of factional competition, even the leader of the regime cannot always guarantee that his allies will attain key political posts. The preferred candidates of Prime Minister Mahathir bin Mohammad (prime minister from 1981 to 2003), for example, were defeated in the 1996 elections.[74] Mahathir frequently had to deal with criticism from party members, the rejections of his candidates, and complaints about his style of leadership.[75]

Factional conflicts within the UMNO have arisen over a variety of issues, like whether to pursue political reform. Much of the party's success, however, has been due to its relatively open internal dynamics, which allow for discussion and the expression of discontent.[76] Those who might consider leaving the party are ultimately contained by the belief that they can "legitimately wield state power through the UMNO-led government."[77] In this way, the UMNO serves as a "safety valve, giving vent to factional rivalries in ways to mitigate those rivalries."[78]

Joining a faction within the UMNO is typically preferable for party elites than leaving the party. Even in tough economic times (when elites have fewer resources to keep their patronage networks flowing), elites are usually better off sticking with the party. In hard times, UMNO elites "find even fewer clientelist resources outside their dominant party. They are thus motivated to join factions, but seldom to defect."[79] In spite of the disregard with which many party elites began to view Mahathir, very few actually left the UMNO.[80] Far from hurting the regime, factionalism in many ways has helped the UMNO survive in power for over fifty years.

Taiwan (1949–2000)

Though Taiwan is now a democracy, for over half a century it was governed by the Nationalist/Kuomintang (KMT) party. The KMT ruled many parts of China from 1928, until it was forced to retreat to Taiwan in 1949. Even though Taiwan is no longer considered authoritarian, the KMT currently holds a majority of seats (71 percent in the 2008 elections) in the Taiwanese legislature and is still a major player in Taiwanese politics.

The KMT was ruled for over 25 years by Chiang Kai-shek, until his death in 1975. Though Chiang Kai-shek was a dominant force in Taiwan, his power was tempered by factionalism within the KMT. As such, Chiang Kai-shek was careful not to push for policies beyond what was acceptable to elites within the ruling party.[81] The party's pragmatism "invited criticism in top level political circles and later broad-based discussion, fanning the flames . . . and the development of factions."[82] KMT legislative sessions were filled with furious debate over the direction of the country and which economic and foreign policies would be most conducive to growth and stability. As factions competed for power and the promotion of their policies, disputes were so intense that it made it difficult to maintain KMT unity.[83]

When Chiang Ching-kuo took over after his father Chiang Kai-shek passed away, factionalism in the KMT remained as intense as ever. Despite Chiang Ching-kuo's efforts to purge potential rivals, factional challengers in the KMT remained.[84] Pervasive factionalism within the KMT kept Chiang Ching-kuo's power in line. It may have even contributed to Taiwan's prudent economic policies, by subjecting proposed policies to criticism from a variety of actors. In many ways, factionalism in Taiwan helped strengthen the KMT regime, "by checking Caesarian rule and allowing the representation of diverse social interests."[85]

Survival of the Regimes

All of the parties of the single-party dictatorships from Asia discussed here are still in power today, despite the fact that each has been characterized by factionalism in one form or another. Rather than destabilizing the regime, factionalization can help prolong it.

These cases illustrate that factionalism requires skillful negotiations on the part of party leaders and forces them to contend with differing viewpoints. Nevertheless, it can be healthy for single-party regimes. It provides an outlet for intra-party elite competition and pushes regimes to adapt in the face of changing times. These, perhaps unintended, effects of factionalism, ultimately enhance the longevity of single-party regimes and ensure the party's continued survival in power.

Single-party Authoritarian Politics in Mexico (1929–2000)

The Institutional Revolutionary Party's (PRI) hold on power in Mexico constitutes one of the longest in modern history. For the greater part of a century, the PRI dominated the Mexican government. The PRI is typically considered a hegemonic party system, as it relied more on the strategy of co-optation than the use of repression or electoral fraud. Key to the PRI's survival in power was its ability to generate mass support and deter elite defections. In this case study, we show how the PRI's use of the full range of strategies, available to single-party dictatorships, helped ensure its survival in power.

The PRI was in many ways a catch-all party, as it located itself in the center of the ideological spectrum, but with a wide radius. This made it harder for leftist and rightist opposition groups to cooperate with one another and coalesce in such a way that they could challenge the PRI's power.[86]

Like many single-party dictatorships, Mexico under the PRI was well institutionalized. The PRI was adept at structuring a highly organized party apparatus, so that it could "compete in elections and control important sectors of society through the PRI's corporatist structure."[87] This high level of institutionalization helps to explain the PRI's durability, as it signified the party's entrenchment in society, the sophistication of its patronage networks, and its ability to regulate party members, as well as voter behavior.

One of the defining features of Mexico under the PRI was the *sexenio*, the strict six-year term limit that presidents were forced to adhere to. This provision ensured that no single individual could amass too much power and provided party elites with an incentive to remain in the game (as they too could soon be president) and wait their turn.[88] Such established provisions for leadership turnover mitigated intra-party tensions by easing competition within the party.[89] Though the *sexenio* meant that there would be hard-fought battles over nomination to the presidency every six years, it also meant that the party would remain more powerful than any one individual and that party elites could always hold on to the promise that they might one day secure the party's nomination for president.

The PRI engaged in expensive efforts to generate support among key sectors of the populace, through its campaign efforts, as well as its patronage networks. Such efforts were critical to the PRI's survival, not only for securing mass support, but for purveying an image within the party of invulnerability. Magaloni describes the tactics of the PRI well:

> During the golden years of the PRI, elections were regularly won by huge margins of victory. One key reason the PRI placed a lot of emphasis in mobilizing voters to the polls even when elections were not competitive was to deter elites from splitting. The PRI developed complex networks of organizations and activities to mobilize voter turnout and distributed particularistic material rewards—everything from land titles to construction materials to public sector jobs—prior to elections. Given that elections were not competitive, high voter turnout was intended to generate a public signal about the regime's strength that was mainly intended to deter disaffected politicians from defecting the ruling party—even when elections were not competitive.[90]

These costly tactics, though at the surface paradoxical, helped ensure the PRI's continued survival in power. Fraud was not enough to keep it in power. The PRI had to ensure that sufficiently tantalizing rewards were doled out to supporters so that it could generate high voter turnout and communicate to potential defectors from the party, that the party was strong. In turn, party elites remained within the party because, doing so, best guaranteed their own access to government office.

Breakdown of the Regime

Factionalism within the PRI was quite common. Joy Langston claims that "from the creation of the PRI in 1929 until the 1997 legislative elections, the sharpest challenges to the regime came from internal splits, not opposition party electoral victories."[91] One of the most famous (and devastating) party splits took place in the 1980s. Left-wing members of the party formed a political group within it called the Democratic Current/Corriente

Democrática (CD), led by Cuauhtémoc Cárdenas, Porfirio Muñoz Ledo, Carlos Tello, Ifigenia Martínez, and Rodolfo González Guevara.[92] The CD took issue with the process of succession under the regime, particularly the ability of the incumbent president to essentially handpick his successor. The PRI tried to influence the behavior of the CD through threats and bribes, but in the end the CD split from the party when Cárdenas was denied the presidential nomination. Soon after, Cárdenas ran as presidential candidate for the Democratic National Front (Frente Democrático Nacional), a loose alliance of leftist parties.

Though many identify the CD's split from the party as integral to the PRI's downfall, this action in actuality was a symptom of larger problems that the party faced. As with many single-party dictatorships, factionalization was not the cause of the PRI's ultimate fall from power.[93] Internal splits over nominations for the presidency, for example, occurred every six years; the party clearly had few troubles surviving them.

The 1994 peso crisis took a disastrous toll on the Mexican economy and undermined the PRI's ability to maintain its patronage networks. Because this was not the first economic downturn in Mexico, voters were not very forgiving.[94] As increasing numbers of voters no longer had an economic incentive to support the PRI, they defected from the party and dedicated their support to the opposition. In response to this, party elites who may have at one point considered defecting from the party saw the opportunity to do so as the party appeared weak.

In June 2000, presidential elections were held. Cárdenas ran under the leftist Party of the Democratic Revolution (PRD) and took 17 percent of the votes; PRI candidate Francisco Labastida received 36 percent; and Vicente Fox, of the conservative National Action Party (PAN) won 43 percent of the votes. Fox was elected president, and the 80 plus years of PRI dominance were officially over.

Summary and Conclusion

Single-party dictatorships often appear to be democracies in disguise. Many have elections and functioning legislatures; some even allow other political parties to compete for posts. Behind their seemingly democratic façade, however, lurks a highly institutionalized and entrenched party machine, a regime that continuously monitors and controls society and will resort to repression or fraud if its dominance is in any way threatened.

Single-party dictatorships are remarkably durable regimes. Their longevity is in many ways attributable to their reliance on nominally democratic institutions. Single-party dictatorships engage in multiple strategies that draw elites (and the public at large) into the political process, giving them something at stake in the regime's survival. The structure of single-party dictatorships is such that party elites are usually better off working together, even when they disagree, than defecting from the party and joining the opposition. As such, these regimes are surprisingly resilient and able to withstand political change and internal division.

In this chapter, we examined a variety of facets of single-party dictatorship. We showed the multiple ways in which these regimes are similar, and also the important ways that they differ. In doing so, this chapter has helped explain how governance by a dominant political party can shape the incentives that political actors face and the strategies that they will pursue to ensure their political survival.

Review Questions

- In what way do single-party dictatorships seem like personalist dictatorships? In what way do they seem like democracies? In what way do they differ from both?
- What role does ideology play in single-party dictatorships?
- How is the relationship between the leader of a single party regime and other party elites characterized?
- Why are single-party regimes the most durable dictatorships?
- In what way were the leaders of the single-party regimes of Communist Eastern Europe unable to consolidate personal power? How did leadership transfers work in Communist Eastern Europe? What caused the downfall of these regimes?
- In what way have the leaders of China, Malaysia and Taiwan been constrained by the party? How have factions enhanced the stability of these regimes?
- Why is Mexico under the PRI classified as a hegemonic party system? What explains the PRI's longevity? What caused its downfall?

Key Points

- Single-party regimes can be characterized according to the role of ideology and the use of repression.

- Single-party regimes are the most durable form of dictatorships because:
  - Party elites have more incentives to remain with the party than to defect
  - The party co-opts the opposition and creates different channels of within-regime participation
  - Factional disputes provide a safety valve to air grievances
  - Rules of succession are institutionalized
- The transitions from one leader to the next in single-party regimes are often relatively smooth.

Notes

1. Geddes, *What Do We Know* (1999).

2. Geddes, *Paradigms and Sand Castles* (2003, p. 53).

3. Huntington and Moore, *Authoritarian Politics in Modern* (1970).

4. Ibid. (p. 23).

5. Ibid. (p. 13).

6. Ibid. (pp. 40–41).

7. Magaloni, *Voting for Autocracy* (2006).

8. Sartori, *Parties and Party Systems* (1975, p. 230).

9. Magaloni, *Voting for Autocracy* (2006).

10. Ibid.

11. Ibid.

12. Ibid. (p. 10).

13. Castañeda, *Perpetuating Power: How Mexican* (2000).

14. Brooker, *Twentieth-century Dictatorships* (1995).

15. Ibid.

16. Hilter's regime is sometimes characterized as personalist.

17. Brooker, *Non-democratic Regimes* (2000, p. 4).

18. Geddes, *Paradigms and Sand Castles* (2003, p. 68).

19. Langston, *Breaking Out is Hard* (2002, p. 82).

20. Geddes, *What Do We Know* (1999)?

21. Ibid., (p. 129).

22. Smith, *Life of the Party* (2005).

23. Geddes, *What Do We Know* (1999)?

24. Magaloni, *Voting for Autocracy* (2006).

25. Nathan, *Authoritarian Resilience* (2003, p. 14).

26. Ibid.

27. Pike, *Origins of Leadership Change* (1989).

28. Koh, *Politics of a Divided Party* (2001).

29. Berg-Schlosser, *Democracy and the One-Party* (1989, p. 123).

30. Cheng, *Embracing Defeat: The KMT* (2008, p. 142).

31. Molomo, *Understanding Government and Opposition* (2000).

32. Tsie, *Political Context of Botswana's* (1996).

33. Makgala, 'So Far So Good'? (2003).

34. Geddes, *What Do We Know* (1999)?

35. Smith, *Life of the Party* (2005).

36. Geddes (1999, p. 131).

37. Granville, *First Domino: International Decision* (2004, p. 7).

38. Ibid.

39. Ibid.

40. Toma, *Revival of a Communist* (1961).

41. Gough, *A Good Comrade* (2006).

42. Batt, *Political Reform in Hungary* (1990).

43. Ibid.

44. Eindlin, *Two Faces of Czechoslovak* (1983).

45. Renner, *History of Czechoslovakia* (1989).

46. Ibid.

47. Ibid.

48. Eindlin, *Two Faces of Czechoslovak* (1983).

49. Granville, *East Germany in 1956,* (2006).

50. Fulbrook, *Anatomy of a Dictatorship* (1997).

51. Ibid.

52. Granville, *East Germany in 1956* (2006)

53. Sarotte, *Dealing with the Devil* (2001); Grieder, *East German Leadership* (1999).

54. Welsh, *Political Transition Processes* (1994, p. 384).

55. Though Taiwan has democratized, the Kuomintang Party (KMT) currently holds a majority of the seats in the legislature and the presidency.

56. Dittmer, *Leadership Change and Chinese* 2003

57. Huang, *Factionalism in Chinese Communist* (2000).

58. Nathan, *Factional Model for CCP* 1973; Huang, *Factionalism in Chinese Communist* (2000).

59. Nathan, *Factional Model for CCP* (1973, p. 54).

60. Ibid., (p. 62).

61. Huang, *Factionalism in Chinese Communist* (2000).

62. Dittmer, *Leadership Change and Chinese* (2003).

63. Hussein, *Some Emerging Trends* (1985).

64. Huang, *Factionalism in Chinese Communist* (2000).

65. Cheng and White, *Sixteenth Central Committee* (2003).

66. Xie, *Semi-hierarchical Totalitarian Nature* (1993).

67. Cheng and White, *Sixteenth Central Committee,* (2003, p. 593).

68. Perry, *Studying Chinese Politics* (2007).

69. Dittmer and Wu, *Modernization of Factionalism* (1995).

70. Nathan, *Factional Model for CCP* (1973).

71. Huang, *Factionalism in Chinese Communist* (2000, p. 29).

72. Case, *Semi-Democracy in Malaysia* (1993).

73. Crouch, *Government and Society* (1996).

74. Case, *1996 UMNO Party Election* (1997).

75. Case, *Comparative Malaysian Leadership* (1991); *New Uncertainties* (2004).

76. Ibid.

77. Alagappa, *Political Legitimacy in Southeast* (1995, p. 72).

78. Case, *UMNO Party Election* (1994, p. 929).

79. Case, *New Uncertainties* (2004, p. 101).

80. Ibid.

81. Roy, *Taiwan: A Political History* (2003).

82. Hood, *Political Change in Taiwan* (1996, p. 469).

83. Ibid.

84. Roy, *Taiwan: A Political History* (2003).

85. Cheng and Haggard, *Taiwan in Transition* (2000, p. 72).

86. Ortiz, *Comparing Types of Transitions* (2000).

87. Ibid., (pp. 68–69).

88. Geddes, *Party Creation*, (2008).

89. Ibid.

90. Magaloni, *Voting for Autocracy* (2006, p. 5).

91. Langston, *Breaking Out is Hard* (2002, p. 65).

92. Ibid.

93. Magaloni, *Voting for Autocracy* (2006).

94. Ibid.

Personalist Dictatorships in Sub-Saharan Africa and Beyond

Personalist dictatorships are perhaps the most colorful of all forms of dictatorship. With all power in the hands of a single individual, policies are often a reflection of personal whims and impulses; no actors exist that can temper the leader's behavior, even if it is eccentric. In this chapter, we provide an in-depth analysis of personalist dictatorships or "one man rule." We discuss the internal structure of these regimes, their patterns of behavior, and the strategies that leaders employ to secure their political survival.

What is Personalist Dictatorship?

Personalist dictatorships are regimes in which a single individual controls politics. In personalist dictatorships, one person "dominates the military, state apparatus, and ruling party (if one exists)."[1] No autonomous institutions exist independent of the leader. Though the leader may ally with or create a political party, it is merely a tool of the leader. Personalist dictators are often current or former members of the military; once in power, however, the military is completely subordinate to them. They differ from military and single-party dictatorships in that neither a party nor the military has a role in policy-making nor in the determination of the selection of successive leaders.[2] Instead the dictator controls all policy decisions and the distribution of political posts.

Personalist dictators rule with extreme freedom, allowing for eccentric policies. Examples abound. Muammar al-Gaddafi of Libya replaced the Gregorian calendar with a solar calendar, changing all of the months with names that he invented himself.[3] Hastings Banda of Malawi decreed that women were forbidden from wearing pants. Francisco Macias Nguema of Equatorial Guinea banned all modern drugs from his country, even during a horrible cholera outbreak.[4] As Samuel Decalo puts it, "Personalist dictatorship may be defined as an authoritarian system of social repression set by an individual—civilian or military—in which, whether social or political structures are pro forma retained or not, all policy dictates derive from him and all of society is viewed as his personal fief."[5]

Personalist dictators handpick a group of individuals to assist them in governing, often referred to as the personalist clique. These individuals are typically friends or family members of the leader. The balance of power between the leader and the clique is tilted significantly in the leader's favor; as such, personalist dictators face few checks on their power. Regimes are characterized as personalist, when "the right to rule is ascribed to a person rather than an office" despite the official existence of a written constitution.[6]

Unlike other types of authoritarian regimes, with personalist dictatorships the line between the leader of the regime and the regime itself is often blurred. Though personalist dictatorships occasionally survive the death or retirement of the leader, intra-regime leadership turnover is relatively rare.

Definition of Personalist Dictatorship

- One-man rule; power is exclusively in the hands of a single individual
- No autonomous institutions
- Military is subordinate to the leader
- Political parties, if they exist, have no de facto power
- Policy choices are determined by the leader
- No checks on the leader's power
- A clique of the leader's friends and/or family members assists in governing

Theoretical Analyses of Personalist Dictatorships

Personalist dictatorships have long captured the attentions of scholars, and the literature devoted to them is quite rich. The fascination with these regimes is in many ways driven by their often capricious and eccentric behavior. With all power concentrated in the hands of a single individual, anything the leader wants the leader gets. Even the most irrational and impulsive policies are possible. In this section, we present key themes in the literature on personalist dictatorships.

Types of Personalist Rule

Sultanism

Sultanism is a regime type that H. E. Chehabi and Juan Linz[7] examine in depth. The term "sultanism" was originally coined by Max Weber.[8] Sultanist regimes are essentially a subset of personalist dictatorships. They are an extreme form of patrimonialism characterized by personal rule and constitutional hypocrisy, "where loyalty to the ruler is motivated by a mixture of fear and rewards to his collaborators."[9] Sultanist regimes are not based on any particular ideology, nor on the leader's personal mission or charismatic legitimacy. Sultanist regimes are distinct from totalitarian dictatorships in that the use of terror is not ideologically motivated and there is no effort on the part of the regime to mobilize the population. Instead, in sultanist regimes, the goal of the ruler is to use power to private ends that can be enjoyed by the ruler and distributed to loyal collaborators.[10]

Absent effective political institutions, sultanist regimes are characterized by the predominance of personal authority, the arbitrary use of power, and the fusion of public and private. Corruption and cronyism are rampant, and the economy is constantly subject to government intervention for the purpose of extracting resources for the leader.[11]

Sultanist regimes maintain power through the extensive use of fear. Political officials maintain their posts contingent on their loyalty to the leader. As such, officials enjoy little job security and can be hired and fired at a moment's notice. Sultanist regimes stay in power by doling out material rewards to key sectors of society; they co-opt parts of society through patronage, undermining the growth of any viable opposition.[12] Co-optation is selective, so as to build the narrow social base of support that the regime needs to maintain control.

Sultanist regimes are unlikely to successfully transition to democracy.[13] Because the leader has penetrated the state and all levels of society, political institutions must be built from scratch. When these regimes do fall, democratization is rare.

Prophetic, Princely, Autocratic, and Tyrannical Dictatorships

Personalist dictatorships are divided into four types by Robert Jackson and Carl Rosberg:[14] prophet, prince, autocrat, and tyrant. The authors use cases from Africa to inform their typology.

The prophet type of personalist leader comes to power with a vision for structuring society. Ideology is heavily emphasized, and the goals of the leader are greater than just staying in power. The princely type of personalist leader rules through patron-client relations. The leader strategically manipulates supporters, forcing them to compete with one another to stay in the leader's good favor. The autocrat type of personalist leader is very similar to the princely type. The autocratic leader rules by ensuring the support of a few key sectors of the society, but does so by command, rather than by strategizing. Lastly, the tyrant type of personalist leader exercises power without restraint. The tyrannical dictator is the most corrupt, with fear used as the main tool for survival. Violence is widespread and often arbitrarily exerted.

Whereas the prophet type of regime is based on the goals of the dictator, the prince, autocrat, and tyrant types are based on the means by which the leader maintains power. The prince rules through strategic manipulation, the autocrat rules by commanding and managing the country, and the tyrant rules by sheer terror. By contrast, the prophet type seeks to reorder society to conform to the leader's ideological vision.

Prophetic, Princely, Autocratic, and Tyrannical Dictatorships (Jackson and Rosberg)

Prophet

- Role of Ideology: strong
- Main goal: restructure society
- Tool of survival: society is loyal since it has been restructured to conform to the leader's vision

⇨

Prince

- Role of ideology: weak
- Main goal: stay in power
- Tool of survival: patron-client ties, divide and rule, strategic manipulation

Autocrat

- Role of ideology: weak
- Main goal: stay in power
- Tool of survival: force and management of the country

Tyrant

- Role of ideology: weak
- Main goal: arbitrary use of power
- Tool of survival: terror and fear

The Structure of Personalist Dictatorships

The structure of personalist dictatorships varies significantly from regime to regime depending on the particular preferences of the leader in charge. In all personalist dictatorships, the leader is at the top of the political hierarchy and wields disproportionate political power.

Personalist dictatorships also rarely—if ever—have institutional provisions for leadership turnover. Because of this, personalist leaders are frequently more paranoid about their political futures than are their counterparts in other dictatorships. Lacking clearly defined rules for how long they will rule and who will succeed them when they retire, personalist dictators often live in constant fear that rivals are plotting to overtake them.[15] In spite of their vast power and freedom, personalist dictators feel that they can trust no one. They have no means of ensuring that their subordinates are telling them the truth, as subordinates have few incentives to do so if it means displeasing the dictator.

Beyond this, however, there are few commonalities in the internal design of personalist regimes. Some have political parties, legislatures, and elections, while others do not. Some have a single military force, while others operate multiple military and paramilitary units. Some personalist dictatorships have a clearly defined internal structure; while in others have rules that are unclear or unknown.

Most personalist dictatorships use some mixture of fear and rewards to stay in power. In some, fear is the predominant tool used, while in others nurturing loyalty is more relied upon. The typical personalist dictatorship is described well by Decalo:

> The personal dictator possesses maximum power to the extent feasible within a given society. Socio-economic patronage and plunder, coupled with status and prestige, are the glue that binds his cohorts to himself. He rules in an absolute imperial manner often for the sole purpose of self-gratification or glorification, molding society in his own image and exploiting it to his own advantage. Personal dictators create a vast societal void within which they often enact their personal fantasies and whims, a vacuum that is particularly destabilizing for successor regimes.[16]

Politics in personalist dictatorships is inextricable from the dominant presence of the regime leader, who can shape society how he pleases, and extract resources from the state unabatedly. The extent to which personalist dictators will pursue such measures depends on the nature of the particular leader in power.

Key Attributes of Personalist Dictatorships

- Leader at the helm of political system
- Internal structure varies markedly across regimes, depending on what the leader's preferences are
- Mixture of fear and rewards used to maintain political power

The Durability of Personalist Dictatorships

Personalist dictatorships are unique in that in no other type of dictatorship does the regime center solely on the political power of a single individual. Though personalist dictatorships are durable regimes, their distinctive structure makes it difficult for them to survive beyond the tenure of the dictator. For this reason, personalist dictatorships exhibit lower average survival rates than single-party dictatorships, which are better designed for handling leadership succession. In this section, we discuss the tools that personalist dictatorships use to maintain their hold on power.

Repression

One of the most obvious tools at the disposal of personalist dictatorships is repression. Violently suppressing internal dissent or challenges to their power is an easy way for personalist dictators to deal with threats. Indeed, personalist dictatorships are known for their brutality. Capable of ruling without restraint—and faced with heightened uncertainty regarding their political survival—personalist dictators often resort to repression and brutality to sustain their hold on power.

This is not to say that other types of dictatorships are not also brutal, as the regimes of Cambodia under the Khmer Rouge or Myanmar under the Burmese military junta illustrate. Though dictatorships of all sorts are prone to the use of violence and repression towards the masses, personalist dictatorships are the most capable of doing this towards *elites*. As discussed in **Chapter 6**, purges of the elite corps are common in personalist dictatorships. Because personalist dictatorships do not contend with an institutionalized or organized elite support group, leaders can treat individual elites with brutality without facing punishment from the larger elite corps.

Elites who are intellectuals are often the targets of personalist dictators' brutality, as they are viewed as potential rivals. Idi Amin of Uganda is a case in point. He is rumored to have killed anywhere from 100,000 to 600,000 intellectuals during his time in power.[17] Intellectuals were also hunted down during the regime of Nguema in Equatorial Guinea[18] and treated with great suspicion during the regimes of Kwame Nkrumah of Ghana and Sékou Touré of Guinea.

In personalist dictatorships, even the slightest internal dissent is usually not tolerated. The power of the personalist dictator goes unchecked, leaving greater room for brutality and repression.[19] Personalist dictators in Africa, for example, have carried out systemic atrocities against their populations, as the regimes of Charles Taylor of Liberia, Amin of Uganda, Jean-Bédel Bokassa of the Central African Republic, and Teodoro Obiang Nguema Mbasogo of Equatorial Guinea illustrate.

Saddam Hussein of Iraq is also remembered for his brutality. When Hussein took power in 1979, he met with all of his senior officials, identified 21 so-called traitors, and then executed the alleged traitors in front of the other officials.[20] Any individuals who made suggestions Hussein disliked were typically killed. During the Iran-Iraq war, for example, the Minister of Health made the mistake of recommending that Hussein step down from power temporarily in order to comply with Iran's stated terms for peace. He was thanked for his candor and then returned to his wife chopped up into pieces in a body bag.[21]

Select Patronage Networks

When personalist dictatorships are not using fear to engender the loyalty of elites (and select sectors of the masses), they are using patronage. Personalist dictatorships are systems that link rulers "not with the 'public' or even with the ruled (at least not directly) but with patrons, associates, clients, supporters, and rivals, who constitute the 'system.'"[22] Low levels of institutionalization make it easy for personalist dictators to create patronage networks that suit their needs. Because leaders control the flow of the state's revenues, they can reward whoever they please. In personalist dictatorships, "the interaction between the big man and his extended retinue defines . . . politics, from the highest reaches of the presidential palace to the humblest village assembly."[23]

The size of the personalist dictator's patronage network is typically kept as small as possible, with resources distributed to select individuals of critical importance to the dictator's survival. The primary recipients of the dictator's largesse are typically members of the dictator's personalist clique or entourage. The leader's family members, ethnic/tribal members, and cronies are usually well-paid in personalist regimes.[24] Because the size of the patronage network is small, poor economic performance is not necessarily destabilizing for personalist dictatorships, so long as there are sufficient funds to pad the wallets of the dictator's key supporters.[25]

By doling out perks to their supporters, personalist dictatorships ensure that these individuals are dependent on the regime for their livelihood, giving them something at stake in the regime's survival.[26] In some personalist dictatorships, in fact, civil servants benefit more from the distribution of patronage than from their actual salaries. According to Jay Ulfelder, the durability of personalist dictatorships "depends largely on bargains among cliques with no claim to grass roots, so ruling elites are freer to ignore popular challenges or to suppress them vigorously when they occur."[27] Such patron-client relationships are fostered in order to bind dictators' followers more blindly to their rule.

Cults of Personality

Personalist dictators also use cults of personality to generate support for the regime. With personality cults, the leader claims to embody the state, such that the concepts of leader and state are fused together, and the "disposition of the regime is synonymous with the personal fate of the supreme ruler."[28] This fusion makes it possible for the dictator to concentrate power. Supporters perceive leaders as "superhuman, blindly believe them, follow them unconditionally, and give them unqualified emotional support."[29] Leaders are romanticized and portrayed as the savior of the masses, making the masses feel dependent on the regime. This leads to an intense and unquestioning loyalty to the leader on behalf of the public.[30]

Charisma is often critical to the leader's success in creating a cult of personality. This charisma is often manifested in "the expression of fervent devotion in a cult of the leader's personality."[31] Followers identify with the leader based on the leader's personal attributes, rather than the values or ideas that the leader represents. The media also plays an important role, as it serves as a vehicle for distributing personalist cult propaganda.[32] Images of the leader pervade society, and objects that glorify the leader are omnipresent.

Personality cults are useful because they help engender the population's obedience to the dictator. By infusing the public space with thematic messages emphasizing the dictator's exceptional powers, leaders generate support for their tenures without having to resort to force; society comes to believe that "the leader possesses exceptional personal, intellectual, oratorical, diplomatic, or other abilities."[33]

Divide and Conquer

To deter the formation of groups that could challenge the regime's power, personalist dictatorships often employ the strategy of "divide and conquer," which entails keeping elites in competition with one another while getting rid of those individuals who start exerting too much power. Personalist dictators must constantly mitigate threats to their power, whether from the military, a political party, or the public at large.[34] To do so, they frequently shuffle positions from one person to the next and hire and fire individuals in ways that generate suspicion and competition among elites. This creates an environment of high uncertainty, where elites are perennially on their toes, preventing the cohesion of any particular group. It also keeps potential rivals from developing their own power bases.[35]

Threats from the military are particularly troublesome for personalist dictators. To keep the threat of a military coup at bay, personalist dictators often divide the military into multiple forces and create paramilitary forces to serve as a challenge to the military. In Iraq, for example, Hussein operated several militias, with the most loyal given the task of guarding Hussein's personal safety. The less loyal Hussein deemed a fighting force to be, the more remote the location it was required to operate from. Personalist dictators further weaken the threat from the military by intervening strategically in military promotions, undermining power-sharing agreements between factions within the military, and forcing powerful officers into early retirement.[36]

Because of the strategy of divide and conquer, personalist dictatorships are often characterized by a high turnover of personnel. This is done to regulate and control rent seeking and to prevent any potential challengers from gaining too much power.[37]

External Threats to Survival

It is uncommon for personalist dictatorships to fall from power due to internal divisions or the defection of elites from the leader's support group. Personalist dictators also rarely voluntarily step down. These conditions make regime change unlikely to be initiated from within personalist dictatorships, as leaders typically hold on to power until the very end.[38] Personal rulers seldom push for political liberalization or relinquish power without a struggle; they have to be forced out. Elites are also unlikely to push for reform, as their political futures are intimately tied to the future of the regime. Lacking an independent power base, elites in personalist dictatorships are "much less likely to find respected places in the post-transition political world than are close supporters of single-party and military regimes."[39] As such, barring the death of the dictator, transitions are often driven from outside of the government, whether through mass uprisings or foreign intervention.

Because personalist dictators cling so tightly onto power, they often do not step down even in the face of serious military threats. Hussein, for example, refused to believe that the end was near when the United States threatened in 2003 that it would soon invade Iraq. Hussein was deposed shortly after by US forces and executed three years later. Personalist regimes' exit from power can be protracted and painful, since leaders "tenaciously" try to "control the transition."[40]

Case Studies

This section provides a selection of case studies to offer a glimpse inside the fascinating world of personalist dictatorships. Because personalist dictatorships have been particularly common in sub-Saharan Africa, we draw from cases in this region. We close with a case study from Haiti to illustrate the dynamics of a personalist dictatorship in which multiple leaders rule. Key points mentioned in this and earlier chapters are highlighted throughout, so as to tightly integrate the theory with reality.

Power unchecked in the Central African Republic (1966–1979)

Bokassa was at the helm of a personalist dictatorship in the Central African Republic for around 13 years. Free to act how he pleased, Bokassa often engaged in erratic behavior; few would challenge his authority. Because no domestic actors could constrain Bokassa's power, his ultimate demise came at the hands of his former benefactor, France. In this case study, we show how power went unchecked in the Central African Republic under Bokassa.

Bokassa took over the Central African Republic in 1966, after overthrowing his cousin, then-President David Dacko, in a coup on December 31, 1965. Bokassa quickly got rid of most government institutions, dissolving the National Assembly and invalidating the constitution.[41] Bokassa's goal was to concentrate power into his own hands and weaken any individual or organization that could pose a threat to him. He designated himself president for life and allowed only one political party to operate, the Movement for the Social Evolution of Black Africa (MESAN), which was built for the sole purpose of serving Bokassa's interests.[42] Bokassa consolidated his grip over the country by holding all of the key civilian and military posts in government. He was in charge of multiple ministerial portfolios, including National Defense, Interior, Information, Agriculture, Military Aviation, Public Service, and Social Security. With few institutions remaining to challenge him, Bokassa ruled with a free hand.[43]

Having destroyed his country's political institutions, no powers existed that could control Bokassa's actions. This vast power and freedom, paradoxically, made Bokassa hypersensitive that rivals were plotting to oust him. To strengthen his hold on power in the face of such perceived threats, Bokassa created a cult of personality. He portrayed himself as the father of the nation and referred to himself by the nickname Papa Bok.[44] He had schools, institutions, military caps, and roads (among others) named after him.[45] His image appeared everywhere, including on clothing, and he typically adorned himself in public with an assortment of medals.[46]

Because of his paranoia that individuals were seeking to overthrow him, Bokassa trusted no one beyond his immediate family.[47] Though he was less skeptical about the loyalty of other members of his ethnic group, for the most part Bokassa kept a close eye on everyone around him.[48] He preferred to surround himself with sycophants, and made sure that key security positions were held by his most loyal kinsmen. Individuals viewed as remotely threatening were fired or reassigned if they were lucky; many simply disappeared.[49]

Because Bokassa's power went unchecked by other domestic actors, his eccentric behavior was also free to run wild. He was incredibly vain and craved constant adulation and glorification.[50] He was also highly extravagant. Bokassa frequently held lavish parties and spent $22 million on his own coronation in 1977 (which comprised 24 percent of the Central African Republic's national revenues).[51] This coronation occurred because Bokassa had, on a whim, created an imperial constitution, converted to Catholicism, and declared himself Emperor.[52] Bokassa frequently wore outrageous attire during his public appearances, such as medallion-encrusted tunics and pompous uniforms. Of course, if Bokassa was ever mocked for such behavior, he would lash out violently.[53]

Bokassa's unchecked power is also reflected in his brutality. He was known to personally take part in the beating and torture of alleged dissidents. Upon taking power, Bokassa killed and purged any suspected rivals; aides seen as disloyal were executed promptly.[54] Even children were subject to Bokassa's extreme brutality. When a group of school children refused to buy uniforms being sold by one of his cronies, Bokassa had them arrested, and many were said to have been murdered.[55] Bokassa was capable of acting however he pleased, regardless of the rationale or cruelty of his decisions.

Breakdown of the Regime

Bokassa's reign over the Central African Republic could not last forever. Though France had initially supported Bokassa, by 1979 it could no longer turn a blind eye to his violent behavior. In September of that year, French troops staged a coup while Bokassa was out of the country and restored Dacko in power (who surprisingly was still alive).

Incompetence in Uganda (1971–1979)

Though Uganda has been ruled by multiple personalist dictatorships, Amin's regime is perhaps the most notorious. Amin dominated Uganda for eight years, maintaining power through a mixture of fear and patronage, like many personalist dictators. In this case study, we highlight the incompetence of the Amin government. This incompetence was the result of two factors: Amin's exclusion of those individuals who could provide him with expertise and Amin's own lack of qualifications for governing.

Amin came to power in 1971 via a military coup that ousted former military colleague Milton Obote, an act that was greeted by cheering crowds.[56] Viewed as a charismatic individual, Amin communicated with the masses directly in tribal languages and frequently made public appearances.[57] Amin was known to be eccentric and was obsessed with being respected. For example, he insisted on being referred to by the title, "His Excellency the President of the Republic of Uganda, General al Haji Idi Amind Dada, VC, DSO, MC."[58] Radio Kampala was ordered to make multiple references to him throughout the day.

In addition to these qualities, Amin was also easily threatened by those around him. Individuals deemed to be more educated or competent than Amin were fired. Promotions in the military were given to individuals who had little experience or education, and uneducated military officers were assigned important positions in the government.[59] Educated officials were often purged on the basis that they were disloyal and typically replaced by novices.[60]

Amin was known to exercise extreme brutality toward his staff out of suspicions of their disloyalty. Aides, cabinet members, and servants were all often treated with cruelty. Any civil servant who disputed Amin was dealt with severely. Because of his obsession with rivals, throngs of Amin's supposed enemies were purged, jailed, or killed.[61]

Amin preferred to surround himself with family members, close friends, and fellow tribe members—since loyalty was of much greater value to him than experience or knowledge.[62] All of these actions greatly reduced the competence of government employees. Amin's constant (and unpredictable) personnel turnovers (intended to keep military and civilian officials on their toes) did nothing to improve this.[63]

Amin's own incompetence only compounded matters. He had little idea how to run a government. Many of his policies were contradictory; most were ineffective. Amin felt uncomfortable presiding over cabinet meetings, refused to read government reports, and put little effort into learning how the government worked.[64] Policy making was done in a spontaneous and an ad hoc manner. Amin preferred to rely on soothsayers, dreams, or his gut instincts to make decisions, than on expert advice.[65] When he did consult with others, it was in the form of campfire chats. Policies were implemented via personal decree and announced through Radio Kampala.[66] Any government institutions that Amin had not dissolved already, he put into states of paralysis through his erratic rule.[67]

The incompetence of Amin's government took a heavy toll on Uganda. Amin overspent government funds, pushing the country into a huge deficit; in response, he merely printed more money.[68] Having plunged the economy into debt, Amin decided to stop paying state employees, in particular the military.[69] Social services were non-existent, as were local government and public works; crop output plummeted and most manufacturing was halted.[70] Simply put, Amin's policies and excesses "drained the nation's human and financial resources."[71]

Breakdown of the Regime

Amin's fall from power was precipitated by his decision in 1978 to annex a piece of Tanzanian territory, known as Kagera Salient. Tanzania responded with force, Ugandan troops were driven out of Tanzania, and Tanzanian troops invaded Uganda to oust Amin. When Amin's troops realized that he would soon be overthrown, they mutinied or deserted.[72] In 1979, Tanzanian forces claimed victory, and Amin was forced into exile in Libya.

Divide and Conquer in Zaire (1965–1997)

Joseph Mobutu became the president of Zaire (today's Democratic Republic of Congo) in 1965 following a bloodless coup that had the backing of the

United States.[74] Mobutu swiftly moved to dismantle government institutions by claiming a state of emergency. He would dominate the political sphere of Zaire for more than 30 years until his overthrow in the First Congo War. The longevity of Mobutu's rule is a testament to the strategies that he employed to stay in power. This case study examines Mobutu's use of one strategy in particular, "divide and conquer," which enabled Mobutu to deny elites (and other sectors of the public) opportunities to collaborate against him.

Upon his assumption of power, Mobutu consolidated power by publicly executing political rivals, secessionists, coup plotters, and other potential threats to his rule. Some of these killings took place before a live audience. Mobutu claimed that you had to create a "spectacular example" to ensure "regime discipline."[74] Mobutu quickly became the sole source of decision making in Zaire. He expected his decisions to be unquestionably obeyed, declaring: "when a chief takes a decision, he decides—period."[75]

One of Mobutu's strengths was his understanding of political symbolism. Mobutu fostered a cult of personality by ensuring that his image was everywhere. Government officials were forced to attach his picture on their lapels and were instructed to wear Mobutu-style suits instead of Western suits.[76] To strengthen his personality cult, Mobutu created the philosophy of Mobutism, which intertwined nationalism with a number of his musings in ways that engendered obedience toward him.[77] He gave himself the title, Father of the Nation and Savior of the People. To promote this vision of himself, every night prior to the evening news Mobutu's image would descend through the clouds from the heavens.[78] By 1975, Mobutu ordered that no one else in the government could be mentioned by name except himself, so that he, in essence, was the only person who mattered.[79]

Mobutu was strategic is his treatment of elites and key sectors of society. He fragmented those sectors that could challenge him and rewarded the individuals and groups that supported him. He used patronage to create faithful fans and distributed it in a dramatic fashion to serve his interests. When state transport workers went on strike, for example, Mobutu responded by personally discussing the problems with their leaders and then firing the Belgian director of the company on television.[80] Mobutu deliberately repressed or co-opted members of the opposition in ways that would buttress his power, while intentionally exacerbating regional and ethnic divisions in Zaire to keep the opposition divided.[81] He used his extensive patronage network to intensify Zairian ethnic divisions and splinter the coalescence of a formidable opposition. Though there was no shortage of opposition parties, they "were based outside the country and seemed unlikely to pose a threat to the regime."[82]

Mobutu also co-opted potential enemies, using a patronage network to "limit the growth of opposition."[83] He used promotions as a way of maintaining proximity to his rivals, while also firing them to create an environment of uncertainty. Nguza Karl-i-Bond, for example, was an opponent of Mobutu during the 1960s. Mobutu co-opted Karl-i-bond by making him foreign minister in the 1970s. Though Karl-i-bond was accused of treason and sentenced to death in 1977, Mobutu spared his life and made him Prime Minister in 1979. Only two years later, Karl-i-Bond was sent to live in exile, but by 1985 he was back on Mobutu's good side and made ambassador to the United States.[84]

Mobutu was particularly adept at dividing and conquering the military. He personally controlled the military and primarily filled it with officers from his own region, Equateur.[85] It was only close relatives, cronies, and members of the Ngbandi tribe who were granted the most important positions in the armed forces, making the military structure highly politicized.[86] Because the military's command structure was not institutionalized or hierarchical, Mobutu rotated officers' positions frequently and encouraged them to report any suspicious activity directly to him.[87] To create a sense of fear among members of the military, Mobutu purged over ten percent of the most promising officers in 1978. He also exploited ethno-regional divisions within the military to prevent it from becoming a cohesive force that could threaten his power. This ensured that there were no autonomous military factions.[88] To further contain the military's power, Mobutu created a 10,000-man "Guarde Civile" under the command of one of his closest associates, General Kpama Baramato.[89] Mobutu deliberately kept the military weak to deter the threat of a coup because he could never be sure of its loyalty.[90]

Mobutu was also tactical in his treatment of high-level government officials. He enjoyed rotating members of his government and cabinet so as to ensure that no individuals became too powerful and to make office holders feel uncertain and vulnerable about their political futures.[91] Government officials were frequently reminded that their terms were precarious and completely dependent on the whims of Mobutu. Access to power under

Mobutu depended on staying in Mobutu's good favor and, occasionally, on his mood, as the following analysis indicates:

> Individuals in public office are totally dependent on him for selection and maintenance of power. By frequently rotating government posts, Mobutu manages to maintain uncertainty and vulnerability. . . . He plays the role of big chief . . . bestowing favors on his subjects based on personal discretion.[92]

Mobutu's relationship with foreign powers was also calculated. He retained the support of key countries by cleverly emphasizing Zaire's strategic importance to the West, both economically and politically. Mobutu diversified sources of external support in order to limit the amount of leverage that any single foreign power had over him. This strategy guaranteed that Mobutu received large amount of economic aid to maintain his patronage network, which was the key to his continued rule.[93]

Of course, the divide and conquer strategy had negative effects on the efficiency of Zaire's bureaucracy. International lending institutions noted that the Zairian bureaucracy was "organized disorganization."[94] It also had negative consequences for the strength of Zaire's military in the face of external threats.

Breakdown of the Regime

Mobutu's skillful political moves kept him safe from internal threats to his power. Like many personalist dictators, his ultimate downfall came at the hands of external actors. Mobutu had openly supported Rwandan ethnic Hutus, angering ethnic Tutsis in the region. Between 1996 and 1997, Tutsi rebels successfully captured much of Eastern Zaire, while Mobutu sought medical treatment abroad. By May 1997, Tutsi rebels aligned with other anti-Mobutu forces in the region and Rwanda to capture the capital, Kinshasa, and force Mobutu into exile.[95]

Intra-Regime Leadership Succession in Haiti (1957–1986)

The Haitian personalist dictatorship under the Duvalier family is distinct in that it lasted well beyond the tenure of the regime's founder, François Duvalier.

Intra-regime leadership succession occurs infrequently in personalist dictatorships; when it does happen, the regime's founder is typically succeeded by his son or another male relative. The Haitian case is no different. Upon François Duvalier's death, his son Jean-Claude Duvalier assumed the leadership of Haiti. This case study details how the Duvaliers maintained their hold on Haiti and the factors that enabled the regime to outlast the term of the regime's founder.

François Duvalier (known as Papa Doc because he was a medical doctor) was elected president of Haiti in 1956. Backed by the military, Papa Doc won in a landslide. His decision to create a new constitution in 1957 sparked the beginning of his authoritarian rule.[96] By 1961, Papa Doc had transformed the legislature from a bicameral to a unicameral body and decided to run for re-election (which was banned in the 1957 constitution). He won these elections by a vote of 1,320,748 to zero. In 1964, Papa Doc announced that he was president for life.[97]

To stay in power, Papa Doc implemented a variety of strategies typical of personalist dictatorships. He fostered a cult of personality by placing portraits of himself everywhere, some of which conveyed the message that he was chosen by Jesus Christ to lead Haiti. In one such portrait, Papa Doc stood next to an image of Jesus Christ with his hand on Papa Doc's shoulder, along with a caption that read, "I have chosen him."[98] Papa Doc portrayed himself as one with the state, claiming that he was the Haitian flag and that anyone who was his enemy was the enemy of the fatherland.[99] These actions all created a paternalistic image of Papa Doc. Papa Doc also used voodoo to manipulate the public. He changed the color of the flag from blue and red to black and red, the colors associated with secret voodoo societies.[100] He capitalized on his knowledge of voodoo to instill fear and obedience in the masses.[101]

To deter the threat of a coup, Papa Doc centralized military and state apparatuses such that all decision-making authority originated with him. He worked to remove the threat of the military by fragmenting the armed forces and creating his own personal security forces.[102] These included the Presidential Guard (Garde Presidentielle) and the private, rural militia known as the Tonton Macoutes (Volontaires de la Sécurité Nationale or VSN). Both were designed to serve as counterweights to the military, which was deliberately kept weak.[103] The VSN was comprised primarily of young men from the countryside who were fiercely loyal to the regime. It acted as a security police in Haiti, detecting and punishing any subversive behavior.[104] The VSN eventually grew to be twice as powerful as the army, since Papa Doc had also purged any influential officers or commanders from army ranks.

These private security forces proved valuable to Papa Doc, as he survived several coup attempts during his tenure. The first, for example, took place on June 28, 1958. Major mistakes on the part of coup plotters—such as their uncertainty regarding the location of needed weapons—undermined their coup effort.[105] Papa Doc's savvy kept him from being overthrown in a coup; his rule was only cut short by his death in 1971.

The transition from Papa Doc to his son, Jean-Claude Duvalier, was relatively seamless. The younger Duvalier (referred to as Baby Doc) had been groomed to take over Haiti after his father's death and was designated by his father to be his successor. There were only a few bumps in the transfer of power from father to son because the elder Duvalier had already destroyed all potentially threatening state institutions. Richard Snyder explains this well:

> By the mid 1960's Papa Doc's insulation from foreign powers, his balanced use of co-optation and repression to inhibit the growth of domestic opposition, and his subordination of the armed forces had eliminated all significant competitors for state power. . . . The stability of Papa Doc's rule and the smooth transfer of power in 1971 to his son, Jean-Claude, were products of this environment devoid of serious challengers.[106]

Only 19 years old when he assumed power, Baby Doc's tenure was less centralized than his father's; he loosened the regime's grip on the countryside as well as on the military.[107] Baby Doc preferred to focus his efforts on stealing from the state rather than on exerting brute power; he did not rely heavily on repression to maintain his rule.[108] Under Baby Doc, Haiti became highly dependent on foreign aid, primarily from the United States, increasing the regime's reliance on foreign powers.[109]

Breakdown of the Regime

Corruption under Baby Doc was rampant. His economic mismanagement was so poor that it began to fuel domestic (and international) discontent. A visit by Pope John Paul II in March 1983, for example, sparked mass protests against Haiti's extreme poverty and increasing inequality.[110] Demonstrations also took place from October 1985 through January 1986. Baby Doc's response was a mixture of carrots and sticks, "vacillating between repression and conciliation."[111] He tried to appease the masses by reshuffling the cabinet, which he hoped would be interpreted as a sign that the regime was trying to purge those responsible for the corruption and destruction of the economy. As protests continued to mount, however, Baby Doc cracked down on the press and used the police and military to subdue the unrest.[112]

At the same time, a group of Haitian army officers—who had opposed Baby Doc's ascension to power from the beginning—saw how vulnerable Baby Doc had become and began to organize to overthrow him.[113] By early 1986, the domestic unrest in Haiti had also grabbed the attention of the United States. The Reagan administration soon insisted that Baby Doc step down from power and leave Haiti. On January 30, 1986, Baby Doc accepted the US' request to assist with his departure from Haiti. He reneged on the deal soon after, however, sparking riots in Haiti and a US announcement of foreign aid reductions. These developments prompted the military coup plotters to demand that Baby Doc leave power immediately. On February 7, 1986, Baby Doc adhered to this request and left Haiti for a life of exile in France following over 30 years of Duvalier rule.[114]

The Role of Personality

A number of scholars have highlighted the role of the leader's personality in dictatorships. In Robert Tucker's (1995) *Politics as Leadership*, for example, leadership is described as the core element of politics. Tucker argues that the personal factor should be included in theoretical models of totalitarian dictatorships. He writes that a "dictator's personality contributes to totalitarianism and should be recognized as one of the regular and important components" (p. 571).

Samuel Decalo (1989) also touches upon the role of personality in his study, *Psychoses of Power: African Personal Dictatorships*. In it he claims that "personal dictatorship is a unique form of autocracy at the tyrannical extreme along the spectrum of authoritarianism, characterized by the personal, aberrant and tyrannical nature of the despotic power exercised" (p. 185). Decalo's work illustrates what can happen when an atypical personality coincides with personalist rule.

Political psychologists look at the role of personality, as well. The traits examined often include paranoia and narcissism, which are frequently intertwined. The combination of these characteristics is very formidable and can lead to brutal and erratic behavior.

Paranoids are hypersensitive and imagine problems that do not exist. Because of this, they prefer to rely on no one. Paranoids constantly expect to unearth plots

⇨

against them. They believe that their supporters are on the verge of betraying them, causing them to overreact to little problems (Post 2003).

Narcissists are also "apt to create enemies where there had been none" (Glad 2002, p. 30). They exhibit paranoid behavior that goes beyond rationality, trusting no one and destroying their most loyal supporters (Rosenthal and Pittinsky 2006). For example, Saddam Hussein always believed that he knew which of his supporters were plotting against him, even before these supporters knew it themselves (Glad 2002). Narcissists have a strong need for admiration. They have a grand sense of self-importance along with an underestimation of other people (Rosenthal and Pittinsky 2006). When narcissistic leaders are angered, they may not hesitate to commit horrible and gruesome acts of violence (Ibid.). Narcissists are preoccupied with attaining power. Even when they have reached the "pinnacle of entrenched power, they continue to crave and seek more of it" (p. 626).

The role of personality is frequently posited as critical in personalist dictatorships precisely because these regimes lack the institutions that can temper the leader's behavior. This institution-free environment can also create and foster personalist dictators' paranoid and narcissistic tendencies.

Summary and Conclusion

Personalist dictatorships enable the likes and dislikes of a single individual to permeate and dominate a country's political sphere. In no other type of dictatorship do leaders rule untamed, where their leadership becomes synonymous with the regime itself. Such freedom can lead to eccentric policies, a volatile and uncertain political atmosphere, and the deterioration of state institutions. With the autonomy to act as they please, personalist dictators have the capacity to be the most ruthless of all authoritarian leaders, but some are also benevolent—or at least see themselves as such. As Alexander Lukashenko of Belarus told a radio station in 2003, "An authoritarian ruling style is characteristic of me, and I have always admitted it. Why? We could spend hours talking about this. You need to control the country and the main thing is not to ruin people's lives."[115]

Though the life of a personalist dictator may in many ways be grand, it is not one free of worry. Personalist dictators must be cunning and shrewd; they must relentlessly act to deter the emergence of rivals, splinter opposition groups, and counter underlying threats from both external and internal armed groups. Personalist dictators trust no one, and their insecurity is compounded by a dearth of institutions that could facilitate power transfers or provide legitimacy to their continued rule.

This chapter delved into the vibrant and multifaceted phenomenon of one-man rule. We examined the political dynamics of personalist dictatorships, how they function, and how they fall. We also looked at the variety of methods that personalist leaders employ to justify and entrench their hold on power. By offering a glimpse into the world of personalist dictatorship, this chapter has shown how politics functions when leaders rule without restraint.

Review Questions

- What is sultanism and how is it distinct from totalitarian dictatorships?
- Why does the structure of personalist dictatorships make them prone to brutality and erratic policies?
- How do prophets, princes, autocrats and tyrants differ?
- Why are dictators in personalist regimes more likely to be paranoid than leaders of dictatorships elsewhere?
- Why do personalist dictatorships tend not to last as long as single-party dictatorships?
- What are the tools used by personalist dictatorships to maintain power?
- How did Bokassa, Amin, and Mobutu stay in power? What factors contributed to the demise of their regimes?
- What explains why Papa Doc's regime in Haiti did not fall apart after his death?

Key Points

- Personalist regimes are unchecked by a party or the military. Power is concentrated in the hands of a single individual.
- Personalist dictatorships have several tools at their disposal to sustain power:
  - Repression
  - Select patronage networks
  - Cults of personality
  - The strategy of divide and conquer
- The primary threats to the survival in personal dictatorships are external.
- Transitions in personalist dictatorships are usually protracted and painful.

Notes

1. Geddes, *What Do We Know* (1999, p. 130).
2. Geddes, *Paradigms and Sand Castles*, (2003, p. 51).

3. Black, *Deterring Libya* (2000).

4. Decalo, *African Personal Dictatorships* (1985).

5. Ibid. (pg. 212).

6. Bratton and van de Walle, *Neo-patrimonial Regimes and Political* (1994, p. 458).

7. Chehabi and Linz, *Sultanistic Regimes* (1998).

8. Ibid.

9. Ibid. (p. 7).

10. Ibid.

11. Ibid.

12. Ibid.

13. Ibid.

14. Jackson and Rosberg, *Personal Rule in Black* (1982).

15. Wintrobe, *Political Economy of Dictatorship* (1998).

16. Decalo, *African Personal Dictatorships* (1985, p. 212).

17. Post and George, *Leaders and Their Followers*, (2004).

18. Ibid.

19. Decalo, *African Personal Dictatorships* (1985).

20. Post, *Psychological Assessment of Political* (2003).

21. Ibid.

22. Jackson and Rosberg, *Personal Rule in Black* (1982, p. 19).

23. Bratton and van de Walle, *Neo-patrimonial Regimes and Political* (1994, p. 459).

24. Ibid.

25. Geddes, *What Do We Know?* (1999).

26. Bratton and van de Walle, *Neo-patrimonial Regimes and Political* (1994).

27. Ulfelder, *Contentious Collective Action* (2005, p. 314).

28. Bratton and van de Walle, *Neo-patrimonial Regimes and Political* (1994, p. 475).

29. Rosenthal and Pittinsky, *Narcissistic Leadership* (2006, p. 625)

30. Tucker, *Politics as Leadership* (1995).

31. Tucker (1977, p. 389).

32. Ibid.

33. Brooker, *Non-Democratic Regimes* (2000, p. 133).

34. Ibid.

35. Bratton and van de Walle, *Neo-patrimonial Regimes and Political* (1994).

36. Barros, *Personalization and Institutional Constraints* (2001).

37. Bratton and van de Walle, *Neo-patrimonial Regimes and Political* (1994).

38. Ibid.

39. Geddes, *What Do We Know?* (1999, p. 25).

40. Bratton and van de Walle, *Neo-patrimonial Regimes and Political* (1994, p. 476).

41. Titely, *Dark Age* (1997).

42. Ibid.

43. Ibid.

44. Ibid.

45. Decalo, *African Personal Dictatorships* (1985).

46. Titely, *Dark Age* (1997).

47. Bokassa's security concerns were somewhat justified, given that he had endured several coup/assassination attempts (in April 1969, December 1974, and February 1976). Each attempt, however, only intensified his paranoia and gave him an excuse to respond to threats with greater severity.

48. Ibid.

49. Ibid.

50. Decalo, *African Personal Dictatorships* (1985).

51. Titely, *Dark Age* (1997).

52. Rubin, *Modern Dictators: Third World* (1987); Crab (1978).

53. Decalo, *African Personal Dictatorships* (1985).

54. Ibid.

55. Titely, *Dark Age* (1997).

56. Source: *1971: Idi Amin ousts Uganda president* (BBC News, January 25, 2005), http://news.bbc.co.uk/onthisday/hi/dates/stories/january/25/newsid_2506000/2506423.stm   (accessed February 16, 2010).

57. Kasozi et al., *Social Origins of Violence* (1994).

58. Legum, *Behind the Clown's Mask* (1997, p. 250).

59. Gertzel, *Uganda after Amin* (1980); Decalo, *African Personal Dictatorships* (1985).

60. Ravenhill, *Military Rule in Uganda* (1974).

61. Kasozi et al., *Social Origins of Violence* (1994).

62. Decalo, *African Personal Dictatorships* (1985).

63. Ibid.

64. Ibid.

65. Ibid.

66. Gertzel, *Uganda after Amin* (1980).

67. Ibid.

68. Kaufman, *Idi Amin, a Brutal*, (2003).

69. Decalo, *African Personal Dictatorships* (1985). Amin often paid his military troops with alcohol.

70. Source: *Country Studies, Uganda* United States Library of Congress (accessed February 16, 2010).

71. Ibid.

72. Ibid.

73. Source: Country Studies, *Zaire (former)* United States Library of Congress (accessed February 16, 2010).

74. Young and Turner, *Rise and Decline* (1985, p. 57).

75. Ibid.

76. Rubin, *Modern Dictators: Third World* (1987).

77. Acemoglu et al., *Kleptocracy and Divide and Rule* (2004).

78. Rubin, *Modern Dictators: Third World* (1987).

79. Young and Turner, *Rise and Decline* (1985).

80. Rubin, *Modern Dictators: Third World* (1987).

81. Snyder, *Explaining Transitions from Neo-patrimonial* (1992).

82. Turner, Decline or *Recovery* (1987, p. 216).

83. Snyder, *Explaining Transitions from Neo-patrimonial* (1992, p. 392).

84. Acemoglu et al., *Kleptocracy and Divide and Rule* (2004).

85. Snyder, *Explaining Transitions from Neo-patrimonial* (1992).

86. Acemoglu et al., *Kleptocracy and Divide and Rule* (2004).

87. Ibid.

88. Snyder, *Explaining Transitions from Neo-patrimonial* (1992).

89. Reno, *Sovereignty and Personal Rule* (1997).

90. Acemoglu et al., *Kleptocracy and Divide and Rule* (2004).

91. Ibid.

92. Ibid. (p. 169).

93. Snyder, *Explaining Transitions from Neo-patrimonial* (1992).

94. Acemoglu et al., *Kleptocracy and Divide and Rule* (2004, p. 170).

95. Source: *Timeline: Democratic Republic of Congo* (BBC News, February 10, 2010), http://news.bbc.co.uk/2/hi/africa/country_profiles/1072684.stm (accessed February 16, 2010).

96. Source: *Country Studies, Haiti*, United States Library of Congress (accessed February 16, 2010).

97. Ibid.

98. Moody, *Haiti: End* (2001).

99. Ferguson, *Papa Doc, Baby Doc* (1987).

100. Ibid.

101. Rubin, *Modern Dictators: Third World* (1987).

102. Ferguson, *Papa Doc, Baby Doc* (1987).

103. Lundahl, *History as an Obstacle* (1989).

104. Ferguson, *Papa Doc, Baby Doc* (1987).

105. Ibid.

106. Snyder, *Explaining Transitions from Neo-patrimonial* (1992, p. 388).

107. Ibid.

108. Ibid.

109. Ibid.

110. Ibid.

111. Ferguson, *Papa Doc, Baby Doc* (1987, p. 88).

112. Ibid.

113. Snyder, *Explaining Transitions from Neo-patrimonial* (1992).

114. Ibid.

115. Source: *Profile: Europe's last dictator?* (*The Guardian*, March 2, 2006).

12 Monarchies in the Middle East and Beyond

Chapter Outline

Monarchies may not appear to be a *type* of dictatorship. After all, the United Kingdom, Sweden, and the Netherlands are all monarchies in a technical sense; they are also all democratic. Such ceremonial monarchies are common throughout the world, though very little political power is actually held by the monarch. This study examines *de facto monarchies*, where the monarch is more than just a figurehead and a royal family is in charge of government and exercises real political power.

Monarchies are relatively uncommon today, especially outside of the Middle East. Though monarchies are not indigenous to the Middle East, most of the world's surviving monarchies are located in this region.[1]

Monarchies Today

Listed below are the monarchic dictatorships in existence today.

- Brunei (1959–present)
- Jordan (1946–present)

⇨

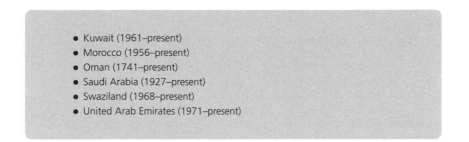

- Kuwait (1961–present)
- Morocco (1956–present)
- Oman (1741–present)
- Saudi Arabia (1927–present)
- Swaziland (1968–present)
- United Arab Emirates (1971–present)

This chapter begins by defining what we mean by monarchies in more detail, before exploring how they are structured and how their political systems function. We also offer key highlights in the rapidly developing literature dedicated to monarchies and close with a selection of case studies.

What is Monarchic Rule?

Monarchies are regimes in which "a person of royal descent has inherited the position of head of state in accordance with accepted practice or the constitution."[2] We exclude from our discussion constitutional or ceremonial monarchies, where political power is in the hands of a civilian government; our focus instead is on monarchies where absolute power is controlled by a ruling family.

In monarchies, policy-making power, access to political office, and control over the military are dictated by a ruling family. The leader of the regime is typically a king or prince, and regime elites are usually members of the royal family. The legitimacy of the regime and of key regime actors is tied closely to bloodlines and family lineage. Leadership succession in monarchies is institutionalized. Though it is not necessary for primogeniture to be used, the transfer of power from one leader to the next must be in accordance with an accepted practice.[3]

In monarchies, a ruling family dominates the political sphere, with key posts held by members of the ruling family and their allies. Some monarchies have legislatures and elections, though they are not vehicles for leadership selection. Some also allow political parties to form and operate. As in single-party dictatorships, however, these institutions are typically tools for the regime's survival rather than means for contesting politics or directing policies.

> **Definition of Monarchy**
>
> - Royal family in power, with king or prince at the helm
> - Clearly defined rules for succession
> - Legitimacy of the leadership based on bloodlines
> - Ruling family in charge of the military and policy
> - Legislatures, political parties, and elections occasionally legal, but subordinate to the family

Theoretical Analyses of Monarchies

Compared to the literature on other forms of dictatorships, few studies have been dedicated to monarchic rule. Though the scholarship devoted to monarchies is expanding quickly, it is still relatively underdeveloped. In this section, we present the central threads of this literature, discussing the different types of monarchies, how they are structured, and the factors that contribute to their durability.

Types of Monarchies

Dynastic and Non-Dynastic Monarchies

Monarchies are split into two groups by Michael Herb:[4] dynastic and non-dynastic. In dynastic monarchies, the royal family forms a ruling institution; in non-dynastic monarchies, the monarch rules alone. Dynastic monarchies differ from non-dynastic monarchies in that the ruling family is better able to check the power of the monarch in the former.

Dynastic monarchies emerged in the Middle East because "rulers' relatives at the dawn of the oil age had powerful bargaining resources which they could use to help rulers stay in power to aid aspiring rulers in achieving power or to attack and depose of sitting rulers."[5] Even before oil revenues started to flow in, the unity of the ruling family gave it great bargaining power vis-à-vis the leader. Bargaining took place over various state assets, such as customs revenues and land. Once oil money began to flow in, a larger bureaucracy and state were needed. This led to a transition from fragmented to unitary rule, where the monarch ruled through a hierarchical administrative structure that was under his direct authority. Subsidiary administrations of the past were destroyed and the ruling family was incorporated into a new central bureaucratic apparatus.[6] Negotiations between the monarch and the ruling family led to the division of state offices and the divvying up of oil revenues, all of which dispersed power throughout the ruling family.[7]

In dynastic monarchies, members of the ruling family control the major state offices and ministries. The ruling family's societal penetration provides the monarch with an information network, and power is distributed throughout the family, enabling it to hold the monarch accountable for his actions. Dynastic monarchies have mechanisms in place for dispute resolution and succession; they are more stable and resilient than non-dynastic monarchies.[8] Members of the ruling family support the system's continuation because they each have a stake in the system; even those who have lost out on top positions are in some way compensated. Dynastic monarchies are comprised of institutions that incentivize "individual princes and sheikhs, in their pursuit of power, to take actions which contribute to the maintenance of family domination over the state."[9]

In non-dynastic monarchies, by contrast, the monarch rules with far less familial collaboration, and power is highly centralized. The monarch's power is in many ways absolute, with power concentrated in the monarch's hands. Because the ruling family is less powerful in non-dynastic monarchies than in dynastic monarchies, the behavior of the monarch largely goes unchecked. Instead, members of the ruling family and other elites are dependent on the personal grace of the monarch to hold their positions and must work to stay in his good favor. Society is kept apolitical in non-dynastic monarchies, and the regime is held together via patron-client relationships. Lisa Anderson refers to non-dynastic monarchies as presidential monarchies because a "strongman dominates a state with relatively few stable political institutions."[10]

Similar to personalist dictatorships, non-dynastic monarchies often fall when the ruler abdicates, as the regime lacks the elite cohesion and institutional strength necessary to ensure a smooth transfer of power from one ruler to the next.[11] When internal dissent arises, non-dynastic monarchs have two choices: repression or abdication. As such, many non-dynastic monarchies fall on account of mass uprisings, as occurred in Iran (1979) and in Afghanistan (1973).

Dynastic and Non-dynastic Monarchies (Herb)

Dynastic Monarchies

- Royal family rules
- Ruling family can check power of the monarch
- Mechanisms in place for resolving disputes and handing succession
- Institutions give members of ruling family incentives to support regime's continuation

Non-dynastic Monarchies

- Monarch rules alone, with near absolute power
- Power concentrated in the hands of the monarch
- Ruling family depends on grace of monarch to hold positions
- Society kept apolitical
- Often fall when ruler abdicates

The Structure of Monarchies

Monarchies differ from other forms of dictatorships in that the regime's structure centers on the legitimacy of a royal family. Though power is often personalized and concentrated in the hands of the monarch,[12] monarchs must contend with the other members of the ruling family who can hold them accountable for their decisions. The precise balance of power between the monarch and the ruling family varies from regime to regime. Outside of the royal family, there are few institutions that have formal checks on the monarch's power; there are also few institutions that can constrain the behavior of the royal family.

In monarchies, the ruling family—led by the monarch—decides who can participate in politics and determines the political rules of the game. Policies are chosen by the ruling family, though many monarchies value the role of consultation in the formation of their decisions and convene consultative meetings to hear the viewpoints of various sectors of the public. The ruling family also controls the distribution of state resources and is in charge of many key sectors of the economy.[13]

Family members in monarchies usually hold all of the important positions in government, such as the key ministerial portfolios and posts in councils.[14] Monarchies in the Gulf have maintained a tight grip on power by ensuring that the major cabinet posts are filled with family members.[15] In Saudi Arabia, for example, the royal family dominates the senior civil and military positions.[16] Power is distributed among family members through various appointments and bureaucratic assignments, all of which helps maintain stability.[17]

Key Attributes of Monarchies

- Locus of power is the royal family
- Ruling family controls policy; consultative assemblies often convened
- Power of the monarch vis-à-vis ruling family varies across regimes
- Key political posts held by ruling family

The Durability of Monarchies

Though little cross-national work has been undertaken looking at the survival rates of monarchic regimes compared to other regime types, monarchies appear to be durable regimes. The monarchy in Oman, for example, has been in power since the 18th century! Though this apparent durability could be due to confounding factors, the average duration of the monarchies in existence in the post-World War II era is around 40 years.

However, the early writings on the durability of monarchies were skeptical of their longevity. Manfred Halpern[18] acknowledges that monarchies have the potential to be flexible (by sharing power), but is pessimistic that they will do so in practice. Similarly, Samuel Huntington[19] argues that it is unlikely that monarchies will be viable in the modern world. His view is that monarchs cannot centralize power and expand their social bases at the same time, nor can they accommodate all of the political demands that accompany modernity and social and economic transformation. Because monarchies are incapable of preventing economic and social change, their regimes are doomed.

In recent years, scholars have switched course and begun to offer explanations for why monarchies are *long-lasting*. According to Robert Graham, monarchies have survived because "they are the most effective means of wielding authority."[20] In Anderson's[21] view, monarchies are durable because of personalist, centralist, and absolutist qualities. In a similar vein, Daniel Brumberg[22] argues that the longevity of monarchies is due to the fact that they have more room to improvise and experiment than other autocracies do. In this section, we present some of the key factors highlighted that contribute to the durability of dynastic monarchies.

Adaptability

As with many leaders, monarchs have to be cunning politicians to keep themselves in power.[23] Critical to their survival is the ability to adapt to modernity and adjust in accordance with social and political changes.[24] To stay in power, monarchs have had to change their outside appearance "to match the issues of the day."[25] Both King Hassan II of Morocco and King Hussein I of Jordan, for example, were master politicians who easily adapted to changing circumstances.[26] This served their regimes well by helping to maintain stability and project an image of the regime's legitimacy.

Because monarchs do not face the same institutional constraints as leaders in single-party or military dictatorships do, they are more capable of adapting to change. There are fewer potential actors who could "veto" such decisions. At the same time, because monarchies have provisions for leadership succession in place, monarchs are less prone to and driven by paranoia than personalist dictators. This makes them better able to identify the threats that they face in a lucid manner and implement the necessary adjustments to ensure their continued survival in office.

Monarchies do not typically tie their legitimacy to any particular ideology. As a result, they can conform to changing environments without having to sacrifice their own principles.[27] Because they do not base their rule on "the rhetoric of revolution and ill-conceived economic policy," monarchies can contemplate reform without fear of "evisceration or abolition."[28]

By adapting to their conditions, monarchies give the opposition little room to maneuver. Once monarchies lose this ability, however, it usually indicates that their regimes are approaching the end.[29] King Faisal II of Iraq, for example, took over the throne in 1938. By the 1950's, however, he had grown out of touch with the Iraqi political and social climate, as had his advisers. His policies and investment choices began to alienate the middle class and widen the gap between rich and poor. Faisal II did not know how to deal with societal grievances and discontent or how to placate the demands of peasants and workers.[30] By 1958, the Iraqi monarchy was overthrown via revolution.

Legitimacy

Critical to the survival of monarchies is their ability to establish the legitimacy of their rule in the eyes of the public. This legitimacy enables monarchies to engender the obedience of their subjects without having to rely on the use of force. It is based on the concept of inherited rule, with great emphasis placed on the importance of noble lineage and traditional values.[31] For this reason, monarchies installed by foreign powers have faced particular difficulties establishing their legitimacy.

To "build their legitimacy and instruments of control," monarchies consciously use the theme of traditional nobility.[32] Monarchies portray themselves as modern-day connections to the past in ways that are reassuring to the masses.[33] Monarchies invent traditions and create "powerful myths" regarding their origins, in an attempt to connect their families with past achievements.[34] Some even fund academic research that contributes to the "reconstruction of the local heritage [turath]."[35]

Monarchies in the Middle East, for example, use "their historical religious status," as well as "rituals and institutions to reinforce their religious legitimacy."[36] In Saudi Arabia, the monarchy capitalizes on its role as the custodian of two holy mosques and host of millions through the Hajj.[37] Saudi kings have also used the Wahhabi interpretation of Islam and the historical alliance between the Al-Sa'ud tribe and Muhammad ibn Abd al Wahhab to reinforce the regime's legitimacy.[38]

The ability to disseminate in the populace an aura of traditional legitimacy enhances the durability of monarchies. In Morocco, King Hassan II emphasized his sharifian lineage by publishing his genealogy each year, demonstrating his direct linkage to the prophet Muhammad. Hassan II claimed to be the Commander of the Faithful, wearing traditional garb and devoting resources to Islamic projects. Article 19 of the Moroccan Constitution states that the king is a "symbol of unity" and that the "monarch is appointed by god."[39]

King Hussein of Jordan also claimed to be a descendant of the prophet Muhammad,[40] as well as a custodian of Haram al-Sharif in Jerusalem.[41] In addition, he patronized Islamic projects such as the renovation of the Dome of the Rock.[42]

In Nepal, the royal family carefully created various myths of ancient glory[43]. Family members claimed to be descendents of the Hindu God Vishnu, the true protector of the Hindu religion. This divine lineage provides the monarchy with the divine right to rule, which is "sanctified and legitimized through complex religious rituals."[44]

Once their legitimacy erodes, monarchies typically do not survive much longer in power. In Egypt, for example, the monarchy often faced legitimacy problems due to King Farouk I's extravagance and the perception among key sectors of the populace that he was no more than a pawn of the British government. Farouk I's corruption, incompetence, and weakness seriously harmed the regime's legitimacy in the eyes of the masses, and in 1952 he was overthrown by the military ending 30 years of monarchic rule.

Family Cohesiveness

The cohesiveness of the ruling family greatly enhances its ability to maintain power. Family ties can provide a strong bond among the ruling elite that deters the likelihood of elite defections. When family members become disgruntled, bargains and/or bribes are usually sufficient to ensure elite loyalty.[45] Individual princes are kept happy through deals that enable them to advance their own particularistic interests. Though not everyone can get what they want, consolation prizes are given out to ensure that all members are better off with the regime intact.[46] Such negotiations help to preserve a tight knit group of loyal family members.

The hierarchy of the family structure also contributes to stability, with sons (i.e. princes) by nature ranked lower in stature than their fathers (i.e. kings). Though the exact balance of power varies across monarchic regimes, the monarch typically has a strong say in intra-regime promotions and can impose sanctions on individuals to ensure discipline.[47] In Saudi Arabia, for example, younger members of the royal family usually respect the family hierarchy, treating senior members with deference no matter how small the age gap between them.[48]

Shared bloodlines do not, of course, guarantee elite cohesion. Intra-family rivalries can prompt internally-led coups, toppling one member of the royal family and installing another. Because such feuding can destabilize monarchic regimes, however, royal family members often prefer to cooperate with one another than to bicker so as to ensure the family's continued rule.

Buying Loyalty

In monarchies, the economy is controlled by a small group of individuals, namely the monarch and members of the royal family. Direct control over the economy enables monarchies to build the clientele networks necessary to secure the support of key sectors of the populace. In Nepal, for example, the king had full discretion over the economy and total control over land distribution.[49] This allowed the royal family to dole out temporary land grants to their most loyal supporters among the elite.[50] With most economic activities in the hands of the ruling family, monarchies can easily offer inducements to engender regime loyalty.[51]

Many monarchies are also rich in oil, further increasing the funds at their disposal to buy loyalty. In Bahrain, for example, oil wealth is used to satisfy influential Shiite families, who constitute a potential source of opposition to the regime.[52] Oil wealth has allowed many monarchies to establish links with key sectors of their societies on terms that are agreeable to the regime. Monarchies without oil wealth have a variety of tools at their disposal to buy off the opposition and reward supporters, such as income from customs dues, land allotments, and other personal businesses revenues. For example, the monarchies of Jordan and Nepal skillfully capitalized on their non-oil resources, using their tourism industries and foreign aid to stay in the good favor of key support groups.

Economic control allows monarchies to selectively distribute patronage, placing monarchs in the role of arbitrator of power among contending forces, like the "father of bickering children."[53] This is an ideal position for the monarch since it enables him to remain above the fray, absolved from guilt and beyond reproach.[54] Privileges are awarded to select groups, with the monarchy essentially buying the support of critical actors. By silencing and/or co-opting pressure groups and other potentially threatening organizations, the regime is freed of constraints on its leadership.[55]

Though repression of political dissidents is common in monarchies, most rely primarily on co-optation to deal with opposition and to cultivate support. Nepal's royal family, for example, ensured that the middle class and the landed elite benefited from the status quo, making these groups an important source of support for the royal family for many years.[56] In the Middle East, many religious leaders are salaried employees working for the state.[57] These individuals are subdued through lucrative positions in the regime. Potential opponents are given state jobs and/or valuable government contracts.[58]

Consultation

The decision-making style of monarchies is one of consultation. In the monarchies of the Gulf region, for example, consultation is a tradition that has enhanced the legitimacy of these regimes and their stability.[59] Families have made central decisions by consensus, providing valuable information to the monarch to aid in the formation of policy. In Saudi Arabia, for example, when King Faisal came to power in 1964, the country's vast oil wealth generated the need for an expanded bureaucracy. A Council of Ministers was established to manage this process. The council was essentially a high-ranked committee of senior princes that advised King Faisal on important decisions. The council assisted with routine matters of administration, as well.[60] The emphasis on consultation in monarchies occurs at various levels, both within the family, through the consultative councils, and with the population at large.

Consultative councils (which exist in Kuwait, Saudi Arabia, Oman, and Bahrain) enable monarchs to appear accessible to the people, lessening resentment and reducing perceived political alienation. These councils serve the function of conveying to the populace that the ruling family is willing to venture outside of its ranks to consult on decisions.[61] They also provide the regime with valuable information about what policies should be followed, helping the family anticipate, monitor, and address discontent before it gets out of hand. Though the consultative councils usually have little de facto political power, they project an image that people's voices are being heard, while also keeping the regime informed about potentially destabilizing societal grievances.[62]

Monarchies also typically have in place other means for consulting with the masses and regime elites. The Sultan of Oman, for example, goes on a yearly expedition around the country, covered by the press, during which he receives complaints. This process is called an open parliament.[63] In many Middle Eastern monarchies, individuals are invited to go to a "diwan" or formal meeting place of leading families.[64] Many monarchies also use a majlis system, which incorporates open forums that serve as a link between the ruler and the citizen in order to preserve traditional modes of political interaction.[65]

In Saudi Arabia, for example, a majlis is used as an advisory council and forum for discussion. It is held by members of the ruling family. Because of the large size of the Saudi royal family, multiple majlis sessions are held, allowing a broad spectrum of Saudi citizens a means of communicating with the government.[66] Citizens can personally petition the king, with the princes acting as intermediaries between citizens and the state.[67]

Kuwait has gone a step further and has a parliament in place. The parliament holds some political power and has even challenged the ruling family at times. Like Kuwait, Jordan also has a functioning parliament that has exercised a small degree of influence. In May 2000, for example, over half of the parliament's deputies "signed a petition demanding a special session of parliament (not then in session) to remove confidence in the government."[68]

These consultative structures make citizens feel like their regimes are accessible to them. As one Bahraini citizen claimed, "I don't worry too much about whether I have a vote or not—after all, I can talk to someone who talks to the ruling family simply by picking up the phone."[69] They provide links between the ruling family and the citizenry that reinforce a common identity.[70] By publicly consulting with other sectors of society, the monarch is seen as acting in the best interests of the people, enhancing the regime's stability.[71]

Elections, Legislatures, and Political Parties

Many monarchies hold elections, have legislatures, and allow political parties to exist. As in other types of dictatorships, the purpose of these institutions is not to allow for democratic political processes, but rather to prolong the survival of the regime (discussed in **Chapter 3**). When, pressure to neutralize threats from larger groups within society mounts, token democratic institutions like elections and legislatures are implemented. These institutions function as theaters of legitimacy that serve the regime's interests.[72]

Elections enhance survival because they enable the negotiation of "a sharing of power between the palace and the parliament."[73] Elections are a means by which the ruling family can disperse power to a limited number of opposition groups, all while "maintaining the role of chief arbitrator."[74] The regime closely controls the electoral process to ensure that pro-regime groups fare well and to strategically divide power among contending forces such that opposition groups do not coalesce into a more formidable political challenger. The regime typically dictates how many parties can run, how they are allowed to operate, and how much funding they can receive. The regime also decides the timing of elections and the rules for translating votes into seats.[75] Many groups are underrepresented in the political process as a result, and opposition parties are forced to deal with major restrictions on campaigning.

The regime can also resort to fraud to win elections. In Kuwait, for example, vote buying has occurred and gerrymandering is often used to support pro-regime candidates.[76] To prevent the opposition from uniting, the regime has also alternated its support for Bedouin, nationalist, and Islamist candidates.[77] Similarly, in Jordan, electoral irregularities have been reported and some elections stolen.[78] Party laws have been manipulated to fragment the opposition and electoral districts have been designed to reduce the influence of the Palestinian population.[79] Electoral fraud is so rampant in Morocco that voter turnout is often low, as voters have little trust that their votes will count.[80] King Hassan II has also used gerrymandering and indirectly-elected legislative seats to maintain control.[81]

All of these factors favor the election of pro-regime candidates and groups and disadvantage those of the opposition. As a result, legislatures in monarchies are typically filled with supporters of the regime and, occasionally, members of the opposition who pose little threat. They serve the purpose of creating regime loyalists who have something at stake in the monarchy's survival. If the election does not go the monarchy's way, it can simply opt to close the legislature.[82]

Many monarchies also allow political parties to organize. The key to legalizing political parties is ensuring that their political participation occurs within the boundaries of the regime. It is also critical that political parties that pose a threat to the regime remain divided so that they do not unify into a destabilizing opposition force. In Jordan, for example, opposition parties are allowed to organize so long as they remain committed to the legitimacy of the monarchy.[83] The king must skillfully manage divisions between Palestinians, trans-Jordanians, and other tribal and regional groups, in addition to different ideological parties.[84] Though political parties are legal in Jordan, the system is designed to encourage independent candidates, rather than strong political parties. Thus, the parties that exist are fractionalized and weak.[85]

Selective Repression

Robust security apparatuses are crucial to the durability of monarchies. They enable regimes to closely monitor public opinion and gather information on the pulse of the population.[86] Many monarchies can afford these security apparatuses through their abundant resources, namely oil.[87] In addition, their security forces are often staffed by foreigners who are unlikely to think twice in suppressing dissent.[88]

In Saudi Arabia, for example, all organizations are closely monitored. The same is true of Bahrain, where the security and intelligence forces have arrested protesters, opposition members, and even injured citizens at religious gatherings. Security forces in Oman have also deterred unrest by severely punishing political activists. Other monarchies in the Gulf monitor expatriate populations to prevent foreign-backed political uprisings. They also keep a close eye on intellectuals, spiritual leaders, and those who study or travel abroad. The combination of "informal networks of informers and professional intelligence services, creates another efficient mechanism of regime security in society: that of an insidious intimidation and fear."[89]

Though the suppression of dissent can deter future dissident activities, many monarchies (particularly those in the Middle East) have exhibited an understanding that the use of repression can backfire. It is often easier to provide incentives for individuals to support the regime's survival than to rely on repression to stay in power. Most of the repression exerted in monarchies is limited to anti-regime activities and is not extended to citizens who play by the rules.[90] Moreover, potential dissidents are typically bribed to conform their behavior rather than imprisoned; the number of arrests is usually kept to a minimum.

Military Loyalty

In monarchies, as in all dictatorships, the military's loyalty to the regime is critical to the regime's survival. Monarchs are not immune to coup plots or assassination attempts. King Faisal II of Iraq, for example, was ousted in a coup in 1958 and executed shortly after. To stay in power, monarchies must ensure that the military is loyal to the ruling family. As Keshab Bhattarai[91] points out, in Nepal, the royal family was able to sustain itself in power despite its disastrous economic policies because of the loyalty of the royal military.

Due to the threat of military ouster, many monarchies seek to control the military by distributing family members throughout the organization. This enables the ruling family to keep an eye on the military so that its loyalty is guaranteed. This is true in Jordan, Saudi Arabia, and Morocco, where male relatives are appointed to key military posts to protect against potential rebellions.[92] Though this strategy does not make the military more effective against external foes, it does serve to prevent coups from occurring.[93] Other tactics used to engender military loyalty include hiring foreign mercenaries (a strategy optimized by many Gulf monarchies) and ensuring that members of the military are well paid.[94]

Succession

Institutionalized rules for determining succession are a key component of the longevity of monarchies. Clear guidelines for leadership turnover create a more predictable and stable political environment and lessen the likelihood of violent and chaotic grabs for power when leaders step down or are otherwise removed from power.

Historically, many monarchies did not have fixed rules in place for succession. All males within the sub-lineages of the ruling families had a right to rule.[95] In some cases, the monarch was chosen by members of the royal families, who would then present their choice to the leading men of the community or to the ulema (Muslim legal scholars) and the majlis for their approval.[96] Because this process often turned violent, however, most monarchies today have institutionalized procedures for succession that satisfy the royal family.

In some monarchies, the process of succession is almost democratic, with consultation and consensus used to make certain that the most skilled family member is selected to rule. In Saudi Arabia, for example, though the king appoints the crown prince, this only occurs after the king has consulted with senior family members to achieve internal agreement about who should take power next. The ruling family has a vested interest in choosing an astute and popular ruler so that the regime is not forced to step down.

Succession in Kuwait has been more complicated since the system was originally too informal and rivalries emerged within the family between two branches of the Sheikh Mubarak's descendants, Jabir (who ruled from 1915–1917) and Salim (who ruled from 1917–1921). To alleviate conflict, Kuwait has alternated between these two branches.[97]

In many monarchies, succession is determined by primogeniture, where the next ruler is always the eldest male in the family or the eldest capable male relative. In Nepal, equal primogeniture was used, which meant that the eldest child, whether son or daughter, was eligible to succeed to the throne. The benefit of primogeniture is that it provides clear guidelines for who will rule. Some form of primogeniture is used in Morocco, Bahrain, Abu Dhabi, Dubai and Qatar.[98]

Though the existence of rules for succession does not guarantee regime stability during leadership transitions, it does enhance it.

Case Studies

This section offers a case study of Iran to illustrate the key facets of monarchic rule in a non-dynastic monarchy. A short case study of Swaziland's monarchy is also presented to provide a case outside of the Middle East of a dynastic monarchy. Weaved in throughout are the ideas emphasized in this chapter, regarding how monarchies work, and the factors that make some monarchies more durable than others.

Concentrated Power in Iran (1925–1979)

The monarchy of Iran is classified as a non-dynastic monarchy, as power was concentrated in the hands of the king (or shah). Though the monarchy survived in power for more than 50 years, it suffered from problems of legitimacy. In this case study, we discuss the factors that contributed to the longevity of this regime, as well as the events that precipitated its downfall.

Reza Shah Pahlavi (referred to as Reza Shah) came to power in Iran in 1925 in a coup overthrowing the ruling Qajar dynasty. Having ruled behind the scenes in the few years prior, Reza Shah was able to seize power due his close relationship with the military, support from foreign powers, and the weakness of the Qajar dynasty.[99] Shortly after, he was named Prime Minister and the parliament (or majlis) voted to abolish the Qajar dynasty and recognize Reza Shah as the new monarch.

Upon assuming power, Reza Shah worked to strengthen his support from the military. He played upon his reputation as a great soldier by nearly always appearing in public in an undecorated military uniform.[100] Reza Shah professionalized the military by organizing it into a semi-Westernized force of 90,000 men.[101] His positive relationship with the military lessened the likelihood that it would stage a coup against him.[102]

Initially, Reza Shah was also popular with the civilian population. He sought to implement substantial economic and social reforms to modernize Iran and turn it into a global power. He worked to transform Iran into a secular society and pushed for greater rights for women and a modern educational system.

To implement these reforms, Reza Shah concentrated power into the hands of the king. He limited the power of the majlis, such that it was eventually just a rubber stamp for his policies, and personally determined who could be elected to it. Political parties that were once strong were banned or had their powers severely limited. Press censorship was also high.[103] Reza Shah wanted the king to stand above all groups in society and for the king's power to go checked by no one. He viewed himself as a father figure for the people of Iran and tried to portray himself in a mystical light. To do so, he commissioned monuments and pictures of himself to be placed all over the country.[104]

The monarchy under Reza Shah suffered from problems of legitimacy, however, given that he had no royal heritage. In an effort to attach legitimacy to his name, Reza Shah added on the name Pahlavi upon assuming power, which symbolized the glories of the ancient past.[105] To solidify the family's royal credentials, he had his son, Mohammed Reza, married to King Farouk I of Egypt's sister Princess Fawzia.[106] Reza Shah also relied on pomp and formality in the family's public affairs to project an image of the family's royalty and re-emphasize to the citizenry that he was the legitimate ruler of Iran.

By the 1940s, however, Iran soon became entrenched in the political battles of the world's great powers during World War II. Reza Shah was forced to abdicate the throne to his son, Mohammad Reza, in 1941 in a deal worked out with the United Kingdom. The transition from father to son was relatively seamless.

Mohammad Reza Pahlavi, (referred to as the Shah of Iran), like his father, also ruled with concentrated power. Only two political parties were allowed to function, the Nationalists and the People's Party, but each lacked any real power or influence. Eventually, nearly all parties were banned or suppressed.[107] The Shah continued his father's tradition of using repression to tighten his control by censoring the media and closely monitoring potential opponents of the regime, like the clergy. All non-trustworthy elements within the military were purged and the bazaar merchant class was suppressed.[108] The Shah also weakened tribal groups in Iran by forming a temporary alliance with them and then subtly encouraging them to compete with one another to reduce their power.[109] The Shah placed himself at the apex of all institutions, making key government bodies dependent on him, such as the bureaucracy, the military, paramilitary institutions like the National Intelligence and Security Organization (SAVAK), and the secret police network.[110] Most state institutions were considered corrupt and inefficient.[111]

Breakdown of the Regime

The monarchy of Iran had always suffered from problems of legitimacy. The Shah was viewed to be a puppet of Western powers by the populace. This image was solidified by the large foreign presence in Iran. By 1978, there were more than 60,000 foreigners living in Iran, two-thirds of them American. This foreign presence intensified "the perception that the Shah's modernization program was threatening the society's Islamic and Iranian cultural values and identity."[112]

The Shah's cronyism did not improve his popularity among the citizenry. Under his tenure, regime loyalists were given monopolies and lucrative business contracts.[113] He was able to keep his supporters happy through Iran's oil revenues. These revenues expanded in the early 1970s when oil prices rose. With the extra income, the Shah embarked on a program to industrialize Iran and massively build up its military. These moves, however, "greatly strained Iran's human and institutional resources and caused severe economic and social dislocation."[114] Public dissatisfaction with the regime intensified, due to rampant official corruption, high levels of inflation, and a rising gap between the rich and the poor.

At the same time, by the late 1970s, the Shah's regime became subject to international scrutiny for its human rights violations.[115] US President Jimmy Carter came to power in 1977 and made human rights a major part of his foreign policy agenda. Such pressures forced the Shah to allow for more freedom of political expression. Those who opposed the regime took advantage of the regime's greater openness and began to organize and stage protests.

By 1978, the size and scope of the protests increased. Strikes broke out across the country. As the opposition movement snowballed, the Shah was forced to flee Iran on February 11, 1979. An Islamic Republic replaced the monarchy immediately after.

Royal Legitimacy in Swaziland (1968–present)

Few monarchies exist today outside of the Middle East. The monarchy of Swaziland is an exception. This brief case study points out some of the key factors contributing to the durability of the Swazi monarchy.

Swaziland was ruled by the British since the early 1900s. By the 1960s, pressures for independence from the United Kingdom began to grow. Several political parties formed, one of them being the Imbokodvo National Movement (INM). The INM was founded by King Sobhuza II, the head of the monarchy that had nominally ruled Swaziland for hundreds of years. The United Kingdom agreed to hold parliamentary elections in 1967 that would grant Swaziland independence under a constitutional monarchy. Sobhuza II and the INM were victorious, and Swaziland became independent in 1968.

Sobhuza II was a charismatic personality who demanded respect. He had strong skills of persuasion and the ability to generate consensus.[116] Sobhuza II placed emphasis on the royal family's legitimacy and its historical centrality in Swazi politics. He focused on Swazi traditions, portraying the "Swazi way of life" as "superior to western lifestyles and practices introduced by colonialism."[117] Sobhuza II was able to project and solidify this image of the monarchy through his "intimate knowledge of Swazi law and custom."[118] He repealed the constitution in 1973 and declared himself the absolute ruler of Swaziland.

In the Swazi monarchy, the economy is entirely controlled by the royal family.[119] The king stands at the top of the social structure and political system.[120] He has maximum executive powers, control over the parliament (which has the nominal function of initiating and debating policy issues), is in charge of the armed forces and military recruiting, and promotes and fires most members of the bureaucracy.[121] The king also enjoys judicial powers.[122] Nevertheless, an inner council of men, known as the Liqoqo, advises the king and a public forum, called the Libandla, provides citizens with the opportunity to discuss different policies.[123]

Military promotions in Swaziland have typically benefited those who have proven themselves loyal.[124] The loyalty of military officers is enhanced through the provision of business opportunities to members of the military upon their retirement.[125] The role of the military has primarily been to support the regime, as opposed to protecting Swaziland from the threat of foreign powers. The constant presence of the army in Swaziland "provides the coercive base to buttress stern policies."[126]

When Sobhuza II died in 1982, the Liqoqo selected one of his sons, fourteen-year-old Mswati III, to be his successor. Two of Sobhuza II's wives ruled Swaziland for the next four years so that Mswati III could finish his education. In 1986, Mswati III was crowned king, marking a seamless transition from one ruler to the next. Despite the fact that most Swazis live in poverty, the monarchy is fairly popular in Swaziland and Mswati III is still in power today.[127]

Summary and Conclusion

Though monarchies are less-studied than other forms of dictatorship, they are no less important. Monarchic regimes sometimes resemble personalist regimes, in that power is concentrated in the hands of a single individual. Yet, monarchies differ from personalist dictatorships in key ways. In some monarchies (such as dynastic monarchies), the power of the monarch is checked by the ruling family, similar to the way party elites check the power of the leader in a single-party dictatorship. Most importantly, in monarchies the legitimacy of the regime is based on royal lineage. This emphasis on family bloodlines means that the process of succession is significantly smoother in monarchic regimes than in other types of dictatorship.

Many unknowns remain about monarchic rule, however, particularly in terms of how monarchies compare with other forms of dictatorship in their policy choices, conflict behavior, and economic performance. Though monarchies appear to be remarkably durable regimes, it is still unclear whether other confounding factors (besides regime type) are actually driving their longevity. Additional research is needed to better isolate the key characteristics of monarchies that drive their behavior and to identify the specific threats that they face to their survival.

Review Questions

- How do de facto monarchies differ from ceremonial monarchies?
- What distinguishes monarchies from other types of dictatorships?
- How do dynastic monarchies differ from non-dynastic monarchies?
- What factors make monarchies durable?

- In what ways do monarchies function like single-party dictatorships? In what ways do they function like personalist dictatorships?
- Why did the monarch of Iran face problems of legitimacy?

Key Points

- Monarchies are distinct from other forms of dictatorship because a person of royal descent is at the helm. The regime's legitimacy is based on bloodlines, and a ruling family is effectively in charge.
- In dynastic monarchies the ruling family checks the power of the monarch and controls major state offices and ministries. In non-dynastic monarchies, power is solely concentrated in the hands of the monarch.
- Monarchies are durable because they: are adaptable, hold traditional legitimacy, are supported by family cohesiveness, use patronage to buy loyalty, are highly consultative, use nominally democratic institutions to ease pressures for democracy, are selectively repressive, have loyal militaries, and have institutionalized procedures for succession.
- Further research is needed on monarchies to establish how their behavior compares with other types of dictatorships.

Notes

1. Anderson, *Absolutism and the Resilience* (1991).
2. Hadenius and Teorrel, *Pathways from Authoritarianism* (2007, p. 146).
3. Anderson, *Absolutism and the Resilience* (1991).
4. Herb, *All in the Family* (1999).
5. Ibid. (p. 22).
6. Ibid.
7. Ibid.
8. Ibid.
9. Ibid. (p. 45).
10. Anderson, *Absolutism and the Resilience* (1991, p. 11).
11. Herb, *All in the Family* (1999).
12. Owen, *State, Power and Politics* (1992).
13. Lust-Okar, *Divided They Rule* (2004).
14. Byman and Green, *Enigma of Political Stability* (1992); Owen, *State, Power and Politics* (1992).
15. Herb, *All in the Family* (1999).
16. Owen, *State, Power and Politics* (1992).
17. Herb, *All in the Family* (1999); Common (2008).
18. Halpern, *Politics of Social Change* (1963).

19. Huntington, *Political Order* (1968).
20. Graham, *Iran: The Illusion of Power* (1979, p. 53).
21. Anderson, *Absolutism and the Resilience* (1991).
22. Brumberg, *Trap of Liberalized Autocracy* (2002).
23. Anderson, *Absolutism and the Resilience* (1991).
24. Ibid.
25. Byman and Green, *Enigma of Political Stability* (1999, p. 27).
26. Anderson, *Absolutism and the Resilience* (1991).
27. Ibid.
28. Kirby, *Want Democracy?* (2000, p. 10).
29. Anderson, *Absolutism and the Resilience* (1991).
30. Tripp, *History of Iraq* (2002).
31. Albrecht and Schlumberger, *Waiting for Godot* (2004); Owen (1992).
32. Nonneman, *Political Reform* (2006).
33. Anderson, *Absolutism and the Resilience* (1991).
34. Owen, *State, Power and Politics* (1992).
35. Anderson, *Absolutism and the Resilience* (1991, p. 13).
36. Lust-Okar, *Structuring Conflict* (2005, p. 48).
37. Albrecht and Schlumberger, *Waiting for Godot* (2004).
38. Ibid.
39. Lust-Okar, *Structuring Conflict* (2005, pp. 48–49).
40. Reich, *Political Leaders* (1990).
41. Lust-Okar, *Structuring Conflict* (2005).
42. Ibid.
43. Bhattarai, *Political Economy of Conflict* (2005); Riaz and Basu, *State-Society Relationship* (2007).
44. Riaz and Basu, *State-Society Relationship* (2007, p. 135).
45. Herb, *All in the Family* (1999).
46. Ibid.
47. Ibid.
48. Ibid.
49. Khadka, *Nepal's Stagnant Economy* (1991).
50. Riaz and Basu, *State-Society Relationship* (2007).
51. Bellin, *Robustness of Authoritarianism* (2004).
52. Owen, *State, Power and Politics* (1992).
53. Lust-Okar, *Structuring Conflict* (2005, p. 48).
54. Richards and Waterbury, *Political Economy* (1996).
55. Byman and Green, *Enigma of Political Stability* (1999).
56. Bhattarai, *Political Economy of Conflict* (2005).
57. Anderson, *Absolutism and the Resilience* (1991).

58. Byman and Green, *Enigma of Political Stability* (1999).

59. Herb, *All in the Family* (1999).

60. Owen, *State, Power and Politics* (1992).

61. Byman and Green, *Enigma of Political Stability* (1999).

62. Herb, *All in the Family* (1999).

63. Ibid.

64. Ehteshami, *Reform from Above* (2003).

65. Ibid.

66. Herb, *All in the Family* (1999); Ehteshami, *Reform from Above* (2003).

67. Herb, *All in the Family* (1999).

68. Herb, *Princes and Parliaments* (2004, pp. 391–392).

69. Byman and Green, *Enigma of Political Stability* (1999, p 30).

70. Nonneman, *Political Reform* (2006).

71. Herb, *All in the Family* (1999).

72. Herb, *Princes and Parliaments* (2004).

73. Herb, *All in the Family* (1999, p. 16).

74. Lust-Okar and Jamal, *Rulers and Rules* (2002, p. 345).

75. Ibid.

76. Lust-Okar and Jamal, *Rulers and Rules* (2002); Posusney, *Multi-Party Elections* (2002).

77. Lust-Okar and Jamal, *Rulers and Rules* (2002).

78. Ryan, *Elections and Parliamentary Democratization* (1998); Herb, *Princes and Parliaments* (2004).

79. Lust-Okar and Jamal (2002); Herb (2004).

80. Herb, *Emirs and Parliaments* (2002).

81. Lust-Okar and Jamal, *Rulers and Rules* (2002).

82. Ibid.

83. Ibid.

84. Lust-Okar, *Structuring Conflict* (2005).

85. Herb, *Emirs and Parliaments* (2002).

86. Byman and Green, *Enigma of Political Stability* (1999).

87. Bellin, *Robustness of Authoritarianism* (2004).

88. Byman and Green, *Enigma of Political Stability* (1999).

89. Champion, *Kingdom of Saudi Arabia* (1999, p. 55).

90. Byman and Green, *Enigma of Political Stability* (1999).

91. Bhattarai, *Political Economy of Conflict* (2005).

92. Bellin, *Robustness of Authoritarianism* (2004); Rubin, *Military in Contemporary Middle* (2001).

93. Herb, *All in the Family* (1999).

94. Rubin, *Military in Contemporary Middle* (2001); Bellin (2004); Champion (1999).

95. Herb, *All in the Family* (1999).

96. Ibid.

97. Peterson, *Nature of Succession* (2001).

98. Owen, *State, Power and Politics* (1992).

99. Kamrava, *Modern Middle East* (2005).

100. Graham, *Iran: The Illusion of Power* (1979).

101. Avery (1965); Cordesman (2003); Gheissari and Nasr (2006).

102. Kamrava, *Modern Middle East* (2005).

103. Graham, *Iran: The Illusion of Power* (1979).

104. Ibid.

105. Ibid.

106. Ibid.

107. Kamrava, *Revolution in Iran* (1990).

108. Graham, *Iran: The Illusion of Power* (1979).

109. Beck, *Revolutionary Iran* (1980).

110. Kamrava, *Revolution in Iran* (1990).

111. Ibid.

112. Source: *Country Studies, Iran,* United States Library of Congress (accessed March 10, 2010).

113. Graham, *Iran: The Illusion of Power* (1979).

114. Ibid.

115. Ibid.

116. Potholm, *Ngwenyama of Swaziland* (1977).

117. Matlosa, *Democracy and Conflict* (1998, pp. 320–321).

118. Potholm, *Ngwenyama of Swaziland* (1977).

119. Kally, *Swaziland Election Dossier* (2004).

120. Potholm, *Ngwenyama of Swaziland* (1977).

121. Rupiya, *Survey of Civil–Military Relations* (2004).

122. Kally, *Swaziland Election Dossier* (2004).

123. Potholm, *Ngwenyama of Swaziland* (1977).

124. Ibid.

125. Dlami, *Success and Competence* (2006).

126. Wiesfelder, *Human Rights in Botswana* (1980, p. 16).

127. Source: Barry Bearak, *In Destitute Swaziland, Leader Lives Royally* The New York Times, (September 5, 2008), http://www.nytimes.com/2008/09/06/world/africa/06king.html?page wanted=1&_r=1&sq=mswati&st=cse&scp=3 (accessed March 10, 2010).

13 Hybrid Dictatorships

As the name suggests, hybrid dictatorships are regimes that share characteristics of two or more types of dictatorships. Among hybrid dictatorships, personalist/military and personalist/single-party hybrids are the most common; single-party/military and personalist/single-party/military hybrids (referred to as triple threats) are rare. This chapter provides a selection of case studies on hybrid dictatorships, detailing how politics works in these blended regimes.

Personalist/Military Hybrid: Pakistan (1977–1988)

Pakistan under General Muhammad Zia-ul-Haq (referred to as Zia) is classified as a personalist/military hybrid dictatorship. Zia came to power in

1977 in a coup ousting Prime Minister Zulfikar Ali Bhutto. Along with the military, Zia ruled Pakistan for the next decade. The regime fell in 1988 when Zia and other top military generals were killed in a mysterious plane crash.[1]

Personalist Elements

When Zia took power, he exerted a personalist style of rule. Zia was a charismatic leader and sought to portray himself as a pious father figure at the top of the Pakistani political pyramid. Few doubted his power or credibility.[2]

After seizing power, Zia immediately weakened potential threats to his power from strong political parties and civilian elites and opposed the implementation of democratic institutions, like elections, legislatures, and political parties. Zia justified this by claiming that "elections have given birth only to goons and chaos and confusion" in Pakistan.[3] Though eventually Zia allowed elections to be held in 1984, more than 95 percent of the votes were cast for him, and he was elected to a five-year term as president.

Zia's disdain for a legislature or parliament led to the creation of an alternative system in which a council comprised of individuals from different fields would act as an advisory board to the president; all 284 of these individuals were to be nominated by the president. Zia eventually reinstated the National Assembly, but did not do so until the National Assembly accepted all of his actions in the past years, including his staging of the 1977 coup.[4] To ensure support for his policies, Zia forged ties with local governments and corrupt politicians who could easily be bought off.[5]

In a sign of his personal control over Pakistan, Zia passed several amendments that served his interests. One such example of this was the eighth amendment, which granted the president the power to dissolve the National Assembly as the president saw fit. This amendment also gave the president the power to appoint the next army chief.[6] Zia also made sure that the judicial system was left impotent by passing constitutional amendments that weakened the supremacy of civilian courts.

Zia worked to weaken political parties in Pakistan. He forbade most political parties from registering with the Election Commission; after October 11, 1979, only four parties were allowed to register.[7] Most parties were dissolved and their funds and properties were confiscated.

Military Elements

Though Zia in many ways exercised personal rule, the military was very involved in the direct management of Pakistan. When Zia came to power, the military emerged as the sole important autonomous actor in Pakistan.[8] It was given responsibilities in major departments of the civil administration and in key sectors of the economy.[9] The military was involved in the state at every level.

The military strategically partnered with Islamic groups when it was in its interests. Islam was used in the regime as a justification to suppress the opposition, create unity within Pakistan, and mask the regime's authoritarian tendencies. While Zia served as Army Chief, he forged close ties to Islamic groups; after taking over as president, he provided arms and economic support to these groups, namely those that supported the military and worked to thwart the power of the civilian opposition.[10]

Islam was also a unifying force for the Pakistani military. Military cadets were trained at Islamic schools and indoctrinated with the belief that the military's role was to protect Islam from outside threats.[11] In order for the military to accomplish this goal, it needed to remain united and abide by a strict military hierarchy. The military's organizational cohesion strengthened Zia's rule.

Personalist/Single-party Hybrid: Cuba (1959–present)

The Cuban dictatorship under Fidel Castro is considered to be a personalist/single-party hybrid dictatorship. Castro seized power in 1959, along with a group of rebels, toppling the regime of Fulgencio Batista in what is known as the Cuban Revolution. He led Cuba for many years, in conjunction with the Communist Party of Cuba (PCC). Castro's brother, Raúl, was named president of Cuba in 2008, following Castro's resignation. The regime is still in power today.

Personalist Elements

Fidel Castro ruled Cuba for nearly 50 years, along with the PCC. This set-up was intentional. The leaders of the Cuban revolution "were reluctant to turn over too much authority to the new party apparatus for fear that their efforts to institutionalize Castro's charismatic authority might dissipate it instead."[12]

Castro was in charge of all major policy decisions, along with a small group of lieutenants who he had fought with prior to assuming power.[13] This inner circle was eventually named the PCC's Political Bureau. Castro controlled "every key lever of power in Cuba, including the judiciary, and [was] responsible for every important appointment."[14] The "vehicle for [his] personal power has been the Cuban Revolution, a profound social movement with global implications."[15]

As with other personalist dictators, Castro relied heavily on repression to stay in power. When the economy worsened in 1992 and 1993, for example, the Cuban regime's tolerance for dissent decreased in tandem. Typical of many personalist dictatorships, the regime's economic policies were met with minimal success, particularly since the fall of the Soviet Union.[16] To mitigate potential unrest, repression was used.

Castro's charismatic personalist and revolutionary discourse also enhanced his rule. He worked hard to keep the messages of the revolution alive and emphasize the importance of social justice. According to William M. LeoGrande:

> At moments when the revolution was riven by sharp cleavages, Castro's authority provided the glue to hold the elite together—through the conflicts between the urban wing of the 26th of July Movement and the Rebel Army, between the veterans of the Sierra and the old communists, between the armed forces and the Interior Ministry in the aftermath of the Ochoa affair, and between reformers and hardliners during the Special Period.[17]

Like a personalist dictator, Castro also played a central role in the making of policy. Decision-making in Cuba inevitably required Castro's input. Elites were forced to compete with one another to gain Castro's attention and lobby him to implement their preferred policies.[18] He was the last word on policy choices and other internal conflicts, diminishing the likelihood that significant splits within the regime would emerge or expand in size.

Single-party Elements

The PCC was created after the revolution; it was not a political force prior. The goal of the party was for it to be the "organizational guarantor of the continuity of Cuba's socialist system."[19] Because it was not part of the struggle against the Batista regime, it evolved into more of a nationalist Cuban party than a representative of the revolutionary working class.[20]

For Castro, the PCC served as a political tool that could unify post-revolutionary Cuba and mobilize the regime's support group.[21] The PCC eventually grew in strength, increasing from 55,000 in 1969 to more than 200,000 members in 1975. By the end of the 1970s, the PCC was institutionally strong enough that it began to resemble a typical communist party. Along with Castro (and later his successor, Raúl), the PCC controls all elements of Cuban life, ranging from mass organizations to the state bureaucracy to the security apparatus.[22]

The legalization of additional political parties in Cuba does not appear to be on the horizon. There are few indications that "a more pluralist multiparty system is being considered either by the leadership or by the party, and there is little evidence at present of a strong clamor for it from the population."[23]

Single-party/Military Hybrid: El Salvador (1948–1984)

The dictatorship of El Salvador from 1948 to 1984 is a single-party/military hybrid dictatorship. Historically, these regimes have emerged infrequently. The regime came to power in 1948 after a number of junior officers overthrew Salvador Castaneda Castro. The military and the Revolutionary Party of Democratic Unification (PRUD) dominated El Salvador for the next 36 years, overseeing a brutal and violent period in El Salvador's history. The PRUD was formed in 1950 by Major Óscar Osorio, who was elected president in 1950. It was later replaced by the Party of National Conciliation (PCN). The regime fell in 1984 during the Salvadoran Civil War, when José Napoleón Duarte won the presidency in what many considered to be a free and fair election.

Single-party Elements

The PRUD was the brainchild of Osorio and supported by a sector of middle class civilians and military personnel who had coinciding interests and a commitment towards modernization. The party addressed the needs of entrepreneurial groups, giving it the support of members of the oligarchy.[24]

In an effort to appear democratic, the regime periodically held elections.[25] Opposition parties were severely disadvantaged in these elections and, during the 1950s, held no seats in parliament. To ensure the victory of the PRUD, intimidation and fraud were widespread. There were also rules in place that stipulated that opposition parties could not have ties to international political organizations,[26] sapping their abilities to fundraise. The regime tightly controlled the electoral process and had full discretion over campaign rules.

The PRUD's descendent, the PCN, was created in 1960 by Colonel Julio Rivera. Like the PRUD, the PCN was committed to economic progress and stability and had the support of the middle and upper classes. In 1962, Rivera won the presidency; the PCN was the only party allowed to participate.[27] The PCN (and prior to this the PRUD) was dominated by the military and served as a vehicle to allow military candidates to compete in elections and run for president, using the "military command structure as a political machine."[28]

Toward the end of the 1960s, as the regime gained more confidence in the organizational strength and popularity of the PCN, it slowly allowed other parties to participate in elections. Though opposition parties eventually won some seats in the legislature, the regime made sure that the opposition never came close to commanding a majority.[29]

Military Elements

The military had long played a key role in Salvadoran politics. It was trained to be disciplined, committed to hierarchy, nationalistic, and anti-communist.[30] The military was involved in the economic and social development of El Salvador and viewed itself as the most capable organization to rule the country.

As is typical of military dictatorships, intra-regime coups were common. The military exerted its will over who would lead the country various times by means of coups and attempted coups.[31] For example, Lieutenant Colonel Jose Maria Lemus, who was elected president in 1956, was deposed in a bloodless coup in 1960 following public demonstrations in the capital calling for his removal. A civilian-military junta took control soon after, led by Lieutenant Colonel Julio Adalberto Rivera and university professor Fabio Castillo. Castillo, however, was a known sympathizer of the Cuban revolution, convincing "the elite and the conservative military officers that the government was influenced by communism."[32] A coup overthrew the junta in 1961, with the new junta affirming its commitment to fight communism and retaining Rivera as a member.

Though the military was not committed to democracy, it did feel strongly that personalist rule was undesirable. Changes to the constitution were implemented in 1962 enabling the military to intervene directly if the rule prohibiting the re-election of the president was not adhered to.[33] This commitment to a single, five-year term for each president helped to stabilize the regime, by reducing the uncertainty regarding the tenure of leaders and leadership turnover.[34]

Triple Threat: Egypt (1952–present)

The Egyptian dictatorship is classified as a triple threat: a hybrid regime that incorporates all three categories of dictatorship. Triple threats are rare; when they do surface, however, they tend to be long-lasting.[35] The Egyptian triple threat regime came to power in 1952 following a coup known as the 1952 revolution that toppled the ruling monarchy. The coup was staged by a group of officers, led by Gamal Abdel Nasser. Nasser was declared president in 1956. He was succeeded by Vice President Anwar Sadat following his death in 1970; Sadat, in turn, was succeeded by Vice President Hosni Mubarak following his assassination in 1981. Today, the Egyptian dictatorship is governed by Mubarak and the National Democratic Party (NDP), which was formed in 1978. The Egyptian military, considered one of the strongest in the Middle East, also plays a major political role.[36]

Personalist Elements

Mubarak, who has ruled Egypt for more than thirty years, shares many features of personalist dictators. Similar to his predecessors, Mubarak has relied on repression and aggressive law enforcement as a means of maintaining power.[37] A state of emergency has been in place since Sadat's assassination.

The regime has continued to crack down on those who oppose it, while engaging in efforts to co-opt the primarily Islamic opposition by making Islam a more prominent aspect of public life.[38]

While Nasser and Sadat ruled in a more charismatic and forceful style, Mubarak has gained a following using other methods. His style of leadership is known for being low-key and business-like. The positive aspect of this leadership style is that it does not generate strong emotions to oust him.[39] Mubarak has also carefully built cross-cutting loyalties in order to "create a web of support for the regime in general, rather than him in particular."[40]

There are few checks on Mubarak's power, despite the regime's insistence that it is democratizing. Mubarak is above parliamentary authority and has substantial freedom to push forth his policy agenda. He can "legislate by decree when parliament is not in session" and bypass parliament altogether through a "government-sponsored referendum."[41] With the exception of the judiciary, all branches of the government are controlled by the executive.[42]

Typical of personalist dictatorships, higher-ranking military officers in Egypt are frequently rotated so that they are never able to establish strong ties or loyalties to any sectors of the military (the organizational necessity for the military to take over in a coup).[43] The Egyptian regime has also emphasized mistrust, making troops hesitant to share information with one another to hamper coordination.

Military Elements

The Egyptian dictatorship has been closely tied to the military since its formation. Nasser relied "heavily on military cadres to implement his social revolution. Officers occupied senior positions in the bureaucracy and the public sector of the economy."[44] It took Nasser over five years to consolidate his authority within the military and to weed out any opposition. He sought to merge the army with the state under the umbrella of his rule.[45] Because of his efforts, the armed forces were more loyal to the regime, than, to the general population.[46]

The role of the Egyptian military in the political sphere has declined slightly over time. The military was the main institution in the 1950s and 1960s, but this has changed somewhat since the 1970s.[47] The proportion of individuals with a military background who are involved in government has declined from 33 percent under Nasser, to 20 percent under Sadat, to 10 percent under Mubarak.[48] The military has accepted a more "subordinate role in Egypt" because its interests have always been safeguarded by the regime.[49] Mubarak has been able to limit the military's direct influence in politics without threatening the military as an institution.

The military's satisfaction is also enhanced by the fact that it is well funded. Egypt is one of the top recipients of US military aid.[50] The Egyptian military has access to the most advanced weapon systems and military training.[51] Only on one occasion (in 1986), have divisions within the military surfaced over pay and conditions. This minor revolt was quickly and fiercely put down by the armed forces.[52]

Because the military has benefited from the status quo, it has worked to preserve it. Indeed, the military has been accused of backing business deals that it directly benefits from.[53] Its substantial economic activities—representing as much as half of Egypt's manufacturing capabilities—serve as a powerful source of patronage for the regime. The military has also benefited from commissions through military contracts and arms production; it is even involved in the production of civilian goods. By 1994, the "military-controlled Administration of National Service Projects ran 16 factories which employed 75,000 workers, producing everything from agricultural machines to medications to ovens and the military's economic mandate has been extended since the early 1990s."[54]

Single-party Elements

The NDP was formed by then-President Sadat. As with the military, the NDP remains in alliance with the regime because it has too much to gain continuing to support it. The NDP has consistently secured at least a majority of seats in the People's Assembly and is the dominant party in the Egyptian political scene.[55]

Like many single-party dictatorships, the bureaucracy—and the number of jobs it creates—is used as a tool to prolong the regime's survival. As evidence of this, the Egyptian bureaucracy is quite expansive.[56] Its interests are intimately tied to the preservation of the status quo. The distribution of bureaucratic jobs is a means by which the regime rewards its most loyal supporters and gives them something at stake in the regime's continuation in power. This is particularly useful given Egypt's high levels of unemployment;

ensuring that there are plenty of government jobs available, to compel individuals, to continue to support the regime, is important for its survival.[57]

The Muslim Brotherhood, a banned political party in Egypt that serves as the most threatening force to the regime, has been allowed to win seats in the People's Assembly (through members of the party running as independent candidates). Allowing the opposition to participate in the political process (albeit in a very limited manner) deters opposition efforts from being exerted toward revolution. Despite the fact that the Muslim Brotherhood had its best showing to date in the 2005 parliamentary elections, the NDP appears to have "dealt with the threat of instability, and it has emerged from the economic and Islamist challenges in many ways stronger than it was in the late 1980s."[58]

Summary and Conclusion

In this chapter, we presented case studies exemplifying hybrid dictatorships. In doing so, we showed how these categories of regime incorporate elements of two or more types of dictatorships. Though hybrid dictatorships are less common than their "pure" counterparts, they are prevalent in the world nonetheless. As such, it is important to gain an understanding of what hybrid dictatorship means and how these blended regimes function in practice.

Notes

1. Source: James Bone and Zahid Hussain, *As Pakistan comes full circle, a light is hone on Zia ul-Haq's death* (The Times, August 18, 2008), http://www.timesonline.co.uk/tol/news/world/asia/article4543628.ece (accessed March 10, 2010).

2. Hyman et al., *Pakistan, Zia and After* (1989).

3. Cohen and Weinbaum, *Pakistan in 1981* (1982, p. 140).

4. Cohen, *Jihadist Threat to Pakistan* (2003).

5. Shah, *Pakistan's 'Armored' Democracy* (2003).

6. Richter, *Pakistan in 1985* (1986); Tiwathia (2006).

7. Richter, *Pakistan in 1985* (1986).

8. Zaidi, *State, Military and Social* (2005).

9. Wilke, *State-Formation and the Military* (2001).

10. Cohen, *Jihadist Threat to Pakistan* (2003).

11. Hussain, *Frontline Pakistan*, (2007).

12. LeoGrande, *Cuban Nation's Single Party*, (2008).

13. Ibid.

14. Palmer, *Breaking the Real Axis* (2005, p. 231).

15. Lockwood, *Caudillos: Dictators in Spanish* (1995, p. 292).

16. As Mark Palmer writes, *these policies are such a failure that Cubans face tight rationing of energy, food, and consumer goods* (2005, p. 231).

17. LeoGrande, *Cuban Nation's Single Party* (2008, p. 57).

18. Ibid.

19. Ibid. (p. 50).

20. Ibid.

21. Ibid.

22. Source: *Country profile: Cuba* (BBC News, November 3, 2009), http://news.bbc.co.uk/2/hi/americas/country_profiles/1203299.stm (accessed March 13, 2010).

23. Source: *Cuba* Economist Intelligence Unit, accessed via http://libraries.ucsd.edu/locations/sshl/resources/featured-collections/latin-american-elections-statistics/cuba/elections-and-events-19912001.html (accessed March 10, 2010).

24. C. Anderson, *Politics and Development Policy* (1961).

25. Walter and Williams, *Military and Democratization* (1993).

26. Ibid.

27. Walter and Williams, *Military and Democratization* (1993); Armstrong and Shenk (1992).

28. Armstrong and Shenk, El Salvador, The Face, (1992, p. 40).

29. Walter and Williams, *Military and Democratization* (1993).

30. Ibid.

31. Ibid.

32. Source: Country Studies, *El Salvador* United States Library of Congress (accessed March 10, 2010).

33. Walter and Williams, *Military and Democratization* (1993).

34. Armstrong and Shenk, El Salvador, The Face (1982).

35. Geddes, *Paradigms and Sand Castles* (2003).

36. McGregor, *Military History of Egypt*, (2006).

37. Alterman, *Egypt: Stable*, (2000).

38. Ibid.

39. Tripp et al., *Egypt under Mubarak* (1989).

40. Alterman, *Egypt, Stable* (2000, p. 113).

41. Blaydes, *Authoritarian Elections and Elite* (2008, p. 25).

42. Brownlee, *Decline of Pluralism* (2002).

43. Rubin, *The Military in Contemporary Middle East Politics* (2001).

44. Abdalla, *Armed Forces* (1988).

45. Ibid.

46. Rubin, *The Military in Contemporary Middle East Politics* (2001).

47. Harb, *The Egyptian Military in Politics: Disengagement or Accommodation?* (2003).

48. Tripp et al., *Egypt under Mubarak* (1989).

49. Harb 2003, *The Egyptian Military in Politics: Disengagement or Accommodation?* (p. 269).

50. *U.S. Arms Clients Profiles—Egypt* Federation of American Scientists, http://www.fas.org/asmp/profiles/egypt.htm (accessed March 12, 2010).

51. Frisch, *Guns and Butter in the Egyptian Army* (2001).

52. Rubin, *The Military in Contemporary Middle East Politics* (2001).

53. Abdalla, *Armed Forces* (1988); Springbord, *President and the Field*, (1987).

54. Blaydes, *Authoritarian Elections* (2008 p. 23).

55. Brownlee, *Decline of Pluralism* (2002).

56. Tripp et al., *Egypt under Mubarak* (1989).

57. Alterman, *Egypt: Stable* (2000).

58. Ibid. (p. 113).

Conclusion

Authoritarian politics is one of the last frontiers of political science. Uncovering systematic patterns in the behavior of dictatorships remains at the forefront of the literature in comparative politics and international relations. This study has synthesized the current state of this ever-growing field. In doing so, it has emphasized two key themes:

1. Dictatorships are not one and the same. They often differ from one another as much as they do from democracies. Lumping dictatorships into a single category can lead to serious misunderstandings about how they will behave and mask important differences in how they function internally.
2. Dictators are distinct from dictatorships. Intra-regime leadership turnover is common in dictatorships; authoritarian regimes often survive well beyond the tenure of any single leader. Viewing dictators and dictatorships as synonymous can cause fundamental confusion in the strategies that motivate leaders and elites and distort our conception of authoritarian political survival.

With these themes in mind, this study has presented key research in the authoritarian politics literature, integrating cutting-edge work in comparative politics and international relations on the subject with earlier studies to provide a complete and detailed picture of how politics works in dictatorships.

Key Highlights

In the first part of this study, we provide an introduction to the world of dictatorships. In **Chapter 1**, we offer theoretical background on how scholars categorize dictatorships and discuss the various typologies that are used to distinguish them. Such classifications are important to identify because they are the stepping stone for comparative analytical work in authoritarian politics. We emphasize that the typology used should be driven by the particular question that the researcher seeks to answer. Because this study focuses on elite-leader and elite-mass relations in dictatorships, we rely on Barbara Geddes'[1] typology, which classifies regimes as personalist, military, single-party, or amalgams of these three. This classification divides regimes according to the key institutions that shape elite politics in dictatorships (namely parties and militaries). We supplement this typology with the category of monarchies to more fully capture the types of dictatorships that have emerged in the post-World War II era.

Chapter 2 delves into the causes of authoritarianism. We look at the range of theories proposed to explain why dictatorship forms as opposed to democracy. Certain conditions appear to be breeding grounds for authoritarianism, namely poverty and economic inequality. Historical and geo-political factors also seem to influence where and when dictatorships surface. Though little systematic research has been done exploring why different *types* of dictatorships emerge, there are clear trends in their regional distribution: personalist dictatorships are more common in sub-Saharan Africa, military dictatorships are more common in Latin America, single-party dictatorships are more common in Asia and Eastern Europe, and monarchies are more common in the Middle East.

In **Chapter 3**, we look at the survival rates of dictatorships. We illustrate how regime type affects the behavior of leaders and elites and, in turn, the regime's survival. Single-party dictatorships are the most long-lasting type of regime, followed by personalist dictatorships, and lastly military dictatorships. Though few studies have comparatively tested the durability of monarchies, monarchies on the surface appear to be fairly durable. More research is needed to test this relationship. This chapter also examines the pivotal role that elections and political parties play in the longevity of dictatorships, showing how these institutions serve as tools that strengthen authoritarian regimes and prolong their survival. The ways in which dictatorships fall from power are also discussed.

Chapter 4 changes the focus from the survival of authoritarian *regimes* to the survival of authoritarian *leaders*. In it, we emphasize the pivotal role of elites in the survival of dictators. Indeed, the dictator's elite support group is most often responsible for the dictator's downfall. The institutional structure of the dictatorship shapes how easy or hard it is for elites to oust dictators. As a result, personalist leaders have the longest survival rates, followed by single-party leaders, and lastly military leaders. This chapter also looks at how dictators are ousted, identifying the types of regimes in which ousters are likely to be violent and when they are likely to destabilize the regime.

Because of the key role that coups play in authoritarian politics—in spurring the formation of new dictators and dictatorships and in marking their downfall—**Chapter 5** is devoted to coups. It examines what coups mean, why and how they occur, and the factors that are required for their success. The next three chapters show how the type of dictatorships affects international and domestic political outcomes. **Chapter 6** explores the relationship between regime type and policy gridlock, or how easy or hard it is for regimes to enact large changes in policy. It identifies the key actors in the decision-making process in dictatorships: leaders and elites. Whether the regime is dominated by a party, military, or neither influences the similarity of the policy preferences of leaders and elites, as well as the ability of elites to "veto" the policy choices of the leader. We show that policy gridlock is most intense in single-party dictatorships, followed by military dictatorships, and lastly, personalist dictatorships.

In **Chapter 7**, we examine the relationship between regime type and the economy. We discuss the literature on domestic political institutions and economic performance, highlighting the types of regimes that have experienced economic miracles, as well as those that have been prey to economic disasters. This chapter also looks at the way in which regime type affects dictators' use of foreign aid and their propensity for corrupt behavior. Personalist dictatorships appear more prone than their counterparts to engage in corruption and to steal from the state in a predatory manner. More research is needed to explain this correlation, as well as to further disentangle the complex relationship between authoritarian regime type and economic performance.

Chapter 8 switches gears and discuses how dictatorship affects international conflict behavior. This chapter shows that regime type influences how well states can signal their resolve during international conflicts, making some dictatorships less likely to be participants in escalatory disputes than others. It also delves into the relationship between regime type and the quality of military intelligence that leaders receive from their advisers. Because personalist dictators receive poorer quality intelligence from their advisory group, they are more likely to commit foreign policy errors.

The following four chapters in this study (**Chapters 9** through **12**) examine each type of dictatorship in depth, merging the theoretical work dedicated to personalist, military, single-party, and monarchic dictatorships with a selection of case studies. They provide detailed analyses of how these heterogeneous regimes behave, how politics works within them, and the factors and strategies that are critical to their survival. The case studies, in turn, illustrate how these ideas function in practice. Lastly, **Chapter 13** looks briefly at hybrid dictatorships, giving real-world examples of each type of hybrid dictatorships to highlight what blended regimes mean in reality.

Dictatorships are pervasive in the world's political landscape, and they also appear to be persistent. Gaining a better understanding of how dictatorships work, who the key political actors are, the incentives these actors face, the institutional environments they operate in, and the tools that they use to enhance their political survival, is a critical endeavor. It enables the development of a more informed foreign policy with respect to authoritarian regimes, while providing for more precise, theoretically- and empirically-driven analyses and assessments of their current and future political behavior.

This study offers a comprehensive analysis of dictatorships, covering a range of theoretical and empirical research agendas devoted to authoritarian regimes and their leaders. It points out the major developments in the field of authoritarian politics, as well as the important questions that remain. In doing so, this study provides a window into the colorful world of dictatorships, reducing some of the mystery and misconceptions that shroud them.

Note

1. Geddes, Paradigms and Sand Castles (2003).

Bibliography

Abdalla, Ahmed. "The Armed Forces and the Democratic Process in Egypt." *Third World Quarterly* 10, 4 (October 1988): 1452–1466.

Acemoglu, Daron and James Robinson. *Economic Origins of Dictatorship and Democracy.* Cambridge, UK: Cambridge University Press, 2006.

Acemoglu, Daron, James Robinson and Thierry Verdier. "Kleptocracy and Divide and Rule: A Model of Personal Rule." *Journal of European Economic Association* 2 (April–May 2004): 162–192.

Acemoglu, Daron and James Robinson. "A Theory of Political Transitions." *The American Economic Review* 91, 4 (September 2001): 938–963

Acemoglu, Daron, Davide Ticchi and Andrea Vindigni. "A Theory of Military Dictatorships." *American Economic Journal: Macroeconomics* 2, 1 (January 2010): 1–42.

Adams, Jefferson. "The Strange Demise of East German State Security." *International Journal of Intelligence and Counter-Intelligence* 18, 1 (December 2004): 1–22.

Adejumobi, Said. "Elections in Africa: A Fading Shadow of Democracy?" *International Political Science Review* 21, 1 (2000): 59–73.

Afoaku, Osita G. "The Politics of Democratic Transition in Congo (Zaire): Implications of the Kabila Revolution." *Journal of Conflict Studies* 19, 2 (1999): 1–21.

Agyeman-Duah, Baffour. "Military Coups, Regime Change and Interstate Conflicts in West Africa." *Armed Forces and Society* 16, 4 (1990): 547–570.

Alagappa, Muthiah. *Political Legitimacy in Southeast Asia: A Quest for Moral Authority.* Stanford, CA: Stanford University Press, 1995.

Albrecht, Holger and Oliver Schlumberger. "'Waiting for Godot': Regime Change without Democratization in the Middle East." *International Political Science Review* 25, 4 (2004): 371–392.

Almond, Gabriel and Sidney Verba. *The Civic Culture: Political Attitudes and Democracy in Five Nations.* Princeton, NJ: Princeton University Press, 1963.

Alterman, Jon B. "Egypt: Stable, but for How Long?" *The Washington Quarterly* 23, 4 (Autumn 2000): 107–118.

Aluko, Olajide. "African Response to External Intervention in Africa since Angola." *African Affairs* 80 (1981): 159– 179.

Alvarez, Michael and John Brehm. "American Ambivalence towards Abortion Policy: Development of a Heteroskedastic Probit Model of Competing Values." *American Journal of Political Science* 39 (November 1995): 1055–1082.

Alvarez, Michael, Jose Antonio Cheibub, Fernando Limongi and Adam Przeworski. "Classifying Political Regimes." *Studies in Comparative International Development* 31, 2 (Summer 1996): 3–36.

Amadife, Egbunam. "Liberalization and Democratization in Nigeria: The International and Domestic Challenge." *Journal of Black Studies* 29, 5 (May 1999): 614–645.

Amelia: A Program for Missing Data (Windows Version). Cambridge, MA: Harvard University. http://GKing.Harvard.edu

Anderson, Charles W. "Politics and Development Policy in Central America." *Midwest Journal of Political Science* 5, 4 (November 1961): 332–350.

Anderson, Lisa. "Absolutism and the Resilience of Monarchy in the Middle East." *Political Science Quarterly* 106, 1 (Spring 1991): 1–15.

Aphornsuvan, Thanet. "The Search for Order: Constitutions and Human Rights in Thai Political History." Paper presented at Australian National University, 2001 Symposium: Constitutions and Human Rights in a Global Age: An Asia Pacific perspective, September 28, 2004.

Aquino, Belinda. *Politics of Plunder: The Philippines under Marcos*. Manila, Philippines: University of the Philippines Press, 1997.

Arendt, Hannah. "The Origins of Totalitarianism: A Reply." *The Review of Politics* 15, 1 (January 1953): 76–84.

Arendt, Hannah. *The Origins of Totalitarianism*. New York, NY: Harvest Press, 1951.

Armstrong, Robert and Janet Shenk. *El Salvador, The Face of Revolution*. Boston, MA: South End Press 1982.

Avery, Peter. *Modern Iran*. London, UK: Earnest Benn Limited, 1965.

Bacchus, Wilfred A. *Mission in Mufti: Brazil's Military Regimes, 1964–1985*. Westport, CT: Greenwood Press, 1990.

Bachman, David. "Institutions, Factions, Conservatism, and Leadership Change in China: The Case of Hu Yaobang." In *Leadership Change in Communist States*, edited by Raymond C. Taras, 129–155. Boston, MA: Unwin Hyman Inc, 1989.

Baines, John M. "U.S. Military Assistance to Latin America: An Assessment." *Journal of Inter-American Studies and World Affairs* 14, 4, Special Issue: Military and Reform Governments in Latin America (November 1972): 469–487.

Banks, A. S, Cross-national time-series data archive (data set). Binghamton, NY: Computer Systems Unlimited, 2001.

Barkey, Henry J. "Why Military Regimes Fail: The Perils of Transition." *Armed Forces and Society* 16, 2 (Winter 1990): 169–192.

Barros, ASC. *The Brazilian Military: Professional Socialization, Political Performance*. Chicago, IL: University of Chicago, 1978.

Barros, Robert. *Constitutionalism and Dictatorship: Pinochet, the Junta, and the 1980 Constitution*. Cambridge: Cambridge University Press, 2002.

Barros, Robert. "Personalization and Institutional Constraints: Pinochet, the Military Junta, and the 1980 Constitution." *Latin American Politics and Society* 43, 1 (Spring 2001): 5–28.

Basajabka, Abu, Kawalya Kasozi, Nakanyike Musis, and James Mukooza Sejjengo. *Social Origins of Violence in Uganda: 1964–85*. Montreal: McGill-Queens University Press, 1994.

Batt, Judy. "Political Reform in Hungary." *Parliamentary Affairs* (1990): 464–481.

Baum, Matthew A. "Going Private: Public Opinion, Presidential Rhetoric, and the Domestic Politics of Audience Costs in U.S. Foreign Policy Crises." *Journal of Conflict Resolution* 48 (October 2004): 603–31.

Baum, Richard, *Burying Mao: Chinese Politics in the Age of Deng Xioaping*, Princeton, NJ: Princeton University Press, 1996.

Bearak, B. "Pakistan Is." *New York Times*, December 7, 2003.

Beck, Lois. "Revolutionary Iran and Its Tribal Peoples." *MERIP Reports* 87, Iran's Revolution: The Rural Dimension (May 1980): 14–20.

Be'eri, Eliezer. "A Note on Coups d'Etat in the Middle East." *Journal of Contemporary History* 5, 2 (1970): 123–129.

Belkin, Aaron and Evan Schofer. "Toward a Structural Understanding of Coup Risk." *Journal of Conflict Resolution* 47, 5 (2003): 594–620.

Bellin, Eva. "The Robustness of Authoritarianism in the Middle East: Exceptionalism in Comparative Perspective." *Comparative Politics* 36, 2 (January 2004): 139–157.

Bendix, Reinhard, *Kings or People: Power and the Mandate to Rule*, Berkeley, CA: University of California Press, Berkeley, 1978.

Bennett, D. Scott and Allan Stam. "EUGene: A Conceptual Manual." *International Interactions* 26 (2000): 179–204.

Berend, Tibor Ivan, *Central and Eastern Europe, 1944–1993,* Cambridge, UK: Cambridge University Press, 1999.

Bergara, M. "A Cross-National Analysis." *California Management Review* 40, 2 (1998): 18–35.

Berg-Schlosser, Dirk. "Democracy and the One-Party State in Kenya". In *Democracy and the One-Party State in Africa,* edited by Peter Meyns and Dani Wadada Nebudere, Hamburg: German Association of Political Science Publication, 1989.

Berrios, Carlos, G. "Civil Military Relations and Democratization in Guatemala." Masters diss.,U.S. State Navy, 1998.

Bertocchi, Graziella, and Michael Spagat. "The Politics of Co-optation." *Journal of Comparative Economics* 29, 4 (2001): 591–607.

Betts, Richard K. "Surprise Despite Warning: Why Sudden Attacks Succeed." *Political Science Quarterly* 95, 4 (Winter, 1980–1981): 551–572.

Bhattarai, Keshab. "Political Economy of Conflict, Cooperation and Economic Growth: Nepalese Dilemma." (May 2005): 1–30.

Bienen, Henry. *Armies and Parties in Africa.* New York, NY: African Publishing Company, 1978a.

Bienen, Henry. "Military Rule and Political Processes: Nigerian Examples." *Comparative Politics,* 2 (1978b): 205–225.

Bienen, Henry. "Military and Society in East Africa." *Comparative Politics* 6 (July 1974): 489–517.

Bienen, Henry and Mark Gersovitz. "Economic Stabilization, Conditionality, and Political Stability." *International Organization* 39, 4 (Autumn 1985): 729–754.

Bienen, Henry and Nicolas van de Walle, *Of Time and Power: Leadership Duration in the Modern World,* Stanford, CA: Stanford University Press, 1991.

Bienen, Henry and Nicolas van de Walle. "Time and Power in Africa." *American Political Science Review* 83 (1989): 19–34.

Binder, Leonard. *Iran: Political Development in Changing Society.* Berkeley, CA: University of California Press, Berkeley, 1962.

Black, Craig R. "Deterring Libya: The Strategic Culture of Muammar Qaddafi." *The Counter-proliferation Papers, Future Warfare Series* 8, USAF Counter-Proliferation Center, Air War College (2000): 1–30.

Blaydes, Lisa. "Authoritarian Elections and Elite Management: Theory and Evidence from Egypt" Paper presented at the Princeton University Conference on Dictatorships, Princeton, NJ, April 2008: 1–31.

Blaydes, Lisa. "Electoral Budget Cycles under Authoritarianism: Economic Opportunism in Mubarak's Egypt." Paper presented at the annual meeting of the Midwest Political Science Association, Palmer House Hilton, Chicago, Illinois, April 2006: 1–24.

Block, Steven. "Political Business Cycles, Democratization, and Economic Reform: The Case of Africa." *Journal of Development Economics* 67, 1 (February 2002): 205–228.

Bloomfield, Adrian. "Anxiety in Europe after sudden death of Turkmen dictator." *Telegraph,* December, 14, 2006, online edition.

Blum, Douglas W. "The Soviet Foreign Policy Belief System: Beliefs, Politics, and Foreign Policy Outcomes." *International Studies Quarterly* 37, 4 (December 1993): 373–394.

Bøås, Morten. "Liberia and Sierra Leone: Dead Ringers? The Logic of Neo-patrimonial Rule." *Third World Quarterly* 22, 5 (October 2001): 697–723.

Boix, Carles. *Democracy and Redistribution.* Cambridge, UK: Cambridge University Press, 2003.

Bone, James and Zahid Hussain, "As Pakistan comes full circle, a light is hone on Zia ul-Haq's death," The Times, 18 Aug 2008, http://www.timesonline.co.uk/tol/news/world/asia/article4543628.ece (accessed on 12 Mar 2010).

Bosco, Joseph. "Faction versus Ideology: Mobilization Strategies in Taiwan's Elections." *The China Quarterly* 137 (March 1994): 28–62.

Bosco, Joseph. "Taiwan Factions: Guanxi, Patronage, and the State in Local Politics." *Ethnology* 31, 2 (April 1992): 157–183.

Box-Steffensmeier, Janet M. and Christopher J. W. Zorn. "Duration Models and Proportional Hazards in Political Science." *American Journal of Political Science* 45 (2002): 951–67.

Brada, Josef C. "Interpreting the Soviet Subsidization of Eastern Europe." *International Organization* 42, 4 (Autumn 1988): 639–658.

Bratton, Michael and Nicolas van de Walle, *Democratic Experiments in Africa: Regime Transitions in Comparative Perspective*, Cambridge, UK: Cambridge University Press, 1997.

Bratton, Michael and Nicolas van de Walle. "Neo-patrimonial Regimes and Political Transitions in Africa." *World Politics* 46, 4 (July 1994): 453–489.

Braumoeller, Bear F. "Explaining Variance: Or, Stuck In a Moment We Can't Get Out Of." *Political Analysis* 14 (2006): 268–290.

Brett, E.A. "Neutralizing the Use of Force in Uganda: The Role of the Military in Politics." *The Journal of Modern African Studies* 33, 1 (March 1995): 129–152.

Brooker, Paul. *Non-Democratic Regimes: Theory, Government, and Politics*. London, UK: Macmillan Press, 2000.

Brooker, Paul. *Twentieth-century Dictatorships: The Ideological One-Party States*. London, UK: Macmillan Press, 1995.

Brown, D.S., and W. Hunter. "Democracy and Social Spending in Latin America, 1980–92." *American Political Science Review* 37 (1999): 1207–1230.

Brown, Stephen. "Authoritarian Leaders and Multiparty Elections in Africa: how foreign donors help to keep Kenya's Daniel Arap Moi in power." *Third World Quarterly* 22, 5 (2001): 725–739.

Brownlee, Jason. *Authoritarianism in an Age of Democratization*. Cambridge, UK: Cambridge University Press, 2007.

Brownlee, Jason. "The Decline of Pluralism in Mubarak's Egypt." *Journal of Democracy* 13, 4 (2002): 6–14.

Brumberg, Daniel. "The Trap of Liberalized Autocracy." *Journal of Democracy* 13, 4 (2002): 56–68.

Brzezinski, Zbigniew. *Ideology and Power in Soviet Politics*. Westport, CT: Westport Press, 1962.

Brzezinski, Zbigniew. "Totalitarianism and Rationality." *American Political Science Review* 50, 3 (1956): 751–763.

Bueno de Mesquita, Bruce and Randolph M. Siverson. "War and the Survival of Political Leaders: A Comparative Study of Regime Types and Political Accountability." *American Political Science Review* 89, 4 (December 1995): 841–855.

Bueno de Mesquita, Bruce, Alastair Smith, Randolph M. Silverson, and James D. Morrow. "An Institutional Explanation of the Democratic Peace." *American Political Science Review* 93 (December 1999): 791–807.

Bueno de Mesquita, Bruce, Alastair Smith, Randolph M. Silverson, and James D. Morrow, *The Logic of Political Survival*, Boston, MA: Massachusetts Institute of Technology Press, 2003.

Bunbongkarn, Suchit. "Thailand in 1991: Coping with Military Guardianship." *Asian Survey* 32, 2 (February 1992): 131–139.

Bunce, Valerie. "Comparing East and South." *Journal of Democracy* 6, 3 (1995): 87–100.

Bunce, Valerie. "Rethinking Recent Democratization: Lessons from the Post-Communist Experience." *World Politics* 55 (January 2003): 167–192.

Bunce, Valerie, and John M. Echols, III. "Power and Policy in Communist Systems: The Problem of 'Incrementalism'." *The Journal of Politics* 40, 4 (1978): 911–932.

Butts, Kent Hugh and Steven Metz. "Armies and Democracy in the New Africa: Lessons from Nigeria and South Africa." *Strategic Studies Institute* (January 9, 1996): 1–35.

Byman, Daniel and Jerrold Green. "The Enigma of Political Stability in the Persian Gulf Monarchies." *MERIA* 3, 3 (September 1999): 20–37.

Cammack, Paul. "Political Development Theory and the Dissemination of Democracy." *Democratization* 1, 2 (Summer 1994): 353–374.

Carothers, Thomas. "The End of the Transition Paradigm." *Journal of Democracy* 13, 1 (January 2002): 5–21.

Carothers, Thomas. "Why Dictators Aren't Dominoes." *Foreign Policy* 137 (July - August, 2003): 59–60.

Carranza, Mario. "Review Essay: Military Coups and Militarization in Latin America." *Journal of Peace Research* 20, 4 (1983): 367–375.

Case, William. "Comparative Malaysian Leadership: Tunku Abdul Rahman and Mahathir Mohamad." *Asian Survey* 31, 5 (May 1991): 456–473.

Case, William. "New Uncertainties for an Old Pseudo-Democracy: The Case of Malaysia." *Comparative Politics* 37, 1 (October 2004): 83–104.

Case, William. "Semi-Democracy in Malaysia: Withstanding the Pressures for Regime Change." *Pacific Affairs* 66, 2 (Summer 1993): 183–205.

Case, William. "The 1996 UMNO Party Election: "Two for the Show." *Pacific Affairs* 70, 3 (Autumn 1997): 393–411.

Case, William. "The UMNO Party Election in Malaysia: One for the Money." *Asian Survey* 34, 10 (October 1994): 916–930.

Castañeda, Jorge. *Perpetuating Power: How Mexican Presidents Were Chosen.* New York, NY: The New Press, 2000.

Celoza, Albert F. *Ferdinand Marcos and the Philippines: The Political Economy of Authoritarianism.* Westport, CT: Greenwood Publishing Group Inc, 1997.

Champion, Daryl. "The Kingdom of Saudi Arabia: Elements of Instability within Stability." *MERIA* 3, 4 (December 1999): 49–73

Chehabi, H.E. and Juan Linz (Ed.). *Sultanistic Regimes.* Baltimore, MD: Johns Hopkins University Press, 1998.

Cheng, Li and Lynn White. "The Sixteenth Central Committee of the Chinese Communist Party: Hu Gets What?" *Asian Survey* 43, 4 (July- August 2003): 553–597.

Cheng, Tun-jen. "Embracing Defeat: The KMT and the PRI after 2000." In *Political Transitions in Dominant Party Systems: Learning to Lose*, edited by Edward Friedman, Joseph Wong, 127–147. New York, NY: Routledge, 2008.

Cheng, Tun-jen, and Stephan Haggard. "Taiwan in Transition." *Journal of Democracy* 1, 2 (Spring 1990): 62–74.

Cheng, Tun-jen and Stephan Haggard. "Taiwan in Transition." *Journal of Democracy* 1, 2 (Spring 2000): 1–14.

Chiozza, Giacomo, and Henk E. Goemans. "International Conflict and the Tenure of Leaders, Is War Still Ex Post Inefficient?" *American Journal of Political Science* 48, 3 (2004): 604–619.

Chirot, Daniel. *Modern Tyrants: The Power and Prevalence of Evil in Our Age.* Princeton, NJ: Princeton University Press, 1994.

Chirot, Daniel. "What Happened in Eastern Europe in 1989?" *Praxis International* 10, 3/4 (1991): 278–305.

Chorley, Katharine Campbell. *Armies and the Art of Revolution.* Boston, MA: Beacon Press, 1973.

Chung-Hon Shih, Victor. "'Nauseating' Displays of Loyalty: Monitoring the Factional Bargain through Ideological Campaigns in China." *Journal of Politics* 70, 4 (October 2008): 1–16.

Clarke, Kevin A. and Randall W. Stone. "Democracy and the Logic of Political Survival." *American Political Science Review* (Forthcoming).

Cohen, Stephen. "The Jihadist Threat to Pakistan." *The Washington Quarterly* 26, 3 (Summer 2003): 7–25.

Cohen, Stephen and Marvin G. Weinbaum, "Pakistan in 1981: Staying On." *Asian Survey*, 22, 2, A Survey of Asia in 1981: Part II (February 1982): 136–146.

Collier, David and Steven Levitsky. "Democracy with Adjectives: Conceptual Innovation in Comparative Research." *World Politics* 49 (April 1997): 430–51.

Collier, Paul and Anke Hoeffler. "Greed and Grievance in Civil War." *CSAE WPS* (March 13, 2002a): 1–43.

Collier, Paul and Anke Hoeffler. "On the Incidence of Civil War in Africa." *Journal of Conflict Resolution* 46, 1 (February 2002b): 13–28.

Collins, P. and M. Dixon, G. Williams. "Nigeria: Capitalism and the Coup." *Review of African Political Economy* 4 (November 1975): 95–98.

Common, Richard. "Administrative Change in the Gulf: Modernization in Bahrain and Oman." *International Review of Administrative Sciences* 74, 2 (2008): 177–193.

Congleton, Roger D. "Political Institutions and Pollution Control." *Review of Economics and Statistics* 74, 3 (1992): 412–421.

Cordesman, Anthony H. *Saudi Arabia Enters the Twenty-First Century.* Westport, CT: Praeger, 2003.

Cordesman, Anthony H. and Khalid R. Al-Rodhan. "The Gulf Military Forces in an Era of Asymmetric War." Working Draft (June 28, 2006): 1–106.

Cox, Gary. "Authoritarian Elections and Leadership Succession, 1975–2000." (November 12, 2007; revised June 17, 2009): 1–45.

Crabb, John H. "The Coronation of Emperor Bokassa." *Africa Today: Smaller States and Larger Neighbors* 25, 3 (July- September, 1978): 25–44.

Crassweller, Robert, *Trujillo: The Life and Times of a Caribbean Dictator,* New York: MacMillan Company, 1966.

Crawford, Vince and Joel Sobel. "Strategic Information Transmission." *Econometrica* 50 (1982): 1432–52.

Crespo, Jose Antonio. "Party Competition in Mexico: Evolution and Prospects". In *Dilemmas of Political Change in Mexico,* edited by Kevin Middlebrook, 57–81. London: Institute of Latin American Studies University of London / Center for U.S. – Mexico Studies, University of California, San Diego, 2004.

Crouch, Harold. *Government and Society in Malaysia.* Ithaca, NY: Cornell University Press, 1996.

Dahl, Robert. *Democracy and its Critics.* New Haven, CT: Yale University Press, 1991.

Dalpino, Catherine. "Thailand's Search for Political Accountability." *Journal of Democracy* 2, 4 (Fall 1991): 61–71.

Davis, John Uniack and Aboubacar B. Kossomi. "Niger Gets Back On Track." *Journal of Democracy* 12, 3 (2001): 80–87.

Decalo, Samuel. "African Personal Dictatorships." *The Journal of Modern African Studies* 23, 2 (June 1985): 209–237.

Decalo, Samuel, *Coups and Army Rule in Africa: Studies in Military Style*, New Haven, CT: Yale University Press, 1976.

Decalo, Samuel. "Military Coups and Military Regimes in Africa." *The Journal of Modern African Studies* 11, 1 (March 1973): 105–127

Decalo, Samuel. *Psychoses of Power: African Personal Dictatorships.* Boulder, CO: Westview Press, 1989.

Dennis, M. and P Brown. *Stasi: Myth and Reality.* London, UK: Longman Press, 2003.

Diamond, Larry. *Developing Democracy toward Consolidation.* Baltimore, MD: Johns Hopkins University Press, 1999.

Diamond, Larry. "Thinking about Hybrid Regimes: Elections without Democracy." *Journal of Democracy* 13, 2 (2002): 21–35.

Diederich, Bernard. *Trujillo: The Death of the Goat.* Boston, MA: Little, Brown, 1978.

Dittmer, Lowell. "Leadership Change and Chinese Political Development." *China Quarterly* (2003): 903–925.

Dittmer, Lowell, and Yu-Shan Wu. "The Modernization of Factionalism in Chinese Politics." *World Politics* 47, 4 (1995): 467–494.

Dix, Robert H. "The Breakdown of Authoritarian Regimes." *The Western Political Quarterly* 35, 4 (December 1982): 554–573.

Dlami, Marietta P. "Success and Competence in Agricultural Business by Retired Military Officers in Swaziland." Paper presented at AIAEE 22nd Annual Conference, Clearwater Beach, FL: 174–182. 2006.

Dolton, P.J. and G.H. Makepeace. "Interpreting Sample Selection Effects." *Economics Letters* 24 (1987): 373–379.

Dominguez, Jorge I. "Leadership Changes, Factionalism, and Organizational Politics in Cuba since 1960." In *Leadership Change in Communist States*, edited by Raymond C. Taras, 129–155. Boston, MA: Unwin Hyman, Inc, 1989.

Dore, Rosemary and Simone Ribeiro, "Political citizenship and the vote of the illiterate in Brazil." Paper presented at International Seminar of the ESREA Research Network "Between Global and Local: Adult Learning & Development" - Magdeburg University, May 28–30, 2009: 49–65.

Downs, George W. and David M. Rocke. "Interpreting Heteroscedasticity." *American Journal of Political Science* 23 (1979): 816–28.

Edwards, George C. "Why Not the Best? The Loyalty-Competence Trade-Off in Presidential Appointments." *The Brookings Review* 19, 2 (2001).

Egorov, Georgy and Konstantin Sonin. "Dictators and Their Viziers: Agency Problems in Dictatorships." *William Davidson Institute Working Papers Series*, 2005.

Egorov, Georgy and Konstantin Sonin. "Dictators and their Viziers: Endogenizing the Loyalty-Competence Trade-off." (May 10, 2006): 1–30.

Ehteshami, Anoushiravan. "Reform from Above: The Politics of Participation in the Oil Monarchies." *International Affairs* 79, 1 (January 2003): 53–75.

Eindlin, Fred. "Two Faces of Czechoslovak Communism." *East Central Europe* 10 (1983): 185–190.

Elkins, David J and Richard E.B. Simeon. "A Cause in Search of Its Effects, or What Does Political Culture Explain." *Comparative Politics* 11, 2 (January 1979): 127–145.

Englebert, Pierre. "Pre-Colonial Institutions, Post-Colonial States, and Economic Development in Tropical Africa." *Political Research Quarterly* 53, 1 (March 2000): 7–36.

Escribà-Folch, Abel and Joseph G. Wright, "Dealing with Tyranny, "International Sanctions and Autocrats' Duration." *IBEI Working Papers* 16 (2008): 2–25.

Eyerman, Joe and Robert A. Hart, Jr. "An Empirical Test of the Audience Cost Proposition: Democracy Speaks Louder than Words." *The Journal of Conflict Resolution* 40, 4 (1996): 597–616.

Fairbanks, Charles. "Revolution Reconsidered." *Journal of Democracy* 18, 1 (January 2007): 42–57.

Farouk-Sluglett, Marion and Peter Sluglett. *Iraq since 1958: From Revolution to Dictatorship.* New York, NY: I.B. Tauris, 2001.

Farrell, Joseph. "Communication, Coordination, and Nash Equilibrium." *Economic Letters* 27 (1988): 209–214.

Fatas, Antonio, and Ilian Mihov. "Policy Volatility, Institutions and Economic Growth." (2005), available at SSRN: http://ssrn.com/abstract=887544.

Fatton Jr., Robert. "Liberal Democracy in Africa." *Political Science Quarterly* 105, 3 (Autumn 1990): 455–473.

Fearon, James. "Domestic Political Audiences and the Escalation of International Conflict." *American Political Science Review* 88 (September 1994a): 577–592.

Fearon, James. "Primary Commodity Exports and Civil War." *Journal of Conflict Resolution* 49 (2005): 483–507.

Fearon, James. "Signaling Foreign Policy Interests: Tying Hands versus Sinking Costs." *Journal of Conflict Resolution* 41, 1 (1997): 68–90.

Fearon, James. "Signaling Versus the Balance of Power and Interests: An Empirical Test of a Crisis Bargaining Model." *Journal of Conflict Resolution* 38, 2 (1994b): 236–69.

Feit, Edward. "Pen, Sword, and People: Military Regimes in the Formation of Political Institutions." *World Politics* 25, 2 (January 1973): 251–273.

Ferguson, James. *Papa Doc, Baby Doc: Haiti and the Duvaliers.* Oxford, UK: Blackwell Press, 1987.

"Fidel Castro Resigns Cuban Presidency After Half-Century in Power." *Associated Press*, February 19, 2008.

Finer, Samuel E. *The Man on Horseback: Military Intervention into Politics.* Harmondsworth, UK: Penguin Press, 1962.

Finer, Samuel E. "State and Nation-Building in Europe: The Role of the Military." In *The Formation of National States in Western Europe*, edited by Charles Tilly, 84–163. Princeton, NJ: Princeton University Press, 1975.

Fish, M. Steven and Robin S Brooks. "Does Diversity Hurt Democracy?" *Journal of Democracy* 15, 1 (January 2004): 154–167.

Fitch, John Samuel. *The Armed Forces and Democracy in Latin America.* Baltimore, MD: Johns Hopkins University Press, 1998.

Fox, John. "Cox Proportional-Hazards Regression for Survival Data." http://cran.r-project.org/doc/contrib/Fox Companion/appendix-cox-regression.pdf (2002)

Frantz, Erica. *Tying the Dictator's Hands: Elite Coalitions in Authoritarian Regimes.* Ph.D. diss., University of California, Los Angeles, 2008.

Frantz, Erica and Natasha Ezrow. "'Yes Men' and the Likelihood of Foreign Policy Mistakes Across Dictatorships." Paper presented at the American Political Science Association Annual Meeting. Toronto, CA, September 3–6, 2009.

Friedrich, Carl and Zbigniew Brzezinski. *Totalitarian Dictatorship and Autocracy.* Cambridge, MA: Harvard University Press, 1956.

Frisch, Hillel. "Guns and Butter in the Egyptian Army." *MERIA* 5, 2 (Summer 2001): 1–12.

Fulbrook, Mary. *Anatomy of a Dictatorship: Inside the GDR 1949–1989.* Oxford, UK: Oxford University Press 1997.

Galbraith, James. *The Predatory State.* New York, NY: Free Press Publishers, 2008.

Gallego, Maria and Carolyn Pitchik. "An Economic Theory of Leadership Turnover." *Journal of Public Economics* 88, 12 (2004): 2361–2382.

Gandhi, Jennifer. "Dictatorial Institutions and their Impact on Economic Performance." Paper presented at the American Political Science Association Annual Meeting. Philadelphia, PA, August 28–31, 2003.

Gandhi, Jennifer. *Political Institutions under Dictatorships.* Cambridge, UK: Cambridge University Press, 2008.

Gandhi, Jennifer and Ellen Lust-Okar. "Elections under Authoritarianism." *Annual Review of Political Science* 12 (June 2009): 403–422.

Gandhi, Jennifer and Adam Przeworski. "Authoritarian Institutions and the Survival of Autocrats." *Comparative Political Studies* 40, 11 (November 2007): 1279–1301.

Gandhi, Jennifer and Adam Przeworski. "Cooperation, Cooptation and Rebellion under Dictatorship." *Economics and Politics* 18, 1 (2006): 1–26.

Geddes, Barbara. "Minimum-Winning Coalitions and Personalization of Rule in Authoritarian Regimes." Paper presented American Political Science Association, Chicago, August, 2004.

Geddes, Barbara. *Paradigms and Sand Castles: Theory Building and Research Design in Comparative Politics.* Ann Arbor, MI: University of Michigan Press, 2003.

Geddes, Barbara. "Party Creation as an Autocratic Survival Strategy." Paper presented at a Conference on Dictators, Princeton University, April 2008.

Geddes, Barbara. "The Role of Elections in Authoritarian Regimes." Paper presented at the American Political Science Association Annual Meeting, Washington DC, September 1, 2005.

Geddes, Barbara. "What Do We Know about Democratization after Twenty Years?" *Annual Review of Political Science II* (1999): 115–44.

Geddes, Barbara. "Why Parties and Elections in Authoritarian Regimes?" Paper presented at the American Political Science Association, Washington DC, September, 2005.

Geddes, Barbara, and Erica Frantz. "The Legacy of Dictatorship for Democratic Parties in Latin America." American Political Science Association Annual Meeting, 2007, Chicago, IL, Aug 30-Sep 02.

Geddes, Barbara and John Zaller. "Sources of Popular Support for Authoritarian Regimes." *American Journal of Political Science* 33, 2 (May 1989): 319–347.

Gelpi, Christopher and Michael Griesdorf. "Winners or losers? Democracies in International Crises, 1918–1994." *American Political Science Review* 95, 3 (2001): 633–647.

Gertzel, Cherry (Ed.). *The Dynamics of the One-Party State in Zambia.* Manchester: Manchester University Press, 1984.

Gertzel, Cherry. "Uganda after Amin: The Continuing Search for Leadership and Control." *African Affairs* 79, 317 (October 1980): 461–489

Gheissari, Ali and Seyyed Vali Reza Nasr. *Democracy in Iran: history and the quest for liberty.* Oxford, UK: Oxford University Press, 2006.

Giliomee, Herman Buhr and Charles Simkins. *The Awkward Embrace: One Party Domination and Democracy.* Amsterdam, Netherlands: Routledge, 1999.

Gill, Emily R. "Modern Authoritarianism: A Comparative Institutional Analysis by Amos Perlmutter." *The Journal of Politics* 47, 4 (November 1985): 1252–1254.

Gillespie, Charles. *Negotiating Democracy.* Cambridge, UK: Cambridge University Press, 1991.

Girling, John. "Thailand in Gramscian Perspective." *Pacific Affairs* 57, 3 (Autumn 1984): 385–403.

Gleditsch, Kristian and Erik Gartzke. "The Ties that Bias: Specifying and Operationalizing Components of Dyadic Dependence." *Working Paper,* 2006.

Gleditsch, Nils Petter. "Do Open Windows Encourage Conflict?" *Statsvetenskaplig Tidskrift* 102, 3 (1999): 333–343.

Godement, Francois. *The New Asian Renaissance.* New York, NY: Routledge, 1997.

Goemans, Hein E. *The Causes of War Termination: Domestic Politics and War Aims.* Ph.D. diss., Department of Political Science, University of Chicago, 1995.

Goemans, Hein E. "Fighting for Survival: The Fate of Leaders and the Duration of War." *The Journal of Conflict Resolution* 44, 5 (October 2000): 555–579.

Goemans, Hein, Kristian Skrede Gleditsch, and Giacomo Chiozza. "Case Description File: June 2007." Archigos: A Data Set of Leaders 1875–2004: http://mail.rochester.edu/~hgoemans/CaseDescriptionJune2007.pdf

Golden, Miriam and Eric Chang. "Corruption and Authoritarian Regimes." Paper presented at the annual meeting of the American Political Science Association, Philadelphia, PA, August 31, 2006.

Goldsmith, Arthur A. "Donors, Dictators and Democrats in Africa." *Journal of Modern African Studies* 39, 3 (2001): 411–436.

Goodwin, Jeff and Theda Skopol. "Explaining Revolutions in the Contemporary Third World." *Politics and Society* 17, 4 (December 1989): 489–509.

Gough, Roger. *A Good Comrade: Janos Kadar, Communism and Hungary.* London, UK: IB Tauris Publishers, 2006.

Gowa, Joanne. "Democratic States and International Disputes." *International Organization* 49, 3 (1995): 511–22.

Graf, William. *The Nigerian State: Political Economy, State, Class and Political System in the Post-Colonial Era.* London, UK: James Curry, 1988.

Graham, Robert. *Iran: The Illusion of Power.* New York, NY: St. Martin's Press, 1979.

Gran, Guy and Galen Hull. *Zaire, The Political Economy of Underdevelopment.* New York, NY: Praeger, 1979.

Granville, Johanna G. "East Germany in 1956: Walter Ulbricht's Tenacity in the face of Opposition." *Australian Journal of Political Science* 52, 3 (2006): 417–38.

Granville, Johanna G. *The First Domino: International Decision Making During the Hungarian Crisis of 1956.* College Station, TX: Texas A & M University Press, 2004.

Greene, William H. *Econometric Analysis.* Fourth Edition, New Jersey: Prentice Hall, 2000.

Grieder, Peter. *The East German Leadership, 1946–1973.* Manchester, UK: Manchester University Press, 1999.

Gugliotta, Guy "The Inner Workings of Dictatorship" *APF Reporter* 9, 2 (1986).

Guisinger, Alexandra and Alastair Smith. "Honest Threats: the Interaction of Reputation and Political Institutions in International Crises." *Journal of Conflict Resolution* 46, 2 (2002): 175–200.

Haber, Stephen. "Authoritarian Government." In *The Oxford Handbook of Political Economy*, edited by Barry Weingast and Donland Wittman, 693–707. Oxford, UK: Oxford University Press, 2006.

Hadar, LT. "Pakistan in America's War against Terrorism: Strategic Ally or Unreliable Client?" *USA Today Magazine* (January, 20–25, 2003).

Hadenius, Axel and Jan Teorell. "Authoritarian Regimes: Stability, Change and Pathways to Democracy, 1972– 2003." *Working Paper #331* (November 2006): 1–39.

Hadenius, Axel and Jan Teorell. "Pathways from Authoritarianism." *Journal of Democracy* 18, 1 (January 2007): 143–156.

Haggard, Stephan. "The Philippines: Picking up after Marcos" In Raymond Vernon editor, *The Promise of Privatization*, edited by Raymond Vernon, 91–121. New York, NY: New York Council for Foreign Relations, 1988.

Haggard, Stephen and Richard Kaufman. *The Political Economy of Democratic Transitions.* Princeton, NJ: Princeton University Press, 1995.

Hagopian, Frances. *Traditional Politics and Regime Change in Brazil.* Cambridge, UK: Cambridge University Press, 1996.

Hale, William. *Turkish Politics and the Military.* London, UK: Routledge, 1994.

Halpern, Manfred. *The Politics of Social Change in the Middle East and North Africa.* Princeton, N.J.: Princeton University Press, 1963.

Halvorsen, Robert and Raymond Palmquist. "The Interpretation of Dummy Variables in Semilogarithmic Equations." *The American Economic Review* 70, 3 (June 1980): 474–475.

Hamann, Kerstin. "The Pacted Transition to Democracy and Labour Politics in Spain." *South European Society and Politics* 2 (1997): 110–113

Handy, Jim. "Resurgent Democracy and the Guatemalan Military." *Journal of Latin American Studies* 18, 2 (November 1986): 383–408.

Harb, Imad. "The Egyptian Military in Politics: Disengagement or Accommodation?" *Middle East Journal* 57, 2 (Spring 2003): 269–290.

Harbeson, John W. ed. *The Military in African Politics.* New York, NY: Praeger Publishers, 1987.

Harden, Blaine. "Zaire's President Mobutu Sese Seko: Political Craftsman worth Billions." *Washington Post:* A1, A27, 1987.

Harrison, S.S. "Bush Needs to Attach Strings to Pakistan Aid". *USA Today,* June 23 2003.

Hartlyn, Jonathan. *The Struggle for Democratic Politics in the Dominican Republic.* Chapel Hill: The University of North Carolina Press, 1987.

Harvey, A. "Estimating Regression Models with Multiplicative Heteroskedasticity." *Econometrica* 44 (1976): 461–465.

Hawes, Gary. "Marcos, His Cronies and the Philippines Failure to Develop." In *Singapore, Indonesia, Malaysia, the Philippines and Thailand,* edited by John Ravenhill, Cheltenham, UK: Edward Elgar Publishing, 1995.

Hawes, Gary. *The Philippine State and the Marcos Regime.* Ithaca, NY: Cornell University Press, 1987.

Hechter, Michael. *Internal Colonialism.* Berkeley and Los Angeles, CA: University of California Press, 1987.

Heckman, James. "Selection Bias as a Specification Error." *Econometrica* 47 (1979): 153–161.

Heeger, Gerald A. "Politics in the Post-Military State: Some Reflections on the Pakistani Experience." *World Politics* 29, 2 (January 1977): 242–262.

Henisz, Witold J. "The Institutional Environment for Multinational Investment." *Journal of Law, Economics, and Organization* 16, 2 (2000): 334–364.

Henisz, Witold J. "Political Institutions and Policy Volatility." *Economics and Politics* 16, 1 (March 2004): 1–27.

Heper, Metin and Aylin Guney. "The Military and the Consolidation of Democracy: The Recent Turkish Experience." *Armed Forces and Society* 26, 4 (Summer 2000): 635–657.

Heper, Metin and Joshua R. Itzkowitz-Shifrinson. "Civil-military Relations in Israel and Turkey." *Journal of Political and Military Sociology* 33, 2 (2005): 231–248.

Herb, Michael. *All in the Family: Absolutism, Revolution and Democracy in the Middle Eastern Monarchies.* Albany, NY: State University of New York Press, 1999.

Herb, Michael. "Emirs and Parliaments in the Gulf." *Journal of Democracy* 13, 4 (October 2002): 41–47.

Herb, Michael. "Princes and Parliaments in the Arab World." *Middle East Journal* 58, 3 (Summer 2004): 367–384.

Hertz, Noreena. *I.O.U.: The Debt Threat and Why We Must Defuse It.* London, UK: Fourth Estate, 2004.

Herz, John. "Idealist Internationalism and the Security Dilemma." *World Politics* 2 (1950): 157–174.

Hibbs, DA. *Mass Political Violence: A Cross National Causal Analysis.* New York, NY: Willey and Sons, 1973.

Higley, John and Michael G. Burton. "The Elite Variable in Democratic Transitions and Breakdowns." *American Sociological Review* 54, 1 (1989): 17–32.

Honaker, James, Anne Joseph, Gary King, Kenneth Scheve, and Naunihal Singh. "Analyzing Incomplete Political Science Data: An Alternative Algorithm for Multiple Imputation. *American Political Science Review* 95, 1 (March 2001): 49–69.

Hood, Steven J. "Political Change in Taiwan: The Rise of Kuomintang Factions." *Asian Survey* 36, 5 (May 1996): 468–482.

Horowitz, Donald L. "Democracy in Divided Societies." *Journal of Democracy* 4 (October 1993): 18–38.

Howe, Herbert. *Military Forces in African States.* Boulder, CO: Lynne Rienner Publishers, 2004.

Huang, Jing. *Factionalism in Chinese Communist Politics.* Cambridge, UK: Cambridge University Press (2000).

Huber, P.J. "The Behavior of Maximum Likelihood Estimates under Non-Standard Conditions." Proceedings of the Fifth Berkeley Symposium on Mathematical Statistics and Probability 4 (1967): 221–233.

Hunt, Benjamin. "The Macroeconomic Effects of Higher Oil Prices." The National Institute Economic Review 179 (2002): 87–103

Hunter, Wendy. *Eroding Military Influence in Brazil.* Chapel Hill, NC: University of North Carolina Press, 1997.

Huntington, Samuel P. "Democracy for the Long Haul." In *Consolidating the Third Wave Democracies,* edited by Larry Diamond, Marc F. Plattner, Yun-Han Chu & Hung-Mao Tien, 3–13. Baltimore, MD: Johns Hopkins University Press, 1997.

Huntington, Samuel P. "Political Development and Political Decay." *World Politics* 17, 3 (April 1965): 386–430.

Huntington, Samuel P. "The Political Modernization of Traditional Monarchies." *Daedalus* 95, 3, Tradition and Change (Summer 1966): 763–788.

Huntington, Samuel P. *Political Order in Changing Societies.* New Haven, CT: Yale University Press, 1968.

Huntington, Samuel P. "Reforming Civil Military Relations" *Journal of Democracy* 6, 4 (1995): 9–17.

Huntington, Samuel P. *The Solider and the State.* Cambridge, MA: Harvard University Press, 1959.

Huntington, Samuel P. *The Third Wave: Democratization in the Late 20th Century.* Norman, OK and London, UK: University of Oklahoma Press, 1991.

Huntington, Samuel P. and Clement Henry Moore. *Authoritarian Politics in Modern Society: The Dynamics of Established One-Party Systems .* New York, NY: Basic Books, 1970.

Hussain, T. Karki. "Some Emerging Trends in China's Domestic Policy." *Economic and Political Weekly* 20, 20 (May 18, 1985): 890–895.

Hussain, Zahid. *Frontline Pakistan: The Struggle with Militant Islam.* New York, NY: IB Tauris Publishers, 2007.

Hutchcroft, Paul D. "Review: Oligarchs and Cronies in the Philippine State: The Politics of Patrimonial Plunder." *World Politics* 43, 3 (April 1991): 414–450.

Hyman, Anthony, Muhammed Ghayur, Naresh Kaushik. *Pakistan, Zia and After.* New Delhi, India: Abhinav Publications, 1989.

Ibrahim, Jibrin. "Political Exclusion, Democratization and Dynamics of Ethnicity in Niger." *Africa Today* 41, 3 (1994): 15–39.

Ibrahim, Jibrin and Abdoulayi Niandou Souley. "The Rise to Power of an Opposition Party: The MNSD in Niger Republic." *Unisa Press, Politeia*, 15, 3, (1996).

Ikpe, Ukana. "Patrimonialism and Military Regimes in Nigeria." *African Journal of Political Science* 5, 1 (2000): 146–162.

Jackman, Robert W. "The Predictability of Coups d'etat: a Model with African Data." *American Political Science Review* 72 (1978): 1262–1275.

Jackson, Robert and Carl Rosberg. *Personal Rule in Black Africa: Prince, Autocrat, Prophet, Tyrant.* Berkeley, CA: University of California Press, 1982.

Jacoby, Tim. "For the People, Of the People and By the Military: The Regime Structure of Modern Turkey." *Political Studies* 51 (2003): 669–685.

Jaggers, Keith and Ted Robert Gurr. "Tracking Democracy's Third Wave and the Polity III Data." *Journal of Peace Research* 32 (1955): 469–82.

Jahan, Rounaq. "Ten Years of Ayub Khan and the Problem of National Integration." *Administration and Society* 2 (1970): 261–298.

Janowitz, Morris. *Military Institutions and Coercion in the Developing Nations.* Chicago IL: University of Chicago Press, 1977.

Janowitz, Morris. "Toward a Redefinition of Military Strategy in International Relations." *World Politics* 26, 4 (July 1974): 473–508

Jeffries, Richard. "The State, Structural Adjustment and Good Governance in Africa." Commonwealth and *Comparative Politics* 31, 1 (March 1993): 20–35.

Jenkins, J. Craig and Augustine J. Kposowa. "Explaining Military Coups d'Etat: Black Africa, 1957–1984." *American Sociological Review* 55, 6 (December 1990): 861–875.

Jenkins, J. Craig and Augustine J. Kposowa. "The Political Origins of African Military Coups: Ethnic Competition, Military Centrality, and the Struggle over the Postcolonial State." *International Studies Quarterly* 36, 3 (September 1992): 271–291.

Jensen, Nathan M. "Multinational Corporations: Political Regimes and Inflows of Foreign Direct Investment." *International Organization* 57 (2003): 587–616.

Jervis, Robert. "Cooperation under the Security Dilemma." *World Politics* 30 (1978): 167–214.

Jilani, Hina. "Human Rights and Democratic Development in Pakistan." (January 1998).

Johnson, A. Ross. "The Warsaw Pact: Soviet Military Policy in Eastern Europe." *Rand Corporation* (July 1981): 1–54.

Johnson, Thomas, Robert Slater, and Patrick McGowan. "Explaining African Military Coups d'Etat, 1960–1982." *American Political Science Review* 78 (1984): 622–40.

Jones, Daniel M., Stuart A. Bremer and J. David Singer. "Militarized Interstate Disputes, 1816–1992: Rationale, Coding Rules, and Empirical Patterns." *Conflict Management and Peace Science* 15, 2 (1996).

Kahin, George Mct., Guy J. Pauker, Lucian W. Pye. "Comparative Politics of Non-Western Countries." *The American Political Science Review* 49, 4 (December 1955): 1022–1041.

Kally, Jackie. "Swaziland Election Dossier 2003." Electoral Institute of Southern Africa (2004): 1–36

Kamrava, Mehran. *The Modern Middle East: A Political History Since the First World War.* Berkeley, CA: University of California Press, 2005.

Kamrava, Mehram. *Revolution in Iran.* London: UK, Routledge, 1990.

Karatnycky, Adrian. "The 2001 Freedom House Survey: Muslim Countries and the Democracy Gap." *Journal of Democracy* 13 (January 2002): 99–112.

Karl, Terry Lynn. "The Hybrid Regimes of Central America." *Journal of Democracy* 6, 3 (1995): 72–86.

Kasozi, Abdu Basajabaka Kawalya, Nakanyike Musisi and James Mukooza Sejjengo. *The Social Origins of Violence in Uganda, 1964–1985*. Montreal, Canada: McGill/Queen's Press, 1994.

Katzman, Kenneth. "Oman: Reform, Security, and U.S. Policy." *Congressional Research Service, United States Library of Congress*, June 28, 2005, http://www.iglhcr.net/crs_country/CRSReport-OmanReformSecurityAndU.S.Policy%28June28,2005%29Updated.pdf (accessed March 10, 2010).

Kaufman, Michael. "Idi Amin, a Brutal Dictator of Uganda, Dies at 80." *New York Times*, August 16, 2003.

Kebschull, H.G. "Operation 'Just Missed': Lessons from Failed Coup Attempts." *Armed Forces and Society* 20, 4 (1994): 565–579.

Keefer, Philip, and Stephen Knack. "Does Social Capital Have an Economic Payoff? A Cross-Country Investigation." *Quarterly Journal of Economics* 112, 4 (1997): 1251–88.

Keele, Luke and David K. Park. "Difficult Choices: An Evaluation of Heterogeneous Choice Models." Paper prepared for the 2004 Meeting of the American Political Science Association, Chicago, IL, September 2–5, 2004.

Kennedy Gavin. *The Military in the Third World*. New York, NY: Charles Scribner's Sons, 1974.

Khadduri, Majid. *Independent Iraq, 1932–1958*. Oxford, UK: Oxford University Press, 1960.

Khadka, Narayan. "Nepal's Stagnant Economy: The Panchayat Legacy." *Asian Survey* 31, 8 (August 1991): 694–711.

Kieh Jr., George Klay and Pita Ogaba Agbese. "From Politics Back to the Barracks in Nigeria: A Theoretical Exploration." *Journal of Peace Research* 30, 4 (November 1993): 409–426.

Kier, Elizabeth. *Imagining War*. Princeton, NJ: Princeton University Press, 1997.

Kind, Hans. "The Philippines: The Sick Man of Asia- Economic Development in the Philippines after 1946." *Working Paper #24* (May 2000): 1–49

King, Anthony. "The World of Command: Communication and Cohesion in the Military." *Armed Forces and Society* 32 (2006): 1–21.

King, Gary. *Unifying Political Methodology: The Likelihood Theory of Statistical Inference*. Cambridge, UK: Cambridge University Press, 1989.

Kinne, Brandon J. "Decision Making in Autocratic Regimes: A Poliheuristic Perspective." *International Studies Perspectives* 6 (2005): 114–128.

Kirby, Owen. "Want Democracy? Get a King." *Middle East Quarterly* 7, 4 (December 2000): 3–12.

Klieman, Aaron S. "Confined to Barracks: Emergencies and the Military in Developing Societies." *Comparative Politics* 12, 2 (1980): 143–163.

Koh, David. "The Politics of a Divided Party and Parkinson's State in Vietnam." *Contemporary Southeast Asia* 23, 3 (December 2001): 533–551.

Kposowa, Augustine J. and J. Craig Jenkins. "The Structural Sources of Military Coups in Postcolonial Africa, 1957–1984." *The American Journal of Sociology* 99, 1 (July 1993): 126–163.

Kriz, Heidi. "When he was King: On the trail of Marshal Mobutu Sese Seko, Zaire's former Kleptocrat-in-Chief" *Metro News*, May 22–28, 1997.

Kruys, GPH. "Intelligence Failures: Causes and Contemporary Case Studies" *Institute for Strategic Studies* (May 2006): 63–96. http://hdl.handle.net/2263/3078

Kugler, Jack, and Yi Feng. "Explaining and Modeling Democratic Transitions." *The Journal of Conflict Resolution* 43, 2 (1999): 139–146.

Kurizaki, Shuhei. 2007. "Efficient Secrecy: Public versus Private Threats in Crisis Diplomacy." *American Political Science Review* 101, 3 (August 2007): 543–558.

Kurlantzick, Joshua. "Burma's Dear Leader." *The Washington Post*, April 23, 2006, online edition.

Laakso, Liisa. "Why Are Elections Not Democratic in Africa? Comparisons Between the Recent Multi-party Elections in Zimbabwe and Tanzania." *Nordic Journal of African Studies* 6, 1 (1997): 18–34.

Lai, Brian and Dan Slater. "Institutions of the Offensive: Domestic Sources of Dispute Initiation in Authoritarian Regimes, 1950–1992." *American Journal of Political Science* 50, 1 (January 2006): 113–126.

Lake, D.A., and M. Baum. "The Invisible Hand of Democracy: Political Control and the Provision of Public Services." *Comparative Political Studies* 34, 6 (2001): 587–621.

Lamont, Duncan. "In the Filing Line." *The Guardian*, September 16, 2002, online edition.

Lane, Ruth. "Political Culture: Residual Category or General Theory?" *Comparative Political Studies* 25, 3 (1992): 362–387.

Langston, Joy. "Breaking Out Is Hard to Do: Exit, Voice, and Loyalty in Mexico's One-Party Hegemonic Regime." *Latin American Politics and Society* 44, 3 (Autumn 2002): 61–88.

LaPalombara, Joseph and Myron Weiner. *Political Parties and Political Development.* Princeton NJ: Princeton University Press, 1966.

Lawson, Kay. "Review: Political Parties: Inside and Out." *Comparative Politics* 23, 1 (October 1990): 105–119.

Lee, Pei-Shan. "The Political Logic of Institutional Choice: Taiwan in Comparative Perspective." *Political Science Review* 13 (2000): 93–124.

Lee, Terence. "Military Cohesion and Regime Maintenance: Explaining the Role of the Military in 1989 China and Indonesia in 1998". *Armed Forces & Society* 32, 1 (2005): 80–104.

Legum, Colin. *Africa Contemporary Record 1975–1976.* London, UK: Holmes and Meier Publishers, 1976.

Legum, Colin. "Behind the Clown's Mask." *Transition* 75 (1997): 250–258.

Legum Colin and John Drysdale (eds.). *Africa Contemporary Record: Annual Survey and Documents; 1968–70.* London, UK: Africa Research, 1970.

Lemke, Douglas. *Regions of War and Peace.* Cambridge, UK: Cambridge University Press, 2002.

LeoGrande, William M. "The Cuban Nation's Single Party." In *A Contemporary Cuba Reader: Reinventing the Revolution,* edited by Phillip Brenner, Marguerite Rose Jimenez and John M. Kirk, 50–62. Lanham, MD: Rowman & Littlefield, 2008.

Levitsky, Steven and Lucan Way. *Competitive Authoritarianism: Hybrid Regimes after the Cold War.* Cambridge, UK: Cambridge University Press, 2010.

Levitsky, Steven and Lucan A. Way. "The Rise of Competitive Authoritarianism." *Journal of Democracy* 13, 2 (January 2002): 5–21.

Lewis, Paul G. *Political Parties in Post-Communist Eastern Europe.* London, UK: Routledge, 2000.

Lewis, Paul H. *Authoritarian Regimes in Latin America: Dictators, Despots, and Tyrants.* Lanham MD: Rowman & Littlefield Publishers, Inc., 2006.

Lewis, Paul H. "Salazar's Ministerial Elite, 1932–1968." *Journal of Politics* 40, 3 (1978): 622–647.

Lewis, Peter M. "Endgame in Nigeria? The Politics of a Failed Democratic Transition." *African Affairs* 93 (1994): 323–240.

Limongi, Fernando and Adam Przeworski. "Political Regimes and Economic Growth." *The Journal of Economic Perspectives* 7, 3 (Summer 1993): 51–69.

Linden, Ronald H. and Bert A. Rockman, eds. *Elite Studies and Communist Politics.* Pittsburgh. PA: University Center for International Studies, 1984.

Linz, Juan. *Totalitarian and Authoritarian Regimes.* Boulder, CO: Lynne Rienner, 2000 (originally published in 1975).

Linz Juan J. and H.E Chebabi eds. *Sultanistic Regimes.* Baltimore. MD: Johns Hopkins University Press, 1998.

Lipset, Seymour Martin. "Some Social Requisites of Democracy: Economic Development and Political Legitimacy." *American Political Science Review* 53 (1959): 69–105.

Lockwood, Lee. "Fidel Castro Speaks on Personal Power." In *Caudillos: Dictators in Spanish America*, edited by Hugh M. Hamill, 292–315. Norman, OK: University of Oklahoma Press, 1995.

LoGerfo, James and Daniel King. "Thailand: Toward Democratic Stability." *Journal of Democracy* 7, 1 (January 1996): 102–117.

Londregan, John B. and Keith Poole. "Does High Income Promote Democracy?" *World Politics* 49 (1996): 1–30.

Londregan, John B. and Keith Poole. "Poverty, the Coup Trap, and the Seizure of Executive Power." *World Politics* 42, 2 (January 1990): 151–183.

Loveman, Brian and Thomas Davies. *The Politics of Anti-Politcs*. Lanham, MD: Rowman and Littlefield, 1997.

Lowenthal, Abraham F. "Review: Armies and Politics in Latin America." *World Politics* 27, 1 (October 1974): 107–130.

Lundahl, Mats. "History as an Obstacle to Change: The Case of Haiti." *Journal of Inter-American Studies and World Affairs* 31, ½ (Spring-Summer 1989): 1–21.

Lust-Okar, Ellen. "Divided They Rule: The Management and Manipulation of Political Opposition." *Comparative Politics* 36, 2 (January 2004): 159–179.

Lust-Okar, Ellen. "Elections under Authoritarianism: Preliminary Lessons from Jordan." *Democratization*, 13, 3 (June 2006): 456–471.

Lust-Okar, Ellen. *Structuring Conflict in the Arab World*. Cambridge, UK: Cambridge University Press, 2005.

Lust-Okar, Ellen and Amaney Ahmad Jamal. "Rulers and Rules: Reassessing the Influence of Regime Type on Electoral Law Formation." *Comparative Political Studies* 35, 3 (April 2002): 337–366.

Luttwak, Edward. *Coup d'Etat: A Practical Handbook*. Cambridge MA: Harvard University Press, 1968.

Magaloni, Beatriz. "Comparative Autocracy" Prepared for the conference *"Research Frontiers in Comparative Politics,* Duke University, April 27–28, 2007: 1–54.

Magaloni, Beatriz. "The Comparative Logic of Autocratic Survival." Paper presented W. Glenn Campbell and Rita Ricardo-Campbell National Fellow and the Susan Louis Dyer Peace Fellow at the Hoover Institution, 2006–07: 1–42

Magaloni, Beatriz. "Credible Power-Sharing and the Longevity of Authoritarian Rule." *Comparative Political Studies* 20, 10 (April/May 2008): 715–741.

Magaloni, Beatriz. "The Demise of Mexico's One-Party Dominant Regime." In *The Third Wave of Democratization in Latin America: Advances and Setbacks*, edited by Frances Hagopian, Scott Mainwaring, 121–148. Cambridge, UK: Cambridge University Press, 2005.

Magaloni, Beatriz. *Voting for Autocracy: Hegemonic party survival and its demise in Mexico*. Cambridge, UK: Cambridge University Press, 2006.

Mahoney, James. *The Legacies of Liberalism: Path dependence and political regimes in Central America*. Baltimore, MD: The Johns Hopkins University Press, 2001.

Mainwaring, Scott. "The Transition to Democracy in Brazil." *Journal of Inter-American Studies and World Affairs* 28, 1 (Spring 1986):149–179.

Mainwaring, Scott, Daniel Brinks, and Aníbal Pérez-Liñán. "Classifying Political Regimes in Latin America, 1945–1999." *Studies in Comparative International Development* 36 (Spring 2001): 37–65.

Makgala, Christian John. "The Relationship between Kenneth Koma and the Botswana Democratic Party, 1965–2003." *African Affairs* 104, 415 (2005): 303–323.

Makgala, Christian John. "'So Far So Good'?: An Appraisal of Dr. Ng'ombe's 1998 Prophecy on the Fate of the BNF." *Botswana Journal of African Studies* 17, 1 (2003): 51–66.

Maniruzzaman, Talukder. "Arms Transfers, Military Coups, and Military Rule in Developing States." *The Journal of Conflict Resolution* 36, 4 (December 1992): 733–755.

Maniruzzaman, Talukder. *Military Withdrawal from Politics: A Comparative Analysis*. Cambridge, MA: Ballinger, 1987.

Manski, Charles F. *Identification Problems in the Social Sciences*. Cambridge, MA: Harvard University Press, 1999.

Maoz, Zeev and Nasrin Abdolali. "Regime Types and International Conflict: 1816–1976." *Journal of Conflict Resolution* 33 (1989): 3–35.

Marinov, Nikolay. "Do Economic Sanctions Destabilize Country Leaders?" *American Journal of Political Science*, 94, 3 (2005): 564–576.

Matlosa, Khabele. "Democracy and Conflict in Post-apartheid Southern Africa: Dilemmas of Social Change in Small States." *International Affairs* 74, 2 (1998) 319–337.

Matsumoto, Mitsutoyo. "Political Democratization and KMT Party Owned Enterprises." *The Developing Economies* 40, 3 (March 2007): 359–380.

Mauro, Paolo. "Corruption and Growth." *Quarterly Journal of Economics* 100, 3 (August 1995): 681–712.

Mauzy, Diane and Robert Stephen Milne. *Singapore Politics under the People's Action Party*. New York, NY: Routledge, 2002.

Mayer, Peter B. "Militarism and Development in Underdeveloped Societies." In *Encyclopedia of Violence, Peace and Conflict*, edited by Lester R. Kurtz and Jennifer E. Turpin, 443–446. San Diego, CA: Academic Press, 1999.

Mazrui, Ali A. "Between Development and Decay: Anarchy, Tyranny and Progress under Idi Amin." *Third World Quarterly* 2, 1 (January 1980): 44–58.

Mbaku, J.M. "Military Expenditures and Bureaucratic Competition for Rents." *Public Choice* 71 (1991): 19–31.

McCleary, Rachel M. *Dictating Democracy: Guatemala and the end of violent revolution*. Gainesville, FL: University Press of Florida, 1999.

McGowan, Patrick J. "African Military Coups d'Etat, 1956–2001: Frequency, Trends and Distribution." *The Journal of Modern African Studies* 41, 3 (September 2003): 339–370.

McGowan, Patrick J. and Thomas H. Johnson. "Sixty Coups in Thirty Years - Further Evidence Regarding African Military Coups d'Etat." *The Journal of Modern African Studies* 24, 3 (September 1986): 539–546.

McGregor, Andrew. *A Military History of Egypt: From the Ottoman Conquest to the Ramadan War*. Santa Barbara. CA: Praeger Publishers, 2006.

McKown, Roberta E. and Robert E. Kauffman. "Party System as a Comparative Analytic Concept in African Politics." *Comparative Politics* 6, 1 (October 1973): 47–72.

Means, Gordon. *Malaysian Politics: The Second Generation*. Oxford, UK: Oxford University Press, 1991.

Means, Gordon. "Soft Authoritarianism in Malaysia and Singapore." *Journal of Democracy* 7, 4 (1996): 103–117.

Meernik, James, Eric L. Krueger and Steven C. Poe. "Testing Models of U.S. Foreign Policy: Foreign Aid during and after the Cold War." *The Journal of Politics* 60, 1 (February 1998): 63–85.

Mezey, Michael L. "The 1971 Coup in Thailand: Understanding Why the Legislature Fails." *Asian Survey* 13, 3 (March 1973): 306–317.

Migdal, Joel S., *Strong Societies and Weak States: State-Society Capabilities in the Third World*, Princeton NJ: Princeton University Press, 1988.

Mintz, A. "The Decision to Attack Iraq: A Non-compensatory Theory of Decision Making." *Journal of Conflict Resolution* 37, 4 (1993): 596–618.

Mintz, A. "How Do Leaders Make Decisions? A Poliheuristic Perspective." *Journal of Conflict Resolution* 48, 1 (2004): 3–13.

Mintz, A., and N. Geva. "The Poliheuristic Theory of Foreign Policy Decisionmaking." In *Decisionmaking in War and Peace: The Cognitive-Rational Debate*, edited by N. Geva and A. Mintz, 81–101. Boulder, CO: Lynne Rienner, 1997.

Mintz, A., N. Geva, S. B. Redd and A. Carnes. "The Effect of Dynamic and Static Choice Sets on Political Decision Making: An Analysis Using the Decision Board Platform." *The American Political Science Review* 91, 3 (1997): 553–566.

Mitchell, R. Judson. "A New Brezhnev Doctrine: The Restructuring of International Relations." *World Politics* 30, 3 (April 1978): 366–390.

Moestrup, Sophia. "The Role of Actors and Institutions: The difficulties of democratic survival in Mali and Niger." *Democratization* 6, 2 (1999): 171–186.

Molomo, Mpho G. "Understanding Government and Opposition Parties in Botswana." Commonwealth & *Comparative Politics* 38, 1 (March 2000): 65–92.

Monga, Celestin. "Eight Problems with African Politics." *Journal of Democracy* 8, 3 (1997): 156–170.

Moody, John. "Haiti: End of the Duvalier Era." *Time Magazine*, June 24, 2001.

Moore, Barrington. *Social Origins of Dictatorship and Democracy: Lord and Peasant in the Making of the Modern World*. London, UK: Penguin, 1967.

Moselle, Boas and Benjamin Polak. "A Model of a Predatory State." *Journal of Law, Economy and Organization* 17, 1 (2001): 1–33

Mulligan, Casey B., Ricard Gil, and Xavier Sala-i-Martin. "Do Democracies Have Different Public Policies than Non-democracies?" *Journal of Economic Perspectives* 18, 1 (2004): 51–74.

Mulvey, Charles. *The Economic Analysis of Trade Unions*. Oxford, UK: Martin Robinson, 1978.

Munck, Ronaldo. "The "Modern" Military Dictatorship in Latin America: The Case of Argentina (1976–1982)." *Latin American Perspectives: State and Military in Latin America* 12, 4 (Autumn 1985): 41–74.

Mutalib, Hussin. "Singapore's 1991 General Election." *Southeast Asian Affairs* (1992): 299–309.

Nathan, Andrew. "Authoritarian Resilience." *Journal of Democracy* 14, 1 (January 2003): 6–17

Nathan, Andrew. "A Factional Model for CCP Politics." *China Quarterly* 53 (January – March 1973): 34–66.

Nathan, Andrew J. and Kellee S. Tsai. "Factionalism: A New Institutionalist Restatement." *The China Journal* 34 (July 1995): 157–192.

N'Diaye, Boubacar. "Mauritania, August 2005: Justice and Democracy, or Just another Coup?" *African Affairs* 105, 420 (April 2006): 421–441.

Needler, Martin C. "Military Motivations in the Seizure of Power." *Latin American Research Review* 10, 3 (Autumn 1975): 63–79.

Needler, Martin. "Political Development and Military Intervention in Latin America." *The American Political Science Review* 60, 3 (September 1966): 616–626.

Neher, Clark D. "Constitutionalism and Elections in Thailand." *Pacific Affairs* 43, 2 (Summer 1970): 240–257.

Neher, Clark D. "Political Succession in Thailand." *Asian Survey* 32, 7 (July 1992): 585–605.

Ngubane, Senzo "Niger's Walk to Democracy?" *African Security Review* 8, 3 (1999). http://www.iss.co.za/Pubs/ASR/8No3/AfricaWatch.html

Nonneman, Gerd. "Political Reform in the Gulf Monarchies: From Liberalization to Democratization? A Comparative Perspective." *Durham Middle East Papers* 80, 6 Sir William Luce Publication Series (June 2006): 1–37.

Nordlinger, Eric A. "Soldiers in Mufti: The Impact of Military Rule on Economic and Social Change in Non-Western States." *American Political Science Review* 64 (December 1970): 1131–1148.

Nordlinger, Eric A. *Soldiers in Politics: Military Coups and Governments*. Englewood Cliffs, NJ: Prentice-Hall, 1977.

Noriega, Roger F. "Venezuela under Chávez: The Path toward Dictatorship." *American Enterprise Institute for Public Policy Research* 3 (2006): 1–9.

Nun, José. "The Middle Class Military Coup." In *The Politics of Conformity in Latin America*, edited by Claudio Veliz, 66–118. New York, NY: Oxford University Press, 1967.

O'Donnell, Guillermo. *Modernization and Bureaucratic-Authoritarianism: Studies in South American Politics*. Berkeley, CA: University of California Press, Berkeley, 1973.

O'Donnell, Guillermo and Phillippe Schmitter and Laurence Whitehead eds. *Transitions from Authoritarian Rule: Tentative Conclusions about Uncertain Democracies*. Baltimore, MD: Johns Hopkins Press, 1986.

Oh, Kong Dan and Ralph Hassig. *North Korea through the Looking Glass*. Washington DC: Brookings Institution Press, 2000.

O'Kane, Rosemary. "Military Regimes: Power and Force." *European Journal of Political Research* 17 (1989): 333–350.

O'Kane, Rosemary. "A Probabilistic Approach to the Causes of Coups d'Etat." *British Journal of Political Science* 11 (1981): 287–308.

O'Kane, Rosemary. "Towards an Examination of the General Causes of Coups d'Etat." *European Journal of Political Research* 11 (March 1983): 27–44.

Olson, Mancur. *Power and Prosperity: Outgrowing Communist and Capitalist Dictatorships*. Oxford, UK: Oxford University Press, 2000.

Olusegun, Obasanjo. *Not My Will*. Ibadan, Nigeria: Iba- dan University Press, 1990.

Ortiz, Reynaldo Yunuen Ortega. "Comparing Types of Transitions: Spain and Mexico." *Democratization* 7, 3 (Autumn 2000): 65–92.

Owen, Roger. *State, Power and Politics in the Making of the Modern Middle East*. London, UK: Routledge, 1992.

Paige, Jeffrey. *Agrarian Revolution*. New York, NY: Free Press, 1975.

Palmer, Mark. *Breaking the Real Axis of Evil: How to oust the World's Last Dictators by 2025*. Lanham, MD: Rowman & Littlefield Publishers, Inc, 2005.

Paribatra, Sukhumbhand. "State and Society in Thailand: How Fragile the Democracy?" *Asian Survey* 33, 9 (September 1993): 879–893.

Partell, Peter J. and Glenn Palmer. "Audience Costs and Interstate Crises: An Empirical Assessment of Fearon's Model of Dispute Outcomes." *International Studies Quarterly* 43 (1999): 389–405.

Paul, Jim. "The Coup, Turkey: The Generals Take Over." *MERIP Reports* 93 (January 1981): 3–4.

Payne, Stanley G. "Twentieth-Century Dictatorships: The Ideological One-Party States." *The American Historical Review* 101, 4 (1996): 1186–1187.

Peceny, Mark, Caroline C. Beer, and Shannon Sanchez-Terry. "Dictatorial Peace?" *American Political Science Review* 96 (March 2002): 15–26.

Peceny, Mark and Christopher K. Butler. "The Conflict Behavior of Authoritarian Regimes." *International Politics* 41, 4 (2004): 565–581.

Penner Angrist, Michele. "The Expression of Political Dissent in the Middle East: Turkish Democratization and Authoritarian Continuity in Tunisia." *Comparative Studies in Society and History* 41, 4 (1999): 730–757.

Perlmutter, Amos. *The Military and Politics in Modern Times*. New Haven, CT: Yale University Press, 1977.

Perlmutter, Amos. *Modern Authoritarianism: A Comparative Institutional Analysis*. New Haven, CT: Yale University Press, 1981.

Perlmutter, Amos. "The Praetorian state and the Praetorian Army: Toward a Taxonomy of Civil-Military Relations in Developing Countries." *Comparative Politics* 1, 3 (April 1969): 382–404.

Perry, Elizabeth. "Studying Chinese Politics: Farewell to Revolution?" *The China Journal* 57 (2007): 1–24.

Peterson, J.E. "The Nature of Succession in the Gulf." *Middle East Journal* 55, 4 (Autumn 2001): 580–601.

Pike, Douglas. "Origins of Leadership Change in the Socialist Republic of Vietnam." *In Leadership Change in Communist States,* edited by Raymond C. Taras, 107–128. Boston, MA: Unwin Hyman, Inc., 1989.

Pinto, Antonio Costa. "Elites, Single Parties and Political Decision-Making in Fascist Era Dictatorships." *Contemporary European History* 11, 3 (2002): 429–454.

Pion-Berlin, David. "The Fall of Military Rule in Argentina: 1976–1983." *Journal of Inter-American Studies and World Affairs* 27, 2 (Summer 1985): 55–76.

Pion-Berlin, David. "Military Autonomy and Emerging Democracies in South America." *Comparative Politics* 25, 1 (1992): 83–102.

Polity IV Project. "Polity IV Project." Political Regime Characteristics and Transitions, 1800–2008. http://www.systemicpeace.org/polity/polity4.htm (accessed February 15, 2010).

Post, Jerrold M. *The Psychological Assessment of Political Leaders: With Profiles of Saddam Hussein and Bill Clinton.* Ann Arbor, MI: University of Michigan Press, 2003.

Post, Jerrold M. and Alexander George. *Leaders and Their Followers in a Dangerous World: The Psychology of Political Behavior.* Ithica, NY: Cornell University Press, 2004.

Posusney, Marsha Pripstein. "Multi-party Elections in the Arab World: Institutional engineering and oppositional strategies." *Studies in International Comparative Development* 36. 4 (December 2002): 34–62.

Potholm, Christian P. "The Ngwenyama of Swaziland: The Dynamics of Political Adaptation." In *African Kingships in Perspective,* edited by René Lemarchand, 129–159. London, UK: Routledge, 1977.

Powell, J.D. "Military Assistance and Militarism in Latin America." *Western Political Quarterly* 18 (June 1965): 382–392.

Power, Timothy J. "Compulsory for Whom? Mandatory Voting and Electoral Participation in Brazil, 1986–2006." *Journal of Politics in Latin America* 1 (2009): 97–122.

Prins, Brandon C. "Institutional Instability and the Credibility of Audience Costs: Political Participation and Interstate Crisis Bargaining, 1816–1992." *Journal of Peace Research* 40, 1 (2003): 67–84.

Przeworski, Adam. *Democracy and the Market.* Cambridge, UK: Cambridge University Press, 1991.

Przeworski, Adam, Michael Alvarez, Jose Antonio Cheibub, and Fernando Limongi. *Democracy and Development: Political Institutions and Material Well-Being in the World, 1950–1990.* Cambridge: Cambridge University Press, 2000.

Przeworski, Adam, Michael Alvarez, Jose Antonio Cheibub, and Fernando Limongi. "What Makes Democracies Endure?" *Journal of Democracy* 7, 1 (1996): 39–55.

Przeworski, Adam and Fernando Papaterra Limongi Neto, "Modernization: Theories and Facts." *World Politics* 49, 2 (1997): 155–183.

Purcell, Susan Kaufman. "Review: Authoritarianism." *Comparative Politics* 5, 2 (January 1973): 301–312.

Putnam, Robert D. "Diplomacy and Domestic Politics: The Logic of Two-Level Games." *International Organization* 42 (Summer 1988): 427–460.

Pye, Lucian. "Armies in the Process of Political Modernization." In *The Role of the Military in Underdeveloped Countries,* edited by John J. Johnson, 69–89. Princeton, NJ: Princeton University Press, 1962.

Pye, Lucian. *Communications and Political Development.* Princeton, NY: Princeton University Press 1963.

Quinlivan, James T. "Coup-Proofing: Its Practice and Consequences in the Middle East." *International Security* 24, 2 (Autumn 1999): 131–165.

Ramsay, Kristopher W. "Politics at the Water's Edge: Crisis Bargaining and Electoral Competition." *Journal of Conflict Resolution* 98, 4 (2004): 459–486.

Ravenhill, FJ. "Military Rule in Uganda: The Politics of Survival." *African Studies Review* 17, 1 (April 1974): 229–260.

Reed, William. "Information and Economic Interdependence." *Journal of Conflict Resolution* 47, 1 (2003a): 54–71.

Reed, William. "Information, Power, and War." *American Political Science Review* 97, 4 (November 2003b): 633–641.

Reich, Bernard. *Political Leaders of the Contemporary Middle East and North Africa: A Biographical Dictionary.* Westport, CT: Greenwood Publishing, 1990.

Reiter, Dan and Allan C. Stam. "Identifying the Culprit: Democracy, Dictatorship, and Dispute Initiation." *American Political Science Review* 97 (May 2003): 333–337.

Remmer, Karen L. "Exclusionary Democracy." *Studies in Comparative International Development* 20, 4 (1986): 64–85.

Remmer, Karen L. *Military Rule in Latin America.* Boulder, CO: Westview Press, 1991.

Renner, Hans. *A History of Czechoslovakia since 1945.* New York, NY: Routledge, 1989.

Reno, William. "Sovereignty and Personal Rule in Zaire" *Africa Studies Quarterly,* 1, 2 (1997).

Riaz, Ali and Subho Basu. "The State-Society Relationship and Political Conflicts in Nepal (1768–2005)." *Journal of Asian and African Studies* 42, 2 (2007): 123–142.

Richards, Alan and John Waterbury. *A Political Economy of the Middle East.* Boulder, CO: Westview Press, 1996.

Richter, William L. "Pakistan in 1985: Testing Time for the New Order." *Asian Survey* 26, 2, A Survey of Asia in 1985: Part II (February 1986): 207–218.

Rindova, Violina P. and Starbuck, William H. "Distrust in Dependence: The Ancient Challenge of Superior-Subordinate Relations." In *Advancement of Organization Behaviour: Essays in Honor of Derek Pugh,* edited by T.A.R Clark, 313–336. Dartmouth, NH: Ashgate Publishing.

Roeder, Phillip G. *Red Sunset: The Failure of Soviet Politics.* Princeton, NJ: Princeton University Press, 1993.

Romer, D. "Openness and Inflation: Theory and Evidence." *Quarterly Journal of Economics* 108 (1993): 869–903.

Rosenthal, Seth A., and Todd L. Pittinsky, "Narcissistic Leadership," *The Leadership Quarterly* 17, 6 (2006): 617–633.

Ross, Dennis. "Coalition Maintenance in the Soviet Union." World Politics 32, 2 (1980) 258–280.

Ross, Michael. "Does Oil Hinder Democracy?" *World Politics* 53, 3 (April 2001): 325–361.

Rothkopf, David. "After This." *Washington Post,* January 20, 2002.

Rowe, Edward Thomas. "Aid and Coups d'Etat: Aspects of the Impact of American Military Assistance Programs in the Less Developed Countries." *International Studies Quarterly* 18, 2 (June 1974): 239–255.

Roy, Dennis. *Taiwan: A Political History.* Ithaca, NY: Cornell University Press, 2003.

Rubin, Barry. "The Military in Contemporary Middle East Politics." *MERIA* 5, 1 (March 2001): 47–63.

Rubin, Barry. *Modern Dictators: Third World Coup Makers, Strongmen, and Populist Tyrants.* New York, NY: Magraw-Hill, 1987.

Rueschemeyer, Dieter, Evelyn H. Stephens and John D. Stephens, *Capitalist Development and Democracy*, Cambridge, MA: Polity Press, 1992.

Rummel, Rudolph. "Democracy, Power, Genocide, and Mass Murder." *Journal of Conflict Resolution* 39 (March 1995): 3–26.

Rupiya, Martin. "A Survey of Civil-Military Relations in the SADC Sub-Region." In *Civil Military Relations in Zambia, A Review of Zambia's Contemporary CMR History and Challenges of Disarmament, Demobilization and Reintegration*, edited by Gilbert Chileshe, Margaret Chimanse, Naison Ngoma, A project of the Defence Sector Programme at the Institute for Security Studies, funded by the Department for International Development (DFID) of the UK government, 2004.

Rutland, Peter. *The Politics of Economic Stagnation in the Soviet Union: The Role of Local Party Organs in Economic Management*. Cambridge, UK: Cambridge University Press, 1993.

Ryan, Curtis R. "Elections and Parliamentary Democratization in Jordan." *Comparative Political Studies* 5, 4 (Winter 1998): 176–1996.

Sanhueza, Ricardo. "The Hazard Rate of Political Regimes." Public Choice 98 (March 1999): 337–367.

Sarotte, M.E. *Dealing with the Devil: East Germany, Détente and Ostpolitk*. Chapel Hill, NC: University of North Carolina Press, 2001.

Sartori, Giovanni. *Parties and Party Systems: A Framework for Analysis*. Cambridge, UK: Cambridge University Press, 1975.

Schapiro, Leonard. *Totalitarianism*. London, UK: Praeger, 1962.

Schedler, Andreas. "Elections without Democracy: The Menu of Manipulation." *Journal of Democracy* 13, 2 (April 2002): 36–50.

Schedler, Andreas (ed.). *Electoral Authoritarianism: The Dynamics of Unfree Competition*. Boulder CO: Lynne Rienner, 2006.

Schirmer, Jennifer. *The Guatemalan Military Project: A Violence Called Democracy*. Philadelphia, PA: University of Pennsylvania Press, 1998.

Schirmer, Jennifer. "The Guatemalan Politic-Military Project: Legacies for Violent Peace?" *Latin American Perspectives* 105, 26, 2 (March 1999): 92–107.

Schultz, Kenneth A. "Do Domestic Institutions Constrain or Inform? Contrasting Two Institutional Perspectives on Democracy and War." *International Organization* 52 (1999): 233–266.

Schultz, Kenneth A. "Domestic Opposition and Signaling in International Crises." *American Political Science Review* 92 (December 1998): 829–844.

Schultz, Kenneth A. "Looking for Audience Costs." *The Journal of Conflict Resolution* 45, 1 (2001): 32–60.

Scobell, Andrew. *Kim Jong Il and North Korea: The Leader and the System*. Carlisle, PA: DIANE Publishing/ Strategic Studies Institute, 2006.

Shah, Aqil "Democracy on Hold in Pakistan." *Journal of Democracy* 13, 1 (2002): 67–76.

Shah, Aqil. "Pakistan's 'Armored' Democracy." *Journal of Democracy* 14, 4 (October 2003): 26–40.

Siebold, Guy L. "The Essence of Military and Group Cohesion." *Armed Forces and Society* 33 (2007): 286–297.

Siegel, Eric. "I Know that You Know, and You Know that I Know: An Information Theory of the Democratic Peace." Paper presented at the 93rd Annual Meeting of the American Political Science Association, Washington, D.C, 1997.

Singer, J. David, Stuart Bremer, and John Stuckey. "Capability Distribution, Uncertainty, and Major Power War, 1820–1965," In *Peace, War and Numbers*, edited by Bruce Russett. Beverly Hills, CA: Sage Publications, 1972.

Skidmore, Thomas. "The Politics of Economic Stabilization in Post War Latin America." In *Authoritarianism and Corporatism in Latin America*, edited by James Malloy, 149–190. Pittsburgh, PA: University of Pittsburgh Press, 1977.

Skidmore, Thomas. *The Politics of Military Rule in Brazil, 1964–1985*. Oxford, UK: Oxford University Press, 1990.

Slantchev, Branislav L. "Politicians, the Media, and Domestic Audience Costs." *International Studies Quarterly* 50 (2006): 445–477.

Slater, Dan. "Iron Cage in an Iron Fist: Authoritarian Institutions and the Personalization of Power in Malaysia." *Comparative Politics* 36, 1 (October 2003): 81–101

Slater, Dan. "Ordering Power: Contentious Politics, State-Building, and Authoritarian Durability in Southeastern Asia." Paper presented at the University of Chicago Comparative Politics Workshop, 2005.

Small, Melvin and J. David Singer. "The War Proneness of Democratic Regimes." *Jerusalem Journal of International Relations* 1 (1976): 50–69.

Smith, Alastair. "International Crises and Domestic Politics." *American Political Science Review* 92, 3 (1998): 623–638.

Smith, Benjamin. "Life of the Party: The Origins of Regime Breakdown and Persistence under Single Party Rule." *World Politics* 57 (April 2005): 421–451.

Snyder, Richard. "Explaining Transitions from Neo-patrimonial Dictatorships." *Comparative Politics* 24, 4 (July 1992): 379–399.

Snyder, Richard and James Mahoney. "Rethinking Agency and Structure in the Study of Regime Change." *Studies in Comparative International Development* 34, 2 (June 1999): 3–32.

Sørensen, Georg. *Democracy, Dictatorship and Development: Economic Development in Selected Regimes of the Third World*, London, UK: Macmillan. 1991.

Springborg, Robert. "The President and the Field Marshal: Civil-Military Relations in Egypt Today." *MERIP Middle East Report* 147, Egypt's Critical Moment (July– August, 1987): 4–16.

Stein, Ernesto and Jorge Streb. "Elections and the Timing of Devaluations." *Journal of International Economics* 63, 1 (May 2004): 119–145.

Stepan, Alfred. *Rethinking Military Politics*. Princeton, NJ: Princeton University Press, 1988.

Stubbs, Richard. "War and Economic Development: Export-Oriented Industrialization in East and Southeast Asia." *Comparative Politics* 31, 3 (April 1999): 337–355.

Svolik, Milan. "Authoritarian Reversals and Democratic Consolidation." *American Political Science Review* 102, 2 (2008): 153–168.

Svolik, Milan W. "Power Sharing and Leadership Dynamics in Authoritarian Regimes." *American Journal of Political Science* 53, 2 (2009): 477–494.

Svolik, Milan. "A Theory of Government Dynamics in Authoritarian Regimes" Paper presented at the annual meeting of the International Studies Association 48th Annual Convention, Chicago, IL, February 28, 2007: 1–47.

Tachau, Frank and Metin Heper. "The State, Politics, and the Military in Turkey." *Comparative Politics* 16, 1 (October 1983): 17–33.

Tamada, Yoshifumi. "Coups in Thailand, 1980–1991: Classmates, Internal Conflicts and Relations with the Government of the Military." *Southeast Asian Studies* 33 (1995): 317–339.

Tanzi, Vito. "Public Expenditure and Public Debt." In *Public Expenditure: The Key Issues*, edited by John Bristow and Declan McDonagh, 6–41. Dublin, Ireland: Institute of Public Administration, 1986.

Taras, Raymond, ed., *Leadership Change in Communist States*. Boston, MA: Unwin Hyman, 1989.

Teiwes, Frederick C. *Politics at Mao's Court: Gao Gang and Party Factionalism in the Early 1950s*. New York, NY: Sharpe Inc, 1990.

Therneau,Terry M. and Patricia M. Grambsch. *Modeling Survival Data: Extending the Cox Model.* New York, NY: Springer-Verlag, 2000.

Titley, Brian. *Dark Age: The Political Odyssey of Emperor Bokassa.* Montreal, Canada: McGill-Queens University Press, 1997.

Tiwathia, Aditya. "The 'General' Problem of Pakistan." *Journal of Scholarship and Opinion* (Spring 2006): 41–49.

Toma, Peter A. "Revival of a Communist Party in Hungary." *The Western Political Quarterly* 14, 1, Part 1 (March 1961): 87–103.

Tomz, Michael. "Domestic Audience Costs in International Relations: An Experimental Approach." *International Organization* 61, 4 (Fall 2007): 821–840.

Tordoff, William. "Decentralization: Comparative Experience in Commonwealth Africa." *The Journal of Modern African Studies* 32, 4 (December 1994): 555–580.

Tordoff, William. *Government and Politics in Africa.* Bloomington, IN: Indiana University Press, 2002.

Transparency International, 2009, http://www.transparency.org/ (accessed January 27, 2010).

Treisman, Daniel. "Decentralization and Inflation: Commitment, Collective Action, or Continuity?" *American Political Science Review* 94, 4 (2000): 837–858.

Tripp, Charles. *A History of Iraq.* Cambridge, UK: Cambridge University Press, 2002.

Tripp, Charles, Edward Roger John Owen, Roger Owen. *Egypt under Mubarak.* London, UK: Routledge, 1989.

Tsebelis, George. *Veto Players: How Political Institutions Work.* Princeton, NJ: Princeton University Press, 2002.

Tsie, Balefi. "Political Context of Botswana's Development Performance." *Journal of Southern African Studies* 22, 4 (December 1996): 599–616.

Tucker, Robert C., "Personality and Political Leadership," *Political Science Quarterly* 92, 3 (Autumn 1977): 383–393.

Tucker, Robert C. *Politics as Leadership.* Columbia, MO: University of Missouri Press, 1995.

Tucker, Robert C. "The Question of Totalitarianism." *Slavic Review* 20, 3 (October 1961): 377–382.

Tucker, Robert C. "Towards a Comparative Politics of Movement-Regimes." *The American Political Science Review* 55, 2 (June 1961): 281–289.

Tullock, Gordon. *Autocracy.* Boston, MA: Klewer Publications, 1987.

Turner, Thomas. "Decline or Recovery in Zaire?" *Current History* 87 (1988): 213–216.

Turunç, Kerem. "The Democratic Shield: How Establishing the Rule of Law Protects Countries from Military Coups." (December 2003): 1–47. http://ssrn.com/author=1144798

Ulfelder, Jay. "Contentious Collective Action and the Breakdown of Authoritarian Regimes." *International Political Science Review* 26, 3 (2005): 311–334.

Valeriano, Brandon and Douglas Gibler. "The Steps to Interstate War in Africa." Paper was presented at the annual International Studies Association Meeting, San Diego, CA, March 25, 2006: 1–36.

Valenzuela, Arturo. "Latin American Presidencies Interrupted." *Journal of Democracy* 15, 4 (October 2004): 5–19.

Van Doorn, J, ed *Armed Forces and Society: Sociological Essays.* The Hague, The Netherlands: Mouton, 1968.

Virost, Milton. "The Colonel in his Labyrinth." *Foreign Affairs* 78, 2 (Mar/April 99).

Wallerstein, Immanuel. *The Capitalist World-Economy.* Cambridge, UK: Cambridge University Press, 1979.

Walter, Knut and Philip J. Williams. "The Military and Democratization in El Salvador." *Journal of Inter-American Studies and World Affairs* 35, 1 (1993): 39–88.

Waltz, Kenneth. *Man, the State and War.* New York, NY: Columbia University Press, 1959.

Wang, T. Y. "Arms Transfers and Coups d'Etat: A Study on Sub-Saharan Africa." *Journal of Peace Research* 35, 6 (November 1998): 659–675.

Wasseem, Mohammad. "Pakistan's Lingering Crisis of Dyarchy." *Asian Survey* 32, 7 (July 1992): 617–634.

Way, Lucan. "Pigs, Wolves and the Evolution of Post-Soviet Competitive Authoritarianism, 1992–2005." *CDDRL Working Papers* 62 (June 2006): 1–64.

Weber, Max. *Theory of Social and Economic Organization.* Translated by A. R. Anderson and Talcott Parsons, New York, NY: Free Press, 1947.

Wedeen, Lisa. "Acting "As If": Symbolic Politics and Social Control in Syria." *Comparative Studies in Society and History* 40, 3 (July 1998): 503–523.

Weeks, Jessica. "Autocratic Audience Costs: Regime Type and Signaling Resolve." *International Organization* 62, 1 (January 2008): 35–64.

Welch, Claude. "Praetorianism in Commonwealth West Africa." *The Journal of Modern African Studies* 10, 2 (1972): 203–221.

Welch, Claude. *Soldier and State in Africa.* Evanston, IL: Northwestern University Press, 1970.

Welch, Claude and Arthur K. Smith. *Military Role and Rule: Perspectives on Civil Military Relations.* North Scituate MA: Duxbury Press, 1974.

Welsh, Helga A. "Political Transition Processes in Central and Eastern Europe." *Comparative Politics* 26, 4 (July 1994): 379–394.

Wiarda, Howard. *Critical Elections and Critical Coups: State, Society and the Military in the Processes of Latin American Development.* Athens, Ohio: Ohio University Center for International Studies, 1978.

Wiarda, Howard. "Review: The United States and the Dominican Republic: Intervention, Dependency and Tryannicide." *Journal of Inter-American Studies and World Affairs* 22, 2 (May 1980): 247–260.

Wiesfelder, R. "Human Rights in Botswana, Lesotho, Swaziland and Malawi." *Botswana Journal of African Studies*, 2, 1 (1980): 5–32.

Wilke, Boris. "State-Formation and the Military in Pakistan: Reflections on the Armed Forces, their State and some of their Competitors." *Working Papers* 2 (2001): 1–36.

Williams, Richard. "Using Heterogeneous Choice Models to Compare Logit and Probit Coefficients across Groups." *Sociological Methods and Research* 37, 4 (May 2009): 531–559.

Wilson, Sven E. and Daniel M. Butler. "A Lot More to Do: The Sensitivity of Time-Series Cross-Section Analyses to Simple Alternative Specifications." *Political Analysis* 15, 2 (January 4, 2007): 101–123.

Wintrobe, Ronald. "Dictatorship: Analytical Approaches." In *Oxford Handbook of Comparative Approaches,* edited by Carles Boix, Susan Stokes, 363–394. Oxford, UK: Oxford University Press, 2007.

Wintrobe, Ronald. *The Political Economy of Dictatorship.* Cambridge, UK: Cambridge University Press, 1998.

World Bank. "World Development Indicators 2003." Washington D.C.: World Bank (2003). CD-ROM.

Wright, Joseph. "Do Authoritarian Institutions Constrain? How Legislatures Impact Economic Growth and Foreign Aid Effectiveness." *American Journal of Political Science* 52, 2 (April 2008): 322–343.

Wright, Joseph. "To Invest or Insure? How Authoritarian Time Horizons Impact Foreign Aid Effectiveness." *Comparative Politics* 20, 10 (2007): 1–30.

Xie, Weizhi. "The Semi-hierarchical Totalitarian Nature of Chinese Politics." *Comparative Politics* 25, 3 (April 1993): 313–330.

Yatchew, Adonis and Zvi Griliches. "Specification Error in Probit Models." *Review of Economics and Statistics* 18 (1985): 134–139.

Young, Crawford. "The African Colonial State and its Political Legacy." In *The Precarious Balance*, edited by Donald Rothchild and Naomi Chazan, 25–66. Boulder, CO: Westview Press, 1988.

Young, Crawford and Thomas Turner. *The Rise and Decline of the Zairian State*. Madison, WI: The University of Wisconsin Press, 1985.

Zaidi, Akbar. "State, Military and Social Transition: Improbable Future of Democracy in Pakistan" *Economic and Political Weekly* (December 3, 2005): 5173–5181.

Zalanga, Samuel. "Ruling Elite Coalitions and State Bureaucratic Capacity: Accounting for Developmental and Predatory States in Malaysia and Nigeria." Paper presented at the First International Graduate Student Retreat for Comparative Research. Los Angeles, CA, May 8–9, 1999.

Zimmerman, Ekkart. "Toward a Causal Model of Military Coup d'Etat." *Armed Forces and Society* 5 (1979): 387–413.

Author Index

Subject Index